FRESH FROM THE MARKET

SARAH WOODWARD
FRESH FROM THE MARKET

ILLUSTRATIONS BY CLARA VULLIAMY

M
MACMILLAN
LONDON

TO THOSE STALLHOLDERS WHO MAINTAIN THE TRADITIONS
AND QUALITY OF OUR MARKETS

First published 1993 by
MACMILLAN LONDON LIMITED
a division of Pan Macmillan Publishers Limited
Cavaye Place London SW10 9PG
and Basingstoke

Associated companies in Auckland, Budapest, Dublin, Gaborone,
Harare, Hong Kong, Kampala, Kuala Lumpur, Lagos, Madras, Manzini,
Melbourne, Mexico City, Nairobi, New York, Singapore, Sydney,
Tokyo and Windhoek

ISBN 0-333-58035-4

A CIP catalogue for this book is available from
the British Library

Typeset by Spottiswoode Ballantyne, Hawkins Road, The Hythe, Colchester

Printed by Mackays of Chatham Plc

CONTENTS

ACKNOWLEDGEMENTS

There are too many people to acknowledge, too many authors whose books have given me inspiration, too many friends around the world who have cooked me dinner, shared their knowledge, and eaten my food. To those left out in this brief list, my thanks go none the less. I am especially grateful to Carol Heaton of Elaine Greene Ltd, for her belief in me and her persistence; Jane Wood of Macmillan, for publishing the book and helping me through the process; my parents, Alan and Elizabeth, for first giving me a taste for travel and food; and especially my mother for all the wonderful meals she has cooked over the years; Louisa Oriel, great cook herself, who first suggested that I should write a book about food; Gilbert Winfield, for setting me on my way in Paris and teaching me how to cook pasta; my brother and his wife, Phil and Martine, for furthering my education in the French way of life; David Kelley of Trinity College, who introduced me to ras el hanout and aroused my interest in the history of food; Janie Matthew, who has accompanied me on endless trips to Berwick Street market and always been willing to both cook and taste; and above all Jonathan Gregson, who has munched his way through endless trial meals, proffered kind criticism, and even washed up afterwards.

INTRODUCTION

The marketplace is the key to good cooking. Not for nothing do the best chefs make much of their willingness to rise at ungodly hours to visit the wholesale markets, of their relationships with their suppliers and their efforts to seek out the highest-quality produce. A good cook needs good materials to work with.

If the right ingredients are so important, how do we get hold of them – and how do we know what to choose? The first lesson is to know where to shop. Using good suppliers takes much of the hard work away – we can let them do the choosing, allowing us to range through the variety of goods on offer and pick what takes our fancy, in the knowledge that it will be seasonal and fresh. Perhaps this is why so many of us rely on supermarkets: we feel sure that with their huge teams of buyers they will get the best although we may have to pay extra for it. The large chains are now trying harder to fulfil high-quality food standards, stocking organic produce, emphasizing sell-by dates, providing a wider choice. The supermarkets have made a deliberate effort to be both practical, through their opening hours, and accessible: it is easier to load the car with everything we want for the week than to lug bags from shop to shop.

But the supermarket, after all, is nothing more than a great big market. Look at the name, now so familiar that we hardly think about it. It is in markets that our national (and international) heritage of food shopping lies. For centuries, all over the world, producers have sent their goods to the local market, to be sold in competition for price and quality. Of course, today many of our markets are centrally owned and organized by retailers. But all around the country there still exist 'traditional' markets, selling seasonal, locally produced goods. These markets may be daily, weekly, monthly; they may be wholesale or retail; they may specialize in one particular type of food, or, more typically, offer a wide variety. These markets are almost always worth seeking out, for here the cook has the opportunity to find out what is in season, to try local specialities, to build a relationship with a particular supplier.

Many of us will be more familiar with such markets from holidays abroad. One of the delights of Provence and Tuscany, of the Basque country or the islands of Greece, the coastal ports of Normandy and Brittany, the southern Italian cities and many other popular destinations, lies in their colourful, bustling markets. That is not to say that British markets should be neglected. They may be fewer in number, they may offer less local produce, but they exist all year round on our doorsteps and many of their producers are trying hard to compete in the face of increasing centralization of retailing. The same is true of small, specialized shops, of farm retailers, of travelling vans. Given the support of the cook, such suppliers have much to offer. Without such support, the best of British produce will simply cease to be produced or will be exported to keener, more discerning customers.

Shopping in a real market or from a small local supplier is not always possible. But wherever the cook shops, he or she needs to use the skills of the market. There is great pleasure to be had in choosing what is best on the day, rather than relying on a pre-set formula. Many restaurateurs pride themselves on their menu, catch or dish of the day, which sets them free from the tyranny of the kitchen. Home cooks should follow the same example. Learning how to pick the best, and to know what to do with it when you get it home, requires a little practice, but confidence is more important than skill. The best is by no means the most expensive. Nor does this method of cooking require enormous dedication and time – precisely the opposite, for the better the ingredients, the fresher the food, the less the cook has to do to make the dish taste good.

This book is about good, seasonal cooking, and the key to this lies in clever shopping. The descriptions of markets are intended as sources of inspiration rather than tour guides. The idea is that you should find out what is available locally. If you are able to visit the markets mentioned, so much the better – they are good or interesting examples. But there are many others, just as there are many good shops and supermarkets. All the recipes are seasonal but that is not to say that some of the summer recipes won't also be good in autumn, and vice versa. Nor is seasonality restricted to UK-produced goods – imports too have their season. The ingredients, however, are generally at their most widely available and best in the seasons suggested for the recipes.

The recipes themselves are drawn across a wide range of culinary cultures, with perhaps an emphasis towards the Mediterranean. Olive oil is used more often than butter and cream, and fresh herbs, fruit and vegetables are a common feature. I prefer simple dishes which allow the ingredients to speak for themselves and don't tie the cook to the kitchen. There are recipes for entertaining and recipes for simple suppers but the gap between the two is not large. Fresh food means fresh cooking and the clever shopper can easily become the clever cook.

A NOTE ON QUANTITIES AND TEMPERATURES

All recipes are to serve 4, unless otherwise stated.

Quantities are given in both imperial and metric measurements. Do be careful not to mix the two – for each recipe you should use either imperial or metric, not a combination. A wine-glass, in my recipes, holds 6 fluid ounces.

Oven temperatures are given in Centigrade, Fahrenheit and Gas Mark. Ovens do vary enormously in their efficiency and therefore a verbal description of temperature is also included. You know your oven best and may like to make adjustments accordingly.

HERBS, SPICES, FATS AND OILS AND A FEW OTHER BASIC INGREDIENTS

Herbs

Fresh herbs are one of the delights of summer. Today, however, many indoor-grown herbs are available all year round, and generally are none the worse for it, although they may lack some of the pungency of the garden variety. Wherever possible I prefer to use fresh herbs, but some herbs do dry well, especially if you pick them at their best from the garden and dry them yourself. Never be tempted to use ready-prepared bouquets garnis, which resemble stale teabags. Try instead compiling your own bouquet from the herbs available or demanded by the dish – tying together a few sprigs of, say, parsley and thyme with a bayleaf is not an arduous task.

The following are the herbs I use most often.

BASIL

Fresh basil is my favourite herb and is essential to many Italian dishes. The dried variety bears no resemblance to the real thing and should not be given shelf space. To preserve a little of the basil flavour for the winter, steep leaves in extra virgin olive oil.

BAY

The flavour of fresh bayleaves far surpasses that of the dried variety. Tie one or two into a bouquet garni, use them to scent marinades and pâtés, thread them on kebabs Turkish style. Dry your own on the branch at home.

CHERVIL

The delicate fronds of chervil are excellent in creamy sauces and soups and with eggs. They are also good added to a salad of baby leaves.

CHIVES

Chives should always be picked young, before the stalks have become hollow and fibrous. They have a powerful flavour and should be used with care. The flowers are edible and can be sprinkled over a salad for a pretty effect in summer.

CORIANDER

Fresh coriander has a wonderfully sharp flavour and a pungent aroma. I find it difficult to grow in the quantities required, and buy huge bunches from the market or local ethnic shops. A bunch will keep for up to a week in the fridge if wrapped in damp newspaper. Fresh coriander is a vital element of much Middle Eastern, North African and Indian cookery. Coriander seeds have an entirely different flavour but are also useful.

DILL

Fronds of dill are delicious with many fish dishes, especially salmon. If you have plenty try making home-cured gravlaks. Dill seeds are also useful but, as with the seeds of coriander, quite different in flavour from the fresh herb.

FENNEL

The feathery fronds of fennel go well with fish and many vegetables, adding a slightly aniseedy flavour. Dry the thick stalks of the plant and throw them on the barbecue when you are cooking fish. Fennel seeds are commonly used in Italy to flavour sausages and in many Indian dishes.

MARJORAM

Marjoram is easy to grow. It adds a fine flavour to tomato sauces and is widely used in Italian cooking. It is virtually interchangeable with its wild cousin, oregano.

MINT

Fresh mint is used in puddings, drinks and savoury dishes. If you have an excess (mint spreads rapidly in the garden), use it to make a mint syrup or heavily sweetened mint tea. Mint also dries well, becoming more concentrated in flavour. In many Turkish dishes, dried mint should be used in preference to the fresh variety.

OREGANO

Oregano or wild marjoram is an essential element of Greek cooking. Try it sprinkled over thick slices of potato roasted in olive oil. Dried oregano is a passable imitation.

PARSLEY

I prefer to use the sweeter flat-leaved Italian or French varieties rather than the curly parsley which is more common in this country. There is no substitute for fresh parsley.

ROSEMARY

A powerful herb which can dominate a dish, a sprig or two of rosemary is, however, a vital ingredient of many Italian dishes. Try fresh needles sprinkled over focaccia. Rosemary is easy to dry at home on the branch and is one of the few herbs to retain much of its flavour when dried.

SAGE

Sage should be used with a very light hand – too much can quite over-power a dish. On the other hand, a few sprigs with calves' liver or in a pâté are delicious. Dried sage can be musty.

TARRAGON

A few leaves of fresh tarragon make all the difference to a chicken roasted in butter. Stick a branch in a bottle of white wine vinegar to make your own tarragon vinegar. Tarragon also dries reasonably well; the dried variety is useful for béarnaise. Be warned that the indoor-grown fresh herb available in winter can have an overpowering liquorice flavour, quite distinct from the subtlety of outdoor-grown tarragon.

THYME

There are many different varieties of thyme, from great bushes to tiny creeping plants which give off a wonderful aroma when crushed under-foot. One of my favourites is lemon thyme, which has a delicate hint of citrus. Use fresh thyme whenever possible, as the dried variety can taste rather musty.

Spices

Spices should be fresh. Roast whole seeds just before grinding (it is useful to have a separate coffee-grinder specifically for spices). Keep ground spices in airtight containers. And don't forget to have a periodic clean-out of the spice cupboard: stale spice can have a positively detrimental effect on a recipe.

The following are the spices I use regularly. Don't worry if you have only a few of them – it is far better to have a small selection of fresh spices than a whole cupboard of rarely used ones.

ALLSPICE

Allspice berries are useful in both sweet and savoury dishes, and especially good in marinades. When ground, the berries rapidly lose their flavour so keep them whole and grind them as necessary.

CARAWAY

The caraway seed has a strong flavour and should be used with care. It is common in northern European cooking and has an excellent affinity with the traditional cabbage and potato dishes of that region. It is also an essential accompaniment to a slice of Munster cheese from Alsace.

CARDAMOM

The wonderfully aromatic cardamom is widely used in both northern Indian and Middle Eastern cookery. The smaller green variety is sweeter than the black. I prefer to use the whole pods, adding one or two to a tagine or a curry, but you can also buy the small black seeds. Put a handful of whole pods in a jar of coffee to give it a Middle Eastern flavour.

CAYENNE PEPPER

Hot cayenne pepper goes stale more quickly than almost any other spice. Keep it in small containers and use it a pinch at a time.

CHILLIES

There is a vast range of chillies and it is important to pick the right variety for a particular dish – the difference between a large, mild green chilli and a red hot Jamaican bell pepper is astonishing. Keep small dried red chillies for grinding when a dish calls for chilli powder.

CINNAMON

Cinnamon sticks can be used whole for scenting casseroles, curries and tagines as well as puddings and even mulled wine. They are difficult to grind successfully at home and therefore ground cinnamon is also useful.

CLOVES

Cloves have a very pungent flavour and should be used with care. They are, however, an essential element not just of some English puddings but also of many savoury dishes. Rather than buying ground cloves, grind them yourself at home.

CORIANDER

Although I usually use coriander seeds in savoury dishes (a few seeds make all the difference to a ratatouille), their orangey scent can also add a distinctive flavour to creams and puddings. They are best kept whole, roasted and ground as necessary.

CUMIN

This is my favourite spice, and is an essential ingredient of Moroccan cooking among many others. For the best flavour, roast the cumin seeds in a dry pan, taking care they do not burn, before grinding to a powder. The powder will retain its wonderful scent for a few weeks – prepare a small batch at a time.

GINGER

There is a vast difference between the fresh green ginger root and the dry powdered variety. Peel the former and chop very finely before frying in many Chinese and Asian dishes; the latter adds piquancy to both sweet and savoury dishes.

JUNIPER BERRIES

The key flavouring in gin, juniper berries are also useful for marinades, particularly for game, and in pâtés.

MACE

Mace, the skin of the nutmeg, was once widely used in English cookery and gives a distinctive flavour to pâtés as well as sweet dishes.

MUSTARD SEEDS

The tiny black seeds of mustard can either be 'popped' in very hot oil or ground as part of a spice preparation. The results of the two methods are very different: the popped seeds are sweet, the ground uncooked ones much hotter.

NUTMEG

Nutmegs should be kept whole, and a little grated as required. The flavour can be overpowering, but a very small amount added to a creamy sauce or a plate of spinach has a subtle effect.

PAPRIKA

Paprika is made from dried sweet red peppers and stales very quickly. Fresh paprika is sweet and comes in varying degrees of 'heat' to the tongue. It is an important element of Eastern European cookery and is especially successful in dishes cooked with yoghurt or sour cream.

PEPPER

Cooking without the sweetest spice is almost unimaginable. There is no place in my kitchen for ready-ground black pepper – always grind your own, to differing degrees of coarseness according to the dish. I almost always use black pepper, but a grinder of mixed red, green and black peppercorns can be useful for steak seasoning. Pickled peppercorns taste more of vinegar than of the spice. The fresh green peppercorns occasionally available in supermarkets must be used quickly and are excellent with steak.

SAFFRON

Saffron is made from the dried stigmas of *Crocus sativus*. A great many flowers are required to produce even the tiniest amount of saffron, and for that reason it has long been known as the world's most expensive spice. If the saffron you buy is not expensive, it is not the real thing.

Saffron should be briefly roasted and then infused in a small amount of warm liquid before lending its extraordinary honeyed, slightly bitter flavour to tagines and puddings, risottos and soups. In my view powdered saffron is no good at all: it has almost always been adulterated. Indian shops are a good source of affordable, authentic saffron.

SESAME SEEDS

Always buy unhulled brownish sesame seeds for flavour, rather than the white hulled variety. The seeds have a full, nutty flavour, which is brought out by dry-roasting in a pan before sprinkling over both puddings and savoury dishes. Sesame seed paste, tahina, is another useful store-cupboard item.

TURMERIC

Often used for colour rather than flavour, the bright yellow ground turmeric can make a dish bitter if used to excess. However, it is an important element in many Indian and North African dishes.

VANILLA

Whole vanilla pods are useful for scenting creams and custards. A vanilla pod left for a few weeks in a jar of white sugar releases the vanilla fragrance into the sugar and you can use the same pod several times.

Fats

BUTTER

I prefer to use unsalted butter for cooking, adding salt as necessary. If butter is to be used for frying, it should first be clarified to prevent it burning: melt the butter and skim off the scum which rises to the surface before straining it through muslin. Alternatively, add a little olive oil to the butter to prevent browning.

GHEE

This is Indian clarified butter. It has a peculiarly sweet, nutty flavour which lends an irreplaceable flavour to many Indian dishes.

GOOSE FAT

If you roast a goose, make sure you keep the fat which drips off the bird. Potatoes roasted in the fat are wonderful, and it is the cooking medium to give an authentic flavour to many Gascon and Basque dishes. You can buy goose fat in tins or glass jars in France and in specialist shops in the UK. Duck fat should also be kept for cooking.

LARD

Commercially available lard adds little to a dish and I very rarely use it.

Oils

COCONUT OIL

Available from Indian shops, coconut oil is useful for giving an authentic flavour to southern Indian dishes. When cold the oil solidifies; stand the bottle in hot water to melt it.

OLIVE OIL

I keep three varieties of olive oil in my kitchen: 'ordinary' olive oil for frying, a mild extra virgin oil for everyday use, and a high-quality cold-pressed extra virgin oil for special dishes and salads. Wherever a recipe in this book calls for extra virgin oil, it is stated. It is a mistake to use extra virgin oil for everything, as it has too 'hot' a flavour for some dishes. As a general rule, the less cooking involved, the better-quality oil you should use.

Apart from the quality and method of production, there is a wide variance in taste between oils from different countries. To lend a particularly authentic flavour, you can use Greek oil for Greek dishes, Italian oil for Italian cooking and so on, although this may be taking matters too far. Personally, I prefer a fruity Tuscan olive oil, but it is very much a matter of taste – experiment until you find a producer you like. Remember, too, that the quality of oil produced from even one olive grove will vary from year to year, like wine.

Always keep olive oil in a sealed bottle and out of direct sunlight. In very cold weather the oil will cloud over.

MUSTARD OIL

Mustard oil should always be heated to give off its sweet, hot flavour. It is useful for northern Indian cookery, but should be bought in small quantities as it quickly turns rancid.

NUT OILS

There are a wide variety of nut oils, of which the most commonly found are those pressed from walnut and hazelnut. Only a very little of either is necessary to lend a distinctive flavour to a dish. Nut oils should be added at the end of cooking.

GROUNDNUT OIL

This is a good oil for deep-frying and can also be used with olive oil to make a salad dressing.

PEANUT OIL

I keep this oil for stir-frying.

SESAME SEED OIL

Sesame seed oil should be thick and brown – avoid the colourless refined variety. Like nut oils, a few drops should be used for flavouring rather than as a cooking medium.

SUNFLOWER OIL

The neutrally flavoured sunflower oil is often mixed with olive oil to make salad dressings and mayonnaise, cutting both the expense and the slightly hot flavour. Sunflower oil is also good for deep-frying.

Bacon

The majority of the bacon sold in this country is a travesty of the real thing, seeping water as soon as you put it in the pan. Real bacon, which gives off fat rather than scum, is hard to find. Look out for a supplier who will cut your bacon from a side, so that you can buy thick slices for lardons when necessary. I often use the Italian pancetta, which is cured in salt and spices rather than smoked, and is available from Italian delicatessens. Pancetta keeps for several weeks in the fridge, so it is worth buying a thick slice or two.

Chocolate

Chocolate can be an ingredient in savoury as well as sweet dishes, but you should never use the kind sold as 'cooking chocolate'. Look for bitter chocolate with a high ratio of cocoa solids – French and Swiss makes are usually the best.

Flour

I prefer to use plain white flour and add baking powder if necessary, rather than buying self-raising flour. Strong plain white bread flour should be a store-cupboard staple, so that you can produce a pizza at a couple of hours' notice. I find wholemeal flour too heavy for pastry or bread and rarely use it.

Garlic

Garlic should always be firm to the touch. If the cloves feel soft or the garlic has started to sprout, discard it – it is better to use none at all. In late summer look out for fat heads of new season's garlic, lightly tinged with pink, which have a wonderfully pungent flavour.

Parmesan

Where a recipe calls for parmesan, always use Parmigiano Reggiano, preferably grated at home from a chunk of the cheese (be sure to ask the delicatessen for cooking parmesan, as opposed to that sold for eating straight). The 'parmesan' sold in tubs is no relation.

Pulses

It is important to remember that, although dried, pulses can still be 'fresh'. Stale lentils, for example, can take twice as long to cook as fresh ones. Pulses should therefore always be kept sealed, bought as and when necessary from stores with a high turnover, and used within six months. My store-cupboard usually contains chickpeas, white haricot beans, lentils, red kidney beans, yellow split peas, green flageolets, cannellini and borlotti beans. Tinned pre-cooked beans can be useful, but they have a soggier consistency than those cooked at home as well as often having added sugar, which renders their liquid useless for many dishes. Dried pulses (with the exception of lentils) should be soaked well and boiled hard for 10 minutes to rid them of impurities before simmering.

Rice

The right type of rice is vital for certain dishes. A risotto should always be made with Arborio or Vialone rice, the plump, slightly yellow Italian varieties which require slow cooking in hot stock. The small-grained Basmati rice from the Himalayan regions of northern India and Pakistan is the ideal variety to accompany both curries and Middle Eastern dishes. It is best cooked by just covering with water and simmering in a covered pan until all the water is absorbed, and is also an excellent rice to use for the Persian method of dry-cooking the part-boiled rice with plenty of butter. Long-grain rice is good for everyday dishes, when the rice is to be simply boiled – I prefer Italian long-grain rice to the American variety. The almost black American wild rice is a useful addition to the store-cupboard; mixed with white rice it makes an excellent stuffing medium. I would always choose wild rice in preference to the healthy but husky brown variety.

Salt

I prefer to use coarse-ground sea salt, either adding a few whole crystals to the dish during cooking or grinding it from a mill. It is quite impossible to imagine cooking without salt, but it should always be used with care – too little can be remedied but too much can be a disaster. The key is to taste regularly during cooking and to remember that as you reduce a sauce the salty flavour accentuates. If you can taste the salt, you have added too much – it should be used as a flavour enhancer.

Stock

A good stock is the basis for many dishes. Get in the habit of making a stock whenever you have a carcass, bones or vegetables left over, so that you have plenty in the freezer. As a good substitute for stock-cubes, freeze highly reduced stock in an ice-cube tray. Chicken, vegetable and fish stocks are the ones I use most frequently.

Tomatoes

The search for juicy, sweet tomatoes is a constant source of aggravation for the British cook. Somewhere along the line our suppliers sacrificed taste for appearance and quantity, producing the perfectly round and utterly flavourless tomatoes which are now, sadly, the norm. If you can find sun-ripened Marmande or plum tomatoes, or grow them yourself, you will know the difference. A partial solution to the problem is to use canned Italian plum tomatoes and tomato paste. Sun-dried tomatoes preserved in olive oil are also useful in the store-cupboard.

Vinegar

A wide range of vinegars is now easily available. These are the ones I use most frequently.

BALSAMIC VINEGAR

Authentic balsamic vinegar comes only from Modena, in the Po Valley in northern Italy. The very best is exorbitantly expensive as a result of the long maturing process, using casks of different woods, and is good enough to sip all on its own. The cheaper varieties also have the distinctive sweet flavour and dark, thick consistency. Balsamic vinegar should be used only in small quantities – a quick swirl in a fresh tomato sauce, a splash in the frying-pan just before serving, a few drips over a bowl of salad leaves.

CHAMPAGNE VINEGAR

Although only tiny quantities of champagne are used in its manufacture, champagne vinegar has greater elegance than an ordinary white wine vinegar. It is particularly good for summer salad dressings and as a base for home-made fruit vinegars – try popping in a handful of raspberries and leaving to macerate for a few weeks.

CIDER VINEGAR

You can smell the apples in a good cider vinegar. It is very good for pickling, for marinades for pork, and for adding a little sharpness to autumn casseroles with apples.

FRUIT-FLAVOURED VINEGARS

A splash of raspberry vinegar can give a welcome lift to a rich dish – it is especially good with duck, particularly a confit. Too much, however, can be overwhelming. Other soft fruits are also used to scent vinegars – try making your own strawberry vinegar by macerating a handful of ripe fruit in some white wine vinegar.

HERB VINEGARS

The most commonly used herb vinegar is that flavoured with tarragon, a crucial ingredient of a good béarnaise. You can make your own simply by pushing a branch of tarragon into a bottle of white wine vinegar and leaving it for a few weeks. Use the same principle to scent vinegars with thyme, sage and rosemary.

MALT VINEGAR

Although this is the traditional British vinegar, I have to admit there is rarely a bottle in my kitchen.

RAISIN VINEGAR

This reddish-brown vinegar is common in Turkey but can be difficult to find in this country. If you do see some, buy it, as it is an excellent medium for pickling.

RED WINE VINEGAR

I prefer white wine vinegars for salad dressings and keep red wine vinegars for adding to casseroles and stews – a few drops can enliven a whole dish. For home-made red wine vinegar, put a 'mother' vinegar in a bottle and add the dregs of red wine bottles as and when they are available, draining the vinegar through muslin before using.

RICE WINE VINEGAR

Keep a bottle of rice wine vinegar for Chinese and Japanese dishes – its distinctive flavour is difficult to substitute.

SHERRY VINEGAR

Sherry vinegar from Spain has a rich, full, slightly sweet flavour and a dark colour. Essential for gazpacho, it is also very good mixed with walnut oil for a salad dressing and in many marinades.

WHITE WINE VINEGAR

White wine vinegar is the classic base for a vinaigrette. It can vary wildly in quality – look for a vinegar which is smooth, with no sharp edges and a distinctively winy taste.

Wine

Wine for cooking must be fit to drink. Better to leave the wine out than use the oxidized dregs of a bottle which has been open for a week – but neither do you need to use an expensive claret. As a general rule, the best wine for cooking is a reasonable bottle from the region in which the dish you are making originated. For example, use a Dão in Portuguese dishes, a Rhône wine for southern French cooking, an Alsatian wine for an Alsatian dish. If you haven't a local wine, use one made from the same grape variety or with similar qualities. Where wine is called for in a recipe, I have made suggestions.

When you cook with wine, the aim is to impart the flavour to the dish but not the alcohol. The dish should boil or simmer after the addition of the wine until the alcohol has been cooked off. Unless of course the dish is not to be cooked at all – one of my favourite puddings is peaches steeped in Beaujolais or a similarly light red wine.

SPRING

SPRING IS A TIME OF TRANSI-
TION, AS WE MOVE SLOWLY FROM
COLD SHORT WINTER DAYS WHEN FOOD NEEDS
to be hearty and hot, to long summer evenings when
the demand is for light, colourful dishes. Spring is the
time when oysters and mussels are slowly replaced
by crabs and lobsters; when Welsh spring lamb
gradually comes into the shops, taking over from the
older hogget; when the first spring salad leaves poke
through the ground. If summer is a period of glut,
spring is a time of reintroduction, of delighted
recognition as each familiar treat, forgotten in the
long months of winter, returns to the market – the
first tiny new potatoes one day, thin green sprues of
English asparagus the next.

The trouble is, many of these delights have been
dulled by the year-round availability of produce,
asparagus in February, new potatoes in November,
'spring' lamb all year round. Of course, some imports
are to be welcomed – spring would be a poor season
for fruit if we could not enjoy the tropical varieties. I
take as much pleasure in the first artichokes from
Italy as in the first British asparagus. The issue is not
importing per se, but importing the right produce at
the right time.

For those cooks who want to follow the spring
season through at a natural pace, the market is the
place to shop. One stallholder promises that she will
have her first tiny root vegetables tomorrow; the
fishmonger suggests a little crab salad, or a sea trout.
Our British markets may not be such a spring treat as
those of, say, the Mediterranean, but the market does
keep the careful shopper in touch with the burgeon-
ing of spring.

STARTERS

Starters from my kitchen generally involve some form of seasonal vegetable. Seasonality should not be slavish. Modern production methods and means of transport ensure that much produce is available outside its historic British growing season. A good example is the range of herbs, which if grown outdoors are restricted to the summer months. Today you can buy most herbs all year round. But there are other vegetables which it is worth waiting for, rather than substituting forced produce. Early asparagus somehow never seems to measure up to our home-grown plants which begin in May; the Jersey potatoes in the same month are a treat; the tiny spring shoots of salad leaves grown out of doors have a special sweetness.

The first month of the British spring often brings dull weather and even duller vegetables. The winter supplies are past their best and the spring imports from the Mediterranean have yet to get going; British produce, even the early vegetables from the Channel Islands, will not be ready for some time. March is the month to rely on cupboard staples for starters: pulses cooked with spices for a Moroccan harira, home-made hummus, bean salads, tabbouleh.

As spring takes hold, the options for the cook increase. The adventurous can pick young weeds from the hedgerows for salads, dandelion leaves being a particular favourite; artichokes from the Mediterranean make a first appearance (although we rarely see the tiny 2 inch variety, so popular in Italy); small leaves of spinach are ideal for salads and tarts. By May, the choice is wide; tiny pale yellow carrots, sweet white turnips, broad beans in pods no longer than your thumb are all ingredients for starters. Jersey, home of the royal potato, starts its spring season up to a month earlier than the mainland, by virtue of being 100 miles further south and enjoying weather on average 3 or 4 degrees warmer. I went there to have a look at the market in St Helier.

Jersey's Early Spring

Jersey is about as near to France as you can get in Britain. And not just physically: Jersey's heritage has as much in common with Normandy and Brittany as it does with the mainland. It is British today because William the Conqueror, Duke of Normandy, was once its owner. The island's split personality is perfectly reflected in the names of the locals – where else could you find a Doug le Masurier, a Brian le Marquand or a Bob de la Haye?

There is one aspect of the island which is distinctly French – the attitude to food. The people of Jersey take their food very seriously indeed. Not surprisingly, for, together with tourism and finance, agriculture is a prop of the economy. The southerly position, the Gulf Stream and the resulting warmer temperatures mean that Jersey can steal a march on the mainland for seasonal vegetables. But it is not just money that drives the Jersey interest in food – there is a real concern for good eating here. You only need to take a look at St Helier's markets to feel it.

The Central Market for produce is a good example of the island's Anglo-French divide. The building is unmistakably British, a perfect example of Victorian kitsch. Built in 1882, it has been preserved with very little change, right down to the outrageous central fountain, fifteen feet high with four tiers supported by plump nymphs. But the role of the market in everyday living is much more Continental – it has been estimated that 35 per cent of the resident population of Jersey pass through it in any one week. The market may be a tourist attraction, but it is also a central element of Jersey life. This is a small place, where everyone knows everyone. So a visit to the market is, as it should be, as much of a social occasion as a shopping expedition.

One stallholder who certainly knows everybody is the redoubtable Maggie Allain, who has worked in the market for over forty years and today runs her fruit and vegetable stall with the help of her three sisters. In late spring, Maggie's stall displays the best vegetables Jersey has to offer. This is produce grown on a small scale for local consumption, supplied direct by local smallholders. Almost all of it has been picked fresh that morning. There are bright green bunches of slender asparagus, ready to be steamed for lunch – try an asparagus risotto. The small pods of broad beans, at least a month ahead of those on the mainland, look sweet enough to be eaten whole; braise them in olive oil with dill and dried mint for a rich Turkish dish. The first courgettes are short and firm, just right for grilling; unfortunately the market doesn't sell the courgette flowers, which give such a splash of yellow to market stalls in the south of France and Italy. Colour comes instead from the bunches of bright orange carrots, topped with their virulent green fronds; eat them raw, or serve them as a starter with pinenuts and griddled spring onions. Try a similar treatment for the dark green calabrese, the florets separated and tossed with chilli peppers and cumin seeds. It is too early for the outdoor-grown tomatoes, but there is greenhouse produce, piles of misshapen, green-striped Marmandes, the sort that our supermarkets reject on the grounds of appearance but that the serious shopper seeks out for flavour. And don't forget the new season's turnips, so different from the woody winter roots, and pretty too, their white flesh dashed with rosy pink. These, Maggie has to admit, come from France; Jersey, she feels, hasn't quite got the hang of root vegetables. Despite its having been the mainstay of the diet during the years of the German Occupation, she believes that the vegetable which grows worst on the island is the swede. Not an insurmountable tragedy.

There is one root Jersey does know about, the tuberous one of the potato. The Jersey Royal is one of the few remaining truly seasonal vegetables – the glasshouse-grown version simply doesn't taste the same. The season is a short one, over by mid June. At its height, in mid May, every stall in St Helier market has its Jersey Royals proudly on display, and the stallholders can tell you precisely which farm they have come from. The experienced shop around to find those grown on the traditional cotils, the steep-sided slopes which necessitate hand-picking, which is less likely to bruise the delicate tuber. The taste of a Jersey potato picked that morning, simply washed clean and steamed or boiled, is a gastronomic experience. They are good enough to be served alone, as a starter with a little hollandaise sauce, or as the main element of a salad, perhaps with bacon and dandelion leaves. Those you buy on the mainland may not be quite so fresh, but the Jersey Ministry of Agriculture estimates that it takes only forty-eight hours for their potatoes to reach the shelves. Choose potatoes of equal size, with no hint of green, keep them in a dark place and cook them as soon as possible to enjoy the unique flavour. And it really is unique: attempts to grow the Jersey Royal outside the island have, to date, all been a failure.

Arguments rage as to whether your potatoes should be cooked with mint. I think not, for the astringent flavour of the herb can overpower the delicacy of the potato. But whether you are pro or anti, you will be disappointed when looking for herbs in St Helier's market. This, I'm afraid, reflects the English side of Jersey. With their early spring and sunny summer, the island has just the climate for herbs – take a look at the herb garden at the delightful Samares Manor for evidence. On my visit to the market I expected to find great fragrant bunches of herbs sitting beside the produce, perfect for spring starters. But the only herbs on offer were a few paltry specimens in plastic pots. There were other omissions too: not an artichoke in sight, although the vegetable garden of Jersey's smartest hotel, Longueville Manor, showed that they grow very well there. On the other hand, neither herbs nor artichokes are a part of Jersey's culinary inheritance; the island remains true to its Norman roots.

A visit to the St Helier central market is a pleasure for the cook. No one minds if you feel the produce, or ask where it came from – indeed, they expect it. Take your time, for the pace of life on Jersey is slow. When you have bought all your vegetables, have a look at the butchers with their displays of Jersey beef, the dark red meat marbled with very yellow fat. The beef is particularly popular with the immigrant Portuguese population, who understand that the fat provides the flavour. Next door you will find the more familiar products of the doe-eyed Jersey cow, thick cream and slabs of butter. Then wander over the road for an even greater treat, the small fish market. Here you will find piles of local plaice and lemon sole, one or two still flapping; small sea bass, ideal for the barbecue; pike brought over from France, for quenelles and pâtés; thick tuna steaks, fresh enough to be served raw. Best of all, though, are the shellfish, fat scallops and clams, ten different sizes of prawn and small sweet local mussels. In the tanks at the back of the stalls there are live lobsters and from time to time crates of huge crabs arrive, a mass of waving claws. In summer the spider crabs, relegated to bait in England, appear in the St Helier market – those that haven't been exported to Spain, where spider crabs are popular for soups and salads. Jersey restocked its oyster beds with the Pacific variety after the natives were ravaged by disease, so you can get oysters all year round; the two high seasons for the oyster growers are Christmas for France and the summer for local consumption. And don't miss the ormers if you can find them – they're a local delicacy similar to the abalone.

The island's cooking, a blend of British and Norman French, is some distance from my own preferences. The emphasisis is on rich dishes, often featuring butter and cream and with little spice, tending to mask the elegant simplicity of the ingredients. But if I am not jealous of Jersey's cooking, I do envy its inhabitants their market – especially in spring, when the early produce is at its best.

ASPARAGUS RISOTTO

The first British asparagus appear in May and are a treat worth waiting for. Look carefully at the tips before buying – any which are discoloured or show signs of sogginess are past their best and should be rejected. Big fat white asparagus (excellent ones come from Italy and Alsace) need nothing more than steaming before being served dripping in butter, or perhaps with olive oil and parmesan (see summer recipe, page 128). But the first British asparagus are often slender green sprues, which are perfect for a risotto. Made with just the tips of the asparagus, this is an extravagant, luxurious dish. The asparagus is steamed over the fragrant rice cooking in stock, the whole then glossed with butter and taken straight to the table. Italian style, the risotto can precede a light main course (grilled fish would be ideal) or alternatively be served as a main dish.

approx. 1 1/2 pints (850 ml) chicken or vegetable stock (*a stock cube won't do here – a risotto is only as good as the stock with which it is made; ideally, make the stock from the ends of the asparagus, with an onion and perhaps a chicken wing or two*)
3 oz (85 g) unsalted butter

10 oz (285 g) Arborio rice
24 tips of asparagus, about 3 inches (7.5 cm) long (*the thinner sprues are good for this dish*)
salt and freshly ground black pepper
4 oz (115 g) freshly grated parmesan (Parmigiano-Reggiano)

To make a risotto you need a wide, reasonably heavy-based frying-pan with a lid, a separate saucepan containing the stock, and a ladle with which to add the hot stock to the rice. The trick is to keep the stock at a constant temperature just off the boil, so that the temperature in the risotto pan barely changes as you add more liquid. This sounds more complicated than it really is.

Once the stock has heated up to just below the boil, melt 1 oz (25 g) of the butter in the frying-pan and add the rice. Make sure all the grains are coated in a little fat by stirring them around. Add the first ladle of hot stock. Stir well until all the liquid is absorbed by the rice and then add another ladleful. Continue this process until the rice is three-quarters cooked, i.e. each grain separate and plump but still with considerable bite. It should take about 15–20 minutes to reach this stage – taste to make sure. Now add the asparagus tips and another ladle of stock. When the rice is ready (another 5 minutes or so – taste again), turn off the heat and cover for 5 minutes before serving – the asparagus will finish cooking in the steam from the risotto. Season to taste. Dot with the remaining butter, sprinkle with parmesan and serve.

AUBERGINE AND BLACK OLIVE PASTE

This highly flavoured concoction of aubergines and olives is designed to be spread on toasted bread. I often serve these crostini as a nibble with drinks or as a light starter, especially in early spring, when they give a hint of Mediterranean flavours to come as the weather warms up. The paste is a rather ominous black colour – top each crostini with a whole olive or a couple of leaves of parsley to counteract this, if you like.

1 large aubergine, approx. 12 oz (350 g)
salt
6 oz (170 g) small black olives, marinated in olive oil rather than brine
3 oz (85 g) fresh white breadcrumbs
1 teaspoon ground cumin (*for the fullest flavour, toast whole cumin seeds in a dry frying-pan before grinding in a coffee grinder*)
1 teaspoon freshly ground black pepper
2 tablespoons extra virgin olive oil
juice of 1 lemon
good-quality white bread (*the Italian olive oil bread, ciabatta, is my favourite*)

Chop the aubergine into 3/4 inch (2 cm) thick slices, sprinkle them with salt and leave them in a colander for 30 minutes, so that the bitter juices drain away. Rinse the aubergine very thoroughly and pat dry. Pre-heat the grill to maximum and grill the slices until the flesh is very tender and the skin is blackened (about 6–7 minutes on either side). Peel off the skin and discard; mash the flesh of the aubergines with a fork or purée in the food processor.

Pit the olives if they still have their stones. Chop them very finely or give them a quick whizz in the food processor (but not enough to reduce them to a paste).

Mix together with a fork the olives, mashed aubergine, bread-crumbs, cumin, pepper, olive oil and lemon juice (if you like a smoother texture, you can again use the food processor, but I prefer the spread to be a little chunky). Pack the resulting mixture into a serving dish and chill well.

Serve the spread, with drinks or as a starter, on toasted pieces of white bread. If you want to keep the spread for a few days, dribble a thin layer of olive oil on top and keep in the refrigerator.

BAKED RED PEPPERS

Although capsicum peppers are now available all year round thanks to imports, in my opinion the sweetest still come from the Mediterranean. The first of these appear in the market in late April and go on through the summer months. The red peppers are the ripest and therefore the fullest in flavour. All foodies now know about roasting peppers, as a result of which many of us have forgotten that they can be just as delicious baked in olive oil, especially when filled with a pungent mixture of anchovies, garlic and capers.

- 4 red peppers, firm and unwrinkled, with no brown patches on the skin
- 2 tablespoons chopped flat-leaved parsley
- 2 large flavourful tomatoes (*misshapen Marmande are best, if you can find them*)
- 2 or 3 cloves of garlic
- 8 best-quality anchovy fillets, preserved in olive oil
- 1 tablespoon capers (*I use those preserved in salt rather than brine – but you must soak these in cold water for 30 minutes before using*)
- 4 tablespoons extra virgin olive oil
- freshly ground black pepper

Slit the red peppers in half from the stalk down. Remove the seeds and stringy white flesh but leave the stalk on. Wash well.

Pre-heat the oven to medium low (130°C/275°F/Gas 1). Arrange the peppers skin side down in a dish into which they will just fit. Chop the parsley very finely. Chop the washed tomatoes into fine slices. Finely chop the garlic. Lay 2 anchovy fillets in the cup of each pepper and sprinkle with chopped garlic, a few capers and some of the parsley. Cover with a few slices of tomato and sprinkle on more parsley. Dribble over $^1/_2$ a tablespoon of olive oil and season with freshly ground black pepper. Repeat for each pepper half.

Bake in the oven for about 30 minutes, until the peppers are tender. Serve with plenty of bread, 2 halves of pepper per person.

CARROT AND PINENUT SALAD

The first of the new season's carrots are so sweet and tender that they deserve pride of place, rather than being used as an accessory. I serve them as the main ingredient of a light and colourful salad for a starter. The salad is good enough to stand alone, but can also be served as part of a selection.

1 lb (450 g) very fresh small carrots, tops on
8 spring onions
2 oz (55 g) pinenuts
1 teaspoon coarse sea-salt
1/2 a clove of garlic
pinch of brown sugar
2 1/2 tablespoons extra virgin olive oil
1/2 teaspoon roughly crushed black peppercorns
juice of 1 lemon
1 tablespoon chopped flat-leaved parsley

Wash the carrots thoroughly and trim them so that only a small sprig of green remains. Trim the tough green ends from the spring onions.

Pre-heat the oven to hot (200°C/400°F/Gas 6). Lay the pinenuts on a baking tray and sprinkle with the sea salt. Roast them in the oven for 5 minutes or so, turning once, until lightly browned. Watch them like a hawk to make sure they don't burn. Leave to cool.

Place the carrots in a pan in which they will lie flat. Add just enough water to cover them, together with a pinch of salt, the garlic, the sugar and 1/2 a tablespoon of the olive oil. Simmer uncovered until all the liquid has evaporated and the carrots are tender. Dress them while still warm with the remaining oil, the black pepper and the lemon juice.

Place a non-stick frying pan or, even better, a griddle, over a high heat. Add no oil. When the surface is very hot, add the whole spring onions and cook, turning once, for 5–7 minutes, until they have blackened in patches and are tender. Chop into chunks and add to the carrots. Remove the garlic and stir in the chopped parsley. Sprinkle over the toasted nuts and serve with plenty of bread.

CHICKPEA AND LENTIL SOUP

This substantial soup is a version of the Moroccan harira, served at sundown during the Ramadan month of fasting. Ramadan falls in the ninth month of the Moslem calendar, but ever since my first encounter with it during a March visit to Marrakesh, I associate it with spring. At dusk each night huge crowds of men gathered around the cauldrons which had been set up in the central square, the Djemaa el Fna, waiting for the signal that eating could begin. The bubbling soup gave off a spicy aroma, scenting the air with cinnamon and ginger, lemon and coriander. The waiting was a true test of faith.

There are many different versions of harira; some include meat, others different pulses, still others are finished with eggs. I stick with chickpeas and lentils, sometimes adding a chicken carcass or a lamb bone to give body to the stock. The soup is designed above all to fill empty stomachs quickly, but what it lacks in elegance it makes up for in flavour. Try it for a family supper on a cool spring day.

Spring

Serves 6–8

6 oz (170 g) dried chickpeas
(*you can use a 15 oz
(425 g) can of chickpeas if
you like, but the soup tastes
better if the water in which
the chickpeas were cooked is
included*)

1 chicken carcass or lamb
bone (optional)

4 oz (115 g) dried lentils (*I
usually prefer the green or
brown variety, but for this
soup I use yellow split
lentils*)

1 teaspoon turmeric

2 teaspoons ground
cinnamon

1 teaspoon ground ginger

1 teaspoon ground cumin

1 teaspoon freshly ground
black pepper

1 teaspoon salt

1 lb (450 g) tomatoes and
1 teaspoon tomato purée
or a 14 oz (400 g) tin
Italian plum tomatoes

2 onions

juice of 1 large lemon

2 tablespoons plain flour

1 tablespoon ghee or
clarified butter

2 tablespoons chopped fresh
coriander

2 tablespoons chopped flat-
leaved parsley

lemon slices

1 small tin harissa paste (*this
fiery paste made from red
chilli peppers is optional –
you can get it from good
delicatessens*)

Soak the chickpeas overnight. The next day, bring them to the boil in 4
pints (2.3 litres) of water (do not add salt at this stage) and simmer for
about 1 hour until tender. If you are using the chicken carcass or lamb
bone, include this in the pan. When the chickpeas are soft, remove the
chicken carcass or lamb bone and add the lentils to the pan together with
the turmeric, cinnamon, ginger, cumin, pepper and salt. Simmer for 20
minutes until the lentils are soft.

Meanwhile, if you are using fresh tomatoes, peel and de-seed them.
An easy way of doing this, if the tomatoes are very ripe, is to halve them
and squeeze them against a grater until only the skin is left; you can also
dip them in boiling water. Chop the onions very finely. When the lentils
are tender, add the onions, the tomatoes, and the tomato purée if you are
using it. Top up with more water if necessary. Add the lemon juice to the

pan and taste to see if the seasoning is right. Cook for another 20–30 minutes.

Just before serving, beat the flour into $^1/_4$ pint (150 ml) of cold water, making sure there are no lumps. Stir the ghee into the soup until it has dissolved, followed by the finely chopped herbs. Finally, stir in the flour water and cook for another few minutes. This unfashionable but good touch gives the soup a slightly glutinous texture.

Serve the soup steaming hot, with a dusting of cinnamon and a slice or two of lemon floating on the surface of each bowl. I serve a little dish of harissa paste separately, for guests to help themselves. If you can't get harissa, you might like to add a few drops of Tabasco.

GLOBE ARTICHOKES – STUFFED AND ROMAN-STYLE

Imported globe artichokes come to the market in April, but the first ones are generally a little tougher or less hearty than those later in the season. Look out, though, for the baby variety from the Mediterranean, which if you are lucky enough to find them are delicious stewed whole in oil. For days when the weather is not right for eating artichokes cold with a vinaigrette, try stuffing them before braising them. This highly flavoured pork stuffing mixture turns the artichoke into a substantial first course or lunch dish.

STUFFED ARTICHOKES

4 large globe artichokes
(*make sure they are firm,
and avoid any whose leaves
are tinged with brown*)
1/2 a lemon
10 oz (285 g) belly pork
6 oz (170 g) pancetta or
unsmoked streaky bacon
1 large egg
2 tablespoons chopped flat-
leaved parsley
4 sprigs of thyme or
1/2 teaspoon dried thyme

1 teaspoon ground
coriander
1/2 teaspoon ground black
pepper
1/4 teaspoon ground mace
1 carrot
1 onion
1 glass dry white wine
1 pint (575 ml) chicken or
vegetable stock
1 teaspoon potato starch
red wine vinegar
string

Trim the artichokes of their stalks and any tough or discoloured outer leaves. With a sharp knife, cut across the artichoke about 1 inch from the top of the leaves, so that you have a flat surface. Rub the cut end of each leaf with the 1/2 lemon to prevent it from discolouring.

Bring a large pan of water to the boil and cook the artichokes for 5 minutes. Remove and leave to cool.

Trim the skin and bone from the belly pork. With a sharp knife, cut the meat into tiny pieces or mince in the food processor. Do the same for the pancetta.

Mix the chopped meats together with the egg, herbs and spices. Add a little salt if you like, but remember that the pancetta is quite salty.

The artichokes should by now be cool enough for you to remove the hairy, bitter choke. With a small, sharp knife cut into the centre of each artichoke from the top. Pull out the soft central leaves and scrape away the hairy choke until you reach the heart. Rinse well under the tap to remove any lingering hairs, pulling the outside leaves apart to create a central cavity. Stuff the meat mixture into the centre of each artichoke and tie around the outside with string.

Heat the oven to medium (150°C/300°F/Gas 2). Peel the carrot and onion and chop roughly. Stand the artichokes in a casserole into which they just fit. Add the chopped carrot and onion and the wine. Bring to the boil and simmer for a few minutes. Add sufficient stock to come halfway up the side of the artichokes and cover the casserole with a piece of buttered greaseproof paper. Put the lid on top and cook in the oven for 45–60 minutes, until the stuffing is cooked and the artichokes are very tender.

Remove the artichokes from the casserole, cut away the string, and put them to keep warm while you make a simple sauce. Strain the liquid and bring to the boil. Reduce by a third. Dissolve the potato starch in a little water and slowly stir into the liquid to thicken it slightly. Add a few drops of red wine vinegar and check seasoning.

Place the artichokes in a pool of sauce and serve.

ROMAN-STYLE ARTICHOKES

The Italians are great lovers of artichokes – they even make a bitter apéritif, Cynar, from them. Every Roman restaurant will have artichokes on the menu in spring. Favourite ways of preparing them include deep-frying in olive oil and, from the city's Jewish community, this recipe for artichokes braised in olive oil with plenty of garlic, parsley and mint. The stalks are left on, as they are also good to eat.

4 small globe artichokes
$^1/_2$ a lemon
2 cloves of garlic
2 tablespoons chopped flat-leaved parsley

1 tablespoon chopped fresh mint or 1 teaspoon dried mint
4 tablespoons olive oil

Cut off the ends of the artichoke stalks and with a potato peeler remove their fibrous outer skin. Tear off any damaged, discoloured or tough outer leaves from the outside of the choke and then, with a sharp knife, cut across the leaves about 1 inch (2.5 cm) from the tip. With the point of the knife, remove the central leaves and the hairy choke, as in the previous recipe. Rub the cut surfaces immediately with the $^1/_2$ lemon, to prevent discolouring.

Chop the garlic, parsley and mint together very finely. Season well and pack this mixture into the central cavities of the artichokes. Place the artichokes flat (i.e. stalk pointing upwards) in a lidded enamel or heat-proof earthenware pan into which they will just fit (metal pans can give an unpleasant taste to the dish and cause discoloration). Pour over the olive oil and add sufficient water to come about a third of the way up the chokes. Cover with foil and put the lid on top. Cook gently over a low heat for about 30 minutes, until the chokes are very tender and most of the liquid has been absorbed. Leave to cool before serving with a squeeze of lemon.

New Potato and Dandelion Salad

The first new potatoes, especially the Jersey Royals, are good enough to be served on their own as a first course, with a hollandaise sauce, or you can use them as the basis for a warm salad. Spring is also the time for the cook to pick young weeds such as dandelions or nettles. The slightly bitter taste of the dandelion is very popular in France, where they are raised by market gardeners, obviating the need to scour the hedgerows. If you choose the latter course, be careful to do so well away from roads or cultivated fields, where insecticides may recently have been sprayed. If dandelion leaves are too hard to come by, you can use other leaves such as lamb's lettuce, rocket, or spinach.

1 lb (450 g) new potatoes
(*Jersey Royals are the best,
but you can also use
varieties grown especially
for salads, such as La Ratte
and Pink Fir Apple – try
to choose potatoes of
roughly equal size so that
they cook at the same rate*)

8 oz (225 g) small
dandelion leaves

5 oz (140 g) smoked streaky
bacon, preferably in 1 or
2 thick slices so you can
cut off cubes or lardons

4 shallots (*they should be
firm, with no green shoots
– if you can't get shallots,
which are at their best in
winter, use a mild red
onion*)

1 small bunch of fresh
chives if available

4 tablespoons extra virgin
olive oil

3 tablespoons red wine
vinegar

salt and freshly ground
black pepper

Wash the potatoes and boil them in their skins until tender, with just a little remaining bite (about 10–15 minutes, depending on size). Meanwhile pick over the dandelion or other salad leaves and wash very well. Chop any of the bigger leaves in half. Chop the bacon into lardons (small oblongs). Peel the shallots or onion and chop finely together with the chives if you have them.

Mix the oil with 1 tablespoon of the vinegar and salt and pepper to taste. When the potatoes are cooked, drain them, slice them in half and dress immediately with the oil and vinegar mixture. Stir in the chopped shallots or onion and chives.

Fry the bacon gently in its own fat until crisp. Stir the crispy lardons into the dandelion leaves, with any fat from the pan. Pour the remaining vinegar into the pan and allow to bubble briefly before pouring over the dandelion and bacon mixture. Finally, stir the potato mixture into the dandelion leaves and serve, with plenty of bread.

PARSEE OKRA OMELETTE

Okra are now available virtually all year round thanks to the transglobal nature of the vegetable market, but they vary wildly in quality. The best are small in size, green throughout rather than tinged with brown, and feel yielding rather than tough to the touch. Despite their provenance from many different countries, as the summer season goes on they seem to become larger and more fibrous. In early spring, and again in autumn, they are at their tenderest and sweetest.

Okra need careful cooking to avoid a glutinuous brown mess. One of my favourite recipes is from the Parsee cuisine of India, given to me by the most generous wife of a Mr Khotawalla, who runs a game reserve near 'Snooty Ooti' in the Nilgiri Hills. The table she set out for dinner was incomparable. This oven-baked omelette was only a small part of the starters on offer but makes a memorable dish all on its own.

2 small onions
12 oz (350 g) okra
3 small fresh green chillies
   (*or fewer, to taste – but do*
   not leave them out
   altogether)
8 oz (225 g) tomatoes
   (*tinned tomatoes do not*
   have the right consistency
   for this dish)

1 tablespoon sunflower or
   vegetable oil
1 teaspoon ground cumin
$^1/_2$ teaspoon salt
$^1/_2$ teaspoon freshly ground
   black pepper
$^1/_4$ teaspoon cayenne pepper
2 tablespoons finely
   chopped fresh coriander
6 large eggs

Chop the peeled onions finely. Wash the okra, top and tail them and cut into $^1/_2$ inch (1 cm) sections. Chop the chillies finely (I leave the seeds in for this dish, but you may prefer to exclude them for less of a bite). Peel the tomatoes by first plunging them in boiling water to loosen the skins, and chop coarsely. Pre-heat the oven to medium (150°C/300°F/Gas 2).

Heat the oil in a frying-pan and fry the onion for a few minutes, until translucent. Add the chopped okra and fry over a medium high heat for 3–4 minutes, until the okra start to give off a glutinous juice but are still green. Now stir in the cumin, salt, pepper and cayenne, followed by the chopped tomatoes and chillies. Cook for another 7–8 minutes over a gentle heat, until the tomatoes are soft and their juice absorbed. Take off the heat, taste for seasoning and leave to cool for at least 15 minutes (if you mix the okra and eggs when the former is still hot, the eggs will scramble).

Make sure the coriander is very finely chopped, with all stalks removed. Beat the eggs and stir in the chopped coriander followed by the cooled okra and tomato mixture.

Grease an 8–10 inch (20–25 cm) china or earthenware quiche dish with a little vegetable oil. Pour in the egg and vegetable mixture and put to bake in the pre-heated oven for 15–20 minutes, until the centre is just set.

Leave to cool a little before serving in thick slices. If you like, serve with a fresh tomato, coriander and onion chutney: simply dice all three together and add salt and lime juice.

SPANISH OMELETTE

Most Spanish tapas bars offer a slice of cold tortilla, a thick omelette whose only ingredients are potatoes and onions. I give the traditional recipe here but you can add bacon, spring onions or peppers as the mood takes you. As with the Parsee okra omelette on page 42, this is an excellent starter to prepare in advance; it is best served just warm. It is also ideal for early spring, before the vegetables (and new potatoes) have got going. I serve it with home-made ketchup.

3 large onions	3 fl oz (75 ml) olive oil
6 large, waxy potatoes	salt
(*floury potatoes will not do for this dish*)	6 large eggs

Peel the onions and cut them into very thin half rings. Peel the potatoes and slice them thinly and evenly. Choose a large non-stick frying-pan and gently heat the oil. Add the potatoes and onions, season with plenty of salt, cover and cook over a low heat until soft – about 20 minutes.

When the potatoes and onions are ready, remove them with a slotted spoon. Drain off the oil, leaving a tablespoon or so in the pan, and keep for another time. Leave the potatoes and onions to cool for 10 minutes or so. Beat the eggs and mix in the potatoes and onions.

Heat the oil that remains in the pan until it is nearly smoking. Add the egg and vegetable mixture and cook for 3 minutes over a high heat. Now turn the omelette over by laying a plate on top of it and turning the pan upside down – be very careful while doing this that no hot fat drips down your arm. When the omelette is on the plate, slide it back into the pan uncooked side down. Cook for another couple of minutes and then leave to cool. The omelette should be thick, slightly browned on the outside and still juicy in the centre. Serve with the ketchup.

HOME-MADE KETCHUP

1 dried red chilli	1/2 teaspoon sugar
1 clove of garlic (*optional*)	1 tablespoon Worcester
4 black peppercorns	sauce
1/2 teaspoon rock salt	juice of 1/2 a lemon
1/4 teaspoon ground cumin	2 oz (55 g) tomato purée
1/2 teaspoon paprika	

Crush the dried chilli, the clove of garlic, the peppercorns and the salt together very thoroughly. Add the cumin, paprika and sugar. Beat the Worcester sauce and lemon juice into the spice mixture, then blend into the tomato purée.

PIZZA

The end of the spring season produces the first bunches of my favourite herb, basil. If we are lucky, it also sees the first lunches on the terrace or in the garden. One of my favourite dishes for such happy days is a home-made pizza, liberally flecked with basil. Pizzas should, of course, be baked in a wood-fired brick oven, but good results can be produced in your own gas or electrically powered one. The pizza is easy to make, economical for large parties and streets better than the majority you will find in pizzerias in this country. A pizza is meant to be a filler before a main dish – try following it with grilled fish or chicken.

The topping I give here is the very simple margherita, my favourite, but once you have got the hang of it you can experiment with all sorts: anchovies, olives and capers on a tomato base, spicy Italian sausage on a tomato and parmesan base, different kinds of cheeses mixed together, shrimps on tomato and so on.

Sufficient to make one large pizza to feed 4

FOR THE PIZZA DOUGH

$^1/_2$ oz (15 g) dried yeast or
  1 oz (25 g) fresh yeast
$^1/_2$ pint (300 ml) warm
  water
$^1/_2$ teaspoon salt
$1^1/_4$ lb (550 g) plain flour
3 tablespoons olive oil

FOR THE TOMATO SAUCE

1 lb (450 g) best-quality
  plum tomatoes and 1
  tablespoon tomato purée
  or a 14 oz (400 g) tin
  Italian canned plum
  tomatoes
1 clove of garlic
2 tablespoons olive oil
2 large sprigs of fresh
  thyme or $^1/_2$ teaspoon
  dried thyme

FOR THE TOPPING

12 oz (350 g) mozzarella
  (*if you can get buffalo
  mozzarella, so much the
  better*)
12 large leaves of basil (*or
  more as the mood takes you
  – but if you can't get fresh
  basil use another fresh herb*
*such as parsley, rather than
dried basil, which bears no
resemblance to the real
thing; alternatively, use a
herb which dries well, like
thyme or rosemary*)
freshly ground black pepper
olive oil

To make the dough, first blend the yeast with a little of the warm water according to the instructions on the packet or from your baker (if you are using easyblend yeast, ignore this stage). Mix the salt with the flour, make a well in the centre and add the prepared yeast. Now add the olive oil, followed little by little by sufficient of the remaining water until you have a soft pliable dough. Knead with your hands for about 8 minutes. *Note:* You can of course use a food processor for this stage, but I have to say I have always had best results by hand, and it is quite a satisfying activity.

Put the dough in a large lightly floured bowl and rub a little olive oil over the surface to prevent cracks. Cover with a clean cloth and leave in a warm place for 1 hour.

Meanwhile make the tomato sauce. Peel the tomatoes if you are using fresh ones (you can do this by dipping them in boiling water, or alternatively halving them and squeezing them against a grater). Chop the garlic very finely. Heat the oil and add the garlic; fry for a minute or two and then add the chopped tomatoes and the thyme. Season well and simmer for 10 minutes until you have a thick paste (if you are using tinned tomatoes, you may have to boil off a little of the liquid). Remove the thyme if you are using a sprig and leave the sauce until you are ready to make the pizza.

Pre-heat the oven to absolute maximum. Oil a large rectangular baking tray with olive oil, and with your fingers (not a rolling-pin), spread the dough across it, to reach the corners (the dough should be as thin as possible without tearing). Roll the edges up a little all the way round. Spread the tomato sauce all over the surface, right up to the edges. Drain the mozzarella very thoroughly and chop into $1/2$ inch (1 cm) chunks. Sprinkle half the torn basil leaves over the surface, followed by the mozzarella chunks, making sure they are evenly distributed. Season with plenty of freshly ground black pepper and dribble olive oil all over the surface.

Bake at the top of the oven for 12–15 minutes, until the edges are crisp and the cheese melted (try to resist the temptation to open the oven during cooking or you will lose heat). Scatter the remaining torn basil leaves all over the pizza, cut into squares and serve.

SPINACH PIE

The early spinach is tender and sweet. Look for small, shiny green leaves with practically non-existent stalks and try them lightly stewed in their own juice, drained thoroughly and dressed with extra virgin olive oil and lemon juice. Use spinach for stuffing filo pastry parcels (see winter recipe, pages 312–13) For an Easter picnic, or more probably an indoor lunch, try this pie, made with olive oil pastry stuffed with spinach sweetened with onions and sultanas.

FOR THE PASTRY

8 oz (225 g) plain flour

$^1/_4$ teaspoon salt

1 whole egg + 1 egg-yolk

2 tablespoons olive oil

4 tablespoons warm water

FOR THE FILLING

2 lb (900 g) fresh spinach, as young as possible

1 clove of garlic

2 tablespoons olive oil

3 small white onions

3 oz (85 g) sultanas

$^1/_4$ teaspoon cayenne pepper

$^1/_4$ teaspoon ground mace (*or nutmeg if you don't have mace*)

juice of $^1/_2$ a lemon

First make the pastry. Sprinkle the flour and salt on to a clean work surface. Make a deep well in the centre of the flour and add the whole egg and the olive oil. Knead it all together (this bit is messy). Now add the warm water, little by little, until the pastry hangs together without being sticky. If you use a food processor to this stage, remove the pastry for kneading. Knead the pastry for 10 minutes or so then wrap in foil or clingfilm and refrigerate for at least 1 hour.

While the pastry is chilling, prepare the filling. Wash the spinach very thoroughly under running water and remove any thick stalks. Bring a large pan of water to the boil and plunge in the spinach, draining it almost immediately. Leave to cool for 10 minutes, then squeeze the spinach dry with your hands and put it in a heavy-bottomed pan over a low heat with the whole, unpeeled clove of garlic and 1 tablespoon of olive oil. Season well and leave to sweat for 15 minutes.

Dice the onions and fry briefly in the remaining tablespoon of olive oil, over a high heat, until slightly browned. Over a high heat, boil off any liquid released by the spinach. Stir in the fried onions, the sultanas, the cayenne pepper, the mace and the lemon juice. Leave to cool.

When you are ready to cook the pie, pre-heat the oven to medium hot (180°C/350°F/Gas 4). Divide the pastry into 2 balls, one roughly twice as big as the other. Roll each ball out on a floured board as thinly as possible. Grease a 10 inch (25 cm) diameter loose-bottomed cake tin with olive oil and line with the larger piece of pastry. Pile in the spinach filling and top with the remaining pastry, rolling the edges together. Brush the surface with the egg-yolk.

Bake in the oven for 50–60 minutes, until the surface is golden. Unmould and leave to cool on a rack. Serve in thick slices, warm or cold.

SPRING SOUP

This soup from Genoa, the land of pesto, celebrates the arrival of the first spring vegetables and needs the freshest of ingredients to be successful. This probably means that you will not be able to make it until the very end of May in Britain, when the first broad beans and peas appear. It is ideal for the gardener, or for those who have access to a good market. However, if you can't get the full range of vegetables, you can always leave one or two out, the principle remains the same. Given the mix of vegetables, it is best made in relatively large quantities; those given below will feed 6–8.

3 globe artichokes (*or 8 oz (225 g) of the very small ones if you can get them*)
8 oz (225 g) spring onions
8 oz (225 g) small green beans
1¹/₂ lb (675 g) unshelled weight of peas
1¹/₂ lb (675 g) unshelled weight of broad beans
8 oz (225 g) new potatoes
salt and freshly ground black pepper

8 leaves of fresh basil
2 eggs
3 tablespoons fruity extra virgin olive oil
6 oz (170 g) piece of fresh parmesan (*or 4 oz (115 g) if you are using ready-grated — but it is much better if you give your guests a hunk of parmesan which they can grate themselves into the soup*)

Remove the choke of the artichokes (see page 38) and the tough outer leaves. Cut the heart and inner leaves into slices ¹/₄ inch (5 mm) thick. Chop the spring onions finely. Top and tail the beans and chop into sections ¹/₂ inch long. Shell the peas and broad beans (you really must use fresh ones for this dish). Peel the potatoes (this is one of the few dishes for which you should peel new potatoes – the earthy flavour of the skins is too strong) and cut them into dice.

Put the sliced artichokes, broad beans and spring onions in a large pan and add 4 pints (2.3 litres) of cold water. Bring to the boil and add salt and black pepper. Cook, simmering, for 10 minutes. Now add the green beans and peas. Simmer for another 5 minutes before adding the diced potatoes. When all the vegetables are very tender (which should take another 10 minutes or so), shred in the basil leaves and take off the heat. Check seasoning.

Mix the eggs with the olive oil and stir this mixture into the soup. Serve immediately, with a hunk of fresh parmesan for grating into the soup, and plenty of bread.

VEGETABLE MEZZE

Middle Eastern and Turkish cuisine are famous for their mezze, the theory of which is no different from the Italian antipasti or the French hors d'oeuvre, a selection of little dishes served before the main course to whet the appetite. Often mezze become a meal in themselves. This is a style of eating which I am particularly fond of and which is perfect for a large gathering. Mezze can include cheese or nuts, meatballs and fried fish, stuffed pastries and vine-leaves, but usually the bulk of the dishes contain some kind of vegetable. These are ideal dishes for the market shopper – you can pick whatever is good on the day, and combine the fresh vegetable dishes with ones from the store cupboard. Below are a few of my favourites for a spring mezze table.

AUBERGINE PURÉE

The best season for both imported and UK-grown aubergines is late spring through summer. My favourite way of cooking them is to roast them under a very hot grill, which gives them a smoky, sweet flavour. In this recipe they are then puréed to make a paste.

2 large aubergines, approx.
  $1^1/_2$ lb (675 g)
2 tablespoons extra virgin
  olive oil
juice of 1 lemon

2 tablespoons chopped flat-
  leaved parsley
salt and freshly ground
  pepper

Roast the whole aubergines under a hot grill until their skins are blackened all over and their flesh tender (this will take about 30 minutes). Rub off the blackened skins, squeeze out as much of the bitter juice as possible and either mash the flesh with a fork or purée it in the processor. Add the oil, a little at a time, followed by the lemon juice, parsley and salt and pepper to taste. Serve cold.

BROAD BEANS STEWED IN THEIR PODS

In Turkey broad beans are cooked whole, in a mixture of oil and water which is simmered for a surprisingly long time, with a rich result.

FOR I LB (450 G) FRESH YOUNG BROAD BEANS
IN THEIR PODS

$^1/_2$ teaspoon salt

juice of 1 lemon

$^1/_4$ teaspoon sugar

4 large spring onions

$1^1/_2$ tablespoons chopped
   fresh dill

1 teaspoon dried mint

$^1/_2$ teaspoon coarsely
   ground black pepper

$^1/_2$ teaspoon ground allspice

4 tablespoons plain olive
   oil

Wash the broad beans thoroughly, cut off the stalks and string them carefully. Sprinkle over the salt, lemon juice and sugar and leave to rest for 15 minutes.

Chop the spring onions into $^3/_4$ inch (2 cm) pieces, including the green ends. Place half the beans in a heavy-based casserole and sprinkle over the spring onions, 1 tablespoon of the chopped dill, the mint, pepper and allspice. Place the remaining beans on top.

Pour over the olive oil and $^1/_2$ pint (300 ml) of water. Bring to the boil, cover and just simmer for $1-1^1/_2$ hours, until the beans are very tender.

Serve tepid or cold, in the juices, sprinkled with the remaining fresh dill, with garlicky yoghurt (page 55) on the side.

BROCCOLI SALAD

Broccoli is of excellent quality in the spring. Although this recipe is Italian rather than Middle Eastern in style, it sits well on a mezze table.

1 lb (450 g) broccoli	4 marinated peperoni
2 tablespoons extra virgin olive oil	(*available in jars from Italian delicatessens*)
1/2 tablespoon balsamic vinegar	1 teaspoon whole cumin seeds

Divide the broccoli heads into small florets about an inch across, removing most of the stalk. Bring a large pan of salted water to a fierce boil and plunge in the broccoli. Cook for 4–5 minutes, until tender but still green. Drain.

Dress the broccoli with the oil and vinegar while still hot. Chop the marinated peperoni into small pieces and add to the broccoli.

Toast the cumin seeds in a dry frying pan until lightly browned all over (take care they do not burn – they should be in a hot pan for no more than a minute or two) and sprinkle over the broccoli. Serve warm.

CHILLIED CARROT SALAD

Harissa is the hot red paste traditionally served with couscous in North Africa. It can be bought here in specialist shops or you can substitute a chilli paste. Handle with care – this salad is fiery.

FOR I LB (450 G) CARROTS
(LARGE CARROTS ARE BEST FOR THIS DISH)

juice of 1 lemon
$^1/_2$ teaspoon coarse salt
2 tablespoons olive oil
2 teaspoons harissa or other
   chilli paste, or to taste

2 teaspoons whole cumin
   seeds
1 tablespoon chopped fresh
   coriander
$^1/_2$ teaspoon coarsely
   ground black pepper

Peel the carrots, chop them into rounds $^1/_2$ inch (1 cm) thick and put them in a pan. Mix together the lemon juice, salt, olive oil and harissa and pour over the carrots. Add sufficient water almost to cover the carrots and simmer until they are very tender, removing the lid for the last 5 minutes to allow some of the liquid to bubble off. Allow to cool.

Just before serving, roast the cumin seeds in a dry pan, taking care they do not burn. Stir the chopped coriander and the pepper into the carrots and top with the roasted cumin seeds.

HUMMUS

Home-made hummus is easy to make provided you have a food processor, and is worth the slight trouble. The traditional version given here does not include tahina; if you like the sesame taste, reduce the quantity of chickpeas and substitute tahina paste. This is an excellent starter for early spring before the new season's vegetables appear.

6 oz (170 g) dried chickpeas *(or a 15 oz (425 g) tin of cooked chickpeas – but dried ones will give a better consistency to the hummus)*
2 fl oz (50 ml) olive oil
juice of 2 large or 3 small lemons

2 teaspoons ground cumin
1 or 2 large cloves of garlic, to taste
salt and pepper
1 teaspoon paprika
1 teaspoon chopped flat-leaved parsley

Soak the chickpeas overnight. The next day, boil them in plenty of water until very tender – about $1^1/_2$ hours. Do not add salt to the water or the chickpeas will go tough.

Purée the slightly cooled chickpeas in the processor with a few table-spoons of cooking water (or liquid from the tin). Slowly add most of the olive oil, dribbling it in at first, until you have a creamy consistency. Now add the lemon juice, cumin, crushed garlic, plenty of pepper and a little salt. As always, taste to check: the hummus should be sharp.

Mix the paprika into the remaining oil. Serve the hummus on a large flat plate, with the reddened oil dribbled over it, and sprinkled with the parsley.

GARLIC YOGHURT

This is a traditional accompaniment in Turkey to a mezze of vegetable dishes. Do not be tempted to use fresh mint; dried is authentic.

1 clove of garlic
$1/2$ teaspoon salt
8 fl oz (250 ml) Greek yoghurt (*I like to use the*

kind made with sheep's milk)
$1/2$ teaspoon dried mint

Crush the peeled garlic clove with the salt. Stir in the yoghurt and leave to stand for a couple of hours before serving, to allow the flavours to infuse. Sprinkle over the dried mint just before serving.

Note: If you like, you can add some chopped cucumber to the yoghurt. Look out for small, firm cucumbers early in the season. Sprinkle the chunks of cucumber with salt and leave to stand for 30 minutes beforehand, to drain away any liquid.

ORANGE AND OLIVE SALAD

Oranges from North Africa are at their best in early spring and make a colourful, refreshing salad when mixed with parsley and olives.

$1 1/2$ lb (675 g) oranges
$1/2$ teaspoon ground cinnamon
pinch of cayenne pepper
$1/2$ teaspoon coarse salt
4 oz (115 g) small black or

green olives, unpitted and preserved in oil
1 heaped tablespoon chopped flat-leaved parsley
extra virgin olive oil

Peel the oranges, making sure you remove any pith, and slice across into fine rings. Arrange them on a plate and sprinkle over the spices and salt. Slice the olives finely and chop the parsley. Stir both into the oranges and dress with olive oil to taste.

TABBOULEH

This burghul wheat salad, found all over the Middle East, is rarely served in Britain with a sufficient quantity of fresh herbs. If you have had a dry and rather boring version before, try this recipe to find out how delicious tabbouleh can be.

6 oz (170 g) burghul wheat
juice of 2 lemons
4 tablespoons extra virgin
   olive oil
salt and pepper
1 huge bunch of flat-leaved
   parsley, to yield 5–6

tablespoons when the
leaves are chopped
1 large bunch of fresh mint,
   to yield 3–4 tablespoons
   when the leaves are
   chopped
8 spring onions

Soak the burghul in cold water for 15 minutes, until it swells. Drain and squeeze out any excess liquid. Mix together the lemon juice and olive oil and stir into the burghul with plenty of salt and pepper. Leave to rest for 30 minutes.

Chop the leaves of the herbs very finely, discarding the stalks (do not be tempted to use a processor or the leaves will disintegrate into a pureée). Chop the spring onions finely. Five minutes before serving, stir the herbs and spring onions into the burghul.

TURNIP SALAD

The new season's turnips are much sweeter and more delicate in taste than the larger, older vegetables of winter. They are also rather pretty. Boiled for a few minutes and then fried in butter or oil, they make an excellent side dish for spring lamb, or for a duck. They can also be served sprinkled with sesame seeds to enhance their nutty taste, as part of a selection of salads.

1 lb (450 g) baby turnips, no more than 1 1/2 inches (4 cm) across
salt and pepper
2 tablespoons extra virgin olive oil

2 teaspoons sesame seeds
juice of 1 small orange
1 tablespoon chopped fresh parsley

Peel the turnips, leaving a little of the stalk attached. (*Note:* if you buy turnips with their leaves still attached, do not throw the leaves away – they are very good boiled and served as a vegetable.) Bring a large pan of water to the boil and cook the whole turnips fiercely for 5 minutes, or until tender. Drain and season.

In a large frying-pan, heat the oil. When it is hot, add the sesame seeds. As soon as they pop (30 seconds), add the turnips. Fry for a few minutes, stirring continuously until the turnips are lightly browned. Put into a dish, with the oily juices, and pour over the orange juice. Serve warm, sprinkled with the parsley.

FISH

Spring is a time for change in the fish supply. Many flat fish start to spawn and decline in quality – tradition suggests that plaice should not be eaten again until May Day. Although the cultivation of oysters means that the 'R in the month' rule does not need to be applied rigidly, native oysters tail off towards the end of April and mussels slowly disappear from the market. Scallops too are coming to the end of their season, although they are still of good quality in March. As the waters slowly warm up, the quality and availability of cold-water fish declines. But there are compensations. Spring is an excellent time of year for salmon and sea trout. Crabs, prawns and lobsters all start to reappear at the fishmonger – and you may even be able to get hold of some crawfish. And there are some excellent imported fish at this time of year.

To guide you through the choice and to tell you what is best on the day, you need an experienced fishmonger. Yet this is perhaps the hardest expert for today's shopper to find. The decline in the number of high-quality independent fishmongers in this country is little short of a national disgrace. The reasons for it are familiar: high costs, low margins, no enthusiasm among the younger generation for sustaining the family business. Although we are now starting to eat more fish again, it may come too late for many of the independents.

And where are our fish markets? Retail fish markets are commonplace at coastal towns on the Continent. Here almost all the markets are exclusively wholesale, although a few (such as Billingsgate) now allow the ordinary customer in to shop. General markets may have one or two fish stalls or a travelling van, but their market share is in decline (sales of fish through market stalls dropped by 10 per cent from 1989 to 1990 alone, according to a Seafish report). Much of this decline is blamed on competition from the supermarkets, which have been slow to wake up to fish but are now in overdrive.

The search for a retail fish market should not be hard in an island nation, but it sadly is. I had almost given up hope of finding one until I visited Bolton.

Bolton – A Tale of Two Markets

I went to Bolton on the recommendation of the Meat and Livestock Commission, to look at the city's recently renovated Victorian market. This huge glass-topped structure, repainted in green and rust and tiled in pink and grey ceramic, has been incorporated into a modern shopping centre, and was held up to me as a prime example of 'what can be done with a market'. It now resembles not so much a market as a theme park. Each shop is its own island among the sea of tiles, the glass units topped with pseudo-Victorian name plates in pastel shades, announcing unlikely titles – no more market caff, but the Café Boulevard.

The market is home to a number of good-quality butchers, with some excellent Welsh lamb and Scottish beef on offer on the day of my visit. But the refurbishment has meant a corresponding increase in rents, and the butchers' prices are under pressure. Custom has not on the other hand increased dramatically, despite their newly sanitized appearance. It may be true that, as the MLC informed me, 'customers don't want a butcher up to his arms in blood, with all sorts of bits of meat hanging around'. Well, yes, but the serious cook does want a butcher prepared to carve a joint a certain way, to trim a cutlet, to provide offal, offcuts and bones as well as premium cuts. Trying to make butchers look like mini-supermarkets is not a recipe for success. The Market Place of Bolton does not have the life and colour which draws me to a market – it is no longer worthy of the name.

Depressed, I trudged back towards the bus station, to take a bus to nearby Bury to sample the famous black pudding from Chadwick's stall in the open market. On the way, it occurred to me that there had been no fish shop in the famous Market Place and I asked an old lady in the street where she bought her fish. 'Why, at the fish market, of course,' she replied, giving me a look which left no doubt that I had confirmed her view that southerners were a bit short of brain power. 'Over there, in

Ashburner Street.' Beyond the labyrinthine tunnels of the bus station stands a long squat building, divided into four sections, with large archways entering into each. The first two sections are marked 'Fruit' and 'Vegetables', and are home to the produce wholesale market, which takes place early in the mornings. The third archway has 'Fish' carved above it. Inside, a fish market takes place three days a week, after the wholesale market has finished. Bolton's transition from wholesale to retail after nine in the morning makes a far wider choice available to the customer. It has also kept business going: several of the traders now rely almost exclusively on their retail sales.

Enter the fish hall, and you find a real market. There is noise, as stall-holders shout out what is on offer and customers discuss the best bargains. There are crowds, pushing past each other to peer at the fish. There are colourful displays, fish piled up on some stalls, artfully arranged on others. Porters wheel in fresh consignments on metal trolleys, risking taking off your legs if you don't watch out. Empty crates stack up behind the stalls and the ice drips on the floor. There are not quite blood and guts, but not far off. Here is real life.

Sentiment and sensation are no good, however, if the range and quality of the food are not up to scratch. That in Bolton fish market is for the most part traditional, and of high quality. Every stall had plenty of cod, with cards marking the port from which it had been bought – Scarborough, Fleetwood, Aberdeen. Common in Continental Europe, this habit of sourcing the produce is one I wish more stallholders followed in this country: it is both useful and interesting. Haddock was excellent, firm and creamy white, cut into thick steaks for grilling. As early spring is not a good time for flat fish, few are in evidence. It is the best time of the year, on the other hand, for wild salmon, and several of the stalls were offering cutlets from a wild fish, as well as huge farmed salmon; the contrast in colours between the lurid pink farmed variety and the slightly brown flesh of the wild fish was striking. If you can afford it, choose the wild salmon every time for taste and texture. Sea or salmon trout are also good in spring, and there were plenty to choose from, as well as rainbow trout – although, as everywhere else, no brown river trout, which are so superior in flavour. The only way to find them today is to take up fly-fishing.

Bolton is also strong on smoked fish: Loch Fyne kippers and oak-smoked ones from the Isle of Man, cod and haddock. The majority of the fish has been dyed bright yellow, but uncoloured versions are available if you ask. These are not just more wholesome but taste better as well; quite why the producers ever started dyeing fish I am not sure, for I find the creamy yellow flesh of a haddock smoked without artificial colourants far more attractive than the bright orange of the processed variety.

Find your colour instead among the shellfish. Spring is a time of transition for shellfish supplies – mussels and oysters are tailing off and lobsters and crabs are coming to the fore. Still, on the early spring day I visited there were plenty of fat and juicy Anglesey oysters. There were live crabs too, their brown claws waving angrily at passers-by. It is hard to buy live crabs in this country, although you rarely see them sold pre-cooked on the Continent. This may be a result of British squeamishness, but it is as much hypocrisy, for a crab cooked at home will suffer no more than one cooked by the fishmonger. On the other hand, it is likely to be far juicier. Scallops too are sold live on the shell in Bolton market, including the large 'queenies'; try them grilled, poached or, as one of the fishmongers suggested, 'lightly fried in garlic butter or baked in white wine'.

Although the majority of the fish at Bolton comes direct from local ports in the north of the country and from Scotland, there is also a fair share of imported varieties from the wholesale markets. In spring this will usually include red mullet and squid, although warmer weather will attract them to our waters later in the season. Imported generally means frozen, and the red mullet suffers greatly from this. Squid on the other hand freeze well, and Bolton had tiny calamari from California which were perfect for stuffing. The most adventurous fishmonger, Mr Buckley Junior, caters for Bolton's ethnic community, with Caribbean fish from Birmingham's wholesale market: trevally, kingfish, emperor fish alongside salt cod and its traditional West Indian accompaniment, ackee. The fish looked good, but not nearly as tempting as his array of white fish from British waters on the other side of his stall: freshness always wins.

But the fish in Bolton does not just have to compete with imports. Almost all the fishmongers now stock poultry and eggs, and these seem to be slowly creeping up on the *raison d'être* of the stalls. One has already succumbed completely. On the day I visited, S. Gittings, Fishmonger, had nothing but chickens and turkeys for sale. Not that I have anything against poultry, but these were hardly prime specimens: bulk rather than quality appeared to be the theme, the chickens frozen and flabby, the turkeys pale and insipid. Their inferiority was marked against the high quality of the fish. The reason for their existence is a familiar one from fishmongers – 'There's no money in fish, we wouldn't make any money if that was all we sold.' Nor is the poultry the only intruder to the fish market: even more unwelcome must be the frozen food centre, selling off cheap rejects from the supermarkets.

Bolton is a rare find in Britain, a good-quality retail fish market. I hope it survives both intruders and developers.

CHOWDER SOUP WITH NEW POTATOES

The American name 'chowder' is derived from the French 'la chaudière', the pot into which the catch of the day was put for cooking. Today it has come to mean a soupy stew of white fish or clams, milk, potatoes and salt pork. I have developed a rather inauthentic and extravagant version, in which half the fish is used to flavour the milky broth, picking out the best bits to poach at the end – perfect if your fishmonger, like mine, sells a fish soup mix, with bits of fish of varying quality. Belly pork substitutes for salt pork and is also discarded after the broth is made; whole slices of firm new potatoes replace larger floury ones which would disintegrate. Finally, juniper, cloves and allspice add an interesting flavour. The result perhaps should not be called chowder, but is a delicious and elegant soup.

1¹/₂ lb (675 g) white fish soup mix (*use at least 2 kinds of fish such as: cod, coley, conger eel, grey mullet, gurnard, haddock, ling, whiting*)
1¹/₂ pints (850 ml) full-cream milk
2 small onions
1 large carrot

1 oz (25 g) butter
4 oz (115 g) slice of belly pork
3 cloves
4 juniper berries
4 allspice berries
2 bayleaves
salt and pepper
1 lb (450 g) new potatoes

Pick out the least bony, best-quality pieces from the fish soup mix and reserve (you should keep about half back). Bring the milk to the boil and allow to cool, skimming off the skin. Slice the onions and carrot and stew them in the butter until tender but not brown (about 10 minutes). Add the slice of belly pork, the spices, the bayleaves, plenty of pepper, the poorer half of the fish, the milk and the same quantity of water. Bring to the boil and simmer for 30 minutes (no longer or the mixture will become gluey). Strain and season to taste.

Scrub the new potatoes and cut into $^1/_2$ inch (1 cm) rounds. Bring the liquid back to the boil and add the potatoes. When they are nearly tender, slip in the remaining pieces of fish. Cook until the pieces of fish are just cooked through (about 10 minutes) and serve immediately.

CUTTLEFISH CASSEROLE WITH SPRING VEGETABLES

I am a great enthusiast of the family of cephalopods, which includes squid, octopus and cuttlefish. Unfortunately, not many people in Britain seem to share my passion, put off I suspect by the rather alarming appearance of these ungainly creatures. It is true that their preparation is no joy, but it is relatively quick and if you have a kind fishmonger he can generally be persuaded to do it for you. The end result looks no more frightening than any other fish. After all, if we are put off by appearance how can we eat monkfish or John Dory?

Cuttlefish seems to be the rarest of the cephalopods in British shops, despite its undoubted preponderance in our seas (think of all those cuttlefish blades on the beach). If you can get hold of tiny ones, they are delicious stuffed with rice and braised. The larger cuttlefish should be sliced and stewed, as in this rustic recipe from the Genoese region which combines the cuttlefish with spring vegetables (the adventurous will keep the cuttlefish ink for a black risotto). The final addition of the bread with parmesan, oil and basil is vital to the depth of flavour of the casserole.

2 lb (900 g) large cuttlefish
(unprepared weight)
2 large white onions
3 large cloves of garlic
8 oz (225 g) young carrots
1¹/₂ lb (675 g) tomatoes
(*I prefer to use fresh rather
than tinned for this dish*)
8 oz (225 g) French beans
8 oz (225 g) tiny new
potatoes
3 tablespoons olive oil
2 sun-dried tomatoes
1 fresh bayleaf

2 sprigs of fresh thyme
salt and black pepper
¹/₄ pint (150 ml) dry white
wine (*a fruity Italian such
as a Pinot Grigio from the
Veneto is ideal*)
1 tablespoon chopped flat-
leaved parsley
4 slices good-quality white
country bread
extra virgin olive oil
1 tablespoon fresh basil
4 oz (115 g) fresh parmesan,
grated

If you have to prepare the cuttlefish yourself, first cut the tentacles off just below the eye. Pull the head and innards from the body and discard. The ink sac will break as you do this, hence the messiness (if you want to keep the ink sac whole for a risotto, remove the body sac very carefully). Rinse the body sac very thoroughly under cold running water. Peel off the tough, speckly outer skin from the body and tentacles and discard. Also pull off the two 'wings' attached to the side of the body and discard. Rinse the body and tentacles again. The cuttlefish is now ready to be chopped into bite-sized pieces for cooking.

Chop the onions coarsely and 2 of the garlic cloves finely. Scrub the carrots; leave them whole if they are very small, or cut larger ones into thick rings. Peel the tomatoes after dipping in boiling water, top and tail the beans and cut in half, and scrub the new potatoes. In a large heavy-based casserole, heat the olive oil. Add the onion and cook over a medium heat, stirring, for 5 minutes, until it is translucent. Add the garlic and carrots and cook for a further 5 minutes. Now add the chopped cuttlefish and turn down the heat. Allow to stew for 5 minutes in the oil before adding the peeled chopped tomatoes and the finely chopped sun-dried tomatoes. Stir in the bayleaf and the sprigs of thyme, tied in a bunch so you can remove them later, and season with salt and plenty of freshly ground black pepper. Pour in the white wine and bubble for a few minutes. Add sufficient water to cover the contents of the pan, cover and leave to simmer.

After 45 minutes add the new potatoes still in their skins, the French beans and the parsley. Continue to simmer, covered, until the potatoes and beans are tender (about 15 minutes).

Rub the slices of bread with the cut side of the remaining clove of garlic and then put each slice in the bottom of a bowl. Dribble extra virgin olive oil all over the bread. Tear the basil leaves and sprinkle over the bread, followed by the grated parmesan. Check the seasoning of the stew, remove the bayleaf and thyme, and spoon the stew over the slices of bread. Serve piping hot.

GRAVLAKS

Gravlaks is the Scandinavian way of preserving salmon, the equivalent of our own smoked fish. The name actually means 'buried salmon', referring to the original practice of digging a hole in which the cured fish was placed to keep it at a constant temperature. Although gravlaks is a well-known dish in Britain, it is one very few people attempt to make themselves. This is a pity, for the flavour of home-cured salmon far exceeds that of the processed and packaged variety. It is especially attractive today, given the relatively low price of farmed salmon. It goes without saying that you must be sure of your supplier and use only the very freshest fish. Fresh dill is also vital.

FOR 1 SIDE OF A MEDIUM SALMON, APPROX. 3–4 LB (1.5–2 KG)

2 tablespoons vodka
1 oz (25 g) coarse sea salt
1 oz (25 g) granulated white sugar
1 tablespoon white peppercorns, coarsely ground
1 good-sized bunch of fresh dill

Cut the side of salmon in half lengthways. In a dish into which it will just fit, lay one strip skin side down. Rub 1 tablespoon of the vodka into the flesh followed by half the salt, sugar and pepper. Repeat the process with the other half of the side of salmon. Arrange the dill, stalks and all, over the surface of the salmon in the dish and place the other half of the side on top, broad end to broad end, as if making a sandwich. Cover with grease-proof paper and put a heavy weight on top.

Leave the salmon in a cool, dark, dry place. A larder or wine cellar is ideal but you can also use the fridge. Each day remove the paper and pour the liquid which has seeped out back into the sandwich. After 2 days remove the weight.

The salmon is ready to eat after 4–5 days. Discard the dill and slice the fish horizontally with a very sharp knife into paper-thin slices. Serve with gravlaks sauce and rye bread.

GRAVLAKS SAUCE

The sauce is basically a very mustardy dressing with dill. The type of mustard is important – English would be far too hot.

2 tablespoons sweet German/Scandinavian mustard or
1^1/$_2$ tablespoons Dijon mustard mixed with
1 tablespoon sugar
3 tablespoons white wine vinegar

2 fl oz (50 ml) extra virgin olive oil
2 fl oz (50 ml) sunflower oil
3 tablespoons chopped fresh dill

Mix together the mustard (and sugar if you are using it) and the vinegar and slowly add the oils as if making mayonnaise. When the sauce emulsifies, speed up the stream. Add the chopped dill and pour over the paper-thin slices of salmon.

MARINATED TUNA

The 'cooking' of raw fish in citric acid is not a new idea – it can be found in cuisines from all over the world. Perhaps the most famous dish is the Central and South American ceviche, white fish marinated in lime juice with plenty of chilli, coriander and perhaps a little tomato. Smart Italian restaurants now serve carpaccio di pesce as well as of beef, nouveau Scandinavians offer salmon marinated in lime juice, dill and vodka, British chefs have become rather keen on 'trios' of raw fish – selections of, say, scallops, monkfish and sea bass chosen for colour as well as flavour.

Despite occasionally pretentious overtones, marinated fish salads make delicious and easy-to-prepare starters. My favourite fish for this treatment is the tuna, whose firm texture and meaty taste stand up well to the assertive flavours of lime juice and coriander. It goes without saying that the fish used for this dish must be very fresh – you must trust your fishmonger.

1 lb (450 g) tuna, cut in one thick slice
6 spring onions
1 tablespoon chopped fresh coriander
2 limes
3 tablespoons extra virgin olive oil

Put the hunk of tuna in the freezer for 1 hour, so that it is firm enough to slice. With a very sharp knife, slice as thinly as possible (the aim is to have paper-thin slices). Lay the slices on a large plate, without overlapping.

Chop the spring onions finely, discarding the green end. Sprinkle the onions and the coriander all over the slices of fish. Mix the juice of the limes with the olive oil and pour over the slices. Leave to stand in a cool place for 1 hour, turning the slices half-way through.

Serve with good bread and a bottle of extra virgin olive oil on the table for your guests to add more to taste.

ROASTED SALMON WITH PASTA

One British stalwart which has in recent years gained in popularity over the Channel is the salmon. Smart French restaurants serve 'le saumon fumé avec ses toasts', exponents of the Italian novella cucina roast the fish and serve it with pasta. This latter technique has a great deal to recommend it, the fish being deliciously moist and the pasta, flavoured with olives, a more interesting accessory than new potatoes. Spring is the season for wild, rod-caught salmon, and if you can find it and can afford it do splash out – you will taste the difference from the flabby farmed variety.

4 oz (115 g) black olives, preserved in oil not brine

8 oz (225 g) plum *or* Marmande tomatoes

4 spring onions

1 tablespoon fresh dill

4 thick salmon cutlets

3 tablespoons extra virgin olive oil

1 lb (450 g) fresh pappardelle or tagliatelle (*I prefer to use the thick flat pappardelle, which are cut from a flat open sheet of pasta rather than a folded one*)

Pre-heat the oven to very hot (220°C/425°F/Gas 7). Stone the olives if they are unpitted and chop them up coarsely. Skin the tomatoes and dice them. Peel any papery shreds from the spring onions and chop them into tiny rounds, discarding the tough green ends. Chop up the dill, discarding the stalks.

Place the salmon in a baking tray and pour over the olive oil. Roast at the top of the oven for 10 minutes. Meanwhile, cook the pasta in plenty of salted water (2–3 minutes for fresh pasta, 10–15 according to make and type for dried – look at the instructions on the packet, and taste before draining).

Remove the salmon from the oven and allow to rest while you prepare the pasta. Pour the oily juices from the baking tray into a pan over a high heat. Add the spring onion and, after a minute or two, the olives and diced tomatoes. As soon as these have heated through (a matter of a minute or so), stir them into the drained pasta together with all the oily juices and the chopped dill. Put a pile of pasta on each plate, place the salmon beside it and serve immediately.

MONKFISH KEBABS ON A BED OF CORIANDER POTATOES

Monkfish has come a long way from the days when it used to be a substitute for lobster. Today it is far too expensive to be served in any disguise. It is a fish which combines well with strong flavours and is one of the few which is sufficiently firm-fleshed to be served in kebabs. If the weather is good enough, these kebabs can be barbecued, but more likely you will grill them. The baked potato mashed with fried onions, coriander and olive oil is a favourite of mine and goes well with meat as well as fish – try it with grilled pork escalopes.

4 baking potatoes
1^1/$_2$ lb (675 g) monkfish tail
6 tablespoons extra virgin
  olive oil
2 limes
2 teaspoons paprika
^{1}/$_2$ teaspoon cayenne pepper
1 teaspoon ground coriander
^{1}/$_2$ teaspoon ground black
  pepper
2 onions (or, *better still, 8 oz*
  (225 g) shallots)
1 large bunch of fresh
  coriander
salt and pepper

Bake the potatoes in their jackets in a medium oven (150°C/300°F/Gas 2) until tender (you could also boil them as is traditional for mashed potato, but this tends to make them waterlogged). Peel, and discard the skins.

Remove any skin from the monkfish and cut the fish into 1 inch (2.5 cm) cubes. Mix together 2 tablespoons of the olive oil, the juice of the limes and the spices and smear this mixture all over the cubes of fish. Leave to rest for 30 minutes.

Chop the onions or shallots very finely and fry, stirring over a high heat, in 1 tablespoon of the oil until crisp. Thread the fish on to skewers and pre-heat the grill to maximum. Chop the leaves of the coriander very finely and mix into the potato flesh together with the crisped onions or shallots and any oil from the pan. Add the remaining 3 tablespoons of olive oil and plenty of seasoning and mash all together. Keep warm.

Under a hot grill, cook the fish quickly until tender, no more than 4 minutes on each side (the lime juice in the marinade will have started the 'cooking' process for you). Meanwhile heat up the marinade. Serve the kebabs on top of a pile of the green-flecked potatoes and dribble over the hot marinade and the juices from grilling.

PRAWNS IN THE STYLE OF VALENCIA

Fresh European prawns start coming back to the fishmonger around April and are simply miles tastier than the watery, frozen varieties. Try to buy them uncooked for maximum freshness and flavour. Large prawns are delicious cooked in their shells: sauté them in olive oil with garlic and fresh green chilli, roast them in the oven with sea salt, grill them over charcoal or under a very hot grill and serve with nothing more than a squeeze of lemon.

For a rich spicy dish, try this method from eastern Spain, which uses a picada, a mixture of nuts, herbs, garlic and fried bread, to thicken and add flavour to the sauce. I still cook the prawns in their shells but this does make for a messy meal; if you prefer, peel the prawns in advance and use the shells to make the stock.

FOR THE PRAWNS

4 unpeeled cloves of garlic
6 tablespoons fruity olive
  oil
1 pint (575 ml) shellfish or
  fish stock (*the best is made
  from prawn shells*)

1 teaspoon cayenne pepper
2 bayleaves
1$^1/_2$ lb (675 g) large, fresh
  prawns

2 oz (55 g) toasted pinenuts
(or *almonds if these are
unavailable*)
1 tablespoon chopped flat-
leaved parsley
2 peeled cloves of garlic

1 slice of good-quality
country white bread,
crusts removed and
lightly fried on both sides
in a little olive oil

Slash the unpeeled garlic cloves on each side. In a heavy pan, heat the oil and cook the garlic cloves for 10 minutes, so that their flavour infuses the oil. Remove the garlic and keep for another dish.

Add the stock, the cayenne and the bayleaves to the oil and simmer for another 10 minutes. Meanwhile, prepare the picada. Purists would have you do this in a pestle and mortar but the food processor is a lot easier. Whizz the nuts until ground then add the parsley, garlic and fried bread. Give another quick whizz so that everything is blended together but has not yet become a mush.

After 10 minutes' simmering, stir the picada into the stock and oil mixture. Add the prawns and cook for another 5 minutes or so, until cooked through. Serve still bubbling, with plenty of bread.

SALT COD IN BASQUE STYLE

Salt cod is a hangover from the days before the deep freeze, and many would argue that it has been retained out of habit rather than for any gastronomic quality. It is true that unless it is properly soaked and cooked, salt cod can be rather nasty. However, well prepared it is excellent, as in this traditional Lenten dish from the Basque country. If you really don't fancy salt cod, you can also try the dish with a fresh firm white fish such as cod or haddock, in which case dispense with the preliminary poaching.

12 oz (350 g) piece of salt
cod, preferably from the
thick end of the tail – the
fish should be white, not
in any way discoloured

12 oz (350 g) onions

2 red peppers

2 green peppers

3 cloves of garlic

2 tablespoons olive oil

1 tablespoon chopped celery
leaves

pinch of cayenne pepper

1 teaspoon coarsely ground
black pepper

1 tablespoon chopped flat-
leaved parsley

4 fl oz (100 ml) dry sherry
(*or you can use dry white
wine instead*)

14 oz (400 g) tin of Italian
plum tomatoes

$1/2$ a lemon

1 lb (450 g) large potatoes

Soak the cod for at least 24 hours in a large bowl of cold water, changing the water several times. Rinse the piece of fish very thoroughly and put it in a heavy-based casserole, preferably enamel or earthenware (metal pans can lend an unpleasant taste to the fish). Cover with plenty of water and bring to the boil. As soon as the water comes to the boil, take the pan off the heat and leave the fish to cool in the liquid.

To prepare the sauce, peel the onions and chop very finely. De-seed the peppers and cut into dice; peel the garlic cloves and chop finely. In a large, heavy frying-pan with deep sides, heat half the oil. Add the onions and fry gently for 5 minutes. When they are translucent, add the garlic and the chopped celery leaves; cook over a low heat for 15 minutes, stirring occasionally. Now add the diced peppers, the cayenne and black pepper and the chopped parsley. Cook, still over a low heat, for another 5 minutes before turning the heat up and pouring in the sherry or white wine. Allow to bubble for a few minutes before adding the tomatoes, chopping them up with a wooden spoon in the pan. Finally, add 4 fl oz (100 ml) of the liquid in which the cod cooked and the juice of the $1/2$ lemon. Stir all together and leave to simmer, uncovered, for 20 minutes or so, until the sauce is thick.

Remove the salt cod from its liquid and flake the fish, discarding the skin and taking care to remove any bones. Put the flaked fish in a gratin dish and pre-heat the oven to medium hot (180°C/350°F/Gas 4). Now prepare the potatoes which will top the dish. Peel them and slice as thinly as possible (it is best if you use a food processor or mandoline for this process, to ensure that the slices are of even thickness). Bring the liquid in which the fish was cooked back to the boil, and simmer the potato slices for 3–4 minutes, until they are tender but not falling apart. Drain carefully.

Stir the tomato sauce into the flaked cod in the gratin dish. Layer the potatoes on top and dribble the remaining olive oil over them. Bake for 30–40 minutes in the oven, until the potatoes take on a little colour. Serve immediately with a crisp green salad and plenty of bread.

SARDINE TIAN

The tian is an earthenware gratin dish used in the Niçois region of France which has come to lend its name to a recipe. It refers to a gratin made with eggs, parmesan, olive oil and, typically, Swiss chard, the whole baked and brought bubbling to the table. Unfortunately, Swiss chard is difficult to get hold of in Britain; quite why I am not sure, as it grows perfectly well in the garden. I find the early spring spinach makes a good substitute. The centre of the tian is lined with filleted sardines: the combination sounds unusual but the end result is delicious for a substantial starter or a light lunch dish.

1 lb (450 g) sardines (*ask your fishmonger if he will fillet them*)	3 eggs
	2 tablespoons chopped flat-leaved parsley
2 lb (900 g) fresh young spinach	6 oz (170 g) freshly grated parmesan
salt and pepper	2 oz (55 g) fresh white breadcrumbs
pinch of grated nutmeg	
2 oz (55 g) rice (*long-grain is best*)	2 tablespoons olive oil

First fillet the sardines, if your fishmonger has not already done so. With a sharp knife, make a slit all the way down the stomach and gut the fish. Cut off the head. Turn the fish over so that it is skin side up and press firmly down on the backbone to flatten it out. Turn it back again and

73

pull out the backbone together with the tail. Pick out any stray bones and rinse well under cold running water.

Wash the spinach very thoroughly and chop coarsely, stalks and all. In a large pan over a gentle heat, cook the spinach until it wilts. Drain, and discard any liquid. Season very well with salt, pepper and the nutmeg.

Bring a large pan of salted water to the boil and cook the rice for 10 to 15 minutes, until tender but still with bite. Drain and rinse under the cold tap.

Pre-heat the oven to very hot (220°C/425°F/Gas 7). Mix together the cooked cooled spinach, the rice, eggs, parsley and 5 oz (140 g) of the parmesan. Oil an earthenware gratin dish and put a 1 inch (2.5 cm) layer of the spinach mixture across the base. Lay the sardine fillets on top, skin side up. Cover with the remaining spinach mixture. Sprinkle the remaining parmesan on top, together with the breadcrumbs. Dribble over the olive oil.

Cook the tian at the top of the oven for 30 minutes. By the end of the cooking time the surface should be lightly browned and the contents bubbling hot. Serve immediately.

SCALLOPS ON TOAST

Scallops are at their best in winter through to early spring. Those you see in summer will always be frozen, and as a consequence likely to give off liquid during cooking. If you can, buy scallops on the shell for a guarantee of freshness and flavour. Although they have a delicate flavour, scallops stand up well to being combined with stronger tastes, hence the old tradition of wrapping them in bacon. I like them grilled, combined with sun-dried tomatoes and fresh basil, pepped up with a little Tabasco, and served on a slice of toasted country bread such as ciabatta. Finish off with a squeeze of lime and a little hazelnut oil for a starter or lunchtime snack.

8 scallops
2 limes
salt and black pepper
1 red onion
1 tablespoon olive oil
1 clove of garlic
8 sun-dried tomatoes soaked
   in olive oil

4 slices ciabatta or other
   good bread
12 basil leaves
Tabasco
hazelnut or other nut oil for
   dressing

If the scallops have been bought on the shell, carefully remove them with a sharp knife and cut away the frilly skirt. Wash carefully and pat dry. With a sharp knife, cut across the bias into 2 or 3 slices. Squeeze a little of the lime juice over the slices, season well and leave to rest for 15 minutes.

Finely chop the onion and fry in the olive oil until very soft but not browned (about 10 minutes). Stir in the garlic and the chopped sun-dried tomatoes and fry for another minute. Heat the grill to medium and toast one side of the slices of bread.

Tear the basil leaves into the onion and tomato mixture and season with black pepper. Spread this over the untoasted side of the bread and put the scallops on top. Grill close to the heat for 3–4 minutes, until the scallops are just beginning to shrink and colour.

Squeeze the lime juice over the toast, add a few drops of Tabasco and a dribble of nut oil, grind over some black pepper and serve immediately.

SHRIMP SOUP

The tiny brown shrimps used in this soup are the most common variety in Britain, although they are increasingly hard to find – try a traditional shellfish stall. These are the shrimps to pot or simply to nibble at with a glass of manzanilla sherry. They make an excellent base for a clear Thai-style shrimp soup, flavoured with ginger, garlic, lemon grass, tamarind and chillies. The broth has a wonderful fragrance and a 'hot and sour' taste. It is vital for this dish that the shrimps should be in their shells, as these give flavour to the soup.

2 large cloves of garlic
1¹/₂ oz (45 g) fresh ginger
(*a piece about as large as
your thumb*)
2 lemons
³/₄ lb (350 g) small brown
shrimps
2 small fresh green chillies
2 or 3 small dried red
chillies
2 sticks of lemon grass

1 inch (2.5 cm) piece of
tamarind or 1 teaspoon
tamarind paste
1 lb (450 g) tomatoes
1 small bunch of fresh
coriander
salt and black pepper
sweet hot chilli sauce
(*bought ready prepared –
the West Indian variety is
excellent*)

Peel and roughly chop the garlic. Peel the ginger and cut it into 5 or 6 thick slices. Cut 1 lemon in half. Wash the shrimps well and put them in a pan with all of the whole chillies, the garlic, ginger, tamarind, lemon grass, halved lemon, whole washed tomatoes and the majority of the coriander (reserve some leaves for a garnish). Cover with 2¹/₂ pints (1.5 litres) of cold water and add plenty of black pepper and a good pinch of coarse salt. Bring to the boil and allow to simmer, covered, for 40 minutes. Take off the heat and allow to stand for a few hours, for the flavours to be absorbed.

To serve, strain the soup and reheat. Taste to check seasoning and stir in the chilli sauce to taste (I use about a dessertspoonful). Finish with the juice from the remaining lemon, float a few of the reserved coriander leaves in each bowl, and serve very hot.

SKATE WITH BLACK BUTTER AND CAPERS

Skate is especially good in the winter and early spring, tailing off towards the end of April. The classic method of cooking it with foaming butter, vinegar and capers remains one of the very best ways of enjoying this fish. Unfortunately, this is a dish which is rarely properly prepared. The fish should be gently poached and topped with best-quality foaming butter, vinegar and capers at the very last minute. Not then a dish for the dinner party, but one for a kitchen supper for friends – the less distance you have to travel from cooker to table, the better.

2 wings of skate, total
  weight approx. 2–2^1/$_2$ lb
  (1–1.25 kg) (*skate actually
  improves for a few days
  after being caught, but
  thereafter can develop an
  unpleasant ammoniac smell
  – sniff it before buying*)
8 shallots

6 tablespoons white wine
  vinegar
1 small bunch of parsley
salt and pepper
4 juniper berries
2^1/$_2$ oz (75 g) unsalted, best-
  quality butter
2 tablespoons capers
  preserved in vinegar

Choose a pan in which both wings will lie flat (if you don't have a large enough pan, try a roasting tin). Chop the shallots and sprinkle over the fish, together with half the vinegar. Add a few stalks of parsley, reserving the remainder. Cover the wings with cold water and add salt, pepper and the juniper berries.

Pre-heat the oven to low (120°C/250°F/Gas ^{1}/$_2$) and warm a serving dish.

Bring the water in the pan very slowly to the boil. Allow it barely to simmer for about 15 minutes (the exact cooking time will depend on the thickness of the wings). The fish is done when the flesh lifts easily off the central bone. Carefully bone and lay the flesh in the warmed serving dish (you can serve the wings whole if you find the boning too tricky). Sprinkle with the chopped parsley.

Drain the liquid from the pan and reserve for another dish. Add the butter to the pan and cook over a low heat until it is foaming and just turning brown. Lift the pan off the heat immediately and pour the foaming butter over the fish. Now heat the remaining vinegar and the capers in the same pan and as soon as the vinegar starts to bubble pour this over the fish. Serve absolutely straight away, with boiled new potatoes and a green salad or vegetable.

SOLE AND RED PEPPER SALAD

The lemon sole is at its best in the winter and early spring months, before the spawning season begins. Look out for baby fish, which have a particular delicacy and sweetness of flavour. When you have tired of serving them plainly grilled or dipped in egg-yolk and fried, try this warm salad, in which the nutty flavour of the roasted peppers and the fragrant walnut oil enhance that of the fish.

1 teaspoon clear honey	4 very small or 2 medium
juice of 1 lemon	lemon sole
4 tablespoons walnut oil	salt and freshly ground
1 sprig of rosemary	pepper
4 red peppers	1 small bunch of young
1 oz (25 g) clarified butter	chives

Make a dressing from the honey, lemon juice and walnut oil. Stand the sprig of rosemary in the dressing to infuse for 15 minutes.

Grill the peppers under a very hot grill until all sides are thoroughly blackened (about 20 minutes). Leave under a clean cloth for 5 minutes then peel. De-seed and cut into strips. Pour the strained dressing over the still warm strips of pepper.

Heat half the clarified butter in a non-stick frying-pan. Fry the sole for just a few minutes on each side. They are done when the flesh lifts easily off the bone. Remove from the pan and skin and fillet immediately. (Alternatively, you can grill the fish under a very hot grill.)

Lay the sole over the red pepper salad, season with salt and a little freshly ground pepper and sprinkle with chopped chives. Serve immediately with good bread (I like Italian ciabatta with this dish).

SQUID SAUSAGES IN RED WINE

Squid are more commonly seen than cuttlefish (see earlier recipe, pages 63–5), and although many of those which reach our markets in the spring have been frozen, they stand up well to this treatment. Later in the year, if the weather is good, look out for fresh squid caught off the British coast.

Squid can be braised, fried, deep-fried or grilled, all with excellent results. I particularly like this Spanish recipe for squid 'sausages', where the squid are stuffed with a mixture of rice, bacon and spring onions before being poached in red wine.

FOR 16 SMALL SQUID
(3–4 INCHES (7.5–10 CM) LONG)

5 oz (140 g) long-grain rice	2 teaspoons paprika
6 oz (170 g) spring onions	$^1/_2$ teaspoon salt
1 clove of garlic	$^1/_2$ teaspoon black pepper
6 rashers of smoked streaky bacon	2 glasses red wine
	1 bayleaf
2 tablespoons finely chopped parsley	

First prepare the squid; this is not a difficult task, although it can be a bit messy. Cut off the tentacles just below the eyes and reserve. Pull out the head and body sac in one piece and remove the small transparent bone which runs down one side of the body, making sure it comes out in one piece. Peel off the mottled skin from the body. Finally, rinse very thoroughly.

Bring a large pan of water to the boil, cook the rice at a swift boil for 5 minutes, and drain. Chop the spring onions very finely with the garlic, and stir into the rice. Chop the bacon as finely as possible, including the fat (it should virtually be minced). Do the same to the reserved tentacles of the squid. Add both to the rice mixture together with the finely chopped parsley, the paprika and the seasonings.

Stuffing the squid is a slightly fiddly job. Be careful not to pack the filling in too tightly or the squid may split during cooking,

and for the same reason do not fill right up to the top – leave about a
³/₄ inch (2 cm) gap. I find it easiest to use a teaspoon to push the stuffing
into the squid.

When you have stuffed all the squid, choose a pan in which they will
all lie flat. Pour in the red wine and an equal quantity of water, and add
the bayleaf. Bring to the boil, turn down to a simmer and gently put in
the squid sausages. The heat will cause the open ends to virtually close.
Leave to just simmer for 25–30 minutes, until very tender. Serve either
straight away or warm.

TROUT WITH BACON

Unless you or a member of your family is a fly-fisherman, you are
unlikely to sample the delights of a freshly caught brown trout – which is
a shame, for there is little to beat such a fish, especially when cooked in the
Black Forest style of blue trout. Rainbow trout needs a little more help to
bring out its flavour, as in this simple dish of trout cooked with bacon
and a splash of vinegar.

4 trout	2 shallots
6 oz (170 g) pancetta or	2 tablespoons white wine
smoked streaky bacon,	vinegar
cut in 1 or 2 thick slices,	1 tablespoon chopped fresh
with plenty of fat	parsley
salt and pepper	
1 tablespoon plain white	
flour	

Gut the fish if the fishmonger has not already done so, and rinse the
insides thoroughly under cold running water. Trim the skin off the
bacon, leaving as much fat as possible, and chop into small oblongs
(lardons). Choose a large heavy-based frying-pan into which both the
trout will fit, and over a low heat fry the lardons until the fat runs.
Meanwhile season the trout very well both inside and out, and roll it in
the flour. When there is plenty of fat in the pan (if the bacon isn't fatty

add a little goose fat or lard) add the trout; fry over a medium heat for 4–6 minutes on each side, depending on the size of the fish. Meanwhile finely chop the shallots. Transfer the fish with the bacon pieces to pre-warmed plates in a low oven.

Fry the shallots in the pan until they take on a little colour. Pour in the vinegar, standing well back, and allow it to spit and sizzle for minute. Pour the vinegar and shallots over the trout, sprinkle with the parsley and serve immediately. Plain boiled potatoes go well.

MEAT

Meat consumption has been in gradual decline in Great Britain for some years. The decline has been selective, with the traditional Sunday joint meats of lamb and beef suffering more than poultry and pork. The figures make shocking reading: household consumption of lamb and mutton, for example, has declined from 376,000 tons in 1980 to only 248,000 tons ten years later; over the same period, beef fell from 700,000 tons to just 444,000. Yet if spring means one thing for the meat eater, it is lamb. The traditional dish for Easter Day, British-reared new season lamb has few equals, especially if you can find lambs from the hill regions. It would be a great pity if we are rearing a generation ignorant of the delights of home-cooked British lamb.

At the same time as the decline in consumption, there has been a shift in retail outlets for meat, with the supermarkets gaining increasing predominance. In particular, supermarkets have emphasized ready-to-cook meats: the chicken pre-basted with olive oil or the seasoned steak have always struck me as remarkably untempting, given the fact that it takes only seconds to season the meat at home, but they appear to have been successful. Pre-cooked meals, which require only reheating, have fared even better in terms of sales, giving rise to fears that the next generation may lose the basic cooking skills.

As a result, the individual family-run butcher has experienced difficult times in the last decade and many have simply closed down, or been bought up by a chain (now themselves running into difficulties). This is a great pity, for a good butcher is a vital aid to the cook. A butcher who is choosy about his suppliers, who knows his customers' preferences, who can trim a particular cut of meat to your choice, a butcher who can tell you which meat is the best quality and value of the week and who understands why you must have veal bones for a particular stock. All this is worth fighting for.

One of the few places where it is still possible to find a gathering of old-fashioned family butchers is in the covered meat markets of the major towns (outdoor meat stalls at the markets now being discouraged by many councils). Many of these were originally devoted entirely to meat, but over the years other stalls have crept in. Nonetheless, finding 5 or 6 butchers in such a market is not uncommon, and many will be third or fourth generation. Cardiff market, in Wales, is one such and it also happens to be on the edge of some of the best lamb-producing country in the world. I visited it to see how the butchers there are facing up to the threat of the supermarkets.

Cardiff Market – Welsh Lamb and More

Cardiff's central market hall attracts visitors for its architecture as well as its food. Standing off St Mary's Street on the way up to Cardiff Castle, the present building was opened in 1891, after its predecessor on the same site lasted for just one year before being destroyed by fire in 1885. The architect, Solomon Andrews, was undeterred by this disaster and came up with a new design for what became known locally as 'Solomon's Temple'. Recently restored for its centenary, the market today still befits the description given at the time of its opening: 'The inside of the market hall is very imposing, and has been greatly admired by many persons from a distance as well as at home, and for general attractiveness is certainly not surpassed.'

The market hall is two-tiered, the original intention having been butchers' shops at the ground level, with a fish market separated off at the eastern end, and 'shops for sale of sundry goods' on the gallery. Today a few sellers of sundry goods (an excellent description) have crept on to the ground floor, but the bulk of it remains devoted to food – and to meat in particular. Butchers still range along both sides of the hall, as they have since the market opened. Some of the shops even predate it – take T. J. Morgan, est. 1861, run today by Andrew and John Morgan, direct descendants of the founder. The family tradition runs strong in Cardiff – W. S. Jones and Sons, established in 1890, today employs three generations of Joneses, father, three sons and a grandson. Moorcraft's, the name of another original tenant, is now in brackets beside a new name, G. White, that of Mr Moorcraft's son-in-law.

Nor, at least at first glance, does the range of meats on offer seem to have changed much. Moorcraft's or White's is a cooked meats specialist. Here, as well as pies, you find cooked pig's feet and bacon knuckles, haslet and brawn, home-made hog's pudding, even chitterlings. In fact, rather a lot of boiled chitterlings, the smaller intestine of the pig. Cooking traditions have not been lost here: according to Mr Moorcraft, he now serves the children of women who were his customers thirty years ago, and recipes have been handed down. He has no doubt that his son-in-law will serve their children too – and chitterlings will still be popular.

But for the unconvinced, there is a lot more to these butchers than tripe. Best of all, in spring there is Welsh lamb. J. T. Morgan, the largest butcher in the market and occupying six bays, sells fifty carcasses of lamb a week in season, as well as 150 odd legs. The meat comes via wholesalers, sourced from all over the Welsh hills. Other butchers, such as W. S. Jones & Sons, buy about a third of their lamb direct – farmers come to them, they go out to the farms. The butchers in Cardiff are spoilt for choice when it comes to buying lamb. Try visiting one of the many livestock markets to get the point. Welshpool, one of the largest, acts as host to 80,000 sheep a week in season.

It's not just, of course, a question of quantity. The quality of Welsh lamb is high, good enough to compete with (and beat) the best France has to offer, except perhaps for those delicious 'présalé' lambs from the salt marshes of Brittany. The legs, the prize cut, are at their best in spring – roast them rare. Buy leg steaks and marinate them in lemon and oil before grilling very briefly or, even better, searing on a skillet. Use the expert skills of the Cardiff butchers to trim your lamb cutlets, so that there is just a nut of pink meat at the end of a short arch of bone, or to leave all eight cutlets together for a carré, whole best end of neck. Get them to bone the shoulder and cut it into cubes for your Moroccan tagine. Ask them to prepare the leg French-style, the central bone removed and only the shank left, for easy carving and quick cooking. Shopping in the market, you can have the cut you want, not one pre-determined by packaging.

These are the expensive cuts, but the butchers (and the customers) of

Cardiff don't let any of the animal go to waste. For long, slow stews buy scrag end of neck. Another cheap cut is the breast, a bit fatty perhaps, but good when served à la Sainte Ménéhould, braised very slowly first, then coated with breadcrumbs and grilled, in the same way as a pig's trotter. Minced lamb mixed with Middle Eastern spices makes the best meat-balls. And then of course there is the offal – liver, kidneys, heart, sweetbreads. In Spain at lamb-slaughtering time, a mixture of all four would be threaded on skewers, encased in the chitterling, and slowly grilled, to be served as a delicacy before the whole roast lamb. More conventionally, try the liver rolled in spices and very briefly tossed in oil, the kidneys cooked with sherry, the sweetbreads sautéed with mushrooms and cream, the heart slowly braised.

In spring and summer, lamb inevitably dominates the butchers of Cardiff. There is beef too, from Scotland as well as Wales, and pork and chicken. Some of it is very good quality. But there is a jarring note. Look at that bacon butcher over there – nice to see a specialist, but why should he advertise himself as a Danish bacon specialist? Wales produces wonderful home-cured bacons, fat and flavourful – a world away from the processed result of the pig injected with water to increase its bodyweight. And why is all his bacon ready sliced, rather than waiting for a customer to dictate the thickness desired? Next door sells chickens; white, flabby-looking things, and yes, they are from a battery farm – chickens which don't taste of chicken, fed on fishmeal and slaughtered too young. The butcher knows it – he eats birds raised free-range on the nearby farm, because 'they taste better'. So why doesn't he sell them? Well, he does sometimes, but they're more expensive and you can't get the volume, though demand *is* slowly increasing.

And then there are the ready-to-cook dishes. Too many of the butchers of Cardiff have taken to doctoring their meats. Fine if done well, as in France; to be fair, there were a few tempting things here, such as veal patties studded with fresh parsley. But the vast majority of the prepared meats couldn't, to my eyes, be more unappetizing. Why roll a piece of rump in steak seasoning, a sickly yellow mix of dried herbs? How long does it take to crush a few peppercorns at home? I wonder what goes into the lurid pinky orange b-b-que (*sic*) sauce which glutinously encases the spare ribs – better to buy a jar of hoisin sauce, if you haven't got time to prepare your own.

The butchers of Cardiff aren't cooks. They have introduced these products only recently, to try to compete with the supermarkets which are inexorably taking away their business. They say their customers like them, especially for the barbecue. Yet gut feeling says they can only lose by following this path. Their prepared meats can't compete with the ready-to-cook meals which come from hundreds of hours of testing by the mass retailers – and the customers who buy them will one day be lured away. The stalwarts of Cardiff market should concentrate on the quality of their sourcing, their butchery, their personal service. That, I hope, is why Mr Moorcraft's son-in-law will see his customers' children in the market in the years to come – not for something they could get in the supermarket.

BEEF TAGINE WITH HONEY AND ORANGES

A tagine is a Moroccan stew, often cooked in the earthenware cooking pot with a chimney-shaped lid which has given its name to the dish. This style of Moroccan cuisine bears great similarity to our own medieval cookery tradition, in its combination of meat and fruit and its use of spices. Here the spiced beef is enlivened by a last-minute addition of Moroccan oranges, which are at their best in the spring. As in some parts of Morocco, the meat is not browned before stewing, producing a more delicate result.

$1^1/_2$ lb (675 g) best-quality stewing beef
1 teaspoon ground ginger
1 teaspoon ground coriander
$^1/_2$ teaspoon ground cinnamon
$^1/_2$ teaspoon paprika
1 teaspoon freshly ground black pepper
a few strands of saffron
8 oz (225 g) spring onions

1 small bunch each of fresh parsley and coriander
1 tablespoon good-quality honey (*try to get orange-flower honey for added flavour*)
1 tablespoon orange-flower water (*optional*)
3 tablespoons olive oil
2 large sweet Moroccan oranges

Trim the beef of fat and cut it into 1 inch (2.5 cm) chunks. Put the meat in a heavy-based casserole and sprinkle over all the spices except the saffron. Chop the spring onions coarsely (including the green ends) and add to the dish. Tie the herbs together in a bunch and place in the casserole, with the end of the string hanging out over the edge. Pour over enough water just to cover the meat and stir in the honey, the orange-flower water and the olive oil. Bring to the boil and then simmer very slowly, covered, for $1^1/_2$ hours.

Soak the saffron strands for 10 minutes in a tablespoon or two of hot water. Peel the oranges, divide into segments and remove all traces of pith. Remove the bunch of herbs from the tagine and add salt to taste. Stir in the saffron water and cook for 5 minutes. Now add the orange segments and heat through for another 5 minutes before serving. Buttered rice goes well.

BOILED BEEF WITH SALSA VERDE

Boiled beef may not sound very exciting, but pot-au-feu or bollito misto has a better reputation. Both refer to boiled meats, although in the Italian bollito misto a boiling fowl and a zampone or stuffed pig's trotter are also included. This is a dish for a restaurant or a large gathering, but a simpler version can be produced using just beef, with a few chicken wings to add flavour. The end result is surprisingly succulent and is served with a piquant sauce based on anchovies, capers and parsley. The sauce is also excellent served with slices of cold beef, roasted very rare.

Serves 6–8

FOR THE BOILED BEEF

3 lb (1.5 kg) piece of chuck
steak, tied into a round
2 onions
2 carrots
2 sticks of celery
1 clove of garlic
8 black peppercorns
4 juniper berries

1 bouquet garni, to include
a sprig of rosemary,
thyme, parsley and a
bayleaf
4 tomatoes
4 chicken wings (*and
chicken giblets if available*)

FOR THE SALSA VERDE

1 clove of garlic	fillets preserved in olive
3 tablespoons finely	oil
chopped flat-leaved	1 tablespoon red wine
parsley	vinegar
2 tablespoons capers	6 tablespoons extra virgin
2 oz (55 g) tin of anchovy	olive oil

Unlike the French pot-au-feu, meats for the Italian bollito misto are put into boiling water, and it is the Italian system which I use. Into a large pan, preferably enamelled, put sufficient cold water to cover the piece of beef and the whole, peeled onions and carrots and the sticks of celery. Add the peeled garlic clove, the peppercorns, juniper berries and herbs tied in a bundle and bring to the boil.

Truss the meat securely into a round bundle if your butcher has not already done so. Halve the tomatoes and grill them briefly until they are soft. When the water is boiling, put in the beef, chicken and grilled tomatoes and turn the heat down to its very lowest setting. For the first few minutes of cooking, skim off the scum as it rises to the surface. Cook the meat, covered, for 3 hours. The liquid should barely simmer, with only the occasional bubble rising to the surface.

To make the salsa verde, crush the garlic clove and pound it with the chopped parsley, capers and anchovies (do not use a liquidizer for this or the mixture will be too fine – a pestle and mortar is the best utensil). Add the vinegar and then beat in the olive oil, slowly at first, as if making mayonnaise.

When serving the beef, be sure to leave it as short a time as possible out of the liquid as it will quickly lose its succulence. Cut it into thin slices and serve with plenty of salsa verde and a few boiled new potatoes.

Rather than serving the cooking liquid before the beef, I prefer to keep it for soup to serve on another day.

CHEESE-STUFFED MEATBALLS

Meatballs don't have a good name but they can be an excellent way of preparing a quick and economical meal. I am very fond of highly spiced meatballs, from both lamb and beef, cooked in the North African style (see both summer and winter recipes, pages 183–4 and 357–9). This Italian dish is less spicy but richer, the meat not only stuffed with melted cheese but also given extra flavour from stronger cheeses like Fontina and parmesan.

1 lb (450 g) lean minced beef	3 oz (85 g) grated Fontina (or Emmenthal) cheese
1 egg	2 oz (55 g) grated fresh parmesan
6 leaves of fresh sage	6 oz (170 g) mozzarella
1 teaspoon fresh thyme leaves or $^1/_3$ teaspoon dried thyme	(preferably buffalo)
	1 oz (25 g) plain flour
	1 oz (25 g) butter

Season the beef mince very well and mix in the egg, the chopped herbs and the 2 grated cheeses. Drain the mozzarella thoroughly and chop into $^1/_2$ inch (1 cm) chunks. Take a walnut-sized piece of beef, roll it into a ball and with your thumb make a deep indentation on one side. Place a chunk of mozzarella in the hollow and mould the beef around it, so that none of the cheese shows. Repeat the process until all the beef is used up – you should have around 30 meatballs. Dust them with the flour.

When you are ready to cook, melt the butter in a frying-pan large enough to take all the meatballs. Fry them quickly on both sides and then turn the heat down a little to give the cheese time to melt. In all, you should cook them for 6–7 minutes. Serve immediately with a squeeze of lemon or with a fresh tomato sauce. Boiled new potatoes and spinach dressed with lemon and oil both go well.

CHICKEN AND FETA PIE

The commercially produced filo pastry is of excellent quality and provides one of the few instances where making your own does not necessarily produce better results. I generally keep a pack in my freezer for starters, puddings and light main courses, such as chicken and feta pie. This Turkish recipe is ideal for lunch on a sunny spring day, served with a simple green salad.

10 oz (285 g) cooked
  chicken breast (*lightly
  grilled is best*)
6 oz (170 g) feta cheese
1 teaspoon ground cumin
1 1/2 teaspoons ground
  cinnamon

1 teaspoon paprika
1/2 teaspoon ground mace
1/2 teaspoon black pepper
4 oz (115 g) unsalted butter
1 packet filo pastry

Chop the chicken breast and feta cheese together very finely and mix in the spices (don't add salt as the feta is very salty). Melt the butter and skim off any scum. Cut the sheets of filo pastry in half across to form a square shape.

Lay a sheet of the pastry on a greased baking tray and brush with butter. Lay a second sheet on top and again brush the surface with butter. Continue the process until you have used 6 sheets. Now sprinkle the chicken and feta mixture all over the surface. Top with a sheet of pastry, brush with butter, and continue the process until you have used all the sheets of pastry. Roll up the ends all around the pie. Brush the top very thoroughly with butter.

Bake for 30 minutes in a medium oven (150°C/300°F/Gas 2) until the surface is golden. Cut into squares and serve immediately.

Meat

CHICKEN WITH DRIED
MUSHROOMS AND CREAM

Spring in the French mountain regions means the season of the morel, which makes a fleeting appearance in certain forests at the end of April. In the Jura, these rare and delicious wild mushrooms are cooked with a cockerel, the local vin jaune and plenty of cream for a rich treat. Not one easy to emulate in Britain – the cult of the wild mushroom has yet to take hold, and morels, vin jaune, and even a cockerel are difficult to find here. But taking the idea and substituting what is easier to buy, a chicken is delicious cooked with a mix of dried and fresh mushrooms, in white wine mixed with sherry as a vin jaune replacement, and finished with cream for a glossy sauce. The ideal accessory to this old-style dish is either buttered noodles or long-grain rice.

1 oz (25 g) dried mushrooms (*morels if you can find them, otherwise dried porcini, available from Italian delicatessens and some supermarkets*)

8 oz (225 g) cultivated mushrooms (*I use organically grown brown caps or champignons de Paris as the French call them*)

1 plump corn-fed chicken, divided into 8 portions

1 oz (25 g) unsalted butter

salt and pepper

$1/_2$ pint (300 ml) dry white wine

1 small glass medium dry sherry (*I use oloroso, but you can also use amontillado*)

6 oz (170 g) double cream

Soak the dried mushrooms for a couple of hours in a little warm water. Wash the fresh mushrooms and dry thoroughly. Joint the chicken if the butcher has not already done so, removing any excess fat.

In a heavy pot, melt the butter. Add the chicken pieces and cook, covered, over a low heat for 20 minutes. Drain off all the chicken fat.

Add the fresh mushrooms to the pan, together with plenty of seasoning, and cook over a low heat for 5 minutes. Now add the wine and sherry and allow to bubble for a minute or two. Add the dried mushrooms and their liquid to the pan and leave to barely simmer for about 40 minutes, until the chicken is tender.

Remove the chicken and keep warm. Add the cream to the mushrooms and liquid and simmer for 10 minutes, until the sauce has amalgamated. Check seasoning and serve the sauce spooned over the chicken pieces.

CHICKEN SALTIMBOCCA

Although the Roman speciality saltimbocca is traditionally made with veal escalopes, I prefer to use chicken breasts. Somehow the sage seems to go better with chicken, and the meat remains juicy even when the cheese has melted, unlike veal which, unless it is of the very best quality, can go dry. This is a dish which requires last-minute preparation, but is also very quick to cook – ideal for a light, rapid supper.

4 breasts of chicken
6 oz (170 g) Fontina cheese
(*if you can't get Fontina,
use another cheese which
cooks well, such as Tomme
from France or at a pinch
Gruyère or Emmenthal*)
4 large or 8 small very thin
slices of Parma ham (*you
can use other raw hams
such as Bayonne or jamon
serrano, but not cooked ham*)
salt and pepper
8 fresh sage leaves
1 oz (25 g) butter (*clarified
for best results – or mix a
little oil with the melted
butter to prevent burning*)

With a very sharp knife, slice the chicken breasts in half, horizontally if they are thick enough, or across the diagonal (too thick a piece of chicken and it will not cook quickly enough). Cut the cheese into 8 slivers to fit the size and shape of the chicken slices, and divide the slices of ham in half if you have large ones.

Season the chicken breasts well all over. On one side of each piece of breast, place a sage leave. Cover with a piece of cheese and then a slice of ham; if the ham is too large, wrap it round the other side of the chicken slice. Repeat for all 8 chicken pieces.

In a pan large enough to take all 8 pieces of chicken, heat the clarified butter or mixed butter and oil. When it is bubbling, put in the chicken pieces, Parma ham side down. Cook very briefly on this side (a minute or two) and then carefully turn over. Cook over a lower heat for about 5 minutes, until the chicken is cooked through and the cheese is melting. Serve straight away, with new potatoes and some green beans or tiny carrots.

LAMB CUTLETS FRIED WITH PARMESAN AND POLENTA

This Italian recipe needs the youngest cutlets of spring lamb to be successful – some of the very best meat comes from Wales. The cutlets are deep-fried in a coating of egg, parmesan and polenta, producing very tender and flavourful meat with a crispy crust, not in any way greasy.

8 lamb cutlets	3 oz (85 g) polenta flour
2 oz (55 g) freshly grated parmesan	2 eggs
	vegetable oil for frying

The lamb cutlets should be trimmed of any fat so that there is only the bone and the nut of meat. Lay the parmesan and the polenta on two large plates. Lightly beat the eggs and put them in a third plate.

Season the cutlets and dip them first in the parmesan, turning them over so that both sides are covered. Shake off any excess cheese and lay the cutlets next in the beaten egg, turning them again. Finally dip both sides in the polenta, making sure that the bone as well as the meat is covered. Repeat for each cutlet. You can carry out this stage up to an hour before cooking the meat

When you are ready to cook, choose a wide shallow pan in which all the cutlets will fit. Add oil to a depth of $^1/_2$ inch (1 cm) and heat until it is almost smoking. Add the cutlets and fry for 2–3 minutes on each side, depending on thickness. Remove, shake off any excess oil, and serve straight away, with a quarter of lemon on each plate. Courgettes, grilled or stewed with tomatoes, go well.

LAMB STEAKS WITH GARLIC, ANCHOVY AND ROSEMARY CRUST

This is not a dish for the youngest of spring lamb, whose delicate flavour might be overwhelmed, but for leg steaks from a more mature animal. The light crust gives additional bite to the meat, which is previously marinated in lemon juice and olive oil. Although this is not a dish for all tastes, it is very popular with those who like highly-flavoured meat dishes. New potatoes and a crisp green vegetable such as beans go well.

2 lemons	2 oz (55 g) tin anchovy
2 tablespoons extra virgin	fillets preserved in olive
olive oil	oil
4 leg steaks of lamb	1 large sprig of rosemary
4 large cloves of garlic	$1/2$ teaspoon freshly ground
	black pepper

Squeeze the juice from the lemons and mix with the olive oil. Lay the lamb steaks in the mixture and leave to marinate for a couple of hours, turning once.

Peel the garlic cloves and drain the anchovies. Pull the spiky leaves off the sprig of rosemary. If you have a food processor, whizz together the garlic, anchovies and rosemary, adding a little of the liquid from the marinade, until you have a paste. Otherwise use a pestle and mortar. When you have a thick paste, stir in the coarsely ground black pepper. Remove the lamb steaks from the marinade and pat dry. Smear the paste all over them.

Pre-heat the grill to absolute maximum (or heat an oiled skillet if you have one). Fry or grill the steaks for no more than 3–5 minutes on each side (depending on thickness and whether you are using a grill or a skillet). The aroma given off during cooking is marvellous. Serve very hot, with a slice of lemon for each steak.

MUSTARD RABBIT WITH POLENTA

Rabbit is an under-appreciated meat in Britain and is more likely to find its way to the Easter table in the guise of a chocolate bunny than a succulent dish. This is not true of many of our Continental neighbours, who have a raft of rabbit recipes. This one combines ideas from France and northern Italy: the meat is marinated in olive oil, smeared with French mustard and served with that staple of Lombardy, polenta. If you buy whole rabbits, use the legs for this dish and keep the saddle for casseroling or making into a pâte.

2 tablespoons olive oil	4 sprigs of fresh thyme
1 tablespoon red wine vinegar	6 oz (170 g) polenta
1 teaspoon sugar	2 tablespoons Dijon mustard
4 rabbit hindlegs	plain flour
	salt and pepper

Mix together 1 tablespoon of olive oil, the vinegar and sugar and pour this mixture over the rabbit legs. Lay the sprigs of thyme in the dish and leave to marinate for at least 4 hours, preferably overnight.

Prepare the polenta according to the instructions on the packet. This will involve pouring polenta in a slow stream into boiling water and then stirring vigorously until the polenta is ready. Proportions of water to polenta are usually in the 3 oz (85 g) to 1 pint (575 ml) range. The time taken to cook varies, especially if you use an 'instant' mix instead of the more traditional variety, which requires 30 minutes or so of stirring. When the polenta is nearly ready, remove the thyme from the marinade, strip it of its leaves and stir them into the polenta. Leave to cool.

When you are ready to cook, heat the grill to maximum. Lift the rabbit from the marinade and pat dry. Smear mustard all over each leg and sprinkle with seasoned flour. Cut the cooled polenta into 4 thick slices. Place the rabbit and polenta on a flat roasting dish. Dribble the remaining olive oil over the polenta. Cook near to the grill to 10 minutes, then turn the meat and polenta over. Cook for another 8 minutes or so and serve piping hot, with a green salad.

PORK TENDERLOIN WITH RED WINE AND CORIANDER SEEDS

Tenderloin is the pork equivalent of fillet steak. It is best cooked quickly over a high heat, although of course unlike fillet steak it should not be served rare, and its tenderness is further improved by a preliminary marinade. In Spain and Portugal red wine and coriander seeds are familiar accompaniments to pork, and I use them here in a simple-to-cook dish which makes an excellent supper. The spring onions give a good contrast of textures.

$1^1/_2$ lb (675 g) tenderloin of pork, in one piece
$^1/_2$ teaspoon black peppercorns
$1^1/_2$ teaspoons coriander seeds
4 fl oz (100 ml) red wine
1 teaspoon white granulated sugar
3 tablespoons olive oil

1 teaspoon fresh thyme leaves *or* $^1/_3$ teaspoon dried thyme
4 large spring onions
1 or 2 cloves of garlic according to taste
coarse salt and freshly ground black pepper
1 oz (25 g) butter

Cut the tenderloin into rounds about 1 inch (2.5 cm) thick and lay in an earthenware dish in which they will just fit. In a pestle and mortar bruise the peppercorns and 1 teaspoon of the coriander seeds. Mix together the red wine, the sugar, half the olive oil, the thyme and the coriander seeds and peppercorns. Pour this mixture over the pork and leave to marinate for about 4 hours, turning once.

To cook, trim the spring onions of their green ends and peel off any papery outer skin. Chop into chunks about $^3/_4$ inch (2 cm) long. Peel and chop the garlic.

Remove the pork from the marinade and pat dry. Strain the marinade and reserve the thyme. Crush the remaining coriander seeds in the pestle and mortar. Mix together the crushed coriander, plenty of coarse salt and freshly ground black pepper and the leaves of thyme stripped from the sprigs. Roll the rounds of pork in this mixture.

Heat the remaining olive oil in a large heavy-based frying-pan over a medium high heat. Throw in the spring onions and as soon as they have stopped spitting add the pork rounds and the chopped garlic. Cook over a high heat for 3–4 minutes on each side, until the pork is cooked through. Remove from the pan together with the spring onion and garlic, and keep warm.

Chop the butter into pieces. Turn the heat down to low and pour the strained marinade into the pan in which the pork cooked. Bring to the boil and reduce quickly by a third. Take off the heat, stir in the pieces of butter to give the sauce a gloss and pour over the meat.

Serve immediately with plain boiled rice and a green vegetable such as French beans.

PROVENÇAL DAUBE OF LAMB

British lamb, particularly that from the Welsh hills, can compete with the best lamb in the world (some would argue that it *is* the best). The first of the new season's lamb appears in early spring, usually at astronomical prices, becoming more affordable towards the end of the season and reaching a peak in the summer months. Before it arrives, however, the fuller-flavoured hogget from lambs nearly a year old is available. This meat is ideal for this hearty stew from Provence.

3 small or 2 large white onions

2 or 3 fat cloves of garlic

1 lb (450 g) best-quality plum or Marmande tomatoes or a 14 oz (400 g) tin

1 tablespoon olive oil

1 1/2 lb (675 g) shoulder of lamb off the bone, cubed and trimmed of fat

1 tablespoon tomato purée (*if you are using fresh tomatoes*)

1 stick of cinnamon

rind of 1/2 an orange

rind of 1/4 of a lemon

1 sprig of rosemary

2 or 3 sprigs of flat-leaved parsley

1 fresh bayleaf

1 thick slice (about 3–4 oz) of pancetta or unsmoked streaky bacon

freshly ground black pepper

1/2 a bottle of heavy red wine from the South of France (*I use Côtes de Ventoux*)

4 oz (115 g) small unpitted black olives, preserved in oil rather than brine

6–8 leaves of basil (*optional*)

Pre-heat the oven to medium (150°C/300°F/Gas 2). Chop the onions into very fine half-rings; peel the garlic and chop finely. Peel and de-seed the tomatoes. In a heavy-based pan with a lid, heat the oil. Fry the onions gently for 10 minutes until translucent but not browned, then add the chopped garlic. Fry for another 5 minutes, stirring to make sure the garlic doesn't catch.

Now turn the heat up and add the lamb, stirring rapidly to make sure the meat is browned on all sides. After a minute or two, add the tomato purée and the peeled, chopped tomatoes. Turn the heat down and cook for a further 5 minutes.

Tie the cinnamon, orange and lemon rinds, rosemary, parsley and bayleaf together with a long piece of string; put them in the pot with the string dangling out for easy removal. Put the piece of pancetta or bacon in the pot. Season the meat with plenty of freshly ground black pepper but no salt at this stage (the olives may make the dish salty). Pour over the red wine, allow to bubble for a minute or two and then cover and transfer to the oven.

Cook for an hour before adding the olives. These should be blanched (dropped in boiling water for 30 seconds and then drained) in advance to remove excess salt.

Cook for another hour or so, until the lamb is meltingly tender. Five minutes before serving, remove the slice of pancetta or bacon and the bundle of herbs and rinds. Check the seasoning and stir in the torn basil leaves if you are using them.

Serve Provençal style with freshly made pasta (tagliatelle or fettucine) and a salad of spring leaves to follow.

ROAST VEAL WITH ARTICHOKES

There is natural concern over the conditions to which veal calves are subjected. The answer is not necessarily to stop eating veal, but always to make sure you ask for animals reared under British standards. The more consumers who follow this route, the greater the chance of eradicating the excessively cruel practices followed on the Continent. Many Dutch calves are already reared under kinder rules for the British marketplace.

Conscience salved, think about a roast of veal for an Easter lunch. The light, pale meat is ideal for spring weather and goes perfectly with the first imported artichokes (which also go well with spring lamb). The cost of veal makes it a special occasion dish, so I usually indulge myself with a rich, creamy sauce. Serve the roast with steamed young vegetables – tiny whole carrots or green beans are perfect.

1 or 2 bones from the knuckle of veal, chopped into pieces by your butcher
2 onions
2 carrots
4 small globe artichokes (*or 8 if you are feeling extravagant*)
1 lemon
1 tablespoon chopped fresh chervil
2 oz (55 g) best-quality unsalted butter

salt and pepper
2 lb (900 g) boned roast of veal (*ask your butcher's advice, but rib end of loin is a good cut; the weight is a lot for 4 but any less and the roast will dry out – and the veal is excellent cold*)
1 glass dry white wine (*a rich buttery Chardonnay works well*)
6 fl oz (175 ml) double cream

First make a stock with the veal bones. Heat the oven to very hot (220°C/425°F/Gas 7) and place the bones in a roasting dish together with the peeled whole onions and the scrubbed carrots. Roast dry for 20 minutes, shaking the pan occasionally so that the bones don't stick. When the bones have coloured, drain off any fat then pour over a pint (575 ml) of water and return the pan to the oven. Reduce the temperature to medium (150°C/300°F/Gas 2) and cook for 45 minutes taking the pan from the oven once or twice to skim off any fat and turn the bones over. Drain off the resulting liquid and leave to cool.

Next prepare the artichoke hearts. Cut off the stalk and pull off any browned outer leaves. Slice across the artichoke about 1¹/₂ inches (3.5 cm) above the base and discard all the tops of the leaves. With a sharp knife, remove the hairy choke which you have now exposed and rinse under the tap to remove any stray hairs. Rub all the cut surfaces with lemon juice to prevent them discolouring. The hearts are now ready to cook. Put them in a small pan with just enough water to cover and simmer until tender, about 20 minutes, but check with a fork (cooking time varies according to freshness and size). Remove the hearts from the water, which you should keep as it will be used in the sauce.

Pre-heat the oven to hot (200°C/400°F/Gas 6). Chop the chervil very finely, discarding all the stalks. Pound the butter and chervil together with some seasoning. With your finger, stuff this mixture into the centre of the rolled joint of veal without untying it. Put the joint in a roasting dish and cook in the centre of the pre-heated oven for 45 minutes.

While the meat is cooking, prepare the sauce. Add the wine and 4 tablespoonfuls of the reserved artichoke cooking liquid to the veal stock and reduce by fast boiling until you have ¹/₂ pint (300 ml) of liquid. Take off the heat, stir in the cream and season to taste. Put the artichoke hearts in the sauce and leave over a low heat, so that it is just on the point of simmering.

When the meat is ready, pour any buttery juices from the roasting pan into the sauce. Carve into thin slices, making sure each contains a little of the chervil stuffing. Place one or two artichoke hearts on each plate and pour over the sauce. Serve with new potatoes.

Spatchcocked Spring Chicken

Spatchcocking refers to the technique of splitting a bird open down the backbone, in order to produce a shape which can be quickly cooked, originally over coals. The technique was a familiar one to eighteenth- and nineteenth-century British cooks. I like to cook small poussins or spring chicken this way, flavouring them in the Italian style with garlic, rosemary and olive oil. The rosemary gives off a marvellously pungent scent as this simple dish cooks.

4 small spring chickens or poussins	salt and pepper
4 cloves of garlic	4 large sprigs of fresh rosemary
4 tablespoons olive oil	8 wooden skewers

With a very sharp knife, split the chicken by cutting all the way along the backbone. Flatten the chicken out by pressing down on the breastbone, so that you end up with a rectangular-shaped chicken. Push a wooden skewer diagonally through the flesh of the chicken and another across the other diagonal, to hold the chicken in place. Rub each bird all over with the cut side of the clove of garlic and then the olive oil. Season well with salt and pepper. Cut the garlic into slivers and slide them under the skin.

Pre-heat the grill to maximum. Dampen the sprigs of rosemary to stop them burning, and place on a metal tray on which all the birds will fit. Put a bird, breast side down, on top of each sprig. Grill near the flame or element for 10 minutes then turn over, dribbling over a little more olive oil as necessary. Grill breast side up for a further 10–15 minutes, until the flesh is white. The skin will blacken in places – don't worry, this adds to the flavour.

Serve the chicken immediately, perhaps with some grilled tomatoes stuffed with garlic and herbs, or just a salad. This is a good dish to follow a plate of pasta.

SPICED LEG OF LAMB

The new season's lamb is a great treat and you will probably want to serve the first joint you lay hands on simply roasted, perhaps scented with rosemary and garlic. Later on in the season, you can try it with honey and lavender (see summer recipe, pages 181–2). For a roast leg of lamb with a difference, consider this North African dish, where the whole leg is basted with spices and lemon juice. The spicing is not aggressive and the lemon juice gives the meat a little sharpness – the combination is delicious. This dish is easy to prepare but does require a fairly full spice cupboard.

2 teaspoons ground coriander

1 teaspoon ground cumin

1 teaspoon whole cumin seeds

$^1/_2$ teaspoon turmeric

$^1/_2$ teaspoon ground ginger

$^1/_4$ teaspoon ground mace

2 cloves, ground

$^1/_4$ teaspoon cayenne pepper

1 teaspoon crushed black peppercorns

$^1/_2$ teaspoon coarse sea salt

juice of 2 lemons

1 leg of new season English lamb, approx. 3–3$^1/_2$ lb (1.5–1.75 kg)

lemon wedges

Mix all the spices and the salt together in a pestle and mortar, lightly bruising the whole cumin seeds. Add the lemon juice to make a liquid paste.

With a sharp knife, make deep incisions in the leg of lamb. Smear the paste all over the meat and leave to stand in a cool place (but preferably not the fridge) for 4–5 hours before cooking.

To roast, pre-heat the oven to very hot (220°C/425°F/Gas 7) and cook for 45 minutes until the spices have formed a crust. Now turn the oven down to medium (150°C/300°F/Gas 2) and continue to cook for another 30–45 minutes. Allow to stand for 10 minutes before serving.

Serve the meat cut in thick chunks, with wedges of lemon to squeeze over. New potatoes boiled and then tossed in garlic, chilli and mustard seeds go well, as does spinach dressed with lemon juice and olive oil.

STEAMED LAMB WITH SAFFRON

This is one of my favourite ways of serving the new season's lamb. It may not sound immediately attractive, but the steaming keeps in the best of the flavour and the basting with butter and saffron makes this a dish fit for a pasha. Two words of warning, however, after all this enthusiasm. (1) Make sure you use real saffron, the stigmas of the crocuses, rather than saffron powder, which is almost always a substitute. Indian shops are a cheap and good source for the real thing. (2) Get the right kit for steaming. Although a wok is perfect for fish, in this case a better bet is a very large pot on top of which you can rest a metal colander, over which you place a lid and tea-towel, or use a steamer. A good tip is to put a small coin in the boiling water beneath the colander: if too much steam escapes and the water dries out, the coin will stop tinkling against the sides of the pan, telling you it is time to add more water.

I prefer to use a gigot or fillet of lamb on the bone for this dish, as it has very little fat. However, it is also a good way to cook a shoulder.

1 heaped teaspoon saffron strands	bone, approx. $2^1/_2$ lb (1.25 kg)
3 oz (85 g) best-quality unsalted butter	6 spring onions
salt and pepper	1 large bunch of fresh coriander
$^1/_2$ fillet of lamb on the	

TO SERVE WITH THE LAMB

1 tablespoon whole roasted cumin seeds	$^1/_2$ tablespoon coarse sea salt
	2 lemons

Pulverize the saffron strands in a pestle and mortar or a grinder, and blend with the butter. Add seasoning to taste.

Trim the joint of lamb of any fat and rub half the butter and saffron mixture over it.

Set up the steaming apparatus. Bring the water to the boil, making sure the bottom of the colander is just above the water surface. Line the colander or steamer with the peeled spring onions and the washed stalks of coriander. Lay the piece of lamb on top.

When the water has come to the boil, place the colander over the pan, making sure it does not touch the water. Cover with a clean tea-towel, followed by as close-fitting a lid as possible. Lay another clean tea-towel on top. Leave to steam for 1 hour, under no circumstances removing the lid.

Pre-heat the oven to maximum. After 1 hour check the lamb: it should be very tender and cooked through. If it is not, check the water beneath (remember the coin?), cover again and steam for another 15–30 minutes.

To finish the meat, baste it in the remaining butter and saffron mixture and place it in the hot oven for 5 minutes. Carve and serve immediately. For added authenticity and flavour, put a plate of roasted cumin seeds and sea salt together with a few slices of lemon in the centre of the table. The only other accompaniments should be bread and a salad – tomato and onion would be good.

PUDDINGS

In my kitchen pudding is almost synonymous with fruit. Quite often I end a meal with just a bowl of fruit and a plate of cheese. When a more elaborate concoction is called for, it is rare that it will not incorporate some kind of fruit, be it dried or fresh.

Yet spring is a lean time for British and indeed European grown fruit. Spanish strawberries appear a month or two earlier than the British ones in June – but, picked underripe for the long journey, they are rarely as succulent or flavourful as those later in the season. It is worth waiting for summer, as it is for Mediterranean peaches, nectarines and melons in top condition.

On the other hand, some of the more exotic varieties which we have grown used to are now at their best. Just because they are not produced locally, it does not mean that we should not be aware of their best seasons. Bananas may be available all year round, but the sweetest come from the Caribbean in March and April. Pineapples too are excellent at this time of year. Oranges from North Africa, and Morocco in particular, are plentiful and juicy in early spring, which also sees the last of the blood oranges. Papaya and mango can both be good, although purists would argue that for the very best of the latter you should hang on for the Alphonse from India in June. Spring is the only time of year you will find the extraordinary loquat or Japanese medlar, with its almost rotten appearance and delicate fragrance. Kumquats are still available for preserving or stewing, and passion fruit are juicy – use their liquid for a delicate soufflé.

Britain, and London in particular, is lucky in having many markets which specialize in ethnic produce. One of the best known is that in Brixton, south London. I visited it to examine the exotic fruits on offer in the spring.

Tropical Brixton Market

No one could claim that Brixton is a pretty market. If you're looking for charm, this is not the place. It is scruffy, even smelly at times, and the roar of the nearby traffic rises above the stallholders' cries. But it is also lively and colourful, and a lot of fun. And its numerous discerning regulars keep the produce both cheap and up to scratch.

The majority of London's markets date back to Victorian times, and Brixton is no exception. The market started towards the end of the nineteenth century in Atlantic Road, and after the Second World War extended into Electric Avenue and under the railway into Pope's Road. Today it numbers some 150 stalls, the majority of them still selling food produce, although as elsewhere there is an inexorable creeping in of trashy clothes stalls. As well as the stalls there are shops which spill out on to the streets, and covered markets in both Granville Arcade and Market Row.

Many of the stalls, especially those selling fruit and veg, have been in the family for three or four generations and some of the current stall-holders have stood on their pitch since just after the war. During that time they have seen incredible changes in the range of produce available. As rationing receded, so the importing of fruit and vegetables by air freight began. One of the stallholders told me that he was the first in Brixton to offer Jamaican bananas, in the early 1950s. Imagine Brixton market without bananas.

Elsewhere in this book, I complain that the effect of the availability of fruit and vegetables from all over the world all year round has dulled our sense of the seasonal. I remain convinced that no one should eat asparagus in December, or strawberries in January – not only are they not as good as the summer varieties, they just don't fit the weather. But this is the position of the privileged. A market such as Brixton is special precisely because it offers exotic varieties which do not grow in Britain. Unlike the supermarket, however, it has a regular base of customers who are both fussy about what they eat and know how to pick the best. The ethnic community of Brixton is largely composed of Afro-Carib-beans, and on any market day you will find many black women nosing through the produce. They know what is good and will not be fobbed off. In particular, they are fussy about their fruit. As one stallholder told me, 'The black people are our favourite customers because they eat lots of fruit – but they certainly keep us on our toes.'

Take the case of the mango. In spring Brixton has to be one of the best places in Britain to buy these delicious fruit. There are small green ones for pickling, large fat orange ones for slicing, juli mangoes, black mangoes, even, according to one sign on a stall, 'sweet sucking mangoes'. In each case the sign over the fruit tells you where they are from – Venezuela, Colombia, Jamaica, Costa Rica and India. A regular habit in France and Italy, this is too rare in British markets. I watched one woman spend a quarter of an hour choosing just two perfect mangoes at one stall – sniffing them, poking them very gently so as not to bruise them, weighing them in her hand. The unruffled stallholder watched patiently, knowing she would come to a decision in the end. Of course, a mango is like a fig – when eaten still warm from the tree it is an experience not to be forgotten, an experience the air-freighted variety can never reproduce. Nor am I suggesting that we all have time to spend a quarter of an hour choosing two mangoes. But the concern of that customer and hundreds like her makes sure the stallholders of Brixton visit the wholesale markets every day and get the right produce at the right price.

Spring is the best time for imported tropical fruit. Brixton today is over-represented on the banana front all year round – firm green ones for savoury dishes as well as soft yellow ones for pudding. But spring sees the arrival of the tiny varieties from the Caribbean, often no longer than your finger, arranged in tight clumps. The very best come from the Windward Isles, their flavour sweet but never sickly, their texture firm but not stringy. They make the most unctuous ice-cream. Pineapples too are excellent at this time of year, towards the end of their season which began in the autumn: sniff them at the stalk end to check they give off a heady scent, prod them with your fingers to make sure they yield, weigh them in your hand to make sure they are heavy in relation to their size. When you have found the perfect specimen, serve it perfectly alone for breakfast or dressed in a rum and lime syrup for pudding.

Bananas and pineapples are commonplace today. In Brixton you will also find fruit with which you may not be so familiar. How about the soursop, a large dark green fruit with a spiny skin, used in the Caribbean to make drinks and ice-creams? Or the durian, that prized but foul-smelling fruit? What about the naseberry, also known as the sapodilla, or the loquat with its elusive flavour, a treat for the fruit bowl? Others may trip you up: the jackfruit and breadfruit are both used as vegetables in Caribbean cooking. Return to more familiar territory with the citrus fruits. Strangest is the ugli fruit, in my view a not entirely successful cross between the grapefruit, the orange and the tangerine, first developed in Jamaica. Far better are the ortaniques, from the same island, a cross between an orange and a tangerine, excellent for topping tarts. The rule of Caribbean provenance is broken for the oranges, allowing in the North African fruit, sweet and juicy as they come to the end of their season. Try sprinkling orange-flower water over them before serving. What about blood oranges for an adult jelly? And don't leave Brixton without buying plenty of limes, a vital component of both sweet and savoury dishes: squeeze their juice over fresh pineapple and papaya or use it to give bite to syrups and ices.

Brixton has plenty to offer besides its tropical fruit. Not everything on display, however, is for the weak of stomach. I consider myself adventurous in taste but even I blanch before pigs' tails and feet dyed a sickly pink, whole cooked cow's feet (even if they are, as the sign informs me, from Scotch beef), skinned goat's heads and yes, bull's testicles. At least the customers here aren't (yet) armed with long two-pronged forks with which to leaf through the tripe on offer at the front of the butchers' stalls, as they are in Ridley Road, London's other leading Caribbean market. The fish stalls, of which there are a great many in the covered arcades, are at first sight only a little more reassuring. Many of the fish are unfamiliar, almost all flown in from warmer waters. Sadly, this means the majority have to be frozen and they often appear a little dull in the eye. Recognizing this, the fishmongers charge different prices for the fresh and frozen varieties of the same fish: a frozen red snapper will often cost half the price of his fresh relative. Perhaps our supermarkets could consider a similar policy – would you be prepared to pay more for truly fresh fish?

Brixton is not the place to go for the best of British- or even European-grown produce. When shopping for asparagus or artichokes, Jersey Royals or sorrel, even strawberries and raspberries later in the season, this would not be my first port of call. But given the dearth of

European fruit in spring, the availability of seasonal exotic fruit (not to mention vegetables) makes it very attractive. And there is such life and colour there. It is a deservedly popular local market, which has kept up with the changing needs of its customers – or maybe its customers themselves have forced the pace.

BANANA ICE-CREAM

Despite their year-round availability, it still seems to me (with the agreement of the trade) that the very best bananas are the tiny, sweet variety that arrive from the Caribbean (especially the Windward Isles) in the spring. They make a wonderful, rich ice-cream, which is good on its own or served with a cake or tart.

$^1/_2$ pint (300 ml) full-cream milk	6 fl oz (175 ml) double cream
4 egg-yolks	8 small ripe bananas
2 oz (55 g) caster sugar	1 lime
	2 teaspoons ground allspice

The base of the ice-cream is a custard. Bring the milk to the boil and allow to cool. Beat the egg-yolks and sugar together until pale and fluffy and stir this mixture into the cooled milk. Cook over the lowest possible heat, stirring all the time, until the custard thickens enough to coat the back of a wooden spoon – this will take about 20 minutes. Never, in your impatience, allow the mixture to boil or it will curdle and you will have to start again. It is best to use a thin-bottomed saucepan which responds quickly to changes in temperature and does not hold the heat – then, if the custard gets too hot, you can lift the pan off the heat for a minute or two without fear of the custard continuing to cook.

When the custard is ready, stir in the cream. Mash the bananas with the lime juice and the allspice and stir this mixture into the custard. Pour it all into a freezer container and freeze, covered, for about 4–6 hours, until set. During that time take the ice-cream out twice and mash it with a fork, to prevent ice crystals forming. Make sure you remove it from the freezer 30–45 minutes before serving.

BLOOD ORANGE JELLY

The best orange season runs from late winter through to early spring, with the mid-season treat of the bitter Sevilles. In March, blood oranges are common and should be snapped up for their slightly sharp flavour and wonderful colour, shown to great advantage in this jelly. Although jellies are often associated with nursery food, they can make very adult puddings when served not too set and spiked with a little alcohol – gin, in this case. You should be able to find orange-flower water in your delicatessen; it gives a slightly spicy scent to both sweet and savoury dishes.

3/4 pint (450 ml) juice (*this will take about 15 blood oranges*)

1 tablespoon orange-flower water (*optional*)

3 tablespoons gin

1 sachet gelatine powder (*sufficient to set 1 pint (575 ml) of liquid*)

Mix together the juice, orange-flower water and gin. Dissolve the gelatine in ¹/₄ pint (150 ml) of hot water and add to the mixture. Pour into a suitable bowl and chill until set. Serve decorated with slivers of orange rind and a few segments of fruit.

CHOCOLATE PUDDING

Chocolate and Easter have become inseparable in our minds, and I therefore include this pudding for Easter Sunday. I have to admit that I am no great lover of chocolate, finding it too rich to end many meals. Perhaps the best way to eat good-quality chocolate is with a hunk of bread and an apple, as a snack. But I do like this recipe, which is somewhere between a pudding and a cake. The truffle-like coating of chocolate and cream makes it veer towards the former.

5 eggs

4 oz (115 g) sugar

4 oz (115 g) best-quality
dark chocolate

1 oz (25 g) butter

2 oz (55 g) ground almonds

2 tablespoons white alcohol,
e.g. eau-de-vie, grappa
(*optional*)

3 oz (85 g) self-raising flour

TO COVER

¹/₄ pint (150 ml) double
cream

6 oz (170 g) best-quality
dark chocolate

Separate the eggs and beat the yolks with the sugar until light and frothy. Melt the chocolate in a double boiler with the butter, stirring occasionally. Mix the melted chocolate and butter into the egg and sugar mixture. Add the almonds and liquor; sieve in the flour and stir all together.

Pre-heat the oven to medium (150°C/300°F/Gas 2). Whip the egg-whites until very stiff and fold into the pudding mixture. Butter an oval or oblong 8–9 inch (20–22.5 cm) cake tin and pour in the mixture. Bake in the oven for 45 minutes, until the cake has risen and a skewer inserted into it comes out clean.

When the cake is cooked, unmould and leave to cool on a wire rack. Prepare the coating by bringing the cream to the boil. When it is very nearly boiling, take off the heat and stir in the chocolate, broken into pieces. Beat together very well, until the mixture has thickened slightly. Leave to cool a little and then transfer to the freezer for 45 minutes to firm up.

When the cake is completely cool, spread on the chilled cream and chocolate mixture. Serve in thin slices, with extra cream as desired.

COFFEE AND MASCARPONE MOUSSE

Mascarpone is a wickedly rich Italian cream cheese, used in tarts, cakes and as a base for mousses. It is good simply whipped up with sugar and egg-whites and served with fruit. You can also whip in a sharp fruit purée (such as damson, see autumn recipe, pages 292–3), or a cup of strong coffee. As the eggs are not cooked, make sure they are free-range and from a reliable supplier.

1 espresso cup of very strong Italian coffee	1 tablespoon brandy or grappa (*optional*)
2 oz (55 g) caster sugar	2 eggs
	6 oz (170 g) mascarpone

Make the coffee, preferably using an espresso maker. It should be very strong. Add half the sugar and the liquor if you are using it, as for a caffè corretto; resist the temptation to drink the coffee immediately and leave it to cool.

Separate the eggs. Whip the mascarpone with the egg-yolks until you have a consistent, light texture. Stir in the cooled coffee and whip the mixture together until there are no lumps and the cream has thickened (6–7 minutes by hand, 2–3 in the processor). Whisk the egg-whites with the remaining sugar until stiff, and fold into the mascarpone and coffee mixture. Spoon into individual serving dishes and chill. Serve within about 12 hours of making the pudding, or it may start to separate.

FLAMBÉED CHERRIES

Cherries only just scrape into the spring section, being the first of the summer fruits to arrive in May. The best might be eaten straight from the paper bag as you wander round the market, but try this recipe for the rest when you get home. Red wine is frequently combined with fruit in French cooking, to great effect.

8 oz (225 g) sweet firm cherries	1 tablespoon redcurrant jelly
1/2 a lemon	1 oz (25 g) unsalted butter
3 oz (85 g) brown sugar	2 tablespoons brandy (*or*
4 fl oz (100 ml) light red wine (*a Beaujolais would be ideal*)	*better still kirsch, if you have it*)

Remove the stalks from the cherries and wash well – do not stone them or they will lose their shape during poaching. Cut the zest of the lemon into thin strips. In a pan large enough to take all the fruit, heat the sugar until it caramelizes and melts slightly. Now stir in the red wine, the juice and zest of the lemon and the redcurrant jelly. Boil fiercely for 2–3 minutes to reduce. Stir in the butter and cook for another minute before adding the cherries. Cook over a lower heat for 2 minutes. Meanwhile, heat the brandy in a ladle, set light to it, and pour it over the cherries. Serve as soon as the alcohol has burned off – cream and ice-cream both go well.

FROZEN ALMOND CUSTARD WITH MINT SYRUP

The first of the mint makes an appearance towards the end of the spring season, in time for the Jersey Royals. Mint is also an excellent ingredient for puddings; snip young leaves over soft fruit such as strawberries, and use larger ones to scent a syrup for ice-creams and mousses. I like this combination of mint syrup poured over a frozen almond custard.

ALMOND CUSTARD

3 egg-yolks
1 1/2 oz (45 g) caster sugar
2 oz (55 g) ground almonds

a few drops of almond essence
1/2 pint (300 ml) full-cream milk

MINT SYRUP

1/2 pint (300 ml) water
2 oz (55 g) sugar

5 or 6 large sprigs of fresh mint

The custard is a standard version with the addition of the ground almonds. Beat the egg-yolks and sugar together until light and fluffy. Mix in the ground almonds and almond essence. Now slowly add the milk, stirring all the time. Heat over the lowest possible flame, continuing to stir – on no account allow the mixture to boil. After about 20 minutes the mixture should thicken sufficiently to coat the back of the spoon. Leave to cool for 30 minutes or so and then transfer to a shallow freezer container with a lid. Freeze for 3 hours, stirring once or twice during that time, until the custard is set but not frozen solid: the consistency should be firm but creamy. If preparing in advance, make sure you take the custard out of the freezer 45 minutes before serving.

To make the syrup, bring the water to the boil and stir in the sugar. When the sugar has dissolved, add the washed sprigs of mint and simmer, uncovered, for 10 minutes. Leave to cool with the sprigs of mint, so that the flavour infuses the syrup, and strain when completely cool.

Serve the frozen custard in round balls, bathed in a little of the mint syrup and perhaps decorated with a sprig of mint.

MANGO MOUSSE

Mangoes are now available virtually all year round, but some of the best arrive in the spring, leading up to those which in many a connoisseur's opinion are the very sweetest – the Alphonse variety from India, whose season starts in May and goes on through the summer. Mangoes are picked underripe to survive the rigours of the journey, but if picked too green they are unlikely to ripen to their full sweetness and should be kept for chutney and pickles. Look for mangoes which are slightly soft to the touch but by no means squidgy, with a splash of rosy pink in the green skin and a strong scent. Keep them in a warm place for a day or two before eating.

Mangoes make a delicious end to a spicy or rich meal, served with just a squeeze of lime juice. I also use them to make this lightly bound mousse, studded with pieces of fruit.

2 large ripe mangoes, approx. 10 oz (285 g) each	2 egg-whites
	2 oz (55 g) caster sugar
	6 fl oz (175 g) double
juice of 1 lime	cream

Peel the mangoes and chop the flesh away from the central flat stone, making sure you keep any juice which flows. Purée the fruit of one mango with the lime juice and any mango juice; cut the flesh of the other into tiny dice.

Whip the egg-whites with the caster sugar until very stiff. Whip the cream until it too stands in peaks. Fold the two together and then fold in the purée. Finally, fold in the diced fruit. Spoon carefully into glass serving dishes and chill for at least 2 hours before serving.

PAPAYA GRANITA WITH VODKA

The papaya or paw-paw is a favourite breakfast fruit in the tropics. Eaten with a squeeze of lime on a sunny terrace before it gets too hot, a slice of papaya is the best start to the day. Those imported to Britain often need careful nurturing in a warm place to reach perfection – give them a good sniff and a squeeze before buying to make sure they are on their way to fully-fleshed juiciness. Papaya flesh makes a beautifully coloured granita, given a kick with a dash of vodka. It should not be served fully frozen, so be sure to take it out of the freezer well before serving.

2 large or 3 small ripe
   papayas – total weight
   around 2$^1/_2$ lb (1.25 kg)
juice of 2 limes
$^1/_2$ pint (300 ml) water
3 oz (85 g) white sugar

2 cardamom pods
2 tablespoons vodka (*for
   extra flavour, use a better-
   quality vodka such as those
   from Russia or Poland*)

Remove all the flesh from the papayas and purée with the lime juice. Make a sugar syrup by boiling together the water, sugar and cardamom pods for 5 minutes. Allow the syrup to cool, remove the cardamom pods and then stir the syrup into the fruit purée. Add the vodka, turn the mixture into a freezerproof bowl, cover, and freeze for 4 hours, stirring every so often to break up the ice crystals. Remove from the freezer an hour or so before serving: the granita should have a slightly slushy consistency, rather than being completely frozen.

PASSION FRUIT SOUFFLÉ

The passion fruit is a tricky fruit to deal with, due to the sharp pips which stud its flesh. But it is the juice which carries all the fruit's sensuous flavour, and only a little is needed to impart a tangy scent to a dish. Try squeezing a few of the fruit over an exotic fruit salad, or mixing a few teaspoons of juice into a crème anglaise. Best of all, make this light and airy soufflé. No flour is needed, as the passion fruit curd gives a sufficient base. The soufflé must, of course, be baked at the last minute and served immediately, for which reason I, being as keen on the conversation as the food, wouldn't serve it at a dinner party.

4 eggs plus 1 extra egg-white	3 oz (85 g) sugar
3 oz (85 g) unsalted butter	juice of 10 passion fruit
	juice of $1/_2$ a lime

Separate the eggs. Melt together the butter and 2 oz (55 g) of the sugar. Add the strained juice of the passion fruit and the lime. Off the heat, stir in the egg-yolks. Heat very gently for 5–10 minutes, until the mixture thickens into a curd – be careful it does not get too hot, or it will curdle. Once thickened, leave it to cool for 30 minutes or so.

Pre-heat the oven to medium (150°C/300°F/Gas 2). Whip the egg-whites until stiff. Add the remaining sugar to the whites and whip again until glossy.

Butter a soufflé dish. Fold a third of the egg-white mixture into the cooled curd and put this mixture in turn in the dish. Now gently fold in the remainder of the egg-white, making sure it is well mixed. Cook towards the bottom of the oven for 15–20 minutes, until the soufflé has risen – resist the temptation to open the oven door during the cooking, or the soufflé may sink. Rush from oven to table.

PINEAPPLE IN RUM AND LIME SYRUP

Pineapples are good from just before Christmas through to the end of spring. But be careful to choose carefully: if picked too under-ripe they may never reach their full juiciness. Conversely, over-ripe fruit are likely to have been bruised during the journey to the market. Look for pineapples which give slightly around the stem, have a powerful scent and feel heavy for their size. For a simple pudding, drench the fruit in a dark rum and lime syrup, as they do in the Caribbean.

1 large pineapple	1 stick of cinnamon
4 oz (115 g) brown sugar	2 cloves
1 lime	1/2 pint (300 ml) water
4 tablespoons dark rum	

This pudding will look best if you can manage to cut the pineapple into rings, using a corer to remove the tough central section, but if you are short of time chunks will do. Either way, make sure you remove all the eyes and reserve the juice for adding to the syrup.

To make the syrup, gently heat the sugar over a low heat for 5 minutes. Now add the juice of the lime, a large strip of zest (reserving the remainder), the rum, spices and water together with any reserved pine-apple juice, and simmer for 20 minutes. Strain the syrup, add the fruit and cook for another 5 minutes. Leave to cool.

Cut thin strips from the remaining zest of the lime and blanch. Sprinkle the strips of lime with brown sugar and bake in a medium oven (150°C/300°F/Gas 2) for 5 minutes. Just before serving, sprinkle the fruit with the strips of lime peel.

RICOTTA TART

Ricotta, a soft white cheese from Italy, is used in both savoury and sweet dishes. The best is very fresh and should be used the same day that you buy it otherwise it has a tendency to dry out and become rubbery. Fresh ricotta is wonderful simply sliced, dusted with sugar and served with summer fruits. Earlier in the year, try this rich cheesecake with a pastry base; the ricotta is flavoured with marsala wine and studded with raisins. This is an excellent pudding to go after the roast lamb on a festive occasion such as Easter Day.

4 oz (115 g) raisins	3 oz (85 g) unsalted butter
3 tablespoons marsala wine (*you can substitute an oloroso or amontillado sherry*)	10 oz (285 g) ricotta
	1 lemon, preferably unwaxed
6 oz (170 g) plain flour	1 whole egg and 1 egg-yolk
2 oz (55 g) caster sugar	4 fl oz (100 ml) double cream
pinch of salt	

Leave the raisins to soak for a few hours in the marsala or sherry.

Make the pastry by sieving the flour with half the caster sugar and a pinch of salt. Crumble in the butter, broken into small cubes, and add 3 tablespoons of iced water (it is important that it should be iced). Quickly knead or process into a ball. Wrap the dough in clingfilm and leave in the fridge for 30 minutes.

Beat the ricotta with a fork for 5 minutes so that it becomes fluffy. Grate the lemon rind into the cheese and add the egg and egg-yolk, the remaining sugar and the double cream. Beat well, then fold in the soaked raisins and the marsala or sherry.

Roll out the pastry, prick it all over with a fork and line a buttered quiche dish. Brush the edges with a little egg-yolk. Bake the pastry blind for 10 minutes in a medium oven (150°C/300°F/Gas 2), then fill the pastry case with the ricotta mixture and bake for a further 40 minutes. Serve just warm.

Rhubarb Tart

The early forced or champagne rhubarb available from the beginning of the year has a very delicate flavour, enjoyed best when the rhubarb is simply steamed, perhaps with stem ginger (see winter recipe, page 399). By spring, however, the stalks are thicker and tougher, their flavour more powerful. Then is the time to make rhubarb tart. There are many recipes for this excellent dish, most of which encase the fruit in a creamy custard. I find that the flavour comes across best if the rhubarb is cooked with just sugar on top of a buttery pastry base. It is important that you peel the rhubarb, otherwise it will be tough.

8 oz (225 g) plain flour	2 eggs
1 oz (25 g) caster sugar	2 lb (900 g) rhubarb
pinch of salt	6 oz (170 g) white
4 oz (115 g) unsalted butter	granulated sugar

Make the pastry a couple of hours in advance to give it time to rest. Sieve the flour and the caster sugar together with the pinch of salt and crumble in the butter, broken into small cubes. Make a well in the centre and pour in one beaten egg, together with a dribble of cold water. Mix all together to make a dough. Leave to stand in a covered bowl in the fridge.

Trim the rhubarb of leaves and any tough ends. Using a potato peeler, peel off all the stringy pink skin. Chop the rhubarb into 3/4 inch (2 cm) segments, chopping any particularly large stalks in half vertically as well.

Pre-heat the oven to medium (150°C/300°F/Gas 2). Roll out the pastry as thinly as possible and prick it all over with a fork. Use the pastry to line an 8–10 inch (20–25 cm) buttered tart tin, making sure the edges come well up. Separate the remaining egg and brush the edges of the tart with the egg-yolk and the base with the egg-white.

Use half the granulated sugar to cover the base of the tart and arrange the rhubarb on top. Sprinkle with the remaining sugar. Cook in the pre-heated oven for 45 minutes. Leave to cool thoroughly before serving.

PINEAPPLE TANSY

The name tansy comes from the bitter-sweet tansy herb which would once have been included in this pudding. Tansy cakes or puddings were traditionally eaten at Easter time, in memory of the 'bitter herbs' of the Passover. Today the name applies generally to this style of dessert, a cross between an omelette and a pancake. You can make a tansy without fruit, or you can include soft fruit like apples, pears and plums. I tried a tansy with pineapple and liked the contrast of textures.

1 small pineapple	pinch of ground cloves
1/2 oz (15 g) butter	4 eggs
2 oz (55 g) brown sugar	4 oz (115 g) natural
1/2 teaspoon ground cinnamon	yoghurt
1/2 teaspoon ground allspice	

Peel and core the pineapple and chop into small chunks. In an attractive heavy-based deep-sided frying-pan (a cast-iron one is best – remember the dish is served straight from the pan), melt the butter. Gently fry the pineapple with half the sugar and the spices until the fruit has softened – this takes about 5 minutes. Allow to cool a little.

Separate the eggs. Beat the egg-yolks and the yoghurt together and stir in the cooked fruit. Whisk the egg-whites until very stiff and carefully fold them into the fruit and egg mixture. Pour into the pan and cook over the lowest possible heat until the mixture has set – about 20 minutes. Meanwhile, pre-heat the grill. When the tansy has set, sprinkle the surface with the remaining sugar and brown under the grill. Serve immediately, straight from the pan. A little soured cream goes well.

SABAYON WITH ORANGE-FLOWER BISCUITS

By rights, this is an Italian dish, zabaglione, the froth of marsala wine and egg-yolks brought foaming to the table from a copper-bottomed pan. But the people of the South of France have their own cold version of this luscious sweet – sabayon, often made with the local sweet Muscat wine and served with fatless biscuits scented with orange-blossom. Elderflower wine is an excellent and cheaper substitute for Muscat and I have found that, in the style of syllabub, an oloroso or amontillado sherry can be a good alternative. Do not, however, be tempted to cut down on the amount of liquor.

FOR THE SABAYON

6 egg-yolks	$^1/_4$ pint (150 ml) of the
3 oz ((85 g) white sugar	chosen liquor

FOR THE ORANGE-FLOWER BISCUITS

2 eggs	2 tablespoons orange-flower
4 oz (115 g) sugar	water
	8 oz (225 g) plain flour

To make the sabayon, beat the egg-yolks and sugar together until creamy in a large bowl to fit over a pan of simmering water (your double boiler probably won't be big enough). Add the liquor in a steady stream and, over the water, continue to beat the mixture for about 15 minutes. It will first become very light and frothy and then thicken, while still retaining its airiness. When it is thick enough to coat the back of the spoon, pour into individual serving dishes and chill.

Note: If the sabayon is going to separate, it will do so very rapidly after you take it off the heat; watch it for 5 minutes or so and if two layers form, return to the pan over the water and continue to beat until it thickens further.

To make the orange-flower biscuits, pre-heat the oven to very hot (220°C/425°F/Gas 7). Roughly whisk together the eggs and sugar and then add the orange-flower water and the sieved flour. Stir with a wooden spoon until you have a sticky dough (you can do this in the food processor). Dust the dough with flour and with your hands roll it out into an oblong shape about $1/2$ inch (1 cm) thick by 2 inches (5 cm) wide. Cut across with a sharp knife at $1/2$ inch (1 cm) intervals. Lay the biscuits on a buttered baking tray and bake at the top of the oven for 10 minutes or so, until they just start to turn colour. Remove the tray, shake to make sure none of the biscuits have stuck, and leave to cool.

SUMMER

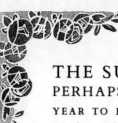
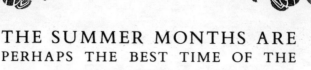

THE SUMMER MONTHS ARE PERHAPS THE BEST TIME OF THE YEAR TO ENJOY SHOPPING FOR FRESH FOOD.

Market stalls are piled with glossy vegetables, their skins shining in the sun, inviting thoughts of salads glistening in olive oil. There are juicy heaps of fruit, much of it gathered from the countries around the Mediterranean – white peaches from Italy, burnished apricots from Spain, purple figs from Greece, sweet yellow melons from the South of France. The fishmonger too joins in this riot of colour: alongside the pale, creamy flesh of the traditional cod and sole are gleaming green and grey striped mackerel, rosy pink shrimps, crabs burnt orange from the boiling pot, and occasionally bright green samphire from the salt marshes. At the butcher's stall there are the early game birds to look forward to, and meanwhile you can choose from tender cuts of lamb for the barbecue and plump, golden chicken for roasting. Perhaps best of all, everywhere there are fragrant bunches of herbs, one of the cook's luxuries of summer.

There is great pleasure to be had in shopping in a market on a warm summer morning. This is not the occasion to go out with a shopping list. Instead, wander between the stalls, choosing by sight, smell and touch. Don't be afraid to poke and sniff, even to ask for a taste: the discerning shoppers of the Continent have a few lessons to teach the more reticent British on this score. When you have filled your basket, go home to a barbecue, a lunch in the garden or a picnic – or, if the weather is true to form, a taste of summer enjoyed indoors.

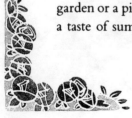

STARTERS

Summer starters should, in my view, be a combination of powerful flavours, simply prepared to allow the freshness and vitality of the ingredients to stand out. This is not a time for fiddly pastry dishes which require time in the kitchen, rich pâtés which will melt in the sun, or intricate mousselines demanding several stages of preparation. The cook wants a dish he or she can prepare with the minimum of fuss, to serve as a light prelude to the main dish.

The wealth of vegetables in the summer season makes them an obvious choice for such starters. Fresh baby vegetables of all varieties are on offer, needing only a little effort to turn them into delicious first courses. Steamed, fried, grilled or barbecued, combined together and dressed with good oils, fresh herbs and perhaps a little spice or other enlivening ingredient, these vegetables are one of the treats of summer.

And where better to buy vegetables than in the market? Here you will find seasonal produce; often you can buy locally grown vegetables, sometimes even picked that morning. You have the opportunity to inspect the produce at close hand, to discuss its origin with the stallholder and to pick the best. Prices are generally lower than in the retailers – you aren't paying for packaging, for one thing. And many market salesmen now provide organically grown vegetables, in response to the increasing demand. Of course, if you have your own vegetable garden, you are luckier still – you can truly pick and choose. For the less fortunate, or the less green-fingered, the vegetable market in summer is a close second best. One of my favourites is in Cambridge, on the edge of the rich and fertile soil of the Fens.

Vegetables from the Fens
in Cambridge Market

Just across the road from King's College chapel and overshadowed by Great St Mary's church, right in the centre of this medieval university town, lies Cambridge's market square. Six days a week it is still used for its original purpose. The market draws its produce from one of the richest horticultural hinterlands in the country; and although much of Fenland has now been given over to mass production of crops for the EC food mountain, not to mention the intrusive rape fields, dedicated producers still exist to take advantage of the region's fertile soil and relatively dry climate. Interspersed between the vast agricultural fields of East Anglia there are still small farms, some barely more than allotments. Many of their owners use organic methods to produce quality vegetables, which then find their way to Cambridge market. Small farmers and their relatives run their own stalls, buying in what they do not grow themselves. So signs declaring 'home-grown' or 'local produce' are not only commonplace in this market, they are also credible.

In the summer months the vegetables of East Anglia come into their own, and it is for them that Cambridge market is especially distinctive. Of course, excellent fruit is also to be had, in particular the sweet local strawberries. There is a splendid fishmonger who comes daily from King's Lynn (although he once confided to me that he ships much of his fish from the West Country, where the choice is greater). On Wednesdays and Saturdays a local farmer has a meat stall, selling home-reared chicken and duck as well as milk-fed pork and lamb and pasture-raised beef. During the BSE scandal he put up signs listing what his cattle were fed to prove their purity, and I took great pleasure in ostentatiously buying a large joint of beef before a hesitant queue. The choice is rounded off by a cheese stall weighed down by wheels of properly matured Cheddar and local Stilton, as well as a wide selection of French cheeses. Its owner will ask you in advance when you want your cheese for, to make sure he gives you one which will be ripe on the day – the sign of a good cheesemonger.

But let's return to the vegetables, the pride and glory of this market. To me, the arrival of home-grown asparagus is a sign that spring has moved on into summer. June sees the stalls of Cambridge market stacked high with bunches of asparagus, ranging from tiny green sprues to fat white varieties, ready to be served in melting butter or a gentle vinaigrette. Baby broad beans also make their appearance around now (a month or so later than those in Jersey), sometimes even small enough to be cooked in their pods, as one stallholder told me she liked them. Shelled, the beans make a splendid salad when briefly cooked and mixed with some smoky bacon or pancetta. The tiny Jersey Royal potatoes have obviously travelled a long way and run out by mid-June, but several stalls have excellent locally grown varieties, such as the French genus La Ratte. These are just right for salads and go on well into summer when the Jerseys have run out. Peas in the pod are on every stall by the middle of June, often alongside baby carrots, pale yellow against their green tops: cook them in just a little water with butter and sugar for a glorious re-introduction to the root vegetable.

By July the carrots have been joined by another baby root, of the beet variety. I have always intensely disliked the vinegary taste of pickled beetroot, and only became a fan of the vegetable after being persuaded in Cambridge to buy a bunch of small, curly-leaved beets by a vendor who told me 'Roast 'em, skin 'em, douse 'em in lemon, oil and parsley and you'll love 'em.' He was right. Courgettes are growing bigger but sensible stallholders still pick them when small. One of my friends in the market regularly brings me in bunches of their bright yellow flowers, for frying after stuffing them with a little soft cheese and ham. Sadly, I seem to be the only customer. The choice of salad leaves is now at its best – lamb's lettuce, oakleaf, summer varieties of endive, sugar Cos, Little Gem, Lollo Rosso, to name but a few. My favourite herb, basil, is sold in huge bunches for a short and glorious period from the end of June by the elegantly coiffed lady whose fruit and vegetable stall right on the edge of the square is a particular favourite of mine. She claims that the greenhouse-grown plants reach 4 or 5 feet in a good year, and having seen the size of the leaves I believe her – this basil is the great-grandfather of the puny plants I keep on my windowsill.

Of course, not all the vegetables available in Cambridge market are plucked from the hinterland of the Fens. The best sweet peppers, globe artichokes, Marmande and plum tomatoes, even garlic, are imported from climates better suited to their growing needs. These basics of

Mediterranean cuisine are essential to my summer cooking plans but must be chosen with care: their longer journey makes them more likely to have suffered on their way to the stall. Peppers should be firm and 'content in their skins', rather than wrinkled and soft. Artichokes should be well-shaped, with no wrinkled brown edges to the leaves; the bite-sized purple variety make an occasional fleeting appearance in Cambridge, when I snap them up for stewing in oil. Tomatoes can be the oddest shapes and still taste sweet: look instead for split skins or bruising to put you off. The garlic, it goes without saying, should be plump and firm, the sort you can roast whole to produce a creamy purée.

As July moves into August the vegetables get larger and some of the herbs, such as coriander, start going to seed. To offset these disappointments, new baby leeks appear, for stir-frying or steaming and slicing into salads. A second wave of new potatoes reaches the market, including my favourite variety, the Pink Fir Apple. But the signs of autumn are already there – tiny onions for pickling, the first parsnips, chanterelle mushrooms from more heavily wooded areas. By the end of the month the variety of salad leaves and herbs has been exhausted and the summer vegetable glories of Cambridge market have gone for another year.

AUBERGINES WITH YOGHURT AND MINT

The glossy purply-black aubergines, both imported and UK-grown, are at their best in the late spring through the summer months – make sure you choose ones with firm skins and no brownish patches or wrinkles. Traditionally in this Turkish recipe the aubergines would be fried in fruity olive oil; I find that they can absorb a frightening amount of oil if cooked in this way and prefer to brush them with the oil and grill them, which has the added benefit of imparting a wonderful smoky taste.

2 large or 3 small
  aubergines
salt and freshly ground
  black pepper
1 clove of garlic
3 tablespoons extra virgin
  olive oil

8 fl oz (250 ml) Greek
  yoghurt (*preferably made
  from sheep's milk*)
1 teaspoon dried mint
3 or 4 sprigs of fresh mint

Wash the aubergines and chop across into pieces approximately $3/4$ inch (2 cm) thick. Place in layers in a colander, sprinkling each layer with salt, and put a heavy plate on top. Leave in the sink to drain for 30 minutes. Cut the clove of garlic in half and rub the cut side around the bowl in which the yoghurt mixture is to be served (earthenware is best). Then crush the garlic and leave to steep in the olive oil. Bring the yoghurt out of the fridge to allow it to reach room temperature.

To cook, pre-heat the grill to hot (around 200°C/400°F). Rinse the aubergine slices thoroughly and pat dry. Drain the olive oil from the garlic, arrange the aubergine slices on the grill and brush the top surface of each with the oil. Allow to grill for about 8 minutes, until the surface is brown but not burnt (it is wise to keep an eye on them at this stage: the cooking time depends upon the firmness of the aubergine and the thickness of the slices, as well as the fierceness of your grill). Turn them over and brush the other side with oil before replacing under the grill. Allow to cook for a further 5–8 minutes: the aubergines should be brown on both sides, the middle tender. Bring out from the heat and allow to rest for a few minutes. Meanwhile, put the yoghurt in the serving dish rubbed with garlic and stir in the dried mint and plenty of freshly ground black pepper. Chop the fresh mint leaves, taking care to avoid the stalks. Lay the aubergine slices in the yoghurt and sprinkle over the fresh mint before serving.

If you want to serve the dish later when warm or cool, mix together the aubergine and yoghurt straight away, but reserve the fresh mint for sprinkling on top just before serving.

ARTICHOKES WITH GARLIC AND ANCHOVY DIP

The globe artichoke season starts in spring and lasts right through the summer months: those in July and August are at their plumpest and juiciest. Look for firm, tightly packed leaves and avoid any with tinges of brown at the tip. With such specimens it seems a shame to eat only the heart, and I prefer to cook them whole, so that the flesh of each leaf can be dipped in a spicy, oily sauce before being sucked out. This is not a dish for elegant eating, but is perfect for a summer lunch in the garden.

4 globe artichokes
2 fat cloves of fresh garlic
   (*try to get new season's
   garlic later in the summer*)
8 anchovy fillets preserved
   in olive oil

8 tablespoons extra virgin
   olive oil (*Italian is ideal*)
juice of $1/2$ a lemon
salt and freshly ground
   black pepper

To cook the artichokes, wash them well and trim the spiky tops of the leaves by cutting across the bulb about 1 inch (2.5 cm) from the pointed top, giving you a flat-topped artichoke which will make it easier to pour in the dressing. Trim the stalk so that the artichoke will stand on its base. Bring a large pan of salted water to the boil and add the artichokes; they will need to boil for between 25 and 40 minutes depending on their size and freshness. To check whether they are done, pull away a central leaf – it should come away easily from the base, and the fleshy end should be juicy and succulent. When the artichokes are cooked, drain them well, making sure you turn them upside down, and set them aside for at least 10 minutes before serving.

To make the dressing, crush the peeled cloves of garlic (this is best done in a pestle and mortar, but you can use the flat side of the knife or whizz them quickly in the processor). Drain the anchovies and pound into the garlic. Add the olive oil, drop by drop at first as if making mayonnaise. Once the mixture has amalgamated, you can speed up the flow. When all the olive oil has been added, add the strained juice of the $^1/_2$ lemon and some freshly ground black pepper.

Some people like to give each person a little pot of dressing in which to dip their artichoke leaves. I prefer to pour it over my artichoke before eating, so that the heart has a chance to absorb the oil before I get down to it.

ASPARAGUS WITH PARMESAN

Asparagus is one of the symbols of early summer to many British cooks. I like all varieties, from the thin green sprues to the fat white stalks of later in the season, but remain convinced that the British-grown asparagus have far more flavour than their earlier imported cousins from the USA and Central America (although those from the Mediterranean are very good). Make sure, though, whatever type you buy, that the tips are still firm. When you have tired of asparagus dripping in butter, try it as the Italians eat it, baked with olive oil and parmesan.

24 fat stalks of asparagus
  (*6 per person – you can
  make do with 4*)
4 tablespoons extra virgin
  olive oil

salt and freshly ground
  black pepper
4 oz (115 g) freshly grated
  parmesan

Pre-heat the oven to medium hot (about 180°C/350°F/Gas 4). Trim the asparagus stalks of their woody ends (this may be 1–2 inches (2.5–5 cm), depending on the asparagus), and peel very finely with a potato peeler. Bring a tall pot of water to the boil and place the stalks upright in it, making sure no tips are in the water. Drain after 5 minutes, being careful not to break the tips, and pat dry. Arrange the asparagus flat in a gratin dish, pour over the olive oil, sprinkle with salt and black pepper and cover with foil. After 15 minutes in the oven, remove the foil and sprinkle over the parmesan. Cook uncovered for another 5 minutes and serve piping hot in the gratin dish.

BASIL AND POTATO GALETTE
WITH CHERRY TOMATOES

As summer draws on, the new potatoes become larger and lose their novelty. Then is the time to try this galette, its crispness providing a perfect base for a small salad of soft sweet cherry tomatoes. The finished galette looks impressive, making it a good choice for the first course of a dinner party.

2 lb (900 g) large firm
   potatoes
salt and freshly ground
   black pepper
juice of $^1/_2$ a lemon
8–10 large fresh basil leaves

2 tablespoons olive oil
8 oz (225 g) cherry
   tomatoes
3 or 4 shallots or 1 red
   onion

Peel the potatoes and grate them coarsely. Sprinkle with salt and the lemon juice to prevent discoloration, then put them in a colander and weight them down (I use a plate with a jar on top). Leave to drain for an hour or so with a bowl underneath – you may be surprised at the quantity of sticky white starch you collect.

The cooking process takes about 40 minutes, requiring only occasional attention. When the potatoes have drained, squeeze any remaining liquid out. Finely shred all but one of the washed basil leaves with your fingers and mix into the grated potato; season well with freshly ground black pepper (but no additional salt). Heat 1 tablespoon of the oil in a large, heavy-based frying-pan over a low heat; add the potato mixture and press down flat across the pan with the back of a wooden spoon. Put an inverted heatproof plate on top and cook over a low heat for 15 minutes. Take the plate off, turn the heat up to medium and cook for another 5 minutes to brown. Turn the galette over by putting the plate upside down on top of the potatoes; holding the base of the plate with a cloth, turn the frying-pan upside down so that the galette ends up on the plate. Heat the other tablespoon of oil and slide the galette back into the pan, uncooked side down. Cook over a low flame for another 15 minutes, then turn the heat up for 5 minutes. At the end of all of this the galette will be ready, the outside brown and crisp, the centre still moist. Cover the surface with chopped tomato, shallot or red onion and the remaining leaf of basil, torn up, and serve, cut into slices.

SALAD OF BABY BROAD BEANS

Too often growers in Britain allow broad beans to grow too large before picking. The larger the bean, the more bitter its taste; look instead for little pods, concealing sweeter beans. Those who grow them in their gardens have a great advantage here. Usually served as an accompaniment to a main course, broad beans can also make an excellent starter. Try them stewed whole in their pods (see spring recipe, page 51) or combined with mild red onion and crisply fried pieces of pancetta or bacon, dressed with balsamic vinegar and nut oil.

2 lb (900 g) unshelled weight of broad beans in the pod
6 oz (170 g) pancetta or unsmoked streaky bacon, cut in 1 or 2 thick slices
2 large red onions
salt

walnut or hazelnut oil
balsamic vinegar
salt and freshly ground black pepper
fresh parsley (*flat-leaved is better, being sweeter than the curly variety*)

Pod the beans. If they are large, slip them out of their thick white jackets to reveal the tender green halves below. Chop the pancetta or bacon into small chunks and fry gently (no fat is necessary). Finely chop the onions and add them to the bacon after it has been frying for 5 minutes; fry for another 5 minutes.

Meanwhile, just cover the base of a separate pan with water, add salt and bring to the boil. Add the beans and cover; if they are young and fresh they will take no more than a minute or two to cook. The beans should be al dente – soft inside but still crisp to the bite. Drain and stir in the bacon and lightly fried onions, together with any pan juices. Add nut oil and balsamic vinegar to taste (I use a proportion of 4 to 1), season with salt and freshly ground black pepper, and sprinkle with chopped parsley. This dish is equally good served hot or cold. If you are going to serve it cold make sure you add the oil and vinegar to the beans while they are still hot, to allow them to absorb the flavours, and don't serve it straight from the fridge.

GRILLED COURGETTES WITH TOMATOES

Tiny courgettes, which have not yet absorbed water to swell, are best just lightly fried or steamed or even served raw. I like to grill the larger variety, having first salted them to allow excess water to drain off. When brushed with oil and placed under a very hot grill, the outsides firm up and colour, forming a seal over the inner flesh which melts to a smoky purée. Served topped with a dice of juicy tomatoes and fresh herbs, these grilled courgettes make a succulent and healthy first course or vegetable dish.

4 courgettes (1 per person)
salt
8 oz (225 g) tomatoes
$^1/_2$ a clove of garlic
a selection or just one of the
  following fresh herbs:
  basil (*my favourite for this*
dish*), parsley, fennel
fronds, chervil, chives,
coriander
1 small green chilli
  (*optional*)
1 lime
2 tablespoons olive oil

Split the courgettes lengthwise, sprinkle with salt and leave to drain for 20 minutes. Meanwhile peel, de-seed and dice the tomatoes. Rub the dish in which they are to be served with a little garlic and stir in the chopped herbs and the finely chopped raw chilli if you are using it. Add the lime juice, season well and allow to stand.

Heat the grill to medium hot (180–200°C/350–400°F). Rinse and dry the courgettes, rub with oil all over, and grill for 10–15 minutes on each side until they are well browned. Serve hot, with the tomato mixture on the side for spooning over.

STUFFED COURGETTE FLOWERS

Market stalls in Italy and France sell bunches of the orange flowers of the courgette plant in season. Difficult to come by in this country, some market stallholders will supply them if asked – or you can pick them from your garden. Perhaps the supermarket chains will soon start to stock them alongside the nasturtium flowers they have already caught on to. Courgette flowers are worth the trouble, for they can be stuffed with a variety of mixtures to produce an elegant starter. I like to use ricotta cheese and a little cooked ham: the soft, creamy cheese and the salty ham are a good contrast to the slightly bitter flavour of the fried flower.

2 large slices of cooked ham (*best-quality home-cooked for preference – processed ham gives off too much liquid*)
4 oz (115 g) ricotta cheese
1 handful of fresh basil leaves

salt and freshly ground black pepper
8 large courgette flowers (2 per person)
oil for deep-frying (*I prefer groundnut or sunflower oil*)

Finely dice the ham and mix into the ricotta. Tear the basil leaves, keeping a few back for decoration, and stir into the mixture along with plenty of seasoning. Wash the flowers and carefully stuff with the cheese mixture, making sure not to overfill them otherwise the sides of the flower may split during frying. Bring the oil to frying temperature, testing with a cube of bread which should immediately turn golden. Slip in the flowers, which may spit – be careful. Allow to fry for 3–4 minutes until they are golden and remove with a slotted spoon. Drain on kitchen paper and serve immediately, sprinkled with the remaining basil leaves.

CRUDITÉS WITH AÏOLI

This classic Provençal dish is the ultimate starter for the market shopper. A little of this vegetable, a handful of that, the best of the day's produce arranged on a plate in a colourful pile for dipping into the aïoli, a glossy garlic mayonnaise which looks its best served in colourful bowls. This can be a starter or, teamed with a few olives and a bite of charcuterie, a main meal. It is the perfect dish for a large group or for a picnic. Choose a selection from the vegetables listed – and this is one time where it really is worth making your own mayonnaise.

At least 4 from the following

carrots (*preferably small ones, green tops still attached*)	like La Ratte, boiled in their skins
celery hearts	radishes
courgettes	small heads of green calabrese (broccoli)
cucumber	
French beans	small heads of white cauliflower
florentine fennel	
mangetouts	tiny whole pods of peas or broad beans
new potatoes such as Jersey Royals, or salad potatoes	

Some of the vegetables need only to be washed, sliced into fingers and sprinkled with a little salt and lemon juice; this goes for carrots, celery hearts (make sure you leave on the tasty leaves), courgettes, cucumber, fennel (again, leave the fronds attached), and radishes. The potatoes, of course, need cooking; they are best served just warm. The French beans, mangetouts, calabrese, cauliflower and pea or broad bean pods need a quick blanch to soften them up: plunge into boiling salted water for no more than a minute and drain well.

Quantities of vegetables will of course depend on the numbers sitting down to the table. But be warned that it is impossible to make a small quantity of aïoli, so I would suggest that this dish should be kept for parties of at least 6, preferably more. It is a friendly dish to eat, made more so if the vegetables are arranged on a colourful platter around a large central bowl of the gleaming aïoli, so that everyone has to reach over and dip in. Anyone not sharing in the aïoli risks finding the garlic fumes a little overpowering.

AÏOLI

To make sufficient for 8 you need

6 large garlic cloves (*this seem a great deal, but the garlic offsets the richness of the eggs and oil; the garlic must be fresh and firm, ideally new season's – the best often has little pink tinges on the skin around the cloves*)

$^1/_2$ teaspoon coarse salt

3 egg-yolks (*at least free-range, preferably fresh from the farm, as they will be eaten raw*)

$^3/_4$ pint (450 ml) good-quality plain olive oil (*Provençal is best, but extra virgin is too 'hot' for my taste in aïoli – you can if you like use plain and half extra virgin for added flavour*)

juice of $^1/_2$ a lemon

Note: when making ordinary mayonnaise, I prefer to use a mixture of olive and sunflower oils, giving a lighter taste. However, aïoli needs to be made with just olive oil to achieve its fruity, powerful effect.

You can make aïoli in the food processor but it will not be quite the same: it somehow lacks the glorious glutinous consistency of the hand-made version. I prefer to set aside half an hour on a sunny weekend, take my bowl out into the garden and make the aïoli by hand. This is hard work but the end result is immensely satisfying.

Pound the peeled garlic cloves with the salt in a pestle and mortar or in a large bowl until they are reduced to a pulp. With a wooden spoon stir in the egg-yolks. Make sure the garlic and yolks are thoroughly amalgamated and then add the first drop of olive oil. A drop means just that, so don't pour straight from the bottle. Stir thoroughly before adding a second drop: patience at this stage will save you time and effort later. Proceed drop by drop, stirring all the time with a wooden spoon, until the mixture starts to thicken. Now you can start to pour the oil in a steady stream. By the time you have added all the oil, the aïoli should be almost hard to stir with your spoon – a good aïoli stands up by itself. Finish by stirring in a little lemon juice, but don't add black pepper as the flecks would spoil the glorious deep yellow of the aïoli.

Word of warning: if you add the oil too fast, the mixture will curdle. Don't despair, but take another egg-yolk and slowly stir in the curdled aïoli – it should reconstitute itself.

If you make the aïoli in advance, do not refrigerate it but leave it to stand, covered, in a cool dark place.

HONEY-DRESSED SALAD OF ROASTED PEPPERS

Capsicum peppers are one of my favourite vegetables and are now easy to buy but too often they are incorrectly served. A raw pepper is not much of a pleasure, its skin bitter, its flesh watery. What a difference when the pepper has first been roasted: the charred skin can be peeled off and the remaining flesh acquires a tender sweetness. Exaggerate that taste with a little honey stirred into the vinaigrette, sprinkle with herbs and you have a colourful dish good enough to be served just on its own.

6 peppers of mixed colours
  – red, green, orange,
  yellow
1 tablespoon clear honey,
  preferably flower-scented
juice of 1 lemon

4 tablespoons extra virgin
  olive oil
salt and freshly ground
  black pepper
1 handful of flat-leaved
  parsley

Heat the grill to maximum and place the peppers underneath it. Allow each uppermost surface to blacken thoroughly before turning – the whole process should take about 20 minutes. Visitors to the kitchen tend to show concern at this stage, but don't worry. Leave the peppers covered with a clean tea-towel for 10 minutes, until they are cool enough to handle. Meanwhile prepare the dressing by heating together the honey and strained lemon juice. Reserve a few slivers of lemon peel for sprinkling over the salad. Take the honey and lemon mixture off the heat when it has amalgamated and slowly add the olive oil, beating it in. Season well.

Peel the peppers on a cutting board – do not do this under the tap, for you want to keep as many of the precious juices as possible. Spread out the peppers, remove the core and seeds and chop into strips. Put the peppers and juices into a bowl. Stir in the dressing, add the chopped parsley and the lemon peel and leave to stand for at least 10 minutes before serving with plenty of country bread.

LETTUCE AND SORREL SOUP

Served warm or cool, this pale green, creamy soup makes an elegant starter. A good way of using slightly tired lettuce or excess from the garden, it should be made with a sweeter variety such as the traditional round or butterhead lettuce, rather than the crispy, more bitter varieties like Little Gem or escarole, which I prefer in salads. The lettuce offsets the slight bitterness of the sorrel leaves, which should be small in size.

2 round lettuces, with plenty of heart
1 large handful of small sorrel leaves
$^1/_2$ oz (15 g) butter
salt and pepper
pinch of sugar
2 pints (1.1 litres) light chicken stock (*home-made is of course best, but you can use a stock cube for this recipe*)
1 egg-yolk (*optional – use only if the soup is to be served warm*)
6 fl oz (175 ml) thick cream
1 teaspoon chopped fresh chives

Wash the lettuce and sorrel leaves and roughly tear. Melt the butter in a heavy-based saucepan and add the leaves, stirring for a minute or two until they are wilted. Season well with salt, pepper and a good pinch of sugar, then add the stock. Bring back to the boil and then simmer gently for 15 minutes. Take off the heat and liquidize. If you are serving the soup warm, combine the egg-yolk with the cream; if it is to be served cool or chilled, use the cream alone. Stir a ladleful of the soup into the cream mixture, then combine with the rest of the soup. Do not bring back to the boil or the soup will curdle. I like to let the soup stand until just warm and then serve it with a swirl of chopped chives and hot bread.

MELON SOUP

Although at first sight this recipe may seem a little odd, it is not really that surprising – melon and cured ham is, after all, a perfectly normal starter, as is a plain slice of melon served unadorned. The success of this uncooked soup depends on the use of very ripe, sweet melons, which are pepped up by the use of fresh ginger and lime juice. Varieties such as Canteloupe or Charentais are best, although Ogen, Galia or Honeydew are adequate substitutes. Test the ripeness of the melons by smell rather than touch. The soup should be served well chilled, which makes it particularly refreshing.

3 small or 2 large very ripe melons
2 limes
2 glasses sweet white wine such as Barsac, Sauternes or Monbazillac (*use a cheap variety*)
pinch of salt
a piece of raw ginger the size of a thumbnail

Scoop the seeds out of the melons, making sure you don't lose any of the juices, and roughly remove the flesh. Put in the liquidizer together with the juice of the limes, the white wine and a pinch of salt. Peel the piece of ginger and grate into the mixture, making sure none of the fibrous strands left on the grater fall in; the point is to get out the juice of the ginger root. Give a brief whizz and add iced water to dilute to the required consistency (the amount of water will depend upon the juiciness of the melons). I generally use bottled natural spring water of a low mineral content rather than tap water, which can give an unpleasant chemical taste – it depends on where you live. Check seasoning and chill until required.

PEA AND MINT SOUP

This soup deserves fresh peas, which are at their best in early summer. Choose small fat pods, taut rather than withered at their stalks and bright green in colour. The combination of peas and mint is a traditional one, given a Turkish flavour by the use of dried as well as fresh mint and the addition of yoghurt. I prefer the soup served warm; it can also be chilled.

1½ lb (675 g) unshelled weight of fresh peas
2 pints (1.1 litres) vegetable stock (*the best stock is made with the pea pods*)
½ oz (15 g) butter

2 sprigs of fresh mint
1 teaspoon dried mint
6 fl oz (175 ml) Greek yoghurt
salt and freshly ground black pepper

Pod the peas. Bring the stock to the boil. Melt the butter in a heavy-based saucepan and add the peas; fry for a minute or two then pour on the vegetable stock. Add 1 sprig of fresh mint. Bring to the boil, then turn down to a simmer and allow to bubble for 15 minutes. Fish out the sprig of mint and liquidize the soup. Stir the dried mint into the yoghurt and season well. Combine a little of the liquidized soup with the yoghurt and then stir into the remainder of the soup. Adjust the seasoning to taste. Serve warm, sprinkled with chopped mint leaves and freshly ground black pepper.

RATATOUILLE

This is another traditional Provençal dish, though the ratatouille served in this country is usually an unattractive parody of the real thing. Good ratatouille preserves the separate flavours of the vegetable constituents, which are stewed in oil and their own juices rather than in a can of tomatoes. Properly prepared, it is too rich to serve as an accompaniment to a main dish, deserving pride of place on its own. It can be served hot or cold and reheats well, so I generally make it in large quantities. The amount given here should be sufficient for 8 at one sitting.

2 large aubergines
3 large courgettes
salt and freshly ground
  black pepper
2 large or 3 small Spanish
  onions
2 large red peppers
2 cloves of garlic
6 tablespoons fruity olive
  oil
1$^1/_2$ lb (675 g) sweet ripe

tomatoes (*the best for this
dish are the Marmande, the
more misshapen the better –
tinned tomatoes do not have
the right texture*)
$^1/_2$ teaspoon coriander seeds
1 sprig of fresh thyme
1 fresh bayleaf
zest of a $^1/_4$ orange
1 handful of flat-leaved
  parsley

Cut the aubergines and courgettes across into 1 inch (2.5 cm) thick slices. Now quarter the aubergine slices and halve the courgette ones. Sprinkle with salt and leave in a colander with a weight on top to degorge; this should take about 30 minutes. Meanwhile, chop the onions into half-rounds, seed the peppers and cut into long strips. Chop the garlic. In a wide heavy-based pan, over a low heat, gently heat the oil. Add the onions and cook until soft. Meanwhile, rinse the aubergines and courgettes and pat dry. When the onions are tender but not brown, add the aubergines, courgettes, peppers and garlic. Cover and cook on a low heat for 30 minutes.

While the vegetables are cooking, peel and de-seed the tomatoes and chop; crush the coriander seeds. When the 30 minutes are up, add the tomatoes, coriander, sprig of thyme, bayleaf, and orange zest to the pan (you may like to tie the herbs into a bunch for easy removal later).

Season with some freshly ground pepper; cover and cook for another 30 minutes. When the dish is ready, the vegetables will be very tender but still whole. Stir in the chopped parsley, check seasoning and serve warm or cold, with plenty of bread for the oily juices.

TOMATO, ORANGE AND BASIL SOUP

For many years, British cooks without gardens were forced to use the perfectly sculpted, utterly tasteless tomatoes grown in hothouses, deprived as they were of the gloriously misshapen, flavoursome varieties of the Mediterranean. This situation is now changing, as retailers wake up to the fact that taste is more important than appearance, but there is still a long way to go. That supermarkets label certain tomatoes as grown 'for flavour' proves the case. Why else would you grow them? Markets and greengrocers sometimes sell sweet home-grown varieties, or imported plum tomatoes; either are ideal for this powerfully flavoured and gaily coloured soup. Served hot, it is perfect for a cooler summer's evening.

3 lb (1.5 kg) flavourful, ripe tomatoes
2 oranges
1 red onion
2 tablespoons olive oil
2 cloves of fresh garlic
1 teaspoon tomato purée
pinch of sugar
1 good handful of fresh basil leaves
1 glass dry white wine
1 bayleaf
1 thick slice of good-quality white bread, crusts removed

Peel, de-seed and roughly chop the tomatoes. Strain the juice from the oranges; remove the pith from a quarter of the skin of one of them and chop the skin finely. Chop the onion finely and fry in 1 tablespoon of the olive oil until soft and translucent but not browned. Add the finely chopped garlic and the tomato purée and fry for a further 2 minutes. Add the chopped tomatoes, orange zest, a pinch of sugar, and all but a few of the torn basil leaves and fry for a minute before adding the glass of wine; allow to bubble for a minute or two before adding the orange juice and the bayleaf. Pour over $1^1/_2$ pints (850 ml) of cold water, season well and bring to the boil, then tear the bread into pieces and add to the soup. Simmer, covered, for 20 minutes. Liquidize if you like a very smooth consistency – I prefer the soup slightly lumpy.

Before serving, adjust the seasoning to taste and stir in the remaining olive oil and a few fresh basil leaves.

WHITE GRAPE SOUP

This chilled, uncooked soup is a traditional dish from the Málaga region of Spain, where it is known as *ajo blanco*. Almonds and pinenuts are mixed with white grapes in a beautiful white liquid thickened with bread, with a powerful kick of garlic. The soup should be served very cold, with ice cubes floating on the surface.

8 oz (225 g) white grapes
(*if you can get seedless
ones, it will make your life
a lot easier*)
4 oz (115 g) almonds,
blanched and skinned
4 oz (115 g) pinenuts
3 fat cloves of new season's
garlic

$^1/_2$ teaspoon sea salt
2 tablespoons extra virgin
olive oil
1 tablespoon white wine
vinegar
2 oz (55 g) fresh white
breadcrumbs
1 pint (575 ml) water

The grapes need to be peeled for this soup: as with tomatoes, boiling water poured over them helps slip off the skin. If you have not got seedless grapes, remove the pips.

Process the almonds and pinenuts with the garlic and salt until you have a smooth paste (traditionally this would be done with a pestle and mortar). Add the olive oil drop by drop, until the paste emulsifies. Now beat in the vinegar, again little by little. Finally, add the breadcrumbs.

Put the paste in a serving bowl and stir in the water. Now add the peeled grapes. Chill for at least 1 hour and serve with an ice-cube in each bowl.

FISH

When the summer weather is good, the demand is for light dishes which do not sit heavily on the stomach during the long hot afternoons or nights. Nutritious, healthy fish fits the bill perfectly. Yet so often it is difficult to get hold of the really fresh variety. It is worth seeking out, however, for little benefits more than fish from being eaten as soon as possible. Straight from boat to pan used to be the old adage, and although in these days of refrigerated transport that is no longer necessary, the taste of freshly caught fish, from river or sea, can be a revelation.

The infinite variety of fish caught from our shores makes it difficult to cover all possibilities. Much fish is good simply grilled or fried and served with a slice of lemon. This is not always true, however, of the grey fillets which our fishmongers are pleased to serve us – much better to get hold of the whole fish wherever possible, or watch a large fish being sliced for you. That way you can look at the eyes, one of the best indicators of freshness.

Unfortunately, in the UK there are too few retail fish markets like those enjoyed in France and Italy, Belgium and Spain – Bolton is the exception rather than the rule. But there are excellent wholesale markets. So seek out, if you can, a local fishmonger who buys fresh from the wholesale markets every day, a travelling fish van from one of the ports, or a supermarket with a fresh fish counter and a sensible buying policy. Better still, visit one of the wholesale markets yourself to see what is being landed off our shores.

Foreign Competition
in Brixham Fish Market

The pretty fishing port of Brixham on the south Devon coast is the home of a large fishing fleet and the setting for one of the UK's wholesale fish markets. One whole side of the harbour wall, right by the fishing smacks, is taken up by a long rectangular building in which, six mornings a week at crack of dawn, fishmongers from all over the country and the Continent as well bid at auction for crate after crate of gleaming fresh fish, caught that night. Only those with licences are authorized to buy here, but when the wholesale business is over the purchasers of the fish are only too happy to pass some straight on (at a good mark up, of course) to the intrepid customer who appears at the door of one of the sheds in which they clean and gut their haul before shipping.

The variety and quantity of fish in the market will overwhelm anyone who ventures in to take a look. The fish is at its most plentiful in the winter season, but even in the height of summer there is a vast acreage of crates. And the choice! In August I found turbot of all sizes, from small fish perfect for poaching for a small dinner party, to fish so large that only a restaurant or a caterer would be interested in buying one whole. The silvery grey sea bass also varied dramatically in size, from small fish which could be cooked whole, to vast specimens which would provide perfect steaks for grilling. There was an abundance of mackerel, their stripes bright and shiny, skins gleaming, ready for the barbecue. Great brutish cod lay alongside the even uglier monkfish; the John Dory weren't that pretty either but would make a delicious dish. A few hake had been landed, and lay in the crates with their teeth bared menacingly. The tentacles of squid and octopus for salads and stews looped over the edges of crates with names like Girl Debra, Sue Ellen and Sea Hunter denoting the fishing boats which had brought in the catch.

There was plenty of flat fish too: tiny lemon soles ready for dipping in egg-yolk and frying quickly in butter to produce a golden first course; Dover soles, slip soles, dabs, plaice, brill and skate wings for serving with black butter. My favourite fish, red mullet, filled crate after crate, the eyes of the fish still prominent and glowing, so unlike the tired specimens with sunken hollow eyes which too often are on offer in supermarkets. Red mullet, like mackerel, is a fish which is especially rewarding when eaten very fresh, and I bought a boxful for barbecuing that lunchtime over a fire scented with fennel twigs.

The shellfish caught my eye: huge blue lobsters and crabs, beady eyes on sticks looking warily around. Most of the scallops are shipped direct to the factory for cleaning but a few bags had found their way to the market. As soon as they had found a buyer, they were lugged next door for shucking, the flesh dropped in salted water. So that's why you can so rarely buy scallops in the shell from fishmongers, who seem to believe we want them ready prepared even if it does mean that by the time they get to the kitchen they are well past their best.

As each crate of fish was auctioned off, its purchaser dropped in a slip of paper to claim ownership. From the names, it seemed as if well over half the fish was being bought for consumers on the Continent. That impression was reinforced as I listened to the voices on the mobile phones which buyers were using to check demand and prices with their customers. Many of them were speaking French, with broad Devon accents. 'Voulez-vous des rougets aujourd'hui?' asked one, checking on the need for red mullet. 'Le prix du loup de mer n'est pas mal,' observed another – sea bass is pretty cheap. And, there was no doubt about it, the French speakers were buying the best-quality fish. One fisherman told me, 'The Continent pays better prices. They can afford it because their customers are keener on fish.' I hope he was wrong about the last bit, for as an island nation we should be enjoying the wealth of food from our seas. Nothing can beat fresh sea-caught fish for a summer lunch, and a visit to Brixham fish market would be enough to convince anyone that we should be able to buy cheap fresh fish of every conceivable variety from our fishmongers and supermarkets – it's certainly being caught, and bought wholesale at ridiculously low prices. But while our retailers remain convinced that we want to buy fillets of cod, hake and coley and not much else, we will continue to lose out. It is up to the consumer to demand the best and the freshest – and stop it going abroad.

As I left the market with my case of mullet and sole, the gulls were wheeling in the air and a few smacks were pulling out to sea from the tiny, sheltered harbour. Several small boys sat on the side, lines dangling hopefully in the sea below, the sun shone on the water. It was a perfect

English summer's morning. The picture postcard scene was spoilt by two intrusions. The first was the sight of a van dropping off frozen breaded plaice fillets at a restaurant right next to the market, no doubt to be sold that night as 'fresh Brixham plaice'. The second was the back view of the 'poissons et coquillages' van pulling out of town, bound on its daily trip across the Channel and to the eager markets beyond.

BAKED GINGERED CRAB

Crabs from all around the British Isles are one of the delights of summer. If you can buy them fresh off the boat for cooking live, they will taste even better – in France crabs are generally sold live. But if you are squeamish, or don't live near the sea or a good fishmonger, try baking the flesh with a little spice to bring out the flavour and moisture which can sometimes be lost in a crab cooked for too long or too long ago.

Serves 2

1 medium-sized cooked crab, approx. $1^1/_4$–$1^1/_2$ lb (550–675 g)
juice of 1 lemon
1 teaspoon fresh grated ginger

good pinch of grated nutmeg
salt and pepper
2 oz (55 g) unsalted butter
2 crustless slices of stale white bread, broken up into crumbs

Ask the fishmonger to clean and prepare the crab for you; this should include cracking the claws, so that the meat is easy to extract. Pick out both the dark and the white meat and mix with the lemon juice, ginger, nutmeg and plenty of seasoning. Cut $1^1/_2$ oz (45 g) of the butter into small cubes and mix with the breadcrumbs; combine with the crab meat. Clean out the crab shell and pack in the crab mixture; dot with the remaining butter. Cover with foil and bake in a medium oven (150°C/ 300°F/Gas 2) for 20 minutes, removing the foil for the last 5 minutes of cooking. Serve hot with bread.

BEAN AND TUNA SALAD

Italian markets in summer boast piles of fresh beans, purpled and speckly or a creamy yellow, perfect for soups and salads. Unfortunately, it is virtually impossible to get fresh borlotti beans in the UK. Even with the dried variety, however, freshness makes all the difference; look for a supplier with a high turnover. It is worth cooking your own to achieve a firm texture and a fuller flavour, especially if you dress the beans when they are warm. This salad is quite different from the tired trattoria version using canned beans and tuna fish. Served cold, it is one of my favourite summer starters.

6 oz (170 g) dried borlotti beans (*you can also use cannellini beans*)
salt and pepper
1 lime
3 tablespoons extra virgin olive oil

8 oz (225 g) fresh tuna
2 red onions
1 tablespoon chopped flat-leaved parsley
1 tablespoon chopped fresh chives
1 clove of garlic

Soak the beans overnight. The next day, add just enough water to cover them by 1 inch (2.5 cm), bring to the boil and boil hard for 10 minutes. Turn down to a simmer and continue cooking until the beans are very tender but not falling apart (this should take about 30–45 minutes, providing the beans are fresh). Drain away any excess liquid (of which there should be little – cook the beans uncovered so that the liquid boils away). Season the beans while still warm with plenty of salt and pepper, the juice of the lime and the olive oil. Leave to cool.

Chop the tuna into small chunks, discarding the skin. Season with salt and pepper and leave for 10 minutes or so. Chop the onions very finely and stir into the beans, together with the fresh herbs and garlic. Just before serving, heat a non-stick frying-pan or a griddle until very hot (add no oil). Add the chunks of tuna and cook very quickly, stirring, no more than a couple of minutes. Stir the tuna into the beans and serve, with more lime juice and oil for guests to help themselves.

CLAM SOUP

Little Venus clams in their shells are too rare a sight at the fishmonger's. If you see them, make sure you buy some. Fiddly to eat, they are nonetheless delicious and worth the trouble. Like mussels, they should be allowed to sit in a covered bowl of salted water for at least an hour before cooking to allow them to clean themselves. Discard any which do not close when tapped or do not open once they have been steamed. You can use them for spaghetti al vongole, pasta tossed with clams, or you can make a white wine and tomato broth in which to steam them open and serve it in a way the Italians would call soup or zuppe although to British eyes it seems to be more of a main dish.

2 sticks of celery, leaves
    attached
1 mild onion
2 cloves of garlic
1 lb (450 g) tomatoes,
    preferably plum (or a
    14 oz (400 g) tin)
2 tablespoons olive oil

2 tablespoons chopped flat-
    leaved parsley
salt and freshly ground
    black pepper
2 glasses dry white wine
2 lb (900 g) clams
$^1/_2$ a lemon

Clean the celery, reserving the leaves, and chop finely, leaving off the stringy end. Finely chop the onion and garlic. Peel and de-seed the tomatoes if you are using fresh ones, and dice. Heat the olive oil in a large, heavy pan and gently fry the onion and celery together until softened and lightly browned – about 15 minutes. Add half the chopped parsley, all the celery leaves and the garlic and fry for another 5 minutes, then stir in the diced tomatoes, together with pepper and salt to taste (I use quite a lot of freshly ground black pepper, to give the broth a little bite). Simmer for 5 minutes until the mixture is pulpy, then pour over the wine and allow to bubble; add the same quantity of water and cook for another 10 minutes. Add the clams and the remaining parsley to the pan and cover; cook over a medium heat until the clams open (a matter of a minute or two). Squeeze in a little lemon juice, and serve immediately with plenty of hot bread to mop up the juices.

FISH SOUP

Fish soup is the ideal dish for the market: its contents simply depend on the day's catch. Don't believe the purists who say you must include this or that: I have made soups with an infinite variety of fish and all of them have been good. So pick and choose from the list given below, and don't be frightened to include some other species if they happen to be to hand. In my view, the only constants for fish soup are a good stock for the base, a pinch of saffron, a strong rouille (a sort of chilli mayonnaise but made with breadcrumbs rather than eggs) for stirring into the finished broth, and plenty of bread. A little sunshine and a glass of chilled white wine also help.

The fish might include

cod	haddock	red mullet
conger eel	hake	red snapper
dogfish	halibut	sea bream
grey mullet	John Dory	weever fish
gurnard	monkfish	whiting

In general I prefer to use firmer-fleshed fish and to avoid fatty fish such as mackerel or salmon for a soup; nor is this the place for delicate flat fish such as plaice or sole. But a huge variety of combinations is possible, according to your own taste and what is available. If you choose to add octopus or squid, remember that they will take longer to cook than the rest of the fish; the reverse applies to shellfish such as mussels, clams or prawns.

I like to use at least 3 or 4 different varieties of fish for my soup, which means I generally make it in fairly large quantities. To make a soup for 8, you need about 3 lb (1.5 kg) total weight of fish. Ask your fishmonger to fillet the fish for you, reserving the skin and bones to make the stock.

FOR THE STOCK

1 onion

2 or 3 celery sticks

$^1/_2$ a fennel bulb

1 tablespoon olive oil

2 lb (900 g) fish trimmings
(*including the trimmings
from the fish you are using
for the soup – ask your*

*fishmonger for an extra fish
head or two*)

2 chopped tomatoes

2 glasses dry white wine

herbs, e.g. dill, chervil,
parsley, fennel fronds

salt and pepper

FOR THE ROUILLE (SUFFICIENT FOR 8)

3 small red chillies

2 cloves of garlic

$^1/_4$ teaspoon coarse sea salt

1 slice of stale white
crustless bread

$^1/_3$ pint (250 ml) olive oil

FOR THE SOUP

good pinch of saffron

3 lb (1.5 kg) weight of fish
before filleting

salt and pepper

8 slices of bread

1 clove of garlic

a little olive oil

First make the stock. Chop the onion, celery and fennel and fry in the oil until soft but not browned. Add the fish trimmings and tomatoes, turn up the heat, and fry for a further minute before pouring over the wine. Add the herbs and plenty of seasoning and pour in $2^1/_2$–3 pints (1.5–1.75 litres) of water. Bring to the boil and then turn down to a simmer for 30 minutes (no more, or the stock will become too gluey). Strain carefully, making sure you leave all the bones behind.

To make the rouille, remove the seeds from the chillies and crush the flesh together with the garlic and salt until you have a fine paste (you can do this in a liquidizer or coffee grinder, although it is most successful with a pestle and mortar). Dip the piece of bread in a very little of the fish stock and squeeze dry with your hands. Form the bread into 2 balls the size of walnuts and mix one into the garlic, chilli and salt paste. Beat in the olive oil, very slowly at first as if making mayonnaise. Once you have added about a quarter of the oil, add the remainder of the bread. If at any point the mixture starts to separate, add a very little hot stock. Once you have added all the oil, you should have a thick, rose-coloured sauce.

For the soup itself, steep the saffron in a little of the hot fish stock. Heat a very little oil and briefly fry the fish fillets, for no more than a minute; then pour over the hot stock. Bring to the boil, add the saffron and seasoning to taste and simmer very gently for 10–15 minutes. The fish fillets will break up into chunks but not fall apart completely. While the soup is cooking, toast the slices of bread on both sides and rub with the cut side of the clove of garlic and a little olive oil.

To serve, first place a piece of toast in the base of each bowl. Ladle a piece of fish on top and then plenty of the colourful, pungent broth. Serve with the fiery rouille on the side, for stirring in.

Note: In many traditional recipes for fish soup, this two-stage process is replaced by cooking the whole fish as if for stock and then puréeing the lot through a very fine sieve or mouli. I prefer the two-stage process for two reasons: (1) it allows you to have chunks of fish in your soup; (2) it eliminates the risk of bones creeping through into the soup, which can happen during the puréeing process.

BARBECUED SARDINES

Anyone who has visited the fishing villages of Portugal will remember the scent in the night air of sardines grilling over a bundle of vine twigs. It is a smell which is less pleasant when lingering in your kitchen for several days, but sardines are ideal for the barbecue. Stuffed with garlic and parsley and quickly cooked, sardines make a powerfully flavoured and appetizing dish.

1 packet of vine-leaves marinated in brine (*or, if you have a vine in the garden, use the fresh leaves*)

2 fresh sardines per person

FOR EACH SARDINE

1 teaspoon chopped fresh parsley, preferably flat-leaved

1 clove of fresh garlic
1 slice lemon

If you are using marinated vine-leaves, soak them for 30 minutes before using. If you have the real thing, so much the better. Thoroughly gut the fish if the fishmonger has not already done so, wash the insides under cold running water for a few minutes, then pat dry. Finely chop the garlic. Stuff the cavity of each fish with the garlic and parsley and pop in the slice of lemon, cut in half. Season well. Wrap each fish in a vine-leaf and put on the hot barbecue. Five minutes on either side should be sufficient, by which time the vine-leaf should be thoroughly blackened. Scrape away the blackened leaf and eat immediately with plenty of lemon.

If you want to cook the sardines under the grill, preheat it to very hot. Omit the vine-leaves as these may catch fire under a grill, and simply grill the fish until brown on each side.

HAKE WITH PEAS

The firm white flesh of hake, at its best in the summer months, is often under-rated. The hake is a fish which takes well to Mediterranean flavours and is especially popular in Spain. It is also cheap and easy to find. Baked in a garlicky tomato sauce and surrounded by fresh peas, this is a good dish for a cooler summer evening.

2 small, or 1 large, onions	2 tablespoons dry sherry
1 carrot	(fino or manzanilla)
2 tablespoons olive oil	4 cutlets of hake or 1 tail of
8 oz (225 g) plum tomatoes	hake, weighing about
1 clove of garlic	$1^1/_2$–2 lb (675–900 g)
1 handful of fresh parsley	8 oz (225 g) fresh shelled
1 teaspoon tomato purée	peas
$^1/_4$ teaspoon cayenne pepper	

Finely chop the onions and carrot and fry gently in the oil until soft and lightly browned, about 10–15 minutes. Meanwhile peel and de-seed the tomatoes and chop. Add the finely chopped garlic and parsley, the tomato purée and the cayenne to the pan and fry for a further few minutes before adding the chopped tomatoes. Cook for a further

5 minutes, stirring occasionally. Pour over the sherry, allow to bubble, then add 1 glass of water and cook, covered and over a low heat, for 5 minutes.

Pre-heat the oven to medium (150°C/300°F/Gas 2). Place the hake cutlets or tail in an earthenware dish that takes them comfortably. Pour over the sauce, cover with foil and cook for 30 minutes. Meanwhile, steam the peas in a little water with a pinch of sugar for 10 minutes or so until soft. When the hake is cooked, remove from the sauce and skin. Stir the peas into the sauce and serve with bread and a green salad.

MARINATED MACKEREL

To be good, mackerel must be extra specially fresh. The best are those bought from the boat, or even caught yourself; but if buying from a fish stall look for a bright eye, gleaming stripes and firm flesh. Line-caught mackerel are better than net-caught, as they will not be bruised. The oiliness of the fish makes it good for grilling but I also like the filleted flesh marinated in lime juice, chilli and coriander, letting the citric juices do most of the 'cooking' before quickly tossing and serving as a salad. The mixture can also be combined with coconut milk to make a south Indian soup.

For 4 as a starter

1 large or 2 small mackerel	1 teaspoon sugar
(*ask your fishmonger to*	salt and pepper
fillet them)	1 tablespoon sunflower or
2 small green chillies	vegetable oil
1 bunch of fresh coriander	4 lettuce leaves
3 limes	

If you haven't got a friendly fishmonger, you will have to fillet the mackerel yourself. Fortunately the fish is served in small pieces, so you don't have to worry about removing whole fillets. Remove the head and tail and with a sharp knife split the skin along the backbone. Slice again down the centre of the fish on each side. Prise the flesh, complete with skin, away from the bones, being especially careful around the stomach cavity. When you are sure the fish is bone-free, scrape away from the skin with a sharp knife. Flake the flesh.

Finely chop the chillies and coriander leaves (you should have about 3 tablespoons when chopped – reserve a little for a garnish). Squeeze the juice from the limes. Mix the chilli, coriander and lime juice with the shredded mackerel flesh and add the sugar and seasoning. Leave to marinate in a cool place for at least an hour, stirring occasionally.

Just before serving, heat the sunflower oil in a wide frying-pan or wok. Add the fish mixture and toss briefly for a minute, literally. Pile a little into the well of each lettuce leaf, sprinkle with the reserved few leaves of coriander and serve.

If you happen to have a lot of mackerel, or you fancy a soup rather than a salad, marinate as before but instead of tossing in the wok, combine with a 14 fl oz (400 ml) tin of unsweetened coconut milk (available from Indian and West Indian stores) and the same quantity of water. Heat, without bringing to the boil, and serve.

OCTOPUS STEW

The ugly octopus is another of those cephalopods which find little favour in Britain. Not so in the Mediterranean, where octopus is prepared with great variety. One of my favourite ways of eating it in Spain is a la plancha, the salted octopus grilled over charcoal and served as tapas. However, such cooking requires that the octopus should have first been tenderized, by beating or salting. Another way to produce a tender effect is to cook the octopus slowly in red wine and olive oil, with plenty of herbs. The resulting stew is fragrant and delicious.

1 large or 2 small octopuses (*about 1 1/2–2 lb (675–900 g) weight – make sure the body sac isn't filled with wet sand before you buy*)
1 large Spanish onion
3 tablespoons olive oil
3 cloves of garlic

1/2 teaspoon coriander seeds, lightly crushed
2 bayleaves (*fresh if possible*)
2 sprigs each of fresh thyme and marjoram or oregano
1/2 bottle full, fruity red wine (*I usually use a Portuguese Dão*)
1 lemon

First prepare your octopus. The first time you do it this will seem daunting, but grit your teeth, sharpen your knife and you will be surprised at how quick and easy it is. First chop off the tentacles just below the eyes and then, gripping just above the eyes, pull the guts out. Throw this lot away and you will immediately feel much better about what is in front of you. Strip the outer flesh away from the body sac and make sure you remove any knobs of membrane (the 'beak') lurking at the head of the tentacles. Peel the body of skin, then rinse very well under cold running water, to make sure you get rid of any lingering sand. Chop the body sac crosswise into 1/2 inch (1 cm) rings. Chop each ring 2 or 3 times to give bite-sized pieces. Separate the tentacles and chop in half or thirds depending on their length. The painful bit is now over.

Chop the onion into small dice. Heat the olive oil in a heavy-based saucepan. Fry the onion for 10 minutes over a gentle flame, until tender and slightly browned; meanwhile chop the peeled garlic cloves. Add them to the onion and fry for another few minutes, until the garlic is tender but not browned. Now turn the heat up slightly and throw in the chopped octopus. Fry, stirring well, until the octopus starts to curl (this will only take a minute or so). Then add the coriander seeds. When these start to pop, add the herbs, tied in a bunch for easy removal. Pour in the red wine. Bring to the boil and then turn straight down to a slow simmer. Cover and leave for $1^1/_2$ hours, checking occasionally to make sure the liquid hasn't dried up – if it is in danger of doing so, add a little water.

When the octopus is meltingly tender, season to taste and then allow to stand a while before serving – it is best, Greek style, warm rather than hot. Just before dishing up, fish out the herbs and stir in the juice of the lemon. I serve this as a main course with a dish of plain boiled rice and a green salad.

POACHED SALMON WITH HERB BUTTER

Over the last decade, salmon sales in the UK for home consumption have outstripped those of any other fish. This has been almost entirely due to the explosion in salmon farming, which has brought with it dramatic reductions in price. Although this is largely to be welcomed, it has meant that many of us have forgotten the true taste of wild salmon. There can be no doubt about it, wild salmon is a cut above the farmed variety, beating it both on flavour and texture.

You can use this recipe for both farmed and wild salmon but I would always choose the wild variety if available (and affordable). Look for grey/brown rather than bright pink flesh, and beware of fatty deposits under the skin; the best tasting salmon are those which are lean. Grilled salmon has a tendency to dryness and I prefer the fish, whether whole or in cutlets, poached in a wine and herb stock and then served with butter flavoured with fennel or dill.

4 thick cut cutlets of salmon

2 oz (55 g) unsalted butter   2 tablespoons chopped fresh
dill or fennel fronds

1 carrot
1 stick of celery
$^1/_2$ a bulb of Florentine
    fennel
2 shallots or $^1/_2$ an onion
$^1/_2$ oz (15 g) butter

salt and pepper
2 glasses dry white wine
sprig of fennel fronds or dill
    (*whichever is to be used for*
    the herb butter)

Make the herb butter by combining the butter and the very finely chopped herbs (this can be done in the food processor). Divide into 4 and chill in the fridge until needed.

To make the stock, finely chop all the vegetables. Melt the butter in a heavy pan and gently fry the vegetables for 5 minutes. Season, then pour over the wine. Bring to the boil and bubble quickly for a minute; add the herbs and $^1/_2$ pint (300 ml) of water. Bring back to the boil and turn down to a simmer, uncovered, for 15 minutes.

Pre-heat the oven to medium hot (about 180°C/350°F/Gas 4). Arrange the salmon fillets in an earthenware baking tray into which they just fit and pour over the strained hot stock – it should be sufficient to cover the fillets if the pan is small enough. Cover with foil and bake for 10–15 minutes, until the salmon is very tender.

To serve, pour the liquid off the fish into a saucepan, leaving the fish, foil removed, in a warm place. Reduce the liquid by hard boiling to about 8 tablespoons. Put the salmon on warmed plates, pour over the liquid and put a lump of herb butter on top of each cutlet.

The traditional accompaniments of peas and boiled new potatoes cannot be bettered, unless you can get hold of some samphire, which should be well rinsed, blanched and then boiled for a few minutes until tender.

PRAWN KEBABS
WITH BAYLEAVES AND CUMIN

You need uncooked prawns for this dish: they should be brown rather than rosy pink in colour. The use of bayleaves is traditional in Turkish cookery and imparts an excellent flavour to the shellfish. You can grill them on the barbecue or use the cooker, making sure in either case that you baste regularly and that the bayleaves don't catch fire. The final sprinkling with toasted cumin seeds adds a distinctive flavour.

FOR EACH KEBAB (1 PER PERSON AS A STARTER, 2 AS A MAIN COURSE)

4 large raw prawns in the shell	freshly ground black pepper
3 fresh bayleaves (*do not use dried leaves, as they will catch fire under the grill*)	$^1/_2$ teaspoon whole cumin seeds
fruity olive oil for basting (Greek is ideal)	lemon or lime wedges
	1 long wooden skewer

Wash the prawns well, making sure you remove any eggs. Thread the kebabs on the skewer, starting with a prawn threaded through from head to tail so that it lies flat, then a bayleaf, doubled over, and so on. Brush all over with olive oil and season with freshly ground black pepper.

Cook the kebabs under a very hot grill, allowing 3–5 minutes on each side according to the size of the prawns. Turn and baste half-way through cooking. The prawns are ready when they turn a rosy pink and their skins begin to crackle.

While the kebabs are cooking, quickly toast the cumin seeds in a frying-pan over a high heat – do not add any oil, you are toasting not frying. Watch very carefully to make sure the seeds do not burn – they should be in the pan no more than a minute. Sprinkle over the kebabs, which should be served with wedges of lemon or lime.

RED MULLET WITH OLIVES

I used to think that the prized red mullet, the 'woodcock of the sea', lived only in the deepest reaches of the Mediterranean, which was why it is usually only available frozen in the UK. In warm weather, however, red mullet is found in British coastal waters, as I discovered on my visit to Brixham. The sad fact remains that it is still difficult to get hold of fresh red mullet and when you do it is very expensive. When on holiday, always look out for the freshly caught variety – I cherish the memory of 4 tiny red mullets cooked for me on the deck of a Turkish fishing ketch, its captain dusting the fish with flour and frying them in olive oil over a primus stove. The frozen fish most common here are best baked in a spicy tomato sauce to which olives have been added for extra bite and flavour. Serve with bread and a bitter salad such as chicory or endive.

1 onion	4 large or 8 small red
1 clove of garlic	mullet (*or 4 small fish if*
1 tablespoon plain olive oil	*serving as a starter*)
1 lb (450 g) plum tomatoes	1 lemon
1 teaspoon tomato purée	4 oz (115 g) black olives
1/2 teaspoon fennel seeds	(*I use the wrinkled black*
1/4 teaspoon cayenne pepper	*Italian variety which have*
1 glass red wine	*been preserved in oil rather*
1 tablespoon extra virgin	*than brine, and find the*
olive oil	*unpitted ones have more*
	flavour)

Chop the onion roughly and the garlic finely. Soften for 10 minutes in the plain olive oil over a low heat, stirring occasionally. Meanwhile peel, de-seed and chop the tomatoes. Add the tomato purée, fennel seeds and cayenne pepper to the softened onion and garlic and cook for a further 5 minutes. Turn the heat up a little and add the tomatoes. Cook for 5 minutes until they have broken down, then pour over the glass of wine. Bubble fiercely before adding the same quantity of water. Season, cover and simmer for 15 minutes, then take off the heat and stir in the extra virgin oil.

Pre-heat the oven to medium (150°C/300°F/Gas 2). Gut the mullet. If I am grilling very fresh mullet, I leave the liver in to give that gamy flavour, but this is not such a good idea for this dish. Slice the lemon and put slices in the cavity of each fish. Lay the mullet side by side in an earthenware baking dish and sprinkle over the olives. Check the tomato sauce for seasoning and then pour over the fish. Cover with foil and bake for 20–30 minutes, depending on the size of the fish – it is done when the flesh comes easily away from the bone. Serve either hot straight from the oven or later as a cool dish.

SEA BASS WITH RAKI

The fine sea bass is at its best from the summer months through to December – try it for an alternative Christmas feast (see winter recipe, pages 345–6). In Provence it is traditionally barbecued over dried fennel twigs, which is fine for herb-scented evenings on the terrace but not so practical in Britain. But the liquorice taste of fennel does go surprisingly well with the fish, and in Turkey is reinforced by flaming the fish in raki, the local blend of grape juice and anis. If you can't get raki, then ouzo, arak or pastis are good substitutes. For a Turkish flavour, serve the fish with steamed burghul wheat.

4 sea bass steaks	1 tablespoon fennel seeds
1/2 teaspoon sea salt	2 tablespoons raki, ouzo,
2 bulbs of fennel	arak or pastis
2 red onions	freshly ground black pepper
2 tablespoons olive oil	2 glasses dry white wine

If you are cooking a whole fish, make 2 or 3 deep slashes on each side. Rub the salt into the fish or steaks and leave to stand for 15 minutes.

Discard the tough outer layer of the fennel and chop off the stalks, reserving the feathery fronds. Chop the fennel bulbs finely together with the onions. In a pan in which the steaks will all fit, heat the oil and fry the onions and fennel gently for 10 minutes until tender. Turn up the heat and add the fennel seeds; when they pop, add the fish. Fry for 1 minute on each side, being careful not to break the steaks when you turn them over; meanwhile warm the raki or other spirit in a ladle. Set light to it, stand back and pour over the fish. Shake the pan to distribute the flames. When they have died down, add the wine; bubble briefly, then turn down to a simmer. Cook the fish for 6 minutes either side. Remove the fish from the pan and keep warm; bubble off any remaining liquid. Serve the fish on a pile of the vegetables.

Steamed burghul wheat goes well with this dish: blanch 8 oz (225 g) of burghul and then steam in a double boiler for 20 minutes. Stir in a few chopped shallots or spring onions, a handful of fresh mint, the juice of a lemon and some extra virgin olive oil. Season well and serve.

SQUID AND SAMPHIRE SALAD

Despite their inelegant appearance, squid are relatively easy to prepare when you have acquired the knack. They are one of my favourites for summer, being easy to serve hot or cold as well as cheap and flavourful. You can enjoy squid deep-fried in a light batter for a quick snack, as it is served on Italian beaches; poached with its ink in a black risotto; or, as here, served just warm in a salad. The salty flavour and juicy texture of the samphire adds a great deal to the dish, but if you can't get samphire the squid is also good served alone.

For 4 as a starter

1 lb (450 g) fresh squid, the smaller the better
8 oz (225 g) samphire
4 oz (115 g) shallots
2 cloves of garlic
1 fresh green chilli
4 tablespoons extra virgin olive oil
2 tablespoons chopped parsley, preferably flat-leaved
juice of 2 limes

Prepare the squid as for the cuttlefish (page 64). Make sure that you remove the transparent bone from the body in one piece. Cut the body into ¹/₂ inch (1 cm) rings and rinse again. Now you are ready to cook.

Remove the fleshy samphire leaves from their roots. Rinse the samphire very well under cold running water to remove some of the salt. Bring a large pan of unsalted water to the boil and blanch the samphire. Drain away the water and bring a new pan to the boil. When boiling, cook the samphire for 2 minutes, until softened but still crisp. Keep warm until needed.

Chop the shallots into thin rings. Finely chop the garlic and the de-seeded chilli. Heat the oil in a wide, heavy-based frying-pan with a lid and add the shallots. Fry for a couple of minutes, stirring to make sure they do not brown, then add the garlic and chilli. Fry for another minute, turn up the heat and throw in the squid. Fry quickly for a minute or two until the tentacles curl, then turn the heat down to low and cover. Cook for 20 minutes, stirring occasionally. Stir in the chopped parsley and the lime juice and take off the heat. The squid should stand for at least 10 minutes before serving.

To serve, pile the drained samphire on a plate and pour the contents of the pan on top. Accompany with extra slices of lime and plenty of bread.

SMOKED SALMON TART

Excellent for a picnic, this rich and creamy tart can be made using inexpensive offcuts of smoked salmon. The fish lies embedded in eggs and cream, spiced with a little nutmeg, the whole encased in buttery pastry. The tart is good served with a cooling cucumber salad for contrast.

FOR THE PASTRY

6 oz (170 g) plain white flour
good pinch of salt

3 oz (85 g) unsalted butter
2–4 tablespoons iced water

FOR THE FILLING

4 oz (115 g) smoked salmon offcuts
2 egg-yolks plus 1 whole egg

1/2 pint (300 ml) double cream
pinch of grated nutmeg

To make the pastry, which is a classic pâte brisée and very easy to prepare, first sieve the flour together with the salt. Break the butter into small cubes and crumble into the flour with your fingers. Add the water (it is important that it should be very cold – leave an ice-cube in a glass of water for a few minutes), in sufficient quantity for the pastry to form into a ball without becoming sticky. There is no need to leave it to rest and this pastry should not be rolled out; simply push with your fingers around the lightly buttered 8 inch (20 cm) flan dish. Prick all over with a fork and bake blind in a hot oven (200°C/400°F/Gas 6) for 15 minutes.

For the filling, chop the smoked salmon into small pieces. Beat the egg-yolks well with the whole egg and combine with the cream and the pinch of nutmeg.

When the pastry base is ready, dot it with the pieces of smoked salmon. Pour over the egg and cream mixture and bake in a medium hot oven (180°C/350°F/Gas 4) for a further 15–20 minutes, until the filling rises a little. You can serve this tart either warm or cold, in which case the filling will sink back.

TUNA WITH SPICY TOMATO

Meaty tuna steaks are excellent for the barbecue or the grill, especially when marinated in a mixture of oil and citrus juices in advance of cooking. I like to accompany them with a fresh chutney of uncooked tomato and coriander with chilli and cumin to provide a little spice. The same treatment works well with other firm-fleshed fish such as swordfish and shark.

4 tablespoons olive oil	1 small green chilli
juice of 2 lemons	2 tablespoons chopped fresh
4 tuna steaks	coriander
8 oz (225 g) tomatoes	1 teaspoon ground cumin
$^1/_2$ an onion	

Mix together the oil and lemon juice and pour over the tuna steaks. Leave to rest for at least an hour, turning once.

To make the chutney, skin and de-seed the tomatoes and chop very finely together with the onion and chilli. Combine with the chopped coriander. When you are ready to cook the tuna, drain off the marinade and heat in a frying pan with the cumin. Pour the hot oil over the chutney.

Cook the tuna steaks under a hot grill (200°C/400°F) for 5–7 minutes on each side depending on thickness. The fish is ready when it turns opaque. Serve with the chutney spooned over each steak.

TURBOT POACHED IN MILK

Turbot was the most prized fish of the Victorian era but, perhaps due to its expense, it has lost favour in recent years. Sometimes, however, smaller fish at more reasonable prices are available at local fish stalls and good fishmongers. If you can get one, a small turbot served whole is a wonderful dish for a dinner party, and turbot is at its best in the summer. In this recipe, the fish is poached whole in a mixture of milk and water, a little of the liquid then being used to make a herby, buttery sauce.

1 small whole turbot, approx. 2½–3 lb (1.25 kg)	2 pints (1.1 litres) full-cream milk salt and pepper

FOR THE SAUCE

½ oz (15 g) plain flour	1 tablespoon chopped fresh
pinch of cayenne pepper	chervil
2 oz (55 g) unsalted butter	½ pint (300 ml) cooking
2 egg-yolks	liquid (*see recipe*)
1 shallot	salt and pepper
1 tablespoon chopped fresh parsley	½ a lemon

To cook the turbot you need a large, deep-sided tray in which the fish will fit diagonally. Pour the milk over the fish and add sufficient water to make sure it is covered. Season with salt and pepper and spread some buttered foil across the top of the dish. Pre-heat the oven to low (120°C/ 250°F/Gas ¹/₂), and bake the fish for about 1 hour, until the flesh comes easily away from the bone.

While the fish is cooling, make the sauce. Work the flour, together with the cayenne, into the softened butter, then mix in the egg-yolks. Finely chop the shallot and combine this and the herbs with the egg and butter mixture. When the fish has been cooking for 30 minutes, draw off ¹/₂ pint (300 ml) of the cooking liquid, topping up to cover with some more water. Over a very low heat, slowly mix the liquid into the egg, butter and herbs, stirring all the time. Take off the heat for a moment or two if the eggs show any sign of scrambling. When all the liquid has been combined, keep stirring over a low heat until the sauce thickens. Before serving, season to taste and stir in the juice of the lemon.

MEAT

In the summer months, my immediate instincts are to take advantage of the vegetables and fruit, and to serve plenty of fish along with rice and pasta dishes. This is not the time for slow-cooking meat casseroles, complicated meat pâtés – save those for the short, dark days of winter. That does not mean there is no place for meat in summer – simply that I prefer quick-cooked meat dishes, with an emphasis on poultry and other white meats, and of course with a place for the summer lambs. Rapid methods of preparation mean that the taste and quality of the meat used is all the more important – it must be able to stand up for itself.

The increasing concern of consumers in recent years for humane rearing of animals destined for the table has brought with it an improvement in taste standards. Nowhere is this more evident than in the chicken, one of my favourite summer meats. A factory bred and raised chicken, fed on an indescribable mixture of offal and fishmeal and slaughtered too soon, simply cannot compare to a plump cornfed chicken which has been allowed to roam, to scratch, to peck – this is not just humane to the chicken, but to the eventual eater of the bird. Pigs, cattle, sheep, not only do they have a better life when reared in closer accordance with nature, they simply taste better. Slaughtering is important, too; the less stressful the conditions under which the animals are killed, the more tender the meat. Unfortunately, current EC regulations look set to close many smaller local slaughterhouses, leading inevitably to longer transportation of live animals.

For the sake of taste, ask your butcher for locally slaughtered meat. Seek out organic meat producers, small specialist suppliers, market stalls selling direct the produce of local farmers, supermarkets stocking free-range birds, high-quality farm shops. Think of meat in terms of the animal that provides it, rather than as a plastic wrapped package. Only by knowing the way in which the animal was reared, slaughtered and butchered will you be able to measure quality.

At the moment, prices for traditionally reared meats are slightly higher but the more people who demand these standards, the more the prices will come down. Perhaps 'peasant' agricultural systems place a higher emphasis on taste than our own large-scale, economically driven and artificially sanitized approach – a visit to a provincial French market may set an example.

Shopping in Chartres
in the Shadow of the Cathedral

Chartres, a sleepy town sixty-odd miles from Paris, is visited by the tourist principally for its magnificent thirteenth-century cathedral. Once you have wandered through it, admiring the boldness of the architecture and the stained glass of brilliant blue, there is little else to do most days of the week, beyond a gentle row on the river Eure or a stroll around the cathedral grounds. But on Saturdays Chartres comes to life. For this is market day, and Chartres is the principal market town of the flat cereal-growing Beauce plains. Just to the south of the cathedral, in the Place Billard, a vast nineteenth-century metal awning covers the square, making sure business goes on whatever the weather. Stalls spill out from under this structure into the adjoining street, making through traffic an impossibility. It seems as if every inhabitant of Chartres comes out on to the streets to stock up for the week ahead.

This is a market unlike any you will see in Britain. Local farmers bring live animals, their makeshift stalls lining the street. Little yellow chicks in wicker baskets, great brown hens for laying, ducklings, baby rabbits, and, as summer moves on, goslings to rear for Christmas, all are crowded on the ground around the stalls. The trade in these animals is mostly between fellow smallholders – the bourgeoisie of Chartres no longer keep a few chickens or ducks in their back yard. Knowledgeable peasants feel breasts, examine claws and eyes and then move off with basketfuls of squawking birds or scrabbling rabbits, many of which, after a few months of freedom and good food, will make their reappearance in the market, this time for the table.

They should get a hint of their future from their owners' stalls, piled with glass jars. The lifeblood of Chartres market are these smallholders, who rear a few animals and vegetables and rely on Madame's skill in the kitchen to turn their produce into desirable treats for the wealthy inhabitants of the town. So there are pâtés de foie gras, made from both duck and goose livers, home-made rillettes (the French equivalent of potted pork), terrines of duck studded with mushrooms, chicken liver pâtés sealed with golden butter. Perhaps Madame also keeps a colony of bees, so there is honey, scented with flowers; or maybe she has a herb garden, from which she picks fragrant bunches for the market. And there will certainly be baskets of freshly laid eggs, both duck and chicken and sometimes goose as well. But there will not be a great quantity of anything, for this is the produce of a few acres, and Madame may well be packing to go back to the farm by midday.

Alongside the gossiping owners of these stalls stands the rather more serious charcutier, with his travelling van packed with every conceivable produce of the pig. If you are shopping for a picnic on a summer's day this is the place to start. Avoid the delicious rillettes this time, for they will melt in the sun; choose instead from one of the many different types of cooked ham – au miel (glazed in honey), au foin (baked in straw), au torchon (baked in a cloth), or simply à l'os (on the bone). Or perhaps you would prefer the jambon persillé, chunks of ham locked in aspic studded with flat-leaved parsley. Buy a whole saucisson sec or salami, for chopping into thick chunks, or choose one of the many larger varieties of saucisson for slicing paper-thin – saucisse de Lyon, de Jesu, au poivre. A few olives, a baguette or two, some fruit, and your picnic is ready.

For the more adventurous picnicker, who likes to build a barbecue, or those lucky enough to be living nearby, as I did for a while, there is even more choice. Itinerant butchers, who make their living moving from market to market, turn up in Chartres on Saturdays. Their summer specialities include tender home-reared squab pigeons, for roasting quickly and serving, the breast still pink, with a salad; quails, ideal for barbecuing wrapped in leaves or for stuffing with a Middle Eastern mixture of rice and dried fruits; and chevreau or kid, a delicate meat which, when the kid is young enough, is delicious simply roasted. In the early part of the summer the lamb is exceptional, whether roasted on a bed of lavender or cubed and grilled or barbecued to a blackened exterior and a smoky pink centre. The steak is sold in huge chunks on the bone, the côte de boeuf which needs to be seared, roasted quickly in a very hot oven and then left to rest before slicing into warm rosy slices. Fortunately, to my mind, these butchers do not stock that poor substitute for beef, horsemeat; that is left to the Boucherie Chevaline, ostracized on the other side of the square.

When you have satisfied your carnivorous instincts, have a look at the fishmonger, who regularly makes the round trip from Brittany. Wander among the fruit and vegetable stalls, admiring the quality and range of soft summer fruits and baby vegetables, some grown locally, some brought up from the Mediterranean. Admire the cheese stalls, with their mounds of creamy butter and thick golden cream. You might like to buy some of the local speciality, Fontainebleau, a cream cheese in mousseline which goes perfectly with the seasonal red berries. Then stroll off, laden with shopping, to have a quiet beer or a coffee in the sunshine in front of the cathedral, and wonder what the market was like when this awe-inspiring church was being built. For it was surely there: this market has the feel of being very little touched by the passage of time.

HOT BEEF SALAD

This salad is derived from a dish I first tasted in Indonesia, at a roadside warung or foodstall. The vegetables in the salad can be varied according to availability: the essence is that they should provide a crunchy contrast to the tender meat. Good quality steak is needed to achieve this tenderness. I like to use a forerib of beef briefly roasted on the bone before slicing, marinating and then stir-frying, but you can also use rump steak. Make sure, whatever cut you choose, that the meat is a dark rich red, denoting proper hanging, and that it is lightly marbled with fat, which is essential for the flavour.

The meat is given an Oriental flavour by resting it while hot in soy sauce and ginger, and the whole is dressed with sesame oil, producing a fine summer supper dish. The preparation sounds more complicated than it is, but as with all stir-frying dishes, this does require some last-minute attention.

FOR THE MEAT

1 small forerib of roasting beef on the bone, approx 2–2¹/₂ lb (1–1.25 kg)

2 tablespoons dry sherry (*it must be dry – fino or manzanilla, but don't use your best; for a more authentic flavour, you could use rice wine*)

4 or 5 cloves of garlic

1 oz (25 g) fresh ginger

4 small chillies (*I use a mixture of green and red*)

1 teaspoon sugar

2 tablespoons dark soy sauce

3–4 tablespoons sweet hot chilli sauce (*optional*)

1 tablespoon sesame oil

1 tablespoon sunflower or peanut oil

FOR THE SALAD

3 or 4 from the following selection (*aim for a contrast of colours and textures, and keep quantities small as the vegetables will be finely chopped*):

carrots, Chinese beans (*the long variety found in Chinese and Indian shops*), courgettes (*presalted to allow the liquid to drain away*), cucumber (*presalted as with the courgettes*), French beans, green peppers, leeks, onions, red peppers, spring onions.

1 small ripe mango

1 tablespoon chopped fresh coriander

sesame oil

1 lime

Pre-heat the oven to very hot (220°C/425°F/Gas 7) and roast the meat for 20 minutes. This is obviously a shorter period of time than you would cook it for if you were simply roasting the meat for serving. immediately, but the marinade and the stir-frying will finish off the cooking process. Take the meat out and let it rest for 5 minutes before slicing, to allow the juices to spread through.

To prepare the marinade, finely chop the garlic, the peeled ginger root and the de-seeded chillies. Mix these together with the soy sauce, sesame oil, sherry, sugar and chilli sauce if you are using it. Remove any excess fat from the joint of beef and carve the meat away from the bone into slices $^1/_2$ inch (1 cm) thick (the Oriental style would be to have much thinner slices, almost slivers, of beef but I find the thicker slices keep the meat more tender). Keep the bone – it makes excellent stock. The meat will be well seared on the outside but very red in the middle. Lay all the slices in the marinade and leave in a cool place (not in the fridge – the meat should cool down naturally, giving it plenty of time to absorb the juices from the marinade). One hour is the minimum resting period, 2 would be better. Turn the meat once during this time.

To make the salad, chop the vegetables into matchsticks, as for stir-frying. If you are using carrots or either type of bean, blanch them for 30 seconds in stock or water. Salt and drain the cucumbers and courgettes; use only the lower root ends of the leeks and spring onions. Remove the flesh from the mango and shred.

When you are ready to eat, remove the meat from the marinade, brushing any pieces of ginger, garlic or chilli back into the dish. Strain the liquid from the marinade and reserve; keep the drained pieces of garlic, ginger and chilli. Heat the sunflower or peanut oil in a wok or large frying-pan, until it is almost smoking. Stir-fry the reserved pieces of garlic, ginger and chilli for 30 seconds, then add the vegetables. Cook for 2 minutes, stirring constantly, then pour over the marinade liquid and allow to bubble for a further 1 minute. Turn the heat right down, cover and leave to simmer for 3 minutes or so. Take off the heat, stir in the chopped fresh coriander and the mango and dress with sesame oil and lime juice to taste. Leave in a warm place for the few minutes it will take to cook the meat.

Wipe clean the wok or frying-pan in which you have cooked the vegetables and place it over a high heat. When the pan is very hot, put in the slices of meat and sear on each side – about a minute. Place on top of the heaped pile of salad vegetables and serve with bread or plain boiled rice.

BOILED CHICKEN WITH EGG AND HERB VINAIGRETTE

Although boiled chicken has gone out of favour in recent years, it can make the most perfect of summer lunches. Simmer a fat boiling fowl slowly with a few vegetables, then leave the chicken to cool a little in its liquid and serve with a herby vinaigrette bound with eggs. This is a dish which takes time but needs virtually no attention and has the added advantage of leaving you with perfect stock for summer soups.

FOR THE CHICKEN

2 large carrots

1 large or 2 small onions

2 sticks of celery

2 small leeks (*assuming the new season's leeks have appeared in the shops*)

1 plump boiling chicken

1 bayleaf

2 or 3 sprigs of fresh parsley

1 small sprig of fresh thyme

FOR THE VINAIGRETTE

3 or 4 spring onions

1 tablespoon chopped fresh parsley

$^1/_2$ tablespoon chopped fresh chives

$^1/_2$ tablespoon chopped fresh tarragon

1 lemon

salt and pepper

2 large fresh eggs

5 tablespoons extra virgin olive oil

Chop the vegetables roughly. Clean the chicken thoroughly, removing any excess fat and the giblets if the butcher has not already done so.

Place the chicken, the vegetables and the cooking herbs in a very large pan. Bring a full kettle of water to the boil and pour over the bird and vegetables – if this is not sufficient water to cover amply, add more. Bring back to the boil and skim off the scum which will rise to the surface. When no more scum rises, turn down to barely a simmer (the occasional bubble should rise to the surface), season to taste, cover and leave for $3-3^1/_2$ hours.

At the end of the cooking the chicken should be very tender. Take off the lid and leave the bird to cool slightly in the cooking liquid – do not remove it from the broth until you are about to serve it, or it will dry out.

Make the vinaigrette just before you eat. Finely chop the spring onions and mix with the herbs. Add the juice of the lemon and salt and pepper to taste. Soft-boil the eggs for 3 minutes, then run cold water over them and peel them carefully over the bowl of onions and herbs, so that the yolk runs into the bowl. Chop the egg-whites. Add the olive oil to the yolk, onion and herb mixture little by little, stirring constantly. Finally, add the chopped egg-whites. Taste to check seasoning.

Serve the boiled chicken dressed with the vinaigrette, with bread and salad. Make sure you keep the broth for soup.

CHICKEN STEWED WITH ONION AND LEMON

Some of my favourite recipes for chicken come from Morocco, where they are expert at producing tender dishes for hot days. I first tasted this dish in a tiny café next door to the enormous souk in Marrakesh. The onions are stewed for a long time so that they acquire the sweetness to counter the sharpness of the lemon juice in which the chicken pieces have been marinated. Served with spicy rice and a green salad, this is a good dish for a large gathering.

FOR 4 DRUMSTICKS AND 4 THIGHS,
ONE OF EACH PER PERSON

3 lemons
2 small green chillies
2 cloves of garlic
2 teaspoons ground coriander
2 teaspoons ground cumin
1 teaspoon ground cinnamon
1/2 teaspoon ground black pepper
1/4 teaspoon salt
3 large Spanish onions
1 tablespoon ghee (*clarified butter, available from Indian shops*) or, failing that, sunflower oil

175

Skin the chicken pieces. Squeeze the juice from the lemons, de-seed the chillies, and chop the chillies and garlic finely. Mix together the lemon juice, chillies and garlic. Mix the spices and salt and rub into the chicken pieces, then lay them in a flat dish and pour over the lemon mixture. Leave to marinate for at least 1 hour, turning occasionally.

Chop the onions into fine rings. Melt the ghee or sunflower oil in a heavy frying-pan with a lid and add the onion. Cover and cook on a very low heat, stirring occasionally, for 45 minutes; the onion should slowly caramelize, browning but not burning. When the onion is ready, strain the lemon juice from the chicken pieces, leaving behind the garlic and chilli. Add the chicken, garlic and chilli to the pan and turn up the heat to medium. Fry with the onions for 5 minutes until the chicken is browned all over. Pour over the lemon juice, add a small glass of water, cover and simmer for 30 minutes, until the chicken is tender. Check the seasoning and serve with basmati rice, briefly fried in a little turmeric before being simmered in water.

CHICKEN ROASTED WITH YOGHURT AND CORIANDER

Fresh herbs are one of the delights of summer, and coriander is a particular favourite of mine. I find it has an excellent affinity with chicken and like to stuff a large bunch in the cavity of a bird for roasting, allowing it to scent the meat without overpowering it. A chicken rubbed with spiced yoghurt before roasting acquires a particularly juicy texture.

1 teaspoon ground coriander	1 free-range chicken, preferably cornfed, approx. 3 lb (1.5 kg)
$1/4$ teaspoon cayenne pepper	
$1/2$ teaspoon turmeric	1 bunch of fresh coriander
4 fl oz (100 ml) Greek yoghurt	$1/2$ a lemon
salt and freshly ground black pepper	1 tablespoon extra virgin olive oil

Pre-heat the oven to medium hot (180°C/350°F/Gas 4). Mix the spices into the yoghurt, together with salt and freshly ground black pepper. With your finger, carefully separate the skin from the breast meat on either side of the breastbone. Hold the chicken so that the legs point upwards and with your finger push the yoghurt mixture between skin and flesh. Wash the coriander leaves, trim the stalks and put the bunch inside the chicken, along with the 1/2 lemon. Rub the olive oil all over the outside of the chicken.

Roast in the oven for 30 minutes, then turn the heat down to medium (150°C/300°F/Gas 2) and leave for another 45 minutes. Just before serving, turn the oven up again, spoon the juices from the cavity over the bird, sprinkle a little salt over the the breast and allow to crisp for 5 minutes. Rest for a few minutes before carving.

DUCK WITH FRESH PLUM SAUCE

Summer duckling is especially good, and as well as whole Aylesbury ducks in the market, magrets of Barbary duck from France are now to be had in some supermarkets. The traditional Chinese dish of duck with pancakes uses a preserved plum sauce, which was the inspiration for this fruity accompaniment. The sharpness of the plum juice cuts the richness of the meat, making an excellent late summer dinner party dish.

1 lb (450 g) dark plums	dark soy sauce
1/2 a wineglass dry sherry	pinch of sugar
sesame oil	4 duck breasts or magrets

The duck breasts require grilling at the last moment; the sauce can be prepared in advance and tastes all the better for it. Wash the plums – there is no need to halve and stone them. Heat a saucepan and add the plums; sizzle for a second or two and then throw in the sherry. Bubble for a minute and then add the same quantity of water; cover, turn down the heat and simmer for 5 minutes. The plums should by now be tender, but the timing will depend fractionally on their ripeness. You need to get them at the point where they start to fall apart but before they become a soggy mush. Push the cooked plums through a sieve into another saucepan, taking care not to lose any of the juices, but to leave the skin and stones behind. Add a few drops of sesame oil, a generous swirl of soy sauce and the sugar; bring back to a steady simmer and reduce to taste (this should not take too long – be careful not to reduce too much or the soy will become overpowering).

When you are nearly ready to eat, pre-heat the grill to maximum. Grill the breasts for 5–8 minutes depending on their thickness or your liking for pink duck meat (I like it pink all through). Rest the duck breasts for 5 minutes in a warm oven before serving, to allow the juices to spread evenly. Meanwhile heat the sauce, stirring in any juices from the meat after draining off the fat. If you are feeling very nouvelle cuisine, slice the duck breasts into a fan on a pool of the red sauce, otherwise put the duck breast and a pool of sauce side by side on each plate. This is a rich dish which needs little with it; mashed potato made with stock instead of milk and a salad of raw fennel and orange are good accompaniments.

ROAST GROUSE

The late summer treat of roast grouse is one peculiar to Britain. Don't be in a rush to buy the birds on 13 August, when they will be overpriced and underhung. By the end of the month the price should have descended from the stratosphere to more manageable levels. And I don't believe the bird is overrated. A grouse roasted in butter, with the traditional accompaniments of watercress and game chips, is a rare rich treat.

For 2 (cost and elegance of eating mean that this isn't really a dinner party dish – far better to serve grouse at a dinner for 2 good friends)

2 grouse
2 pieces of pork fat, each large enough to cover a bird, or 4 rashers unsmoked streaky bacon (*the former is better as it does not impair the fine flavour*)
salt and black pepper

1 oz (25 g) unsalted butter
2 slices of stale white country bread, crusts removed
2 large potatoes
1 bunch of watercress
lemon juice
fresh oil for deep-frying (*I use groundnut oil*)

Almost all game birds need some protection from the fierce heat of the oven if they are to emerge tender and moist from roasting. Traditionally in the UK we provide this by wrapping them in bacon; but I prefer the French method of using pork fat to surround the bird, tainting neither the pan juices nor the meat itself with the strong taste of bacon. Of course, getting hold of suitable strips of pork fat means having a friendly butcher, and you may well need to use bacon after all; in either case, make sure the breast of the bird is well covered and tie the fat in place so that it cannot curl away from the meat while cooking. Work some salt and black pepper into the knob of butter and then divide, placing half in the cavity of each bird.

Pre-heat the oven to very hot (220°C/425°F/Gas 7). Place each bird on its side on top of a slice of bread on an oven tray. Allow to roast for 10 minutes, then turn the oven down to medium hot (180°C/350°F/Gas 4) and turn the bird over on to the other side. After another 10 minutes, remove the protective wrapping of fat or bacon, place the bird breast uppermost, baste with the buttery juices from the cavity and cook for a further 5–10 minutes, depending on how well done you want the birds (which will in turn depend upon how long they were hung). Rest for 5 minutes in a warm place before serving on top of the slices of bread, with the buttery pan juices poured over. I sometimes fry the grouse livers in a little butter and brandy and spread this mixture on to the bread, but some may find this too powerful a flavour.

I serve my grouse in the traditional way with watercress and game chips. The latter are easy to make and opening a packet of crisps is no substitute. One large potato per person is plenty; the potatoes should be firm. Peel and slice with a mandoline or food processor into thin slices, as if for a gratin. Blanch the potato slices in salted boiling water to which a few drops of lemon juice have been added – the slices should literally go straight in and out of the water. Heat the oil. Pat the potato slices dry. When the oil is hot enough (i.e. when a piece of bread will float on the surface and become crisp but not immediately blacken) add half the potato slices, making sure you do not overcrowd the pan or they will stick to the bottom. Fry until the slices are golden brown – this will take about 5 minutes depending on the potatoes. Remove the slices with a slotted spoon and drain on kitchen paper. Repeat with the remainder. Sprinkle with salt and serve alongside the grouse and watercress.

GUINEAFOWL WITH PEAS AND TOMATO

The guineafowl is another good bird for the summer, with a taste somewhere between chicken and pheasant. It is now more commonly reared in this country and is available from some supermarkets, as well as local butchers and markets. As with pheasant, if you roast the bird whole the breasts may dry out and I prefer to cook the breasts and legs separately. This recipe for braised guineafowl breasts takes advantage of the fresh peas now available to produce a dish derived from the Basque cooking of northern Spain, served with an accompaniment of mashed potatoes made with stock and oil.

4 breasts of guineafowl (*if you buy whole guineafowl, keep the legs for grilling or roasting and the carcasses for splendid stock*)
1 tablespoon olive oil
1 clove of garlic
1 sprig of fresh marjoram or oregano

8 oz (225 g) shelled weight of peas
4 tomatoes
$^1/_2$ pint (300 ml) chicken or guineafowl stock
4 large potatoes
salt and pepper

Quickly sear the guineafowl breasts in the oil until browned on each side. Lay them in an earthenware dish and scatter with the chopped garlic and herbs. Surround with the peas and the peeled chopped tomatoes. Bring the stock to the boil and pour into the dish. Bake uncovered in a medium hot oven (180°C/350°F/Gas 4) for 30 minutes.

Meanwhile, peel the potatoes and boil until soft. When the guineafowl is cooked, drain away and reserve most of the liquid, leaving the peas and tomato. Keep in a warm place. Mash the potatoes with the liquid from the guineafowl, a little olive oil and plenty of seasoning. Pile on a plate, spoon the vegetables around and place the breasts of guineafowl on top.

LAMB KEBABS

Lamb is a favourite meat for the barbecue, being ideally suited to quick cooking. I like to take chunks from a shoulder of British lamb and marinate them in a yoghurt-based mixture filled with spice before barbecuing or, if the weather fails, grilling.

$1^1/_4$ lb (550 g) boned shoulder of lamb	1 teaspoon ground black pepper
$^1/_2$ tablespoon ground cumin	juice of 1 lemon
$^1/_2$ tablespoon ground coriander	1 tablespoon tomato purée
$^1/_2$ teaspoon cayenne pepper	$^1/_2$ teaspoon salt
	8 fl oz (250 ml) Greek yoghurt

Trim the lamb of any fat and cut into 1 inch (2.5 cm) chunks. Mix together all the spices with the lemon juice, tomato purée and salt and then fold into the yoghurt. Thoroughly coat each chunk of meat and leave to marinate for 2 hours, turning occasionally.

To cook, pre-heat the grill to maximum or make sure the barbecue coals are glowing. Shake off any excess yoghurt and cook very quickly, turning occasionally, so that the meat chars on the outside but retains a smoky pink middle. Serve immediately, with chunks of lemon for squeezing over and perhaps some grilled tomatoes stuffed with herbs and garlic.

ROAST LAMB WITH LAVENDER

By the summer months British lamb is widely available. See if you can get lambs reared entirely on milk for a particularly good flavour. Another type to look out for are the 'présalé' lambs of Brittany, which acquire their unique flavour from being reared on the salt marshes. Leg of lamb is good roasted on a bed of rosemary – or try substituting the rosemary with sticks from a lavender bush for a subtler, more fragrant effect, and basting the meat with a little flowery honey. Lavender and rosemary sticks are both good thrown on the barbecue before cooking lamb.

1 or 2 cloves of fresh garlic	preferably flower-scented,
1 small leg of lamb, approx	e.g. acacia blossom
3 lb (1.5 kg)	5 or 6 stalks of lavender,
freshly ground black pepper	with flower heads
1 tablespoon clear honey,	

Pre-heat the oven to hot (200°C/400°CF/Gas 6). Chop the peeled garlic cloves into fine slices. With a sharp knife, make incisions in the meat and push in the garlic slices. Season the joint with freshly ground black pepper. Smear the honey all over the surface of the meat. Arrange the lavender stalks in the baking tray and place the meat on top, making sure none of the stalks or flowerheads are uncovered or they will burn. Just by resting on the flowers while it is cooking the meat is infused with a marvellous fragrance.

Put the lamb in the oven. Keep the oven temperature high throughout the cooking and baste regularly with the pan juices. The cooking time will depend on the size of the joint and how pink you like your meat. For this recipe I like mine rosy and roast a medium-size leg for 1–1$^1/_4$ hours. It is very important that the lamb should to be left to rest in a warm place for 10 minutes before carving to allow the juices to suffuse through the meat. Carve at the table, allowing those present to admire the golden shine that the honey gives the meat and to enjoy the wafts of garlic and lavender that the joint gives off as you cut into it.

I often serve lamb cooked this way with Italian roast potatoes – thick slices of unpeeled red-skinned potatoes sprinkled with thyme and roasted in olive oil in the meat pan around the joint. These should go in the oven at the same time as the lamb. A simple green vegetable such as French beans or a green salad completes the dish.

SPICY LAMB MEATBALLS IN LEMON SAUCE

As summer draws on, you may have had your fill of roast, grilled and barbecued lamb. Now is the time to think of new ways of cooking the meat. Minced lamb is generally available from a compliant butcher and from many supermarkets, and makes excellent meatballs. These are not the boring meatballs of school dinner days, but rather highly spiced mouthfuls floating in a rich, lemony sauce, another delicious example of cooking from the Middle East. With rice and a salad, this makes a simple supper dish.

1 lb (450 g) minced lamb
3 oz (85 g) basmati rice
spice mix (*see below*)
salt
1 whole egg
2 onions
1 tablespoon vegetable oil

1 clove of garlic
1 small green chilli
2 lemons
pinch of sugar
2 tablespoons fresh
   coriander

Spices
One of my favourite spices for lamb is a Middle Eastern spice mixture known as ras el hanout, which I buy in the Arab quarter in Paris whenever I am there and store in jars for adding to tajines, couscous and

other Arab dishes such as this one. I have never managed to elucidate from the storekeepers what goes into their patent mix of ras el hanout, for each store has its own recipe, which is a closely guarded secret. If you can find ras el hanout in a specialist Middle Eastern food store, then you are lucky; if not, try the following mixture, which gets close, although it is by no means authentic (the real version contains such easy to obtain items as dried rosebuds). Make more than you need immediately, so that you can store it for other dishes.

1 tablespoon ground cinnamon	$1/_2$ tablespoon ground ginger
1 tablespoon ground cumin	$1/_2$ tablespoon ground allspice
$1/_4$ tablespoon cayenne pepper	$1/_4$ tablespoon finely ground black pepper
$1/_2$ tablespoon turmeric	4 cardamom pods, ground
$1/_4$ tablespoon finely ground cloves	

Mix the lamb mince, dry rice, 2 tablespoons of the spice mix, seasoning and egg together in a large bowl with your hands. Roll the mixture with the palms of your hands into balls about the size of a walnut. Finely chop the onions and fry in the oil for 10 minutes, until they are quite soft and lightly browned. Add the chopped garlic and chilli and fry for another 5 minutes, then add the meatballs, turning gently until they are coloured on all sides. Add the juice of the lemons and enough water to cover, with a good pinch each of salt and sugar. Bring to the boil, cover, and turn down to a simmer for 25 minutes. Chop the coriander leaves, add to the pan and cook for a minute or two longer. Check for seasoning and serve with rice, coloured with a little turmeric, and a tomato salad.

OSSOBUCO

This dish from northern Italy is justly famous, for the stewed veal shins in a rich sauce make a marvellous dish. This is one of the few casseroles I cook in summer, when the fresh herbs for the last-minute kick of the gremolada are available. Although the initial assembly of ingredients is a little time-consuming, this is a slow-cooking dish which can be left alone and takes well to reheating. In Milan the dish would be served with a buttery risotto yellow with saffron, but you may find this a little too much and prefer plain rice. No vegetables beyond a green salad are necessary.

You do need good-quality veal, but fortunately this no longer means calves which have endured the cruel rearing practices of crating. Calves reared under British standards produce good if not quite such white meat without being reared under such restrictive living conditions. Many butchers and supermarkets now sell this veal ready prepared for ossobuco, in thick-cut slices around the central marrow bone.

2 large carrots
3 medium onions
4 sticks of celery
1 oz (25 g) butter
2 large cloves of garlic
zest of $^1/_2$ a lemon
3 or 4 sprigs of fresh thyme
3 or 4 sprigs of flat-leaved parsley
2 fresh bayleaves
1 lb (450 g) plum tomatoes or a 14 oz (400 g) tin plum tomatoes
2 tablespoons olive oil
2–2$^1/_2$ lb (1–1.25 kg) shin

of veal, in 4 slices about 1 inch (2.5 cm) thick, on the marrow bone
1 oz (25 g) plain flour
$^1/_2$ pint (300 ml) Italian dry white wine
1 pint (575 ml) beef stock (*many Italian cooks use stock-cubes and this is a dish where they are fine*)
2 teaspoons tomato purée (*if you are using fresh tomatoes*)
salt and pepper

FOR THE GREMOLADA

zest of $^1/_2$ a lemon
1 large clove of garlic
1 tablespoon chopped Italian flat-leaved parsley
4 sage leaves, chopped, if available (*do not substitute*

dried sage, if you cannot get fresh simply leave it out)
1 sprig of rosemary, leaves chopped
8 leaves of fresh basil

Peel the carrots and onions and chop finely, together with the celery. Melt the butter in a heavy-based deep casserole into which the veal will just fit in one layer, and fry the vegetables gently until soft, 15–20 minutes. Finely chop the garlic and add for the last 5 minutes.

Chop the lemon zest into 2 or 3 strips and tie in a bundle with the thyme, parsley and bayleaves. Take the softened vegetables off the heat and add the bundle of herbs to the pan. Skin the tomatoes if you are using fresh ones, remove the seeds and chop the flesh finely. Turn the oven to medium (160°C/325°F/Gas 3).

In a frying-pan sufficiently large to take all the veal, heat the olive oil. When the oil is hot but not smoking, dip both sides of each slice of veal in the flour and fry quickly on both sides to seal. Lay the meat on top of the vegetables.

Pour off any excess oil from the frying-pan and add the wine, stirring well to loosen any residue from the meat. Boil for a couple of minutes, then pour the wine over the meat. In the same pan, heat the stock with the tomato purée (if you are using it), the chopped tomatoes and seasoning to taste (omit salt if you are using a stock-cube). When the liquid is boiling, pour it over the meat. The combined stock and wine should be sufficient to cover the veal; if it is not, add a little hot water. Bring the contents of the casserole to a slow simmer, cover, and transfer to the oven. Cook for $2^1/_2$–3 hours, until the meat is meltingly tender. After an hour or so, check the level of the liquid; if it looks low, add a little more water.

To make the gremolada, finely chop together the lemon zest, garlic and herbs. Stir this mixture into the dish 5 minutes before serving. Take piping hot from oven to table.

QUAILS STUFFED WITH PINENUTS, RICE AND SULTANAS

Quails are increasingly reared in Britain and are now widely available. This little bird has a delicate flavour ideal for summer dishes and is quick to cook. For this dish of Persian origin, you need a friendly butcher to bone the bird; failing that, try the next recipe. Once boned, the cooking is very simple, the cavity of the bird being filled with a mixture of spiced rice and dried fruit and nuts before braising. Good served hot, the birds can also be served cold as an elegant picnic dish.

2 oz (55 g) sultanas
4 oz (115 g) basmati rice
2 oz (55 g) pinenuts
2 teaspoons ground
  cinnamon
salt and freshly ground
  black pepper

$^1/_2$ teaspoon grated lemon
  peel
1 teaspoon rosewater
  (*optional*)
4 boned quails

Briefly soak the sultanas in a very little boiling water to plump them up. Meanwhile, bring a pan of water to the boil and cook the rice for 5 minutes. Mix together the pinenuts, rice, cinnamon, seasoning, lemon peel, and rosewater if you are using it. Spoon this mixture into the cavity of each bird and tie up firmly with string into a sausage shape.

Put the birds in a pot into which they just fit and cover with boiling salted water. Simmer for 30 minutes, until very tender. Remove the string and serve. The cooking liquid will later make excellent stock.

GRILLED QUAILS WITH GRAPES

Quails can very easily be grilled whole for a simple, delicate dish. They can also be barbecued, but are best first wrapped in a couple of damp leaves to keep them moist (vine leaves would be traditional, but you can use a crisp lettuce). Either way, they are good served on a bed of seeded and lightly fried grapes, for a Bacchanalian feast to be eaten with the fingers.

approx. 15 white grapes per
  quail (*seedless grapes will
  make your life a great deal
  easier*)
2 quails per person (or 1 if
  for a first course)

2 tablespoons olive oil
1 sprig of fresh oregano or
  marjoram per quail
salt and freshly ground
  black pepper
$^1/_2$ a glass dry white wine

Turn the grill up high. Seed the grapes if necessary and cut each one in half. Rub the quails all over with some of the olive oil and tuck a sprig of marjoram in the cavity of each. Season well. Put the quails on their sides under the grill. Grill for 5 minutes on either side and then 2–3 minutes breastbone uppermost. Meanwhile fry the seasoned grapes for a couple of minutes in the remainder of the oil; pour on the wine, let it bubble for 5 minutes, then leave covered over a low heat until needed.

Serve the grilled quails on a bed of grapes. Quails are best eaten with the fingers, so provide plenty of napkins.

ROAST PORK ITALIAN STYLE

Pork is not a traditional summer meat, a hangover from the days before refrigeration. Yet a roast of pork stuffed with the feathery fronds of a fennel bulb or two and some of the new season's garlic, basted with olive oil and roasted quickly to keep it juicy, can be a good summer dish. And any leftovers are delicious cold. To go with the pork, try braised bulbs of fennel and Italian-style roast potatoes cooked around the meat.

For 6

3 bulbs of fennel, with plenty of feathery fronds
3 plump cloves of fresh garlic
$^1/_2$ teaspoon fennel seeds
freshly ground black pepper
6 tablespoons fruity olive oil
$2^1/_2$–3 lb (1.25–1.5 kg) boned rolled loin of pork

2 lb (900 g) potatoes *(the red-skinned Desirée variety are best for this dish)*
coarse sea-salt
1 glass dry white wine
1 bayleaf
1 small bunch of fresh marjoram or oregano (or $1^1/_2$ teaspoons dried)

Trim the feathery fronds from the fennel. Peel the garlic and crush it with the fennel fronds. Add the fennel seeds and plenty of freshly ground black pepper and pound together to form a paste, adding a few drops of olive oil if necessary.

Pre-heat the oven to very hot (220°C/425°F/Gas 7). Stuff the centre of the pork loin with the garlic and fennel mixture (you may like to unroll the meat, but I prefer just to push the stuffing into the cracks with my fingers). Roast the meat uncovered for 30 minutes.

Meanwhile, scrub the potatoes but do not peel them. Cut them into rounds 3/4 inch (2 cm) thick and rinse them again to remove the starch.

After the meat has been in the oven 30 minutes, drain off the fat. Arrange the potatoes around the meat and pour over 5 tablespoons of the olive oil, pouring some over the meat itself. Sprinkle both the potatoes and the meat with coarse sea-salt. Turn the oven down to 200°C/400°F/Gas 6.

To braise the fennel, cut each cleaned bulb into quarters. Heat the remaining tablespoon of olive oil in a heavy-based pan which will take all the bulbs flat. When the oil is sizzling, add the bulbs cut side down and cook for 10 minutes, until well browned. Now pour over the glass of wine, add seasoning and the bayleaf, and cook covered for 20 minutes or until the fennel is very tender.

When the meat has been in the oven for a total of 1 hour, turn the potatoes over and sprinkle the marjoram or oregano over them. Baste the meat with the olive oil from the pan. Cook for another 20 minutes and then remove the meat from the roasting dish and let it stand for 10 minutes. Meanwhile, turn the oven up to maximum to crisp the potatoes.

Serve the meat cut into thick slices, with olive-oily pan juices poured over and the fennel and potatoes on the side. A quarter of lemon is good squeezed over the meat.

PUDDINGS

Summer pudding is to many people the ultimate summer dessert. It is a prime example of what such a dish should do, using the freshest of seasonal fruits with the simplest other ingredients to make a pudding which is vibrant in taste and colour, the perfect end to a meal. Almost all the puddings I like in summer use fruit in some way and fruit is an area where British markets come into their own in summer. Of course, they differ from the markets of Provence, Tuscany, or other Mediterranean areas, with which many of us are familiar from our holidays. Peaches, melons, nectarines, grapes, all have to be imported and so lose that just-picked quality. But Britain produces wonderful berries: raspberries from Scotland are sought after on the Continent, our strawberries are far sweeter than the early Spanish-grown equivalents, bilberries grow wild on our moors. In high summer, market stalls all round the country are piled with these seasonal fruits, making a much more attractive picture than the chilled packages in the supermarkets (which, moreover, are sold at a higher price). Visit a market in summer to buy fruit and you may be surprised at the bargains on offer.

Fruity Soho: Berwick Street

The location of the Berwick Street market is not promising. The picture of stalls piled down a dirty London street in the heart of the sex and sleaze of Soho is a long way from the street markets we find on our holidays in the Mediterranean and dream of when we come home. But it's worth persevering, because first impressions can deceive. Berwick Street market may not be picture-postcard attractive; but it has got a lot to offer to those of us disinclined to arise at the crack of dawn to go to the even less scenic New Covent Garden. Much of the fruit and vegetables on offer in this Soho street market come from Covent Garden's wholesalers, the very same who supply some of London's most celebrated restaurateurs. Not only are there tremendous bargains to be had, but the range is exceptional. Here, in the right season, you can find wild mushrooms like chanterelles, pleurottes, puffballs; rarer vegetables such as salsify, samphire and seakale; vast bunches of fragrant herbs; every type of salad leaf; that rare commodity, a ripe plum tomato; and a stunning display of fruit.

In the summer it is the fruit stalls that draw me to Berwick Street. I like extravagant fruit bowls, brimming over with soft white peaches, red berries and yellow cherries. The prices in this market make buying fruit in quantity a pleasure. Tiny plastic punnets are a rarity here. Instead, strawberries and raspberries are scooped into brown paper bags from the huge piles on the stall. It is a noisy market where East End voices still shout in competition: 'Fifteen lovely peaches for a pound.' 'Who'll give me a quid for these melons?' 'Just look at these juicy strawberries.' As the day goes on the voices get hoarser, the bargains greater and the smell of warm, ripe fruit in the air becomes more powerful.

At Berwick Street you must choose your fruit carefully. The prices are low because the fruit is often at the peak of ripeness and therefore not of interest to the wholesale purchasers, who must have fruit that can stand transportation or have a reasonable shelf life. Berwick Street is not the place for the weekly shop; it is for fruit to be eaten within a day or two of buying. But, on the other hand, here you will not find peaches that sit on your windowsill for days, never ripening to the anticipated fleshy juiciness. As with any market, watch carefully as the stallholder picks out your fruit, and be suspicious of any who hide behind their stall to fill up your bag or who object if you examine the fruit too carefully. I once had a terrific row with a vendor who wouldn't let me pick out my own basket of figs but insisted on choosing for me; I should have known – when I got home I found that the figs were cracked, their juices long evaporated and the flesh going to seed. But this is the exception rather than the rule. The stallholders generally combine a good line in sales patter with a brusque friendliness. They respect anyone who knows their fruit as well as they do and will generally grant you a taste if you ask politely.

Summer is the time for berries. In late July Berwick Street boasted sweet and juicy myrtilles or bilberries, the type my sister-in-law picks wild in the Vosges of Alsace; these had been cultivated, some in California, some in Dorset, lacking perhaps the herby subtlety of the wild variety but compensating with their juiciness. Eat them as the Italians do, just with sugar and lemon, or use them to make a stunning open tart. Loganberries and the tastier tayberries from Scotland offered an alternative to raspberries; all three are good as the filling for a sweet pancake. Tiny wild strawberries looked even more delectable than their larger cultivated cousins, to be served with nothing more than a sprinkling of sugar and a squeeze of lemon. Heavily fruited sprays of redcurrants were perfect, the currants firm and juicy; use them in a sauce for a saddle of hare baked in cream, in tarts and purées, as a vital ingredient for summer pudding. There were white currants as well as redcurrants, too rare a sight and another good reason to make a summer tart. And what about the gooseberries, one of the few remaining truly seasonal fruits, the ultimate basis for a fool?

The range of soft fruits on offer stood up well to the temptations of the berries. Yellow cherries from Washington State, sweet and juicy and the size of small apricots, broke the rule that taste is too often sacrificed to size; the more traditional red cherries, this time from Italy, were just as tempting. I would put some in the fruit bowl but the rest could go into a clafoutis, the rich sweet batter hiding the dark, soft fruit. Alongside the familiar yellow peaches were white-skinned Italian varieties, perfect for slicing into a glass of wine, and for a special treat, 'Snow Queen' white nectarines. The scent of the Cantaloupe melons was so strong that it surrounded the stall like cloying bath essence; ripe, sweet melons like these are perfect for making into soup, enlivened with a little ginger and sweet white wine. Apricots, burnished golden and gleaming in the summer sun, were irresistible; and fortunately a quick taste showed that they were juicy rather than woolly. Try baking them with butter and brandy to accentuate the slightly sharp flavour – or add them to the fruit bowl. And what a fruit bowl it will be, the best and brightest fruits piled high, perhaps served in an ice-bowl decorated with flower petals for a special occasion, the perfect, simple end to a meal.

To go with your fruit, you might like to buy a few cheeses from the stall which specializes in rejects from the supermarkets. These are cheeses which are deemed too ripe by the buyers, which usually means that they are just right for eating, unlike the solid versions on offer on the shelves. You might find a slice of Brie, its centre creamy yellow and soft rather than chalky white and hard, as the supermarkets seem to believe it should be served. Or a Pont l'Évêque, skin slightly sticky to the touch, the cheese giving off a pungent aroma. Or you could buy a hunk of Parmigiano-Reggiano from one of the many Italian shops in the quarter, not just for grating over their excellent fresh pasta, but for eating in its own right – parmesan goes especially well with ripe pears. While you're there, buy a tub of mascarpone or a few spoonfuls of very fresh ricotta to serve with your fruits. For the main course, try the fishmonger; there is one in the market and another in nearby Brewer Street. Pick up a brace of grouse, a guineafowl or a wild rabbit from the butcher in the market street, who specializes in game, or the excellent Randall & Aubin's in Brewer Street. And you will want to fill your basket with plenty of summer vegetables, which are as varied in range as the fruit.

You will go home laden down with good things to eat, for Berwick Street is the very best of London markets. And you will not be short of ingredients for summer puddings.

APRICOT AND CINNAMON TART

Choose golden-yellow, slightly firm apricots for this delicately scented tart. If the fruit is at all squashy it risks being slightly woolly in taste. The apricots are partly cooked in advance on the stove and then baked in a creamy yoghurt on a buttery pastry base, dusted with cinnamon and brown sugar. This tart is best served warm, with a little more yoghurt to accompany it.

FOR THE PASTRY

6 oz (170 g) plain white flour

pinch of salt

3 oz (85 g) unsalted butter

1 egg

1 oz (25 g) sugar

FOR THE FILLING

1 lb (450 g) apricots

1/2 oz (15 g) butter

1 tablespoon sugar

4 fl oz (100 ml) Greek yoghurt

4 fl oz (100 ml) double cream

1 egg

1 teaspoon ground cinnamon

1 teaspoon brown sugar

To make the pastry, sieve the flour with a pinch of salt. Break the butter up into small pieces, make a well in the centre of the flour and add the egg and the butter. Blend together with your fingers, then add the sugar. Add a little chilled water (about 2 tablespoons) and form into a ball; the pastry should not be too sticky. Wrap the ball of pastry in greaseproof paper, clingfilm or foil and rest in the fridge for at least 1 hour.

For the filling, wash the apricots, halve them, and remove the stones. Melt the butter in a saucepan and add the apricots and sugar. Cook over a low heat for a couple of minutes and then add a tablespoon of water. Cover and cook for 5 minutes; the apricots should be soft but not falling apart.

When you are ready to make the tart, pre-heat the oven to medium hot (180°C/350°F/Gas 4). Roll out the pastry and fill an 8–10 inch (20–25 cm) buttered tart or quiche dish, the sort with a detachable bottom.

Prick the pastry all over with a fork and bake blind for 15 minutes. Arrange the part-cooked apricots over the pastry base. Whip together the yoghurt, cream and egg and pour over the apricots. Combine the cinnamon and crunchy brown sugar and sprinkle over the top. Bake the tart for 20 minutes in a medium hot oven (180°C/350°F/Gas 4). Serve warm.

ROASTED APRICOTS WITH BRANDY

This simple pudding is one of my favourite ways of serving apricots. Their centres filled with a little cheap cooking brandy (Spanish is ideal) and a small knob of butter, the apricots are baked to a juicy softness, before being served with their buttery juices.

2 lb (900 g) apricots	brandy
2 oz (55 g) unsalted butter	1 oz (25 g) brown sugar

Wash the apricots, halve them, and remove the stones. Pre-heat the oven to medium (150°C/300°F/Gas 2). Arrange the apricots on a buttered baking tray, well side up. Fill the well of each with a small knob of butter and a little brandy. Sprinkle over the sugar and bake for 20 minutes. Serve very hot.

BILBERRY (MYRTILLE) TART

Native bilberries are rarely seen and make a great treat. Look out for the tiny, ground-hugging bushes if you go walking on a moor – on an August trip to Dartmoor I was quickly able to gather a basketful. Occasionally bilberries appear in the shops in the summer. In Italy they are a great favourite served just dusted with a little sugar and lemon. The French arrange them on a buttery open tart, as here. Be careful not to overcook the berries, though, as the key to this tart is that they should keep their shape.

FOR THE PASTRY

6 oz (170 g) plain white
   flour
pinch of salt

3 oz (85 g) unsalted butter
1 egg
1 oz (25 g) sugar

FOR THE FILLING

1 egg-white
1¹/₂ lb (675 g) bilberries

1 oz (25 g) caster sugar
icing sugar

Make the pastry as for apricot tart (see pages 194–5), including baking blind for 15 minutes in a medium hot oven (180°C/350°F/Gas 4). Brush the pastry base with the egg-white and arrange three-quarters of the washed bilberries over the pastry base. Sprinkle with the sugar and bake for 25–30 minutes. Scatter the remaining uncooked bilberries over the tart, dredge with a little icing sugar and serve warm or cold.

CHERRY CLAFOUTIS

The nearest thing in British cooking to a clafoutis would be a Yorkshire pudding with fruit in it or perhaps a toad-in-the-hole with berries instead of sausages. But despite this unappetizing description a clafoutis makes an excellent if filling pudding, the light sweet batter providing an excellent foil for the sharp fruit. My favourite is the traditional variety made with cherries. Make sure you buy small sweet black cherries for this dish – the larger, more watery varieties will not provide the right contrast of texture and flavour.

Note: A clafoutis is made with unstoned cherries, allowing the fruit to keep its shape and preventing the juices from weeping out into the batter. Warn your guests before they take their first enthusiastic mouthful or you may have a few dentist's bills on your hands.

¹/₂ pint (300 ml) full cream
   milk
1¹/₂ lb (675 g) cherries
6 oz (170 g) plain white
   flour

4 oz (115 g) caster sugar
a pinch of salt
2 oz (55 g) unsalted butter
4 eggs

First boil the milk and leave to cool. Pre-heat the oven to medium low (140°C/285°F/Gas 1). Butter an ovenproof dish with shallow sides and scatter the washed, unstoned cherries across the bottom. Sieve the flour and mix in the sugar and a pinch of salt. Melt the butter, without allowing it to brown, and beat the eggs. Slowly add the eggs into a well in the centre of the flour, followed by the melted butter and the warm milk. Stir well together to remove any lumps. Pour this batter over the cherries.

Bake in the centre of the oven for about 45 minutes, until the batter rises and the top browns. Leave the oven door open for the last 5–10 minutes of cooking, to make sure the batter doesn't immediately sink when you take the dish out. Sprinkle with a little more sugar and serve immediately.

GOOSEBERRY FOOL

The gooseberry is a very versatile fruit: it makes excellent sauces for smoked fish such as mackerel, and for rich fatty meats like goose (no surprise, given the name). As a pudding, however, I have always found a dish of stewed gooseberries rather a disappointment, probably due to the bitterness of the seeds. Sieve those seeds out, however, leaving the essence of the fruit to be folded into whipped cream for a fool, and you have an elegant pudding. For an extra eighteenth-century flavour, I like to scent my fools with orange-flower water.

1 lb (450 g) green gooseberries	1 piece of lemon rind
3 oz (85 g) white sugar or to taste, depending on the ripeness of the berries	$^1/_2$ pint (300 ml) whipping cream
	1 tablespoon orange-flower water

Wash the gooseberries and put them in a pan with the sugar and lemon rind. (As they will be sieved, there is no need to top and tail the berries.) Put the covered pan over a low heat and steam the gooseberries in their own liquid until very soft (about 20 minutes). Sieve the purée very thoroughly and chill. When the purée is cold, whip the cream and combine with the orange-flower water. Stir in the fruit, taste to check sweetness (you may want to add a little more sugar, but I like this fool fairly tart), and spoon into serving dishes. Chill until required.

LEMON AND LIME GRANITA

This water ice requires the minimum of beating, as the crisp ice crystals which form are part of its cooling charm. The citrus flavours of lemon and lime make a refreshing pudding, and the water ice can be prettily served in a scooped-out lemon.

4 oz (115 g) sugar	3 lemons
$^1/_2$ pint (300 ml) water	3 limes

Make a syrup by bringing to the boil the sugar and water in a small, heavy-based saucepan. Stir to make sure the sugar has dissolved, and boil uncovered for 5 minutes. Allow to cool.

Squeeze the juice from the fruit and strain to remove the pips. Stir the juice into the cooled syrup, pour into a large freezerproof bowl, cover and freeze for at least 2 hours. Stir after 30 minutes to break up the ice crystals; stir again after 1 hour. Remove the granita from the freezer 5 minutes before serving and stir again.

Note: if you leave the granita in the freezer for longer, remove at least 30 minutes before serving to achieve the right consistency, which should be slightly slushy.

NECTARINES IN WINE

This dish is best made with white nectarines, although the more common yellow variety will do. It is simplicity itself: the fruits are peeled, sliced and marinated in red wine before serving as a heady end to a dinner party.

For 4

6 large white nectarines	2 glasses light red wine (*a*
1 oz (25 g) caster sugar	*Beaujolais is my favourite*)

Peel and slice the nectarines. Sprinkle with sugar and leave for 30 minutes. Divide between 4 glasses, pour over the red wine and leave to chill for at least 1 hour before serving.

QUICK JAM OF RED SUMMER FRUITS

Jam may be a misnomer for this quick and delicious way with red summer fruits, but there is a strict ratio of sugar to fruit which must be adhered to. Use different fruits, or different mixes according to what you have available, but always add half the weight of the fruit in sugar. The juicy fruit in caramelized sugar is quite delicious.

6 oz (170 g) strawberries	9 oz (255 g) granulated
6 oz (170 g) raspberries	white sugar
6 oz (170 g) redcurrants	

Wash all the fruits very well. Hull the strawberries and cut in halves or quarters if large. Remove all the stalks from the redcurrants. Stir the sugar into the fruits.

Heat a heavy-based frying-pan. Add the fruits and cook, stirring, for a few minutes, until the juice runs and the sugar caramelizes lightly. Serve hot – vanilla ice-cream goes very well.

RASPBERRY PANCAKE

When or if you tire of raspberries and cream, try fresh raspberries wrapped in light pancakes, which are then quickly flambéed in a little liqueur and served warm dusted with a little sugar.

4 eggs
4 oz (115 g) plain white
  flour
pinch of salt
1/2 pint (300 ml) full-cream
  milk (*or half milk and half*
  single cream)

2 oz (55 g) unsalted butter
1 oz (25 g) caster sugar
1 lb (450 g) raspberries
liqueur (*preferably eau-de-vie*
  de framboise or another
  white liqueur such as
  kirsch)

To make the pancake batter, first separate the eggs. Sieve the flour, add a pinch of salt, and make a well in the centre. Add the beaten egg-yolks and then the milk, slowly at first. When all the milk is beaten in, the batter should have the consistency of thick cream.

When you are ready to cook the pancakes, whip the egg-whites until stiff and fold into the batter. Heat a heavy, wide, non-stick frying-pan over a high heat and melt a little of the butter. Fry the pancakes one at a time in butter, adding just enough batter to cover the surface of the pan. If the pancakes are very thin, you won't have to turn them, an exercise I always find tricky. When each pancake is done (i.e. just beginning to colour – a matter of a minute or two at most), dust with caster sugar and put on a plate in a low oven to keep warm. When you have enough pancakes, fold each around a pile of washed raspberries. Heat a little liqueur in a ladle, set it alight, and pour it over the stuffed pancakes. Serve immediately.

ROSE-PETAL TART

Roses were regularly used in eighteenth-century British kitchens and
rosewater continues to be a standard ingredient in Turkish cuisine. The
delicate fragrance of a rose-scented pudding, be it a creamy yoghurt or a
delicate tart of cream cheese as here, is quite a revelation to the modern
cook. The tart itself is made with rosewater, but for those who can find
unsprayed roses the top can be sprinkled with crystallized rose-petals,
which look pretty and taste delicious.

6 sheets filo pastry
2 oz (55 g) unsalted butter
4 oz (115 g) caster sugar
6 cardamom pods
6 fl oz (175 ml) cream
  cheese (*I use the rich*

Italian cheese mascarpone)
4 fl oz (100 ml) natural or
  Greek yoghurt
$1/2$ teaspoon grated lemon
  zest
2 tablespoons rosewater

FOR THE ROSE-PETALS

1 handful of unsprayed rose-
  petals

1 egg-white
1 oz (25 g) caster sugar

Filo pastry is one type of pastry that it is simply not worth trying to make
at home. Instead, buy a frozen packet of filo from a good delicatessen or
supermarket, allow to defrost and then make the tart case. First butter a
tart or quiche dish. Cover the filo pastry with a clean, damp tea-towel
while you are working with it. Melt the butter. Take a sheet of pastry at a
time, brush one side with melted butter then lay, buttered side up, in the
dish. Do the same with the next sheet, laying it across the first at right
angles. Lay the next sheet at a 45 degree angle. In this way the oblong
sheets of pastry can be moulded to fill the round dish. When you have
used all 6 sheets, trim the pastry which hangs over the edge of the dish
with a knife. Bake blind in a medium hot oven (180°C/350°F/Gas 4) for
15 minutes.

Make a sugar syrup by boiling the sugar, cardamom pods and $1/4$ pint
(150 ml) water hard for 5 minutes – stir to ensure that all the sugar has
dissolved. When the syrup has cooled a little, pour over the cooked pastry

case (this will stick the sheets of filo together). Put the pastry case back in a medium oven, uncovered, for a further 10 minutes.

Mix the cream cheese, yoghurt, lemon zest and rosewater together and spoon into the pastry case. Bake for a further 20 minutes in a medium oven and leave to cool.

To crystallize the rose-petals, dip each petal first in egg white and then in caster sugar. Arrange on a sheet of greaseproof paper on a baking tray, and leave in the lowest possible oven for about 6 hours. The crystallized petals keep well in an airtight jar. Sprinkle them on the top of the tart.

PEACH AND REDCURRANT SOUP

The redcurrant is another fruit which, like the gooseberry, I prefer sieved and puréed to remove the bitter seeds (this rule does not apply, incidentally, to its rarer cousin, the white currant, which is excellent cooked whole in an open tart). Combine this rich red purée with freshly sliced peaches for a fragrant fruit soup.

For 4

8 oz (225 g) redcurrants
1 oz (25 g) sugar
2 cardamom pods

1 glass sweet white wine
(*I use a Muscat*)
4 large or 6 small ripe peaches

Wash the redcurrants (no need to top and tail them) and put them in a pan with the sugar and the cardamom pods if you are using them. Add the wine, cover, and simmer for 10–15 minutes, until the fruit is pulpy. Sieve carefully, taking care to leave behind the seeds. Peel and slice the peaches, add to the redcurrants, and chill well before serving.

STRAWBERRIES WITH MINT AND BALSAMIC VINEGAR

This is hardly a recipe, more a way of serving strawberries if you have tired of the usual dollop of cream and sugar. The serving of fruit with vinegar was common in Roman cuisine, as a way of bringing out the full flavour of the fruit, and is more successful than it sounds. Modern Italians still serve strawberries with balsamic vinegar – make sure you get the real thing, from the Modena region.

For 1 lb (450 g) of strawberries, you need 2 tablespoons of balsamic vinegar and a good handful of fresh mint leaves (these should be small and bright green for the sweetest flavour). Wash and slice the strawberries. Chop the mint finely and sprinkle over the fruit together with the vinegar. Add a grind of black pepper and marinate for at least an hour before serving.

SUMMER PUDDING

I have never met anyone who does not enjoy summer pudding, which is to me a pudding of genius in its simplicity. It is also ideal for the market shopper. Try it all through the summer with a range of different red and black fruits, according to what's available. The traditional recipe, given here, calls only for redcurrants and raspberries, but you could add blackberries, bilberries, blueberries, damsons, plums or strawberries.

1 lb (450 g) raspberries	slightly stale white bread
8 oz (225 g) redcurrants	*(this is one time when*
3 oz (85 g) sugar	*sliced bread comes in handy)*

Put the washed raspberries and the topped and tailed redcurrants in a pan with the sugar and cook for a couple of minutes over a gentle flame, until the juices run. The aim is to soften the fruit only – you do not want it to become mushy. If you are using different fruits, such as plums, you may have to cook them a little longer but the same principle applies.

Remove the crusts from the bread and line a deep bowl with the slices, making sure they are overlapping. Put the fruit and juices in the bread case and cover with more slices of bread. Put a plate on top and a heavy weight on top of this. Refrigerate for at least 4 hours, preferably overnight, then turn out and dust with a little icing sugar. A sprig of mint on top of the pudding looks pretty.

TEA AND MINT WATER ICE

This is iced tea taken a step further and makes a refreshing end to a meal, with its minty undertones. Vary the tea according to taste – I like Lapsang Souchong for its smoky quality but other good choices are Earl Grey, Orange Pekoe and jasmine tea. It will lack something, however, if made with an ordinary, blended tea.

1 pint (575 ml) strong tea
e.g. Lapsang Souchong
(*make it 1 1/2 times the
normal strength*)

1 large bunch of fresh mint,
washed
2 oz (55g) sugar
1 lemon

Make the tea and leave to infuse with the mint for 30 minutes. Strain and bring back to the boil; mix in the sugar and lemon juice. Boil for 2 minutes, then allow to cool before freezing. Stir 2 or 3 times during the freezing process, to break up the ice crystals.

AUTUMN

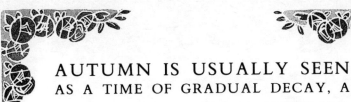

AUTUMN IS USUALLY SEEN
AS A TIME OF GRADUAL DECAY, A
FALLING AWAY, RATHER THAN OF NEW LIFE.
Golden leaves flutter to the ground, plants are nipped
by the first frosts, livestock are brought inside to
shield them from the bitter winds. Yet if the cook
steps outside the kitchen there is plenty of life to be
found, in the fields and forests, the hedgerows and
orchards. Many of the delights of the autumn months
grow in the wild. There are mushrooms, too many of
which are simply left to rot. Hedgerow fruits are
ready to be picked – blackberries for pies, elderberries for wine and sauces, sloes for flavouring gin.
There are native crab-apples, too, in the hedges; and
in the orchards there is an abundance of apples,
plums, pears, quinces and even occasionally medlars,
the small brown-skinned fruit which is eaten when it
is on the verge of rotting. Game reappears in the
marketplace and the fishermen's catches tend to
improve at this time of year. Rarely can the cook
choose from so much home-grown produce.

STARTERS

Cooler weather calls for more substantial meals, and the first course sets the tone. Rather than summer's light introduction to a meal, an autumn starter needs to take the edge off an appetite sharpened by the wind. This is no time for raw vegetable salads, although a salad made up of gutsier, warm ingredients mixed with leaves will be welcome. Vegetable dishes demand an earthier, more substantial flavour – and what is there to beat the mushroom? Cold soups go out of the window now, to be replaced by thick, steaming liquids made from powerful-tasting ingredients. Warm tarts, their filling lightly risen in buttery pastry, are the perfect prelude to a roast bird.

These are tastes from the north rather than the south of Europe, flavours designed to beat off long black nights rather than to be indulged in on warm sunny evenings. Few places in France have incorporated northern traditions into their cooking more than Alsace. So I visited Strasbourg market to enjoy the range of produce and bring back some ideas to my kitchen.

Strasbourg, the Market Town of Alsace

Autumn is my favourite time of the year in Alsace. The trees of the Vosges are slowly changing colour, their fallen leaves making a colourful carpet through which spring wild mushrooms. The fruit trees which line the valley roads are heavily laden with tiny purple plums, the quetsch from which the Alsatians distil a fiery white eau-de-vie. The wine villages south of Strasbourg are celebrating the harvest with their weinfest: medieval streets fill with crowds quaffing mugfuls of the sugary, cloudy new wine. Everywhere there is good food to be enjoyed, food which is perfectly suited to cool, bright autumn days and misty evenings.

Alsace has been much fought over, and its chequered history is reflected in today's diet. French and German influences have blended to produce a cuisine and a viticulture which are unique. Many visitors to France will experience their first taste of Alsatian cuisine in the bustling Parisian brasseries to which it has been exported. After a meal in one of these, for example the famous Chez Jenny off the Place de la République, the diner might leave with the impression that Alsatians eat nothing but the pickled cabbage, choucroute, served with sausages and cooked pork or ham, perhaps preceded by the odd slice of foie gras, the whole washed down with jugs of fruity white wines with German-sounding names – Gewürztraminer, Riesling, Edelzwicker, Sylvaner. Certainly the pig, the goose and the cabbage have made a significant contribution to the food of the people of Alsace, but there is much more to their regional cuisine, as I discovered on my autumn visit to Strasbourg, the main market town of the region and the capital of Alsace.

Strasbourg boasts several food markets, the largest of which until recently took place in the Place Sainte Marguerite. However, this site is now being developed to house a museum of modern art, and the traditional market was shifted to the Quai Turckheim, where it takes place on Wednesday and Friday mornings. A short walk away across the covered Vaubon bridge over the River Ill lies Petite France, the tanners' district of medieval Strasbourg and now a favourite spot for tourists to admire the half-timbered houses which line the streets. Another few minutes' walk and you arrive at the glorious red cathedral which dominates the city centre – if you are able to resist the temptation of the weinstube or inns on the way, where you can enjoy a glass of Riesling and a tarte à l'oignon. But keep these treats in store for later – the market is at its best in the morning.

The first thing that will strike you when you enter the market is, as expected, the astounding range of pork products. Huge smoked Black Forest hams hang behind row after row of sausages – for steaming or boiling with the choucroute, or smoked versions ready to be sliced for a starter. If you want to offer a plate of charcuterie as a first course, this is your dream market. Home-made rillettes of potted pork and goose sit beside salamis studded with hazelnuts or pistachios, rolled in herbs or black peppercorns, made with wild boar meat instead of domesticated pig. There are rough pork pâtés and smooth duck or goose pâtés. There are pâtés flavoured with juniper, made with the trimmings of the game from the Vosges – venison, marcassin or young wild boar, hare, birds of all descriptions. Thick slices of tourte au Riesling, a solid pie made from minced pork and veal cooked in the local white wine, are equally tempting. Perhaps best of all to British eyes is the bacon, its skin blackened from smoke, its taut flesh a rosy pink studded with white fat. This is not bacon which will seep water when you fry it, unlike the travesty of the product which we in Britain put up with. Use it to make that delicacy from the neighbouring county, quiche Lorraine, and compare this quiche to the impostors which we choose to flatter with the name.

Locked within glass cases on the stalls is the solid gold of the market, the foie gras, livers of fattened geese and duck. From the gastronomic (if not the ethical) point of view, a slice of foie gras must surely be the best starter of all, served chilled with nothing but a slice of toast and a glass of spicy Gewürztraminer. But if your purse or your morals won't stretch that far, there is an alternative: cooked chicken livers from the black-footed farmyard chickens can be whipped with cream and butter to make a passable substitute. In any case, don't miss out on the geese altogether – you can buy a whole bird, a half, a quarter or just a leg or breast. Would that our own butchers were so accommodating. And make sure you pick up a jar of goose fat, the vital ingredient for perfect roast potatoes.

The German element in their past is reflected in the Alsatians' liking for salads, served as a starter with charcuterie or goose and duck to add substance. One of the most popular salads consists of grated sausage, cheese and white radish, with fresh horseradish on the side, not a lettuce leaf in sight. Yet several stalls sell nothing but lettuces – autumn varieties of frisée, oakleaf, batavia, escarole and lamb's lettuce, at their best when the weather turns cooler. The locals buy smoked duck's breast for shredding over the salad; a similar effect can be achieved by frying the skin from a duck breast until crispy. English tastes might not enjoy the popular salad of gésiers d'oie, fried goose gizzards served with frisée. Try as a milder alternative a salad of chicken livers fried in butter and tossed with grapes or sultanas.

Around a third of the market is given over to those products of the pig, goose and duck for which Alsace is famous. But there is much more besides. Root vegetables are at their juiciest in autumn, and Strasbourg market offers a splendid choice. Tiny red radishes, for serving as they do in the bierkellers with just a pile of coarse salt, lie alongside long thin white ones, to be grated and covered with a mustardy dressing for crudités. The blackened root of the horseradish, an unusual sight in Britain, is sold here in huge piles; it can be grated and served fresh with cold meats such as presskopf, pressed pig's head, or preserved in a sauce to last through the winter, in the traditions of the Middle Ages. New season's onions, sparkling white with translucent skins, are used for a variety of dishes: just sliced raw in salads; as the vital ingredient of the delicious tarte à l'oignon; as a topping for the tarte flambée or flammekueche which is the evening speciality of many of the weinstube – a flat pizza-like bread spread with onions, bacon and crème fraîche and baked in a bread oven on huge wooden platters. Or, for variety, buy some of the large sweet shallots known because of their shape as 'cuisses de poulet' or chicken thighs.

For colour, try the beetroot, to be used in salads with crème fraîche and dill, or to be served alongside a pot-au-feu, the meat stew for which ready-prepared bundles of vegetables and herbs are sold. Cooked with autumn nuts, beetroot makes a wonderful rich red soup. Bright orange pumpkins are split into quarters, enough for a creamy soup or a vegetable dish, fried in butter. Red cabbages, though these are almost black in colour, are the ideal accompaniment for goose when casseroled with apples and chestnuts. Nearby are bunches of small greeny-white turnips still on the leaf – the ones which have escaped the preserving in salt which produces the 'navets salées', an ancient dish still popular in Alsace. The cardoon, a form of thistle which originates in the Mediterranean and is a rare sight in British markets, is casseroled with beef marrow in Alsace; the celery is sold topped by enormous leaves, for flavouring soups and stews as well as salads. And over the vegetable stalls wafts the sharp smell of fresh coriander and the sweeter one of mint, sold in vast quantities for making Arab mint tea.

A few stalls sport one of the real delicacies of Alsace in autumn – wild mushrooms gathered from the fields of the wine- and hop-growing regions and the woods of the Vosges. Mushrooms sprout here in such enormous quantities that on any walk or drive through the countryside, particularly a day or two after rain, you will see eager bounty hunters peering at the undergrowth, their wicker baskets at the ready. This is no job for the uninformed amateur, for many of the mushroom species are extremely, even deadly, poisonous, and to the untrained eye they are easy to confuse with the edible fungi. The local people have picked mushrooms all their lives, and can usually spot from fifty yards a good cep or chanterelle, horn of plenty or milk cap. But for those in doubt, the local pharmacy provides a danger-spotting service – take in your basket of mushrooms and the local chemist will tell you which are safe to eat. To be safer still, buy in the market – although of course the mushrooms you have picked yourself will always taste better. The huge ceps command a high price, for they are a real delicacy, whether grilled, baked or fried. The same applies to the chanterelles, whose woody fragrance makes them an excellent starter when fried with garlic, shallots and parsley.

Interspersed among the vegetables are small stalls stacked with local cheeses, home-made by the farmers' wives who bring them to the market. Chèvre or goat's cheese is available in varying stages of ripeness, from the soft and watery production of that week to the hardened, lemony crottins. Alongside are sold the new season's nuts, mainly walnuts and hazelnuts, for sprinkling over a grilled goat's cheese salad or, copying the example of the weinstubes, for serving on their own with a glass of the vin nouveau as an apéritif. The pride of Alsatian cheese, though, is the small, round cow's milk cheese known as Munster. Often served with caraways seeds, its pungent smell hangs in the air around the cheese stalls. A delicious autumn starter I enjoyed later in a brasserie overlooking the cathedral was a feuilleté of Munster, cheese, apples and caraway seeds baked in a light, buttery puff pastry.

I could go on. About the fish stalls, piled with a wide range of sea fish brought from afar and, better still, freshwater fish from the nearby rivers – wild brown trout, very fresh for truite au bleu, smoked eel and pike, white fish for the matelote or Alsatian fish stew. The honey-sellers, with their different varieties depending on whether the bees feed in the pine forest, on chestnut trees, or amid flowering meadows. The fruit stalls catch the eye, with their fruits of the forest: bilberries, rosehips, redcurrants, blackberries. And the bread stalls, with their cartwheels of pretzels and spicy kugelhopf cakes, a local delicacy. Strasbourg market, in touch with the seasons, reveals an unexpected range of Alsatian cuisine. Oh, and you can buy excellent choucroute there as well.

BEETROOT AND NUT SOUP

Most beetroot sold in this country has been pre-cooked and pickled in vinegar. No wonder few of us like it. How different is the beetroot that you have bought raw, roasted or boiled in its skin and then gently fried with a little butter and parsley. This beetroot will taste sweeter and juicier, and above all the flavour of vinegar will not predominate. This ruby red soup, a distant relative of the classic Northern European borshch, uses the new season's hazelnuts and walnuts to complement the nutty taste of the root. The spices are regularly used with beetroot in northern India and bring out its flavour to the full.

2 lb (900 g) raw beetroot	1 teaspoon whole fennel
4 oz (115 g) shelled weight	seeds
mixed walnuts and	1 teaspoon whole cumin
hazelnuts or Kentish cobs	seeds
(*the flavour will be much*	$^1/_2$ tablespoon vegetable oil
improved if you use new	$^1/_2$ teaspoon salt
season's 'wet' walnuts and	1 teaspoon white sugar
cobs, which have not had	freshly ground black pepper
their natural oils dried out	2 tablespoons sour cream
of them)	1 tablespoon finely chopped
	parsley

Wash the beetroot, prick the skins several times with a fork, and roast in a medium oven (150°C/300°F/Gas 2) for 2 hours. If you have less time, you can boil the beetroot for 45 minutes, again in their skins, but they will bleed a little. Peel and cut into chunks. Make sure all the bitter outer skin has been removed from the nuts.

Lightly crush the spices. Heat the vegetable oil in a heavy-based casserole and when the oil is very hot fry the spices for a minute or two, until just browned (take care they do not burn). Turn down the heat and add the nuts and beetroot together with the salt and sugar and some black pepper to taste. Fry for another couple of minutes, then pour over 2 pints (1.1 litres) of water. Bring to the boil, cover, and leave for 30 minutes to simmer.

When the beetroot is thoroughly tender, liquidize the soup. Pour into bowls and add a swirl of sour cream and a sprinkling of parsley to each. Serve immediately.

CARROT AND CORIANDER SOUP

Soup is always appreciated as a starter when the weather grows cooler, warming you up and taking the edge off your appetite so that you are ready for a more delicate main course to come. The sharpness of coriander combines well with the sweetness of carrots in this brightly coloured soup, which can be topped with a few toasted cumin seeds for extra flavour and bite.

The quantities given here are generous for 4, as the soup is cheap to make and keeps well.

3 lb (1.5 kg) carrots
1/2 oz (15 g) butter
3 tablespoons fresh
    coriander (*if fresh*
    coriander is not available,
    you can use 3 teaspoons of
    ground seeds, although the
    effect will be different)

3 pints (1.75 litres) water
2 teaspoons cumin seeds
    (*optional*)
salt and pepper
4 fl oz (100 ml) crème
    fraîche or, failing that,
    single cream

There is no need to peel the carrots – simply scrub, top and tail and chop them roughly. Melt the butter in a large, heavy-based saucepan and fry the carrots gently for 5 minutes.

Stir in the chopped coriander, reserving a few leaves for a garnish if you are not using the cumin seeds. Season well, then add the water and bring rapidly to the boil. Cover and simmer actively for 20 minutes. Meanwhile, toast the cumin seeds in a dry frying-pan over a high heat; this should be done very quickly, making sure the seeds do not burn.

Liquidize the soup and adjust the seasoning to taste. The soup takes reheating well, in fact positively benefits from it. Just before serving, stir in the crème fraîche or cream and sprinkle with the toasted cumin seeds or reserved coriander leaves. Serve with plenty of hot granary bread.

CHESTNUT SOUP

Towards the end of the autumn season, imported sweet chestnuts from Italy and Spain appear in the shops. Time for the braziers to be set up on street corners, the scent wafting from their roasting chestnuts often more appetizing than the charred nuts themselves. Cooked at home, chestnuts make an excellent addition to savoury dishes: use them with apples when casseroling red cabbage, as a garnish for a venison casserole, or as a separate sauce for a roast turkey. In northern Europe, chestnuts are made into a substantial soup, given additional richness by the use of game stock.

1 lb (450 g) fresh chestnuts	stock (*the best stocks are*
1 onion	*made from the carcass of a*
1 carrot	*roast bird, or from*
1 oz (25 g) butter	*trimmings of venison or*
1/2 teaspoon ground mace	*hare*)
salt and pepper	1/2 glass amontillado sherry
2 pints (1.1 litres) game	(*optional*)

Wash the chestnuts and score them once across the rounded side. Bring a large pan of water to the boil and boil the chestnuts hard for 15 minutes. Peel them as soon as they are cool enough to handle, making sure you remove the bitter skins.

Roughly chop the onion and carrot and fry gently in the butter. After 5 minutes, add the chestnuts, the mace and plenty of seasoning. Cook for a further minute or two, then add the game stock. Bring to the boil, cover and simmer for about 30 minutes, until the nuts are very soft. Liquidize.

Before serving, stir in the sherry if you are using it (this gives an additional depth to the soup). Serve with toasted bread.

CHICKEN LIVER MOUSSE (FAKE FOIE GRAS)

Chicken liver pâté is often seen as a relic of student dinner parties from the seventies – a cheap, but rather unappetizing dish. This Alsatian recipe for chicken liver mousse is a quite different proposition, a rich, unctuous concoction which deserves its subtitle of fake foie gras.

These quantities will be sufficient for 6 as a starter; the mousse keeps for about a day, longer if topped with a layer of clarified butter.

8 oz (225 g) chicken livers
2 glasses dry white wine
3 oz (85 g) unsalted butter, softened
salt and pepper

pinch each of ground allspice and mace
1 tablespoon ruby port
3 fl oz (75 ml) crème fraîche or half double and half sour cream

Wash the chicken livers and remove any fat or greenish-tinged bits. Bring the wine to the boil and plunge in the livers, making sure they are thoroughly covered. When the wine comes back to the boil, count 3 minutes then remove the livers. Drain and allow to cool.

Mince the livers as finely as possible (this is best done in a food processor). Beat in the softened butter a little at a time, together with seasoning, the spices and the port. Whip the crème fraîche or cream mixture until stiff and gently fold in. Spoon the mousse into small pots and chill well. Serve with toast.

COURGETTE AND PINENUT FLAN

By the time autumn comes along, my enthusiasm for courgettes has somewhat diminished after the delight of early summer. The courgettes are fatter, more watery, coming closer to marrows. Yet they won't go away, especially if you grow them in the garden, so you need to think up new recipes. This Niçois tart is a good way of using larger courgettes and has a delicate, subtle flavour combined with a crunchy texture.

FOR THE FILLING

3 reasonably large
  courgettes, total weight
  approx. 1 lb (450 g)
salt
1/4 of an onion
2 oz (55 g) pinenuts

4 fl oz (100 ml) double
  cream
3 egg-yolks
pinch of grated nutmeg
freshly ground black pepper

FOR THE PASTRY

6 oz (170 g) plain white
  flour
pinch of salt

3 oz (85 g) unsalted butter
2–4 tablespoons chilled
  water

Peel the courgettes and grate coarsely. Salt and leave to degorge for up to an hour.

Make the pastry by sieving the flour with a good pinch of salt. Chop the butter into cubes and blend in with your hands until you have a fine crumble, then add the chilled water. Form the pastry into a ball. Grease a flan dish and push the pastry around it with your hands – there is no need to let it rest or to roll it. Bake blind in a medium hot oven (180°C/350°F/Gas 4) for 15 minutes.

Grate the onion. Bring a pan of water to the boil and blanch the onion for 2 minutes. Squeeze any remaining liquid out of the grated courgettes and mix with the drained, blanched onion. Spread the pinenuts over the base of the flan case. Arrange the courgettes and onion on top. Mix together the cream and egg-yolks and pour over; sprinkle the top with a very little nutmeg and some freshly ground black pepper. Bake in a medium hot oven (180°C/350°F/Gas 4) for a further 15–20 minutes, until the filling rises. Serve hot or warm.

CURRIED CELERIAC SOUP

The celeriac is a relatively unusual vegetable in our markets and shops, and most often makes its way to the table as part of a dish of crudités, grated into a mustardy mayonnaise. It is, however, a good vegetable for cooking – boil chunks and sauté them in butter as a side dish for game. It also makes good soup, as in this lightly curried version. The watercress is not strictly seasonal, but is usually available and adds a peppery bite to the Indian spices, as well as a little colour.

1 large or 2 small celeriac, approx. 1$^1/_2$ lb (675 g)	1 tablespoon sunflower or other oil
3 medium potatoes	$^1/_2$ teaspoon ground cumin
1 onion	$^1/_2$ teaspoon turmeric
1 clove of garlic	$^1/_4$ teaspoon ground ginger
1 inch (2.5 cm) piece of fresh ginger	1 teaspoon ground coriander
1 large mild green chilli	1 teaspoon garam masala
	1 small bunch of watercress

Peel the celeriac and chop roughly; do the same to the potatoes. Finely chop the onion, garlic, fresh ginger and de-seeded chilli. Fry together over a medium heat in a large pan in the oil for 10–15 minutes until lightly browned. Add the spices and fry for a further couple of minutes, then add the chopped celeriac and potato, turning the pieces so that they are coated with the spices. Cover with 2 pints (1.1 litres) of water and bring to the boil, then turn down the heat and simmer for 30 minutes or so. When all the vegetables are soft, liquidize the soup thoroughly.

Remove the watercress leaves from their stalks. Just before serving, check the seasoning of the soup and float a dessertspoon of watercress leaves in each bowl.

GRILLED GOAT'S CHEESE SALAD WITH FRESH WALNUTS

A wide variety of goat's cheeses are now available, both in the markets and in the shops. Many are locally produced, with Wales and the West Country leading the field for Britain in the face of tough competition from abroad, France in particular. Some supermarkets now stock goat's cheeses specifically for cooking, but I find them rather rubbery and prefer to use slices from a soft white freshly made log of goat's cheese. Avoid cheeses with added flavouring ingredients such as herbs or peppers, as these tend to give an overwhelming flavour which spoils the simple balance of the dish. The new season's 'wet' walnuts take a bit of time to crack open, but their juiciness makes the trouble worthwhile. Once this is done, the salad is easy to prepare.

8 oz (225 g) 'wet' walnuts
mixed salad leaves such as
   oakleaf, lamb's lettuce,
   radicchio, rocket, frisée
4 × 1 inch (2.5 cm) thick
   slices of French bread
6 oz (170 g) slice from a

log or bûche de chèvre,
   cut into 4 slices, or
2 small whole goat's
   cheeses, cut in half
walnut oil
lemon juice
freshly ground black pepper

First crack the walnuts and remove them from their shells. Don't worry if the nuts break into pieces. Bring a pan of water to the boil and blanch the nuts for 30 seconds. While they are still warm, slip off the outer skin, which has a bitter taste.

Wash the salad leaves and arrange on serving plates. Pre-heat the grill to its maximum and toast one side of the slices of bread. Lay the cheese on top of the untoasted side and put back under the grill until the cheese begins to bubble.

Meanwhile dress and toss the washed salad leaves in walnut oil and lemon juice. Lay the toast on top of the salad, sprinkle with the walnuts and pepper and serve immediately.

LEEKS VINAIGRETTE

This typically French treatment for leeks is one of my favourite ways to kick off a meal in the autumn. Leeks have a particular sweetness at this time of year, and deserve as plain a treatment as possible. Don't smother them in a sauce béchamel; rather, stew them gently in a little oil and dress while still warm for a light, flavourful and healthy starter.

8 smallish leeks (2 per
person), all of fairly equal
size
1 tablespoon olive oil for
cooking, plus extra virgin
olive oil for dressing

1 teaspoon coriander seeds
2 fresh bayleaves
pinch of sugar
Dijon mustard
white wine vinegar

Chop the green top off the leeks, as well as the root end. Peel off any tough outer skin and make sure the leeks are roughly equal lengths. Make a deep cross in the tip of each and stand, root end down, in a tall jug of water for up to 30 minutes, to allow any dirt trapped in between the layers to float out. Finish cleaning with a quick burst under the cold tap.

Heat the olive oil with the coriander seeds in a lidded pan into which the leeks will just fit. When the seeds pop, add the leeks and bayleaves and fry gently for a minute on either side. Now add half a wineglass of water and cover. Cook for 10 minutes or so until the leeks are tender but not falling apart.

Make a vinaigrette with a pinch of sugar, a teaspoon of mustard (far less if you are using fierce English mustard rather than the mild Dijon variety), and 1 part white wine vinegar to 4 parts olive oil. When the leeks are ready, brush off the coriander seeds, season lightly and dress immediately. The leeks can be served warm, which seems most appropriate in autumn, or cool (but not straight from the fridge).

ONION TART

In Alsace, onion tart is the traditional precursor to choucroute. Although many would find such a meal daunting in its entirety, an onion tart does make a splendid starter before a light main dish, as well as being a meal in itself when served with salad at lunchtime or for a simple supper. The sweetness of the onions in their light creamy filling and the buttery flakiness of the pastry are a delicious combination.

FOR THE PASTRY

6 oz (170 g) plain white
flour
pinch of salt

3 oz (85 g) unsalted butter
1 egg
2–3 tablespoons iced water

FOR THE FILLING

1¹/₂ lb (675 g) sweet white
onions
2 oz (55 g) unsalted butter
2 egg-yolks

6 fl oz (175 ml) double
cream
salt and pepper
pinch of grated nutmeg

To make the pastry, first sieve the flour with a good pinch of salt. Cut the butter into cubes and crumble into the flour with your fingers. Add the beaten egg and about 2 tablespoons of iced water, sufficient to make a dough. Roll the pastry into a ball, wrap in clingfilm, and leave in a cool place for about an hour.

Peel the onions and chop into very fine rings, discarding the central core. Melt the butter in a heavy pan and gently stew the onions until they are very soft. They should not brown, just slowly melt in the butter. This should take 30–40 minutes in all – stir the onions from time to time.

Pre-heat the oven to medium hot (180°C/350°F/Gas 4). Roll the pastry out as thinly as possible and lay in an 8–10 inch (20–25 cm) buttered quiche dish. Bake blind for 10 minutes.

Lay the stewed onions across the base of the pastry case. Mix together the egg-yolks and cream and season with salt, pepper and the nutmeg. Pour this mixture over the onions and cook for 20–30 minutes in a medium hot oven (180°C/350°F/Gas 4) until the filling rises up and just browns on top. An onion tart will keep, but is at its best when served straight from the oven.

PIGEON SALAD

British wild wood-pigeons have some way to go before they can compete with the succulent tenderness of their farm-reared cousins in France or Italy. Nevertheless, young wood-pigeons can be delicious when quickly roasted. Alternatively, marinate and then quickly grill the breasts, leaving the carcass and legs for a soup. 1 wood-pigeon will stretch between 2 for a light starter, but for a lunch dish you would probably want 2 breasts per person. The use of cinnamon with pigeon is traditional in Moroccan cuisine, as in their pigeon pie, pastilla.

2 wood pigeons

FOR THE MARINADE

1 tablespoon good-quality red wine vinegar	2 tablespoons olive oil 3 or 4 sticks of cinnamon

FOR THE SALAD

1 frisée lettuce	only 4 oz (115 g) of wild
1 lemon	mushrooms)
walnut oil	1 clove garlic
8 oz (225 g) brown cap or other good mushrooms (*chanterelles would be a special treat – due to their intense flavour you need*	1 tablespoon olive oil 1 tablespoon chopped fresh parsley ground cinnamon freshly ground black pepper

First remove the breasts from the birds. With a sharp knife, make an incision down either side of the breastbone and cut away the flesh of the legs where they join the body. With your fingers carefully remove the breasts. Mix together the marinade ingredients and leave the breasts to rest for at least an hour in the marinade turning once.

Wash the lighter leaves of the frisée, discarding the dark green bitter outside leaves. Arrange on 4 separate plates. Prepare a dressing of 1 part lemon juice to 3 parts walnut oil.

Pre-heat the grill to maximum. Lift the pigeon breasts from the marinade, shaking off any excess liquid, and grill quickly, for approximately 5 minutes on each side, or less if you like the breast very pink. Allow to rest for 5 minutes before carving.

Meanwhile, wipe the mushrooms clean and slice thickly. Chop the garlic very finely. Sauté the mushrooms with the garlic in the olive oil until soft. Stir in the parsley, season and keep warm.

When the pigeon is cooked, carve each breast into 2 or 3 slices. Toss the lettuce in the dressing, pile the mushrooms on top and lay over the pigeon breasts. Dust with ground cinnamon and black pepper and serve.

POACHED QUAILS' EGG SALAD

Quails' eggs are now readily available in the shops, a by-product of the increase in the farming of quails. I have always found them rather boring when served hard-boiled with the inevitable celery salt and cayenne pepper but, then, I am not very fond of hard-boiled eggs, full stop. Poached quails' eggs, however, have always seemed to me to be rather indulgent, perhaps because of the high ratio of yolk to white. The poaching process is a little fiddly but is quick to execute once you have got the hang of it – practise before serving this dish at a dinner party. The result is a good warm salad for a first course.

Dijon mustard	6 oz (170 g) smoked streaky
pinch of sugar	bacon, preferably in one
white wine vinegar	or two thick slices
extra virgin olive oil for	2 slices of dry white bread
dressing and ordinary	1 dozen quails' eggs
olive oil for cooking	cayenne pepper
1 oakleaf lettuce	celery salt

Bring a large pan of water with a few drops of vinegar to the boil. Make a dressing with a good teaspoon of mustard, a pinch of sugar and 1 part vinegar to 4 parts extra-virgin olive oil. Wash and pick over the lettuce and arrange on serving plates. Remove the rind from the bacon and chop into small chunks; take the crusts from the bread and cut into bite-sized pieces. Fry the bacon in a little oil until crispy; keep warm while you fry the bread into croûtons in the bacon fat.

To poach the eggs, break them carefully one at a time and slip into the fast-boiling water. Immediately use 2 spoons to mould the free-floating white around the yolk; then slip in the next egg. By the time you have moulded this one, the first egg will be ready. Lift out with a slotted spoon and continue the process until all 12 eggs are poached.

Sprinkle the bacon and croûtons over the lettuce, gently lay 3 eggs on each plate and pour on the dressing. Sprinkle cayenne pepper and celery salt over the eggs and serve immediately.

PUMPKIN SOUP

There is a widespread belief in Britain that pumpkins deserve to have eyes hollowed out of them to make lanterns for Hallowe'en, for they are good for little else. The Italians know better, using pumpkin to stuff ravioli and as a vegetable, stewed in butter. Pumpkin flesh provides the base for this delicate creamy soup, which is an elegant starter.

2 lb (900 g) peeled pumpkin flesh (*preferably from 1 small whole pumpkin rather than a slice from a larger one, as the smaller pumpkins are sweeter*)
1 oz (25 g) butter
1 teaspoon grated fresh ginger
$^1/_4$ teaspoon turmeric
$^1/_4$ teaspoon grated nutmeg
1 teaspoon sugar
salt and freshly ground black pepper
$1^1/_2$ pints (850 ml) full-cream milk
$^1/_2$ pint (300 ml) water
4 fl oz (100 ml) single cream

Make sure all the stringy strands which attach the seeds have been stripped away from the core of the peeled pumpkin. Chop the flesh roughly. Melt the butter in a heavy-based pan and fry the ginger for a minute before adding the pumpkin, spices, sugar and seasoning. Fry for 10 minutes until soft, then add the milk and water. Bring to the boil, making sure the milk doesn't boil over, and simmer for 20 minutes or until the pumpkin is completely soft. Liquidize, check the seasoning and reheat with the cream. Serve topped with freshly ground black pepper.

QUICHE LORRAINE

The quiche on sale in many British shops and restaurants is nothing more than a travesty of the real thing. A quiche should be a light, buttery tart, its filling gently risen, light and airy. Some cooks include cheese in their quiche Lorraine, but I have never experienced this in a quiche served in Lorraine itself. This version uses nothing more than good bacon, eggs and cream.

FOR THE PASTRY

6 oz (170 g) plain white flour

3 oz (85 g) unsalted butter

1 egg

2–3 tablespoons iced water

FOR THE FILLING

4 oz (115 g) thick cut smoked streaky bacon

3 egg-yolks plus 1 whole egg

1/2 pint (300 ml) double cream

freshly ground black pepper

To make the pastry, first sieve the flour with a good pinch of salt. Cut the butter into cubes and crumble into the flour with your fingers. Add the beaten egg and about 2 tablespoons of cold water, sufficient to make a dough. Roll the pastry into a ball, wrap in foil, and leave in a cool place for about an hour.

Pre-heat the oven to medium hot (180°C/350°F/Gas 4). Roll the pastry out very thinly and lay in a buttered quiche dish. Bake blind for 10 minutes.

Chop the bacon into small cubes or lardons and fry gently for a minute or two until the fat runs. Remove the bacon from the fat. Beat the egg and egg-yolks together and add the cream. Season well with freshly ground black pepper.

All the preparation to this stage can be carried out in advance. However, the final cooking should be left until 30 minutes before you want to serve the quiche, which should be carried straight from oven to table.

Lay the pieces of bacon on the pastry base and pour over the egg and cream mixture. Bake for 20–30 minutes in a medium hot oven (180°C/ 350°F/Gas 4) until the filling rises up and browns on top. Serve immediately, before the filling falls back.

MUSHROOMS – WILD AND FIELD

Mushroom-hunting is almost a national sport in France and Italy, but has yet to catch on in Britain. There are plenty of wild mushrooms around in autumn and they are well worth looking out for. Make sure you are armed with a good guide to those which are edible and those which are dangerous. A picture book is not enough: pictures can often be confusing, and you should rely on thorough descriptions of appearance and habitat. Better still, take an experienced mushroom-gatherer with you – my French sister-in-law has taught me far more than any book.

My favourite wild mushroom is the cep or *Boletus edulis*, which has the added advantage that it is easy to recognize. Ceps are now available, at a price, in good markets and from specialized stores, and Italian stores stock the dried variety (porcini in Italian) for soups and stews. Other good wild mushrooms are chanterelles, parasol mushrooms, horns of plenty (or more threateningly in French, trompettes de mort), and milk caps.

If you get a good haul of wild mushrooms, try not to wash them but simply wipe them clean with a damp cloth. Cut out any rotten pieces where insects have had a bite, and slice the mushrooms up, including the stalks. Or, if you have some prize ceps, leave them whole. You can grill or roast whole mushrooms with a little olive oil, or fry sliced ones with shallot, garlic and parsley (the best way is to fry the mushrooms twice, once in a little vegetable oil to release their juices, then again in butter with the garlic, etc.)

If you have only a few wild mushrooms, try making a risotto to eke them out, where the mushroom juices will mingle perfectly with the rice, or stir the cooked mushrooms into some fresh tagliatelle, boiled and buttered. If you cannot find or buy wild mushrooms, then you can still buy some excellent field mushrooms in the market. Look out for large caps with shaggy brown skins, preferably with their stalks still attached. One of my favourite ways of cooking this type of mushroom is to stuff and then bake them.

STUFFED FIELD MUSHROOMS

8 large field mushrooms
3 shallots
1 clove of garlic
3 tablespoons extra virgin
    olive oil
3 oz (85 g) fresh
    breadcrumbs
3 slices of Parma or other

good quality raw ham,
    such as the Spanish jamon
    serrano or the French
    jambon de Bayonne
1 tablespoon very finely
    chopped parsley
salt and freshly ground
    black pepper

Remove the stalks from the mushrooms. Wipe the caps free of all dirt with a damp cloth, and place in a lightly oiled baking dish. Pre-heat the oven to hot (200°C/400°F/Gas 6).

Clean the mushroom stalks and chop finely. Chop the shallots and garlic and cook gently in 1 tablespoon of the olive oil until translucent but not browned – about 5 minutes. Then add the chopped mushrooms and cook for another couple of minutes, until the mushrooms start to soften. Stir in 2 oz (55 g) of the breadcrumbs, the ham chopped into little pieces (including the fat) and the parsley. Season well. Spoon this mixture into the mushroom caps, scatter with the remaining breadcrumbs and dribble over the remaining olive oil. Bake for 15–20 minutes, until the mushroom caps are tender, and serve piping hot.

MUSHROOM AND BACON SALAD

This salad can be made with a variety of salad leaves, but I like it best with lamb's lettuce, otherwise known as corn lettuce or mâche. If you can get pleurottes or chanterelles, this will be a particular treat; if not, use field mushrooms. The mushrooms are first fried to give off their liquid, the bacon is then added to the pan to lend a salty, smoky flavour, and the whole is stirred while still hot into the leaves before dressing with balsamic vinegar and olive oil.

8 oz (225 g) field
mushrooms or 4 oz
(115 g) wild mushrooms
(*their stronger flavour and
less watery consistency
means that you need less,
but if you have a
sufficiency then the more
the better*)
4 oz (115 g) lamb's lettuce
2 thick slices of smoked

bacon or pancetta
2 tablespoons plain olive oil
2 thick slices of white
country bread, crusts
removed
1 clove of garlic
1 handful of fresh chives
(*optional*)
freshly ground black pepper
extra virgin olive oil
balsamic vinegar

Wash the mushrooms to remove any grit clinging to them and pat dry (if you have wild mushrooms, carefully wipe them clean). Wash the lamb's lettuce, separating each cluster of leaves from the roots. Chop the bacon or pancetta into chunks. Heat 1 tablespoon of the plain olive oil in a heavy-based frying-pan over a medium flame and throw in the mushrooms. Fry for just a few minutes if using wild mushrooms, a little longer for field mushrooms. Drain the resulting liquid and keep for some other use; put the mushrooms in a warm place. Turn down the heat, add the remaining olive oil to the pan, and put in the bacon or pancetta and the bread cut into bite-sized pieces.

While this is frying (for about 5 minutes) finely chop the garlic and chives and arrange the lamb's lettuce in a salad bowl. Just before serving add the garlic and chives to the pan together with the mushrooms and fry for a further minute, stirring well. Season with freshly ground black pepper and pour the contents of the pan over the lamb's lettuce; toss and serve immediately. For the dressing, I like to copy the Italians and put extra virgin olive oil and balsamic vinegar on the table for the guests to help themselves, unless you have really good balsamic vinegar, worth its weight in gold, in which case you may well wish to protect it from your guests and dress the salad in advance.

VINE-LEAVES STUFFED WITH NUTS

All over the Middle East, Turkey, Greece and North Africa, vine-leaves are stuffed with a variety of savoury mixtures to make an appetizing starter. Today you can buy ready stuffed vine-leaves in Britain, but the pleasure, and the taste, will be far greater if you make them yourself. One of my favourite fillings is a mixture of pistachio nuts and wild rice, producing an elegant autumn dish, to be served cold as a starter.

To make 20 individual stuffed vine-leaves

1 packet vine-leaves preserved in brine, containing at least 25 leaves (*or the same number of fresh ones, if you have them*)

3 oz (85 g) long-grain rice

3 oz (85 g) wild rice (*some supermarkets now sell ready-mixed rices*)

1/2 teaspoon turmeric

1 teaspoon ground cinnamon

1 teaspoon ground cumin

1 teaspoon ground coriander

1/2 teaspoon salt

4 oz (115 g) whole, uncooked pistachio nuts

2 lemons

4 tablespoons olive oil

1 teaspoon dried mint

If you are using preserved vine-leaves, soak them for 30 minutes in tepid water, changing the water half-way through the soaking. If you are lucky enough to have fresh leaves, blanch them for 2 minutes in lightly salted water.

Rinse the rice very thoroughly to rid it of starch and combine it in a bowl with the spices and the salt. Chop the pistachios roughly and add them to the mixture.

To fill each vine-leaf, lay it on the work surface vein side up. Spoon a little of the rice and nut mixture on to the centre of the leaf, from which the veins spread out. Fold over the base, fold in each side so that you have a width of approximately 1 1/2 inches (3.5 cm), and then roll up the leaf. Set aside and repeat the process until you have sufficient, reserving about 5 of the leaves.

Line a heavy-based pan with the reserved leaves (this will stop the stuffed vine-leaves from sticking). Lay the stuffed leaves across the base of the dish – they should just fit. Pour over the juice of the lemons, the olive oil, the dried mint and sufficient water to just cover. Put on the lid and bring to a simmer over a gentle flame – the water should barely bubble. Cook for 1 hour, until the rice is tender. Allow the stuffed vine-leaves to cool in the liquid before carefully removing them. Serve just tepid or cool.

FISH

For many people fish is a quintessentially summer dish. True, cooler autumn days bring a desire for heartier dishes, powerful flavours and filling food. Summer's lightly poached cutlets of salmon do not seem so attractive now. But what about seafood risotto or a whole fish baked with Indian spices, West Indian shellfish curries or herring grilled with a crispy mustard crust? Colder weather may mean you cook fish in different ways – it shouldn't mean you stop eating it.

The choice of fish available in the autumn months is especially plentiful and varied. As the seas around the British Isles cool, locally caught fish become firmer, their flesh whiter. The size of the catch increases, bringing a wider choice and lower prices. Some varieties of fish appear only in autumn, like the small blue shark landed off the Cornish coast.

The real treat of autumn is our native shellfish. Britain's shores are particularly rich in molluscs, which for centuries were the everyday food of the poor. We all know the stories of poor Londoners in the eighteenth century pleading for something other than oysters. Somewhere along the line, however, many of us have lost the taste for these simple and delicious foods, so that nowadays much of our shellfish is exported.

The Belgian passion for mussels is at least partially fed by the fruits of the sea from the Pays des Galles – Wales. Colchester oysters are a delicacy in France, where they are double the price of cheaper local varieties – about 40 francs a dozen. The few Colchester oysters that remain this side of the Channel retail in quite another price stratosphere. We keep more of our cockles, but, sadly, so that we can murder them in malt vinegar. Where I live in the East End of London, vinegared cockles, mussels and whelks are still popular for Sunday lunch, but you rarely see a pile of live shellfish.

All of which is gloomy news, for shellfish makes ideal autumn food. On a bright September day, oysters served with nothing more than a squeeze of lemon and a glass of white wine are the perfect starter. When the sky clouds over and the rain comes down, a steaming pile of mussels floating in their fragrant broth is a heartening sight. Cockles quickly cooked in the shell until they open are quite different from the vinegared variety, juicier and far fuller in flavour. So follow the old adage, and when the R reappears in the month look out for shellfish. There are signs that it is making a comeback: some supermarket chains now stock mussels, for example. Native oysters are still too expensive, but prices are coming down; the more we eat, the cheaper they will become. And there are markets where shellfish is available in abundance, as I found out when I went on a September visit to Swansea in South Wales.

Swansea – Market for the Gower Peninsula

The approach to Swansea market is not at all encouraging. You turn off a pedestrianized row of shops known as Oxford Street, which has about as much charm as its namesake in London, into a small alleyway lined with rather ordinary vegetable stalls. Entering the market itself, which has stood on the same site since 1830, you are greeted by a motley array of stalls featuring children's toys, plastic washing-up bowls, cheap clothing, not a scrap of food in sight. Swansea may have been for centuries the market town for the Gower peninsula and its backdrop of fertile valleys, but at first sight it seems unlikely that the tradition has been maintained. Sniff the air enclosed in this covered site, however, and there is a rewarding hint of things to come. The market smells good. There is a whiff of fish, overlaid by a salty tang. Push forward into the centre of the market and you will see the source of this enticing smell – a ring of cockle stalls.

Swansea lies on the edge of one of the most beautiful stretches of coastline in the British Isles. The Gower peninsula is an area of outstanding natural beauty encircled by beaches. On the north side of the peninsula, along the Burry estuary, lie the largest cockle beds in Britain. Gower cockles – and other shellfish besides – find their way all over the country and further afield, but many are still sold in Swansea market as they have been since the Middle Ages.

The cockle stalls today are encased in a protective veneer of glass, at the recent request of the Health and Safety Executive. The women serving no longer wear the Gower costume of apron, plaid shawl, striped dress and cockle bonnet, unless they are posing for a publicity photograph. The cockles are now gathered in trailers pulled by Landrovers or tractors, instead of sturdy Welsh cobs. But this is still a traditional business. Each of the six stalls in the centre of the market is a family-owned business, handed down through generations. The cockle-gatherers go out with the tide, and no more efficient way of gathering the cockles has been found than the old back-breaking method of collecting them by hand. The 'factories' in which the cockles are processed are small affairs, employing a handful of people each, usually members of the family. And the cockles sold in the market are no tourist gimmick: they are regular food for the local people.

Processed cockles, prised from their shells by steaming or boiling at the factories, are the most popular buy. In Swansea they are fortunately sold with vinegar on the side rather than doused in it. But as I was told by the almost inevitably named Mrs Williams, standing beneath the faded picture of her mother-in-law on a donkey laden with wicker baskets of cockles, 'We prefer to eat them in the shell.' She steams them in a very little water; I would substitute white wine and throw in some garlic, parsley and shredded leek. Either way, the cockles from the Gower peninsula are delicious. Available all year round, they are at their best in the autumn, when Swansea council holds a cockle festival to celebrate the town's good fortune.

The cockle stalls sell other seafood, of course. Best are the local mussels, small and sweet and fresh enough to be eaten raw, although I prefer to steam them in the same way as the cockles. Laverbread, too, is on offer, ready boiled and rolled in oatmeal to make it crisper when fried. Although prepared locally at the cockle factories, most of this seaweed is brought down from Scotland or across from Ireland, Gower supplies of *Porphyra umbilicalis*, as it is less commonly known, having run short. Laverbread is popular for breakfast with fried bacon, or stirred into fried cockles; it also makes a fine sauce for a roast leg of Welsh lamb.

There is much to Swansea market besides the cockle stalls, for these are not the only family-run affairs. Nearby are the pork butchers, many of whom come to market only on Fridays and Saturdays, spending the rest of the week at their real business of farming. They offer home-cured bacon, thick-sliced, the lean a soft pink surrounded by yellow fat, perfect for flavouring vegetables. This is meat from properly brought up pigs, slaughtered locally, the meat hung before curing, producing bacon that won't reduce to water when sizzled in the pan. Then there are the lamb butchers, with whole halves of lamb hanging in their windows, besides legs properly encased in fat, which will be succulent when roasted, the fat drained away. Smaller stalls offer eggs, boiled beetroot, home-made Welsh scones, a few tomatoes, a little parsley. As in France, this is mostly the produce of the smallholding. A cheese stall sells fine Welsh cheeses, such as the powerful Llanboidy. And, curiously enough, there are delicious locally made pecorino and ricotta, produced by an Italian who has chosen to settle in the Welsh hills. The vegetable stalls are limited in choice but high in quality, the stallholders mostly selling their own produce – tight cabbages, perfect for casseroling with bacon, tiny yellow pickling onions, many varieties of potato, bright green watercress. But there wasn't a leek in sight; they appear later in the season.

So far, everything I had seen came from the Gower peninsula and the hills beyond – just as it should be in a local market. But there is one area in which Swansea market draws its supplies from far and wide and that is in the fish department. Swansea still has a port and a small fishing fleet, which supplies some of the stock for the market's four fish stalls. But each offered such a quantity and variety of fish that I knew they must also buy from further afield.

One stall in particular boasted a display almost to rival that of Harrods. Its owner, Christian Phelps, spends his early mornings on the telephone to wholesalers all over the country (probably including some of the mobile-phone-toting buyers I had seen at Brixham). His efforts produce a remarkable array of fish. On the day of my visit it included pink and grey striped tiger prawns from Madagascar, each one weighing a quarter of a pound; thick slices of blue-skinned shark from Cornwall; tiny calamari, shipped from California, alongside larger local squid; and a whole conger eel, its teeth bared menacingly, confronting an equally vicious-looking hake. There was a selection of colourful fish for steaming or baking with Oriental spices – red snapper, golden thread, black-banded and sea bream, red gurnard. The flat fish included tiny flounders and lemon sole, plaice and megrim. Cod was available fresh, salted or oak-smoked. And, of course, there were shellfish: oysters of different sizes, mussels, crabs and prawns. Only the cockles were missing – but then Christian wouldn't compete with the cockle families.

Christian supplies a number of local restaurants, but his main customers are the people of Swansea. That he, and the three other stalls in the market, are able to offer such an excellent selection of fish speaks well of his customers' eating habits. The people of Swansea haven't so much discovered the pleasure of eating fresh fish, they have simply never abandoned it.

At the time of going to press, the traditional way of life of the cockle families is threatened by EC regulations. Cockles can no longer be sold in the shell on the market and purification requirements mean that many of the families' individual factories are closing down, to be replaced by one large plant. The future of the Penclawdd cockle industry looks grim.

BAKED MUSSELS ON THE SHELL

There is a wide variety of mussels available in the autumn months. I prefer the small sweet British and French mussels steamed open and served in their own juices or perhaps with a little wine. The larger, fleshier Spanish mussels, on the other hand, need a little more treatment to bring out their flavour. I grill them with spicy tomato and a breadcrumb topping before serving on the half shell.

24 large Spanish mussels
4 plum tomatoes
4 shallots
2 cloves of garlic
1 dried red chilli
3 tablespoons extra virgin
   olive oil
1 teaspoon tomato purée
salt and freshly ground
   black pepper

$^1/_2$ teaspoon dried oregano
   (*dried is fine, although of*
   course the fresh herb is
   better – in which case you
   will need to use double the
   quantity)
1 oz (25 g) dry white
   breadcrumbs

Let the mussels soak for at least an hour in some salted water, covered with a cloth – they will clean themselves, removing much of the grit trapped in their shells. To speed the process up, give them a handful of oatmeal on which to feed.

When the mussels have soaked, scrub them under running water, making sure you scrape off any small barnacles clinging to their shells. Discard any mussels which have broken shells, or which do not close when you tap the shell. Debeard the mussels by pulling out the small strings sticking out of one side of the shell. Place each prepared mussel in a clean bowl of cold water.

To make the sauce, peel and de-seed the tomatoes and chop finely. Chop the shallots, garlic and chilli, and gently fry them in half the olive oil until soft but not brown – about 5 minutes. Add the tomato purée and let it take colour before adding the tomatoes to the pan. Season and add the oregano. Turn down the heat, add a tablespoon of water and cook, covered, for 20 minutes until the tomatoes are very soft.

Open the mussels by putting in a covered pan over a high heat; after 3 or 4 minutes all the mussels should have opened. Discard any that don't. Remove the half of the shell to which the mussel has not adhered and place the other half on the grill pan. Spoon a little of the hot sauce into each shell, covering the mussel. Season the breadcrumbs and sprinkle on top. Dribble over the remaining olive oil.

Pre-heat the grill to three-quarters of its maximum temperature. Place the mussels under the grill and cook for 4–5 minutes, until the breadcrumb topping is nicely browned. Serve immediately.

ORIENTAL BAKED FISH

A whole fish baked with Oriental spices is easy to cook and gives off a powerful fragrance when brought to the table. I like to use a combination of chilli, garlic, ginger, coriander and lemon grass and simply bake the fish in foil surrounded by the flavouring ingredients, which ensures that you don't lose any of the delicious juices.

2 inch (5 cm) piece of fresh ginger
4 cloves of garlic
2 large green chillies
2 fish, each approx. 1–1¹/₂ lb (450–675 g) (*fish which respond well to this sort of treatment include red snapper, sea bream and grey mullet*)
salt and pepper
¹/₂ tablespoon sunflower or peanut oil
2 limes
4 sticks of lemon grass
2 tablespoons chopped fresh coriander

Peel the ginger and crush the garlic cloves. De-seed the chillies and finely chop with the garlic and ginger. Clean the fish if the fishmonger has not already done so, and make several slashes across the skin on each side, right down to the bone. Rub plenty of salt and pepper into the flesh of each fish. Pre-heat the oven to hot (200°C/400°F/Gas 6).

When you are ready to cook, heat the oil in a frying-pan. Fry the garlic, chilli and ginger briefly (for a minute or two). Chop each lime into 4 slices and place in the cavity of each fish together with half the fried garlic, chilli and ginger. Take 2 pieces of foil large enough to wrap the fish in and lay 2 sticks of lemon grass on each. Sprinkle over half the coriander and put the fish on top. Cover each fish with the remaining coriander and the rest of the garlic-chilli-ginger mixture. Fold up the foil parcel. Bake in the oven for 20–30 minutes, depending on the size of the fish – it is ready when the flesh lifts easily off the bone. I like to open the fish parcels at the table, allowing everyone to catch a whiff of the spicy scents. Serve with boiled rice and some stir-fried vegetables.

BRILL COOKED IN CIDER

The brill is a flat fish related to the turbot and is almost the turbot's equal in flavour, having a delicate yet delicious taste. In Normandy a whole brill is often cooked in the oven in cider and cream with mushrooms, producing a tender fish course with a rich sauce and a hint of apples.

> 1 whole brill, approx. 2^1/$_2$– 3 lb (1.25–1.5 kg)
> 8 oz (225 g) mushrooms (button mushrooms are best)
> 4 shallots
> 1^1/$_2$ oz (45 g) butter
> 1 pint (575 ml) dry cider
>
> (*a traditional, non-carbonated cider is best – try a French cider or a West country scrumpy*)
> 4 oz (115 g) double cream
> 2 oz (55 g) stale white breadcrumbs

Ask the fishmonger to scale and gut the brill. At home, wash the fish and carefully pat dry. Clean the mushrooms – leave button mushrooms whole, otherwise slice them. Chop the shallots finely. Melt half the butter and gently fry the shallots for a few minutes, making sure they don't brown; when they are soft, add the mushrooms. Season well, cover and cook for 5 minutes.

Pre-heat the oven to medium (150°C/300°F/Gas 2). With the remaining butter, grease a dish large enough to take the whole fish. Lay half the cooked mushrooms and shallots on the base of the dish and put the brill on top. Pour over the cider, mix the cream into the remaining shallots and mushrooms and arrange over the top of the fish. Sprinkle over the breadcrumbs.

Cook uncovered in the oven for 25–30 minutes depending on the size of the fish. It is ready when the flesh lifts easily off the bone. Serve this rich dish with nothing more than plain boiled potatoes.

CONGER EEL SOUP

The conger eel is caught in large quantities off British shores but has yet to become a popular element of the British diet. Except, that is, in the Channel Islands, where conger eel soup made with cabbage and marigold petals is a traditional dish. My own version of conger soup is rather more Mediterranean in flavour.

1 onion	1 piece of conger eel tail,
2 cloves of garlic	weighing about 2 lb
1 small dried red chilli	(900 g), chopped into
1 tablespoon plain olive oil	3 or 4 pieces
1 lb (450 g) plum tomatoes	2 glasses dry white wine
and 1 teaspoon tomato	3 egg-yolks
purée or a 14 oz (400 g)	2 tablespoons extra virgin
tin plum tomatoes	olive oil

Finely chop the onion, garlic and chilli. In a large pan, fry all together over a low heat in the plain olive oil for 10 minutes, until the onion is softened. Meanwhile peel and de-seed the tomatoes if using fresh ones, and stir the tomato purée into the pan. Follow with the chopped fresh or tinned tomatoes and fry the whole for 5 minutes. Now add the pieces of conger eel. Cook for 2 minutes on either side and then pour over the wine. Allow to bubble before adding 2 pints (1.1 litres) of cold water. Season, bring to the boil and simmer for 45 minutes.

Push the contents of the pan through a fine sieve, making sure you press down well on the pieces of conger to ensure that the essence of the fish passes through to the broth. Leave to cool for 10 minutes. Stir the yolks into the broth and put back on the heat, stirring continually until the soup is thoroughly hot and slightly thickened; take care not to allow it to boil. Check the seasoning, take off the heat and stir in the extra virgin olive oil before serving piping hot with plenty of bread.

FRIED COCKLES WITH BACON AND LAVERBREAD

This very simple Welsh dish makes an excellent brunch or light lunch. It is best made with cockles which have not been preserved in vinegar, as the cockle ladies in Swansea market understand; but at a pinch you can use the vinegared variety, as long as you soak them well beforehand. The seaweed laverbread nowadays mostly comes from Scotland and Ireland rather than Wales. If you can't find fresh laverbread, it is available in tins from good delicatessens.

8 rashers of good-quality unsmoked bacon
1 lb (450 g) shelled cockles
4 oz (115 g) laverbread
4 slices of bread
1 tablespoon chopped fresh parsley
pepper
$^1/_2$ a lemon

Chop the bacon into small pieces and fry until the fat runs. Add the cockles and fry for another few minutes. Stir in the laverbread and heat through. Meanwhile, toast the bread. Stir the parsley into the cockle mixture, season with pepper and lemon juice, pile on to the toast and serve immediately.

GOANESE GREY MULLET

The grey mullet is a firm-fleshed fish which takes well to strong flavours. The fish is widely available in Britain in the autumn months, and can be simply grilled or baked as well as treated more exotically. In Goa, the former Portuguese colony in Southern India, grey mullet is rubbed with coconut milk, ginger and garlic and stuffed with a spicy herb mixture before grilling, to allow the fish to absorb the flavours.

- 1 clove of garlic
- 1 inch (2.5 cm) piece of fresh ginger
- 4 tablespoons unsweetened coconut milk (*available in tins from Indian and West Indian stores*)
- 2 grey mullet, each approx. 1–1¼ lb (450–550 g)

- 1 Spanish onion
- 1 tablespoon vegetable oil
- 2 teaspoons ground cumin
- 1 teaspoon turmeric
- 2 tablespoons chopped fresh coriander
- 1 lime

Grind the garlic and the ginger to a paste together with the coconut milk (this can be done in a food processor or a pestle and mortar). Wash and gut the fish and make several deep slashes across the flesh on either side, down to the bone. Smear the paste all over the fish, making sure some gets down into the slashes. Leave to marinate for 30 minutes.

Chop the onion into fine half rings and fry in the vegetable oil for 15–20 minutes, until well browned. Add the cumin and turmeric and fry for another few minutes before stirring in the coriander. Take off the heat.

Pre-heat the grill to medium hot (180°C/350°F). Sear the fish in the frying-pan, browning it on both sides. Stuff with the onion and coriander mixture and grill for 10 minutes on each side, until the flesh comes easily away from the bone. Serve with wedges of lime.

GRILLED MACKEREL IN VINEGAR WITH DAMSON AND OKRA CURRY

Mackerel offer both good value and quality towards the end of autumn, especially when very fresh – look for bright-eyed fish with gleaming stripes. The fattiness and strong flavour of mackerel means that the fish takes well to sharp and fruity flavours, hence the traditional serving of mackerel with gooseberry sauce. There are also many ancient recipes for pickled mackerel, the fish preserved in vinegar. I combine these ideas when serving mackerel by dressing the hot grilled fish with vinegar and surrounding it with a curry of damson and okra, a wonderful contrast to the fish itself in taste, texture and colour.

You can of course serve the mackerel without the curry or vice versa.

FOR THE CURRY

8 oz (225 g) damsons	1 teaspoon ground cumin
1 lb (450 g) okra	1 teaspoon ground
8 oz (225 g) tomatoes	coriander
2 inch (5 cm) piece of fresh	$1/2$ teaspoon freshly ground
ginger	black pepper
3 cloves of garlic	1 teaspoon sugar
2 small green chillies	flat-leaved parsley, to
1 tablespoon sunflower oil	garnish
1 teaspoon garam masala	$1/2$ a lime

FOR THE FISH

2 large or 4 small mackerel	8 tablespoons white wine
salt and black pepper	vinegar
1 lime	1 tablespoon chopped fresh
8 shallots	parsley

Make the curry first. Wash the damsons thoroughly, halve and remove the stones. Top and tail the washed okra. Peel the tomatoes and chop.

Finely chop the peeled ginger and garlic and the de-seeded chillies, then heat the oil and fry them over a medium heat for 5 minutes, stirring. Add the spices to the pan and fry for a further minute before adding the okra and the chopped tomatoes, together with the sugar (if the damsons are very tart, you may like to add a little more). After another minute or two add the damsons; pour over a glass of water, turn down to a low heat, cover and leave for 25 minutes. Stir in the parsley and lime juice.

Meanwhile cook the fish. Turn the grill up to very hot and rub the skin of the fish with salt and pepper. Put a couple of slices of lime in the cavity of each fish. Grill on each side for about 10 minutes, depending on the size of the fish – the flesh should come easily away from the bone, which you can test with a fork. The skin will brown and bubble up; this is intentional.

Finely chop the shallots and gently heat with the vinegar. When the liquid is hot but not boiling, take off the heat and sprinkle over the chopped parsley as a garnish.

When the fish are done, peel off the blackened skin. Arrange on a serving plate and pour over the hot vinegar and shallots; leave in a warm place for 10 minutes to infuse. Check the curry for seasoning – if it is too tart, add a little more sugar. Serve the mackerel surrounded by the purple curry and with a dish of plain boiled rice.

GRILLED OYSTERS

Nine times out of ten, I like to eat my oysters straight from the shell, with nothing more adventurous than a squeeze of lemon. With our plump and juicy native oysters, which reappear in September and stay with us throughout the autumn, it seems a shame to do anything more than open them (not in itself an easy task) and eat them. But there are times when a cooked oyster is called for – raw oysters are an acquired taste, if an easy one to acquire, and I recommend serving oysters cooked if you are unsure of your guests' feelings towards them. For cooking, Pacific oysters (available all year round) are just as good although I would always choose natives for eating raw.

16 oysters
3 leeks
2 glasses white wine (*you need good wine for this dish: I like to use a Californian or Australian Chardonnay, as the buttery fatness complements the oyster perfectly – drink the rest of the bottle with the oysters*)

freshly ground black pepper
2 tablespoons chopped flat-leaved parsley
1/4 pint (150 ml) double cream
1/2 oz (15 g) butter
soy sauce
1 lemon

First, open the oysters. This is a difficult task which is made a good deal simpler if you have an oyster knife, a small wooden-handled tool with a short, flat, thick blade. The first time I ever bought oysters for eating at home was on Christmas Day in Chartres; after half an hour struggling to open one of them I returned shamefaced to the fishmonger opposite to be shown the technique. The beginner should wear thick gloves during the opening ceremony, as oyster shells are sharp.

Holding your oyster flat side of the shell uppermost, pointed end towards you, scrape away any loose shell from one side; then insert the knife flat into the join or hinge about a third of the way down from the pointed end of the oyster. Twist the knife through 90 degrees to prise open the shell. Scrape any meat adhering to the flat side into the cupped shell and detach the oyster from the muscle with the blade. Scrape out any adhering shards of shell, taking care not to lose the liquid, and lay the oyster flat, on ice if you are not going to cook them immediately.

When you are ready to cook (which should be within an hour of opening the oysters) pre-heat the grill to maximum. Chop the white part of the washed leeks into shreds about 1 inch long. Now pour a little of the wine into each oyster shell and season well with freshly ground black pepper. Put the oysters under the hot grill for 3–5 minutes, according to size of oyster and taste. Meanwhile mix the chopped parsley into the cream. Add this mixture to the oysters and cook for another 2 minutes or so before serving, just enough for the cream to heat through.

Heat the butter in a frying-pan and quickly fry the shreds of leek until they are wilted but not brown, about 3–4 minutes. Season with soy sauce and lemon juice and put a pile of leeks around the outside of each serving plate. Place the oysters in the centre of each plate, surrounded by the leeks, and serve immediately.

HERRINGS WITH A MUSTARD CRUST

Herrings are both good and plentiful in the autumn months and make cheap and nutritious dishes. I like herring grilled with mustard, its sharpness balancing the full flavour of the fish. Traditionally, herrings are rolled in oatmeal before grilling or frying, but I prefer to use the Italian cornmeal, polenta, whose smaller grains give a crisper texture. You can serve grilled herrings with fried apples – I also like them with fried cucumber (see below).

4 small herring	2 tablespoons polenta
2 tablespoons Dijon mustard	2 oz (55 g) butter
(*do not use the much fiercer*	
English mustard)	

Ask your fishmonger to gut the herrings, remove the head and take out the backbone, leaving you with a kipper-shaped fish (this is easy to do at home if you don't have a friendly fishmonger).

Pre-heat the grill to maximum. Smear one side of each fillet all over with mustard and then roll them in the polenta. Dot with a little butter and grill, not too close to the element or flame, for 10 minutes until the crust has turned golden brown. Turn the fish over and smear the other side with the remaining mustard; sprinkle over the rest of the polenta and dot again with butter. Grill for a further 10 minutes. Serve immediately with wedges of lemon.

FRIED CUCUMBER

1 whole cucumber	2 teaspoons black mustard
1/2 tablespoon vegetable oil	seeds
1 teaspoon coarse sea salt	2 tablespoons sour cream

Chop the cucumber into chunks. Heat the oil and add the salt and mustard seeds; when the seeds start to pop, add the cucumber. Fry, stirring occasionally, for 10 minutes, until the cucumber is golden. Add 1 tablespoon of water, cover, and cook for a further 5 minutes. Take off the lid, boil off any excess water, stir in the sour cream and serve immediately.

MUSSELS IN WHITE WINE

When I was a child living in Brussels, we regularly used to eat our Sunday lunch in a restaurant just off the magnificent Grande Place. I used to long for the autumn so that I could once again enjoy my favourite meal, a huge tureen of mussels, the top of which I could hardly see over. The mussels were cooked in a winy liquid, and I used to eat every last one, using a mussel shell as a pincer, until I could spoon out the sauce from the bottom of the pan. I enjoy the dish just as much today, although now I serve it as a starter with bread rather than as a main course with frites.

4 lb (2 kg) mussels	$^1/_3$ bottle white wine
salt	(*Alsatian wine such as*
2 onions	*Sylvaner or Riesling is*
1 clove of garlic	*ideal*)
2 leeks	2 tablespoons chopped fresh
1 oz (25 g) butter	parsley

Let the mussels soak for an hour or so in some salted water, covered with a cloth – they will clean themselves, removing much of the grit trapped in their shells. To speed the process up, give them a handful of oatmeal on which to feed.

When the mussels have soaked, scrub them under running water, making sure you scrape off any small barnacles clinging to their shells. De-beard them by pulling out the small strings sticking out of one side of the shell. Discard any mussels with broken shells, or which do not close when tapped. Place each prepared mussel in a clean bowl of cold water.

Choose a large pan which will take all the mussels. Finely chop the onions and garlic. Chop the leeks into slivers and rinse thoroughly. Melt the butter and fry the onion, leeks and garlic gently for 10 minutes, until soft but not brown. Now turn the heat up and add the mussels, together with the wine. Put the lid on and allow to bubble until all the mussels are open, about 5 minutes. Remove any mussels which have not opened. Stir in the chopped parsley, season well and serve, making sure you warn your guests not to eat any closed mussels which you might have missed.

SEAFOOD RISOTTO

Whenever I can find a selection of shellfish, I like to make a seafood risotto. The absorbent Arborio rice makes a perfect foil to the richness of the seafood, which is cooked in the shells, giving greater flavour to the dish. This is a meal in one, ideal for a casual Sunday lunch or for a large group – it needs only a green salad to go with it, a plate for the pile of empty shells and plenty of paper napkins.

For 6

2 lb (900 g) mussels in the shell

1 lb (450 g) clams or cockles in the shell

1 lb (450 g) whole, raw prawns (*I often use a variety of sizes – if you can get 1 or 2 large tiger prawns as well, they will make the dish especially attractive*)

2 pints (1.1 litres) chicken stock (*I prefer to use chicken stock, as I find fish stock makes the dish overpowering*)

1 onion

2 oz (55 g) unsalted butter

10 oz (285 g) Arborio rice

Prepare the mussels as in the previous recipe. Follow the same procedure for the clams and cockles, which do not need de-bearding. Wash the prawns and remove any eggs.

You will need a very large, heavy-based and deep-sided frying-pan to cook this dish. The key principle of cooking risotto is that the stock should be kept hot, so that the temperature in the risotto pan with the rice stays relatively constant as you add liquid. You should therefore heat the stock in a separate pan.

Finely chop the onion and fry in the butter over a gentle heat for 10 minutes until soft but not brown. Add the rice, and stir to coat all the grains in fat. Add a ladleful of hot stock and stir until the rice has absorbed all the liquid; repeat the process. Continue until the rice is three-quarters cooked (which should roughly correspond to you having used $3/4$ of the stock and will take 15–20 minutes), then add the unshelled prawns to the pan, heads and all. Open the mussels and cockles over a high heat in a separate pan, strain the resulting liquid and pour it into the risotto. Continue cooking, adding more stock if necessary, until the rice is perfectly plump and tender, then stir in the opened mussels and cockles and serve immediately.

SHARK SAUCE NORMANDE

For a brief period in the autumn, small blue shark are landed off the Cornish coast: they often appear in the shops and markets for only a few weeks. Shark with a rich sauce normande may seem an unusual combination, for shark is hardly a Norman speciality. I was first served the dish by a restaurateur from Normandy now living on the French Caribbean island of Guadeloupe. At the time I suspected that the setting had a great deal to do with my ecstatic memory of the food, but re-creating the dish in the less exotic surroundings of my own kitchen, I discovered that it was almost as good as I remembered, the rich sauce a perfect foil to the tender shark meat. The title of 'sauce normande' is as given by my friend in Guadeloupe. This is by no means the authentic sauce, which should include mussel liquor.

4 pieces shark, each about $1^1/_2$ inches (3.5 cm) thick,
total weight $1^1/_2$–2 lb (675–900 g)

FOR THE SAUCE

$^1/_2$ pint (300 ml) fish stock	1 glass dry white wine
2 or 3 dried mushrooms	$^1/_4$ pint (150 ml) double
2 oz (55 g) butter	cream
1 oz (25 g) flour	2 egg-yolks
1 teaspoon Dijon mustard	$^1/_2$ lemon

Make the sauce in advance of cooking the fish. Make a fish stock by simmering fish trimmings with a piece of onion, a stick of celery and perhaps a little fennel, if you have it handy. Meanwhile, soak the dried mushrooms in a wine-glass full of warm water so that they release their perfume.

Melt 1¹/₂ oz (45 g) of the butter and stir in the flour, together with the mustard. Cook for 2 or 3 minutes over a low heat, until the roux takes on a little colour. Stir in the fish stock a little at a time, followed by the white wine and the liquid from the soaked mushrooms (retain the mushrooms themselves for use in another dish). Allow to boil uncovered for 5 minutes or so, stirring all the time, until the sauce thickens and is very smooth. Leave the final stage of preparation until the fish is cooked.

To cook the shark, pre-heat the grill to medium hot and grill for 8–10 minutes on each side (or less if you have a thinner steak), until the flesh turns opaque. Skin and keep warm.

To finish the sauce, beat together the cream and egg-yolks. Bring the sauce back to almost but not quite boiling and stir in the mixture, together with any juices from the cooked shark. Heat through (but do not allow to boil) and finish with a squeeze of lemon. Serve in a separate jug.

SKATE, TURNIP AND POTATO SALAD

Skate, one of my favourite fish, is of especially good quality in the autumn. The pink-tinged wings are easy to cook and stand up to strong flavours, as in the classic dish of skate with black butter and capers (see pages 77–8). I also like to serve skate in this Scandinavian-inspired salad, the fish draped over waxy potatoes and small turnips, the whole bound by a hollandaise flavoured with dill and lime. This makes an excellent starter or a main lunch dish.

The following quantities make a starter for 4 people.

8 oz (225 g) small turnips
8 oz (225 g) small potatoes
  (*waxy, salad varieties such as La Ratte or Pink Fir Apple are best*)
2 small to medium skate wings

4 oz (115 g) unsalted butter
2 limes
2 egg-yolks
8–10 sprigs of fresh dill
salt and freshly ground black pepper

The salad works best if the ingredients are still tepid from cooking, so don't make it too far in advance.

First, prepare the salad ingredients. Peel the turnips and cut them into quarters, or cubes if they are large. If you have salad potatoes, there is no need to peel them; simply wash and cut into quarters or halves, depending on their size. Boil the potatoes in salted water until soft but not falling apart, then drain them and put them, covered, in a low oven to keep warm. At the same time, steam the turnips in a covered pan with a little water, a knob of butter and a pinch of sugar until they too are soft; keep warm with the potatoes. Gently fry the skate wings in $^1/_2$ oz (15 g) of butter for 4–5 minutes on each side, depending on thickness – the flesh should come easily away from the bone. Skin and keep warm in the oven.

Now make the sauce. Chop the chilled butter into cubes and squeeze the juice from the limes. In a double boiler or a heatproof glass bowl which will fit over a pan of water, mix together the egg-yolks and lime juice. Heat the water until it is hot but not quite boiling and place the glass bowl over the pan, making sure the bottom does not touch the water. Beat the butter into the egg and lime mixture a cube at a time. Make sure the water underneath doesn't boil or the mixture will scramble – if it looks like getting too hot, lift the bowl off the pan for a moment. When all the butter has been amalgamated, the sauce should be of pouring consistency. If it appears too thick, add a few drops of warm water; if too thin, keep stirring over the heat until it thickens. When the sauce is ready, take off the heat, stir in the very finely chopped dill, reserving a few fronds for a garnish, and add salt to taste.

To assemble the salad, arrange some of the potatoes and turnips on each plate. Remove the flesh from the skate with a fork – it will come off in long strips. Lay some of the fish over each pile of vegetables and then pour over the sauce. Sprinkle with the reserved dill and freshly ground black pepper, and serve.

SMOKED HADDOCK WITH STIR-FRIED VEGETABLES

Smoked haddock is one of the treats of British fishmongers. Make sure you buy the undyed variety, which has not been treated with artificial colouring; it may not be such a brilliant yellow, but will taste far better. Fortunately, undyed haddock is becoming increasingly available; some fishmongers, like the admirable Ashtons in Cardiff market, now indicate which of their fish contain colouring. Smoked haddock makes an excellent soup (see winter recipe, pages 348–9). Alternatively, stir-fry it with autumn vegetables for an unusual dish.

1 lb (450 g) smoked haddock	1 dessertspoon (or to taste) sweet hot chilli sauce (*Chinese or West Indian varieties are good*)
3 carrots	2 tablespoons dry sherry
3 leeks	
1 fennel bulb	
$^1/_2$ oz (15 g) fresh ginger	$^1/_2$ tablespoon sesame oil
1 clove of garlic	2 limes
1 tablespoon peanut oil or other oil for frying	

Soak the piece of haddock for up to an hour, changing the water once. Then skin and shred the fish into flakes.

Peel the carrots, remove the green end of the leeks, and trim the fennel. Chop all the vegetables into matchsticks. Finely chop the ginger and garlic. Heat the frying oil in a large pan or wok over a high heat, add the ginger and garlic, and fry for a minute, stirring continuously. Now add all the chopped vegetables and fry for 2–3 minutes, stirring all the time. Stir in the fish, then add the chilli sauce, sherry and 1 tablespoon of water. Allow to bubble, turn down the heat and cover. Cook for 5 minutes.

Season with the sesame oil and plenty of lime juice and serve, either with rice as a main course or bread as a starter.

PRAWN CURRY

The best prawns I ever tasted were served on the shaded balcony of a friend's house in Managua, Nicaragua. We had bought the shellfish that morning from some small boys at a beach on the Pacific side of the country, and as soon as we got home the prawns were cooked with spices. This is the recipe we used.

2 lb (900 g) large raw
  prawns
1 teaspoon cumin seeds
1 teaspoon coriander seeds
1 teaspoon black mustard
  seeds
1 teaspoon black
  peppercorns
1 teaspoon turmeric
1 hot dried red chilli pepper
1 onion
2 cloves of garlic

1 inch (2.5 cm) piece of
  fresh ginger root
6 firm tomatoes
2 tablespoons vegetable oil
  (*coconut oil is especially
  good for this dish, if you
  can get it – it solidifies
  when cold and you must
  heat it up in the bottle to be
  able to pour it*)
2 limes
1/2 teaspoon salt

Wash the prawns well and remove any eggs. Grind the cumin, coriander, mustard seeds, peppercorns, turmeric and chilli pepper in a coffee grinder kept especially for the purpose, or in a pestle and mortar.

Finely chop the onion, garlic and ginger. Peel and de-seed the tomatoes and chop. Heat the oil in a wide, heavy-based frying-pan and gently fry the onion, ginger and garlic together for 10 minutes. Add the ground spices and cook, stirring, for a further 2 minutes. Add the tomatoes and salt and cook for another 2 minutes. Then pour over 1/3 pint (250 ml) cold water.

Turn the heat up and quickly bring the water to the boil. Cook over a high heat, stirring, until almost half the liquid has evaporated.

Add the prawns and stir well to make sure they are thoroughly coated. Turn the heat down as low as possible, cover the pan, and cook for 6–8 minutes, depending on the size of the prawns; they are done when they have turned thoroughly pink. Stir in the strained juice of the limes, check the seasoning and serve.

Prawn curry is particularly good served with a fresh mango chutney: chop a ripe mango, mix in a little chopped garlic, chilli and onion to taste, add some fresh coriander and squeeze over some lime juice. The only other dish necessary is a bowl of plain boiled rice.

MEAT

Cool autumn days call for hearty meat casseroles, dishes which can be left to cook long and slowly in the oven while you go out for breezy walks to enjoy the changing colours of the countryside or simply read a book by the fireside. Such dishes are equally well suited to the rigours of life in the city, for they can be cooked in advance and reheated with no ill effects. Cheaper cuts of meat can be left to marinate, often for a day or two, until you are ready to cook them to a melting tenderness. This method of cooking may require some advance planning, but it need not be demanding in terms of actual time in the kitchen.

Autumn brings new choices to the meat counter. One of the cook's greatest pleasures this season is the reappearance of game in the marketplace. Heralded by the early grouse of August, by October the game is plentiful and varied. Personally, I find the sight of a game dealer's stall or shop hung with wild rabbits, birds in the feather and perhaps the odd haunch of venison positively appetizing. Yet it seems from listening to the comments of passers by that I am unusual in this attitude. 'Oh, how cruel – look at those poor animals' is a common response to such a colourful array. Yet which has a better quality of life – the battery-reared chicken or the wild duck, free from the moment of its hatching until the moment of its death?

The consumer also benefits from the quality of life of wild animals shot for the table. No danger here of artificial growth hormones or unnatural foodstuffs upsetting the cycle. Game is good for you, a fact recognized in the increasing popularity of venison, a lean meat with a distinctive but not too forceful flavour. The new enthusiasm for venison has led to (or perhaps been provoked by) the establishment of numerous deer farms by farmers looking for new sources of earnings. These initiatives have brought down the price of venison and made it more available through securing supply to the supermarkets. Farmed venison may prove to be the first step in reintroducing a generation of consumers to the delights of game.

Farmed deer apart, however, game is generally not easy to get hold of. All game dealers have to be licensed by the local councils, who report a decline in numbers. Many traditional family businesses dealing in game are running out of steam in the face of low margins and a general lack of enthusiasm from the customer. The dealer dies, or retires, and no one takes his place. You are lucky now if your local market boasts one game dealer, where in the past there used to be two or three. Of course there are exceptions: Oxford covered market is one, with its serried ranks of birds in the feather. But for each market like Oxford there are many more such as Norwich, in the heart of game country yet without a single game dealer in its central market square – the last one retired a few years ago. In my childhood in Northumberland, my father regularly returned home from the city market bearing game. So I decided to revisit Newcastle to see whether the haul of the shoots on the Northumbrian moors still finds its way to the market stalls.

The Old Butcher Market in Newcastle upon Tyne

The covered market in Newcastle has stood upon the same site since 1843. Now known as the Grainger market, after the street on which it stands, it was originally called simply the Butcher market. The name change came as a result of protestations from the non-food sellers who now make up more than half the market, selling a variety of goods from flowers to kitchen utensils, children's clothes to second-hand books. True to the 1950s feel of the place, there is even a Lucky Strike stall, with an archaic range of packaged toiletries for the winner. Yet the original name still feels much more appropriate, for here are more butchers' stalls gathered in one place than in any other market I have visited.

You can sit in the old-fashioned café in the centre of the market eating an English breakfast of black pudding, back bacon, pork sausage and fried egg with a stottie bap on the side, washed down with a mug of strong tea, and gaze on meat in every direction. In front of you, whole oxtails are suspended from a rack, waiting to be made into soup. To the side, a young man in a bloodstained apron is threading skins on to an old-fashioned sausage-making machine, before filling them with the meat mixture sitting in the huge vat beside him. Just round the corner from the café is a traditional tripe store, selling black pudding, white pudding, cow-heels and pigs' trotters – not a sight for the weak of stomach, but welcome nonetheless for keeping such products available to the customer.

Autumn is an especially good time for pork, which until just before the Second World War was still a seasonal meat, available fresh only from September through to February. Pigs are big business in the countryside around Newcastle, and it shows in the market. Whole stalls are dedicated to the sale of bacon – collar bacon, middle, back, streaky, smoked, unsmoked, green, local oyster bacon, smoked gammon, bacon shanks and Ayrshire roll. As one butcher, whose stall has stood on the same site since the last century, explained to me in Geordie, 'War fussy 'bout our pig like.'

That shows not just in the bacon, but in the whole legs of pork hanging above the butchers' stalls, their skin waiting to be scored to produce a better crackling. Hams, on the other hand, are not such good quality, their meat too pink and too wet – no equivalent here of the dried and smoked whole hams you find in other great pig-eating areas, from Strasbourg to Bologna. But the black puddings are something to boast about, their taut skins encasing highly spiced meat specked with white globules of fat. Even if you don't like that sort of food, be pleased that this part of our culinary heritage hasn't disappeared.

The people of Newcastle, when they can afford it, remain wedded to their Sunday roast and the preferred meat is beef. The move towards leaner meat, welcome though it is on health grounds, can go too far: strip all of the fat from a joint of meat and you lose a great deal of the flavour. The joints on sale in Newcastle show the delicate marbling of fat through the beef which produces a fuller taste, and the fat is the creamy-yellow colour which indicates a grass-fed animal. The beef is a deep red, indicating proper hanging; the butchers of Newcastle hang their beef for a good two weeks.

Amid the pork, the beef, the lamb, the offal, it is quite difficult to spot the game, which after all is what I am searching for this bright autumn morning. In fact, there is little of it left. Newcastle market, as I remember it from my childhood days in the early 1970s, used to have four game dealers. In common with so many markets around the country, their numbers have dwindled in recent years. One retired, one went bankrupt, one changed hands and, although still licensed, sells little game, leaving only one old stalwart. But what a hanger-on! Mr Kettlewell's stall has stood on the same spot in the Butcher or Grainger market since 1844, just a year after the market place was first opened for trading. Originally the stall was called Smith's, but Mr Kettlewell's grandmother inherited it and changed the name when she married, only to divorce her husband but hold on to the stall.

Today's Mr Kettlewell maintains the standards of his ancestors and offers as wide a range of game as he can lay his hands on. He buys wherever he can, from shoots not just over the beautiful moors above and to the west of Newcastle, but in the Cheviots which separate England from Scotland, the Scottish border country, the lakelands to the west – anywhere the game is plentiful and cheap. For cheap it must be: his customers buy on price as much as quality. Mr Kettlewell appears single-handedly determined to persuade them to return to cooking game, handing out recipe sheets to the doubtful, explaining to the thrifty how many dishes can be conjured from one hare, making his own venison sausages to introduce the wary. Even he despairs at times: 'People here don't know how to cook these things any more, and if they cook them badly once, and the meat turns out tough, they blame me.'

In the face of this seeming adversity, Mr Kettlewell maintains one of the broadest selections of game I have seen. On the early November day on which I visited, the range of birds, besides the usual pheasant, included the wild ducks mallard, widgeon and teal; Northumbrian partridge; and woodcock, the bird perhaps most prized by the Victorians and after which the red mullet takes its honorary name of woodcock of the sea. An unusual sight was that of the tiny wader bird, the snipe, properly prepared with its innards intact and its plucked head threaded through the body with the long beak; the roasted brains and liver are considered a delicacy. Yet Mr Kettlewell was not satisfied: he bemoaned the lack of blackcock and grey hen, neither of which he had been able to procure despite extensive searches. In truth, he had little custom for such obscure and inevitably expensive birds – some of those for sale had, to his sorrow, already had to be frozen, given the lack of demand.

Other birds on offer included fat and juicy quail, farm-reared but none the worse for it, perfect for grilling for a quick supper dish. Guineafowl transpired to have been imported from Belgium and France, although farming of this excellent bird is now increasing in this country. Not a native, it is very rarely found living wild in Britain, except where it has been introduced as a watchbird to pheasant shoots: the appalling squawking noise a guineafowl makes when disturbed being guaranteed to wake a watchful keeper on the lookout for poachers. Guineafowl is good roasted but even better casseroled – try it with cabbage. The pre-Christmas geese had not yet appeared but could be ordered from the farm where they were being fattened. Hare was sold whole or in half packs, the saddle for baking, the legs for casseroling, the blood necessary for a civet could be obtained if ordered in advance. Wild rabbits were plentiful, their price reflecting the numbers in which they are currently plaguing farmers – casserole them or marinate and grill the legs for a delicious and economical dish. Both wild and farmed venison was on offer, from cheap stewing packs for the casserole, to expensive saddles and haunches for roasting at Sunday lunchtime. Try a joint of venison for an alternative Christmas feast.

The Grainger market in Newcastle is an excellent place to buy meat, but the selection of game available there is what makes it special for me. Shop holders like Mr Kettlewell are the type of enthusiast that cooks must encourage if we are to continue to be able to buy our own local produce. The Victorians took game for granted – take a look at Mrs Beeton. We are now regaining our taste for it, but perhaps too slowly for the likes of Mr Kettlewell. He has no heir, and cannot see anyone else wanting to take over his stall under current trading conditions. It is up to the cooks of Northumberland to prove him wrong.

BAKED SADDLE OF HARE WITH CREAM AND REDCURRANTS

As soon as the corn is cut, hare appears in the markets and shops. Although older hare is best casseroled or made into a civet (a stew which uses the animal's blood and liver as a thickening agent), I think the saddle of a younger hare is at its most succulent when roasted or baked. This also makes a relatively economical dish, for the hindquarters can then be used for pâtés, pies or casseroles. If simply roasting a saddle, you need to lard it by threading the meat through with strips of pork fat, using a larding needle (no longer an easy implement to come by). This rich recipe from Belgium avoids this process by baking the saddle in cream. I find the tartness of redcurrants lifts the sauce, as well as providing a splash of colour.

A saddle weighing around $1^1/_2$ lb (675 g) will feed 2 generously or 3 at a pinch; although the meat is rich, it will not stretch to 4, so perhaps this is a dish for a romantic evening.

1 saddle of young hare	$^1/_2$ pint (300 ml) double
4 shallots	cream
2 tablespoons red wine	8 oz (225 g) redcurrants
vinegar	

Ask your butcher to joint the hare, leaving the saddle whole. When you get home, strip the tough, translucent membrane from the saddle, exposing the purple flesh.

Pre-heat the oven to low ($110°C/225°F/Gas$ $^1/_4$). Find a dish into which the saddle only just fits, and put it in upside down. Finely chop the shallots and sprinkle over the hare. Mix the vinegar into the cream to slightly sour it, and pour it over the hare; if the dish is small enough, the saddle should be completely covered. Put a lid or some foil over the dish and place it in the oven.

It is best not to look at the hare during the cooking process, as in the early stages of cooking the sauce may well separate – it is not worth giving yourself a nasty shock, for it will come back together after about an hour of cooking. At this stage baste the saddle. While the hare is cooking, strip and wash the redcurrants.

After $1^1/_4$–$1^1/_2$ hours' cooking in total, the saddle will be done. The exact length of time will depend on the size of the saddle and whether you like the meat slightly pink. At this stage, lift the meat out of the sauce, carve it into long strips along the length of the saddle, and put to keep warm.

Strain the sauce into a pan, making sure you pour in any meat juices from the carving, and place over a gentle heat. Stir in the redcurrants and heat through. Check the sauce for seasoning and if necessary add a pinch of sugar.

Serve the slices of hare on a pool of sauce dotted with redcurrants, with a pile of fresh white tagliatelle or other noodles on the side.

BEEF IN CIDER WITH APPLE DUMPLINGS

A beef casserole is just the sort of dish I appreciate on a cool autumn day. The beef is cooked slowly with a selection of vegetables, in a liquid which will then form the sauce. Every European country has its own recipe, from the Provençal daube which uses red wine, tomatoes and garlic, through the Flemish carbonnade, where the meat is cooked in the local Belgian beer, to Irish beef and Guinness stews. One of my favourite of these dishes comes from the West Country, where beef and root vegetables are cooked in cider, producing tender meat and sweet vegetables in a sauce with a hint of apple. Apple dumplings, made from potato with a core of grated apple and smoked bacon and tossed in dripping to brown them, complete the dish.

FOR THE CASSEROLE

$1^1/_2$ lb (675 g) stewing beef, e.g. chuck

1 onion

$1/_2$ tablespoon goose or duck fat or beef dripping

8 oz (225 g) celeriac

8 oz (225 g) small turnips

1 tablespoon plain flour

$1/_4$ teaspoon ground mace

salt and pepper

1 pint (575 ml) strong cider (*scrumpy is best – try to find a non-carbonated cider*)

2 bayleaves

FOR THE DUMPLINGS

1 lb (450 g) potatoes	¹/₂ teaspoon salt
4 rashers of smoked streaky bacon	¹/₄ of a lemon
1 large cooking apple (*a favourite variety of mine is the Lord Derby, but as these are hard to come by, you will probably use a Bramley*)	3 oz (85 g) plain flour
	1 egg
	1 tablespoon goose or duck fat or good-quality beef dripping

Trim the beef of fat and cut it into chunks. Choose an enamelled casserole – aluminium will turn the cider black. Finely chop the onion and fry it in the fat or dripping until soft. Meanwhile, peel the celeriac and turnips and cut into cubes. Bring a pan of water to the boil and blanch the turnips, to take off any edge of bitterness.

Pre-heat the oven to medium low (130°C/275°F/Gas 1). When the onion is soft, add the other vegetables to the pan. Fry for a few minutes then turn up the heat and add the beef. Sear well on all sides, then stir in the flour and mace. Season and add the cider, which should be sufficient to cover the meat and vegetables. Tuck in the bayleaves, cover the pan and transfer to the oven. Cook for 2 hours.

To make the dumplings, boil the potatoes whole in their skins until they are soft, about 20–30 minutes according to size. Do not prick them to test or they will become waterlogged; check they are ready by squeezing firmly, holding the potato in a cloth. While they are cooking, dice the bacon very finely and gently fry in its own fat. Peel the apple and coarsely grate the flesh; sprinkle with half the salt and all the lemon juice and allow to stand for 10 minutes. Drain away the resulting liquid and add the grated apple to the now cooked bacon; stir for a minute or two so that the apple starts to melt. Take off the heat.

When the potatoes are cool enough to handle, peel them and coarsely grate the flesh into a large bowl. Stir in the sieved flour, the egg and the remaining salt. Quickly, with your fingers, mould the mixture together (this is a messy job – initially the dumpling dough is very sticky). Do not under any circumstances be tempted to use a processor or the dumplings will be leaden. Have extra flour on hand to sprinkle over as necessary. On a floured surface, form the dumpling mixture into 2 long sausage shapes; chop each across into 8 slices, so that you have 16 dumplings in all.

Make a small well in the centre of each dumpling and spoon in a little of the apple and bacon mixture. Form the dumpling around this centre so that it is completely covered. Sprinkle with flour and set aside until you are half an hour or so away from eating.

To cook the dumplings, bring a large pan of salted water to the boil. Gently slide in the dumplings and continue to boil. The dumplings are cooked when they rise to the surface (about 8–10 minutes). Have ready a pan with a tablespoon of melted goose or duck fat or dripping. Transfer the cooked dumplings to the pan and fry on all sides until lightly browned.

To serve, check the seasoning and spoon the piping hot casserole into warmed serving plates, arranging 4 dumplings at right angles around each plate.

BRAISED STUFFED WILD DUCK

Available from licensed game dealers around the country, wild duck is also beginning to appear in certain supermarkets and can be a good introduction to game, for its flavour is less powerful than that of some other birds. The most commonly seen variety is mallard, but widgeon and the much smaller teal also make an appearance at good game dealers. A mallard and, at a pinch, a widgeon will stretch between 2, but a teal will only feed one. Wild ducks are good roasted when well larded; I also like to braise them with a savoury stuffing.

4 oz (115 g) dried apricots
(*I prefer to use wild
apricots, which need plenty
of pre-soaking, but you may
prefer for convenience's sake
to use apricots which need
no soaking*)
$^1/_2$ an onion
$1^1/_2$ oz (45 g) butter
salt and pepper

2 or 3 celery sticks, with
leaves attached
3 oz (85 g) wild rice
3 oz (85 g) long-grain rice
2 mallards
2 tablespoons whisky
2 glasses dry white wine
$^1/_2$ an orange
1 sprig of fresh thyme
2 or 3 fresh bayleaves

If necessary, soak the apricots according to the instructions on the packet. To make the stuffing, chop the onion finely and fry in a third of the butter until translucent. Finely chop the celery, reserving the leaves, add to the onion and fry for another few minutes. Bring a pan of water to the boil, wash the wild and long-grain rice under cold water to rid them of starch, mix them together and boil for 1 minute. Drain well and stir into the fried onion and celery, together with the chopped celery leaves and the finely chopped dried apricots. Season well.

Make sure the innards of the ducks are thoroughly cleaned out and that any loose feathers are removed. Sear the ducks in another third of the butter, making sure they are browned on all sides. Heat the whisky in a ladle, set light to it, stand back and pour over birds. Allow the flames to die down completely before removing the birds from the pan.

Pre-heat the oven to medium (150°C/300°F/Gas 2). Stuff the birds with the rice mixture and place breast side down in a heavy lidded pan in which they will only just fit. Pour over the white wine, the juice of the orange and sufficient water to cover the birds. Tuck in the thyme and the bayleaves together with a strip of the orange peel. Cover and cook for 45 minutes. After this time, turn the birds breast uppermost and uncover the pan. Continue cooking for another 20–30 minutes, until both the birds and the stuffing are tender. Remove the birds from the pan and keep warm; reduce the sauce by fast boiling until it is a third of its original volume. Finish with the remaining knob of butter, carve the birds into halves and spoon the stuffing around them together with the sauce. This rich dish needs only a salad to accompany it – a watercress and orange salad is especially good with duck.

CALVES' LIVER WITH DEEP-FRIED SAGE

Offal is not very popular in Britain, which is a shame, for it offers a wide range of satisfying and largely economical dishes. The best, if by far the most expensive, introduction to the delights of offal is through calves' liver, which is a world apart from those dreadful memories of liver at school. In Italy, calves' liver is traditionally served with fresh sage leaves; I find these can give a rather overpowering taste, and prefer them deep-fried, which both softens the flavour and provides a crispy contrast to the unctuous quality of the liver. Sage grows on well into the autumn, so fresh leaves should not be too difficult to find even if you don't have a bush in your garden.

fresh oil for frying (*e.g. sunflower, groundnut*)	1 tablespoon olive oil
8–10 sage leaves per person	4 large or 8 small slices of calves' liver, thin cut
1 oz (25 g) butter	1 lemon

This is a very simple dish to prepare, but requires last-minute cooking. To cook the sage leaves, bring a small pan of the oil to the point where it is almost smoking – test with a small cube of bread, which should brown almost immediately. Stand back and put in the sage leaves, no more than 15 at a time. As soon as they stop spitting and start to curl (a matter of a minute or two), lift out the leaves and put to dry on absorbent paper.

To cook the liver, heat the butter and oil together in a non-stick frying-pan. When the oil is hot but not browning, put in the slices of liver. Provided the meat is cut thin enough, the cooking time is very quick: 1 minute on each side should be enough to sear the meat, leaving the inner flesh a rosy pink. Do not overcook or the liver will toughen and curl up. Allow to rest for a minute or two before serving with the sage leaves sprinkled over and a quarter of lemon on each plate.

Good accompaniments are potatoes and onions sautéed in olive oil, and courgette fritters (thin strips of courgette dipped in a flour and water batter and fried in $1/2$ inch (1 cm) of sunflower oil).

CHICKEN WITH POMEGRANATE
AND WALNUT SAUCE

Pomegranates make only a brief appearance in our shops, the first fruit arriving in September and the last disappearing in early January. Look for fruit with hard skins streaked with red for the sweetest flavour. The seeds of the pomegranate must be carefully squeezed to extract their juice without the tannin prevalent in the pith. The result is a beautiful translucent mauve-red juice, wonderful for breakfast. Ancient Persian cuisine used pomegranate juice to great effect in adding a sweet-sour flavour to meat dishes. In this classic recipe given to me by a friend brought up in Iran, the meat is chicken, and the sauce thickened with another autumn special, 'wet' walnuts.

1 lb (450 g) 'wet' walnuts in the shell (*for convenience you can use 6 oz (170 g) dried, shelled walnuts, but they will not contain as many of the nut oils*)	1 onion
	1 tablespoon vegetable oil
	4 pomegranates
	1 unwaxed lemon and juice of $1/2$ a lemon
	$1/2$ tablespoon sugar
4 chicken thighs and 4 chicken drumsticks	4 cloves
	salt and pepper

Shell the walnuts and blanch them. Make sure you have slipped off all the bitter skin. Grind the nuts into small pieces (but not so far as to produce a paste). If the chicken pieces are very fatty, remove the skin (although I prefer to leave the skin on if possible, as it improves the flavour of the dish).

Finely chop the onion and fry in the vegetable oil for 10 minutes, until soft. Meanwhile remove the juice from the pomegranates. The easiest way to do this is to scoop out all the seeds into the liquidizer, give a quick whizz and strain; if you simply use a juice extractor, you are likely to release the tannin contained in the pith. Stud the unwaxed lemon with the cloves.

Add the chicken pieces to the frying onion, and brown on all sides. Then stir in the ground walnuts. After a minute or two, add the lemon juice, the sugar, the whole lemon, the pomegranate juice, and salt and pepper to taste. Add sufficient water to cover.

You can make this dish in the oven or on the stove. Cook in the oven, pre-heated to medium low (130°C/275°F/Gas 1), or cook slowly over a low flame for an hour, until the chicken is very tender. Remove the lemon, check the seasoning to taste and serve with plain boiled rice.

DUCK WITH RED PEPPER SAUCE

A domesticated duck is a difficult bird to roast, but when it is got right, the meltingly tender flesh encased by crispy skin, there is little to beat it. The most common duck for sale in Britain is the farmyard Aylesbury, a large white bird with plenty of fat. This is not, in my opinion, a duck for serving slightly rare; I prefer the British method of cooking the meat relatively slowly until it is brown throughout, which ensures that you do not end up with overdone breast and underdone legs. The sweet, full flavour of the red pepper sauce, which is enriched with the duck's liver, combines well with the duck meat.

1 large Aylesbury duck, with giblets, approx. 4–5 lb (2–2.5 kg)	*1 glass white wine, sprig of thyme, bayleaf)*
1/2 pint (300 ml) duck stock, made from the giblets *(to make the stock you will need 1/2 an onion, 1 carrot, stick of celery,*	1 oz (25 g) butter 1 tablespoon olive oil 3 red peppers 2 tablespoons ruby port salt and freshly ground black pepper

First, make the stock from the duck's giblets, excluding the liver. Chop the onion, carrot and celery and stew in half the butter for 15 minutes until soft. Add the giblets and pour over the white wine; bubble for a minute or two. Add the herbs and some black pepper together with 3/4 pint (450 ml) water and simmer, covered, for 30 minutes. Then take off the lid and reduce the liquid to 1/2 pint (300 ml). Strain.

To cook the duck, wipe the inside clean with a cloth and rub the olive oil all over the bird. Many cooks pierce the skin of the bird all over with a fork, to allow the fat to run out from the top; I find this makes for greasy skin and dry meat and prefer to allow the fat to drip out more slowly. Simply prick the duck a couple of times on each side, where the legs join the breast.

Pre-heat the oven to medium low (130°C/275°F/Gas 1). Place the duck on its side on a wire rack in the oven tray (the rack is important – it stops the bird stewing in its own fat). After 30 minutes, pour off the fat (make sure you keep it for roasting potatoes) and place the bird on its other side. It should cook for another 30 minutes in this position, during which time you can get on with the sauce.

Pre-heat the grill to maximum and place the unpeeled peppers underneath it. Char on all sides, making sure the skin is thoroughly black; this will take about 20 minutes (you can also do this over an open flame, but this method requires more effort from the cook). Leave the blackened peppers to cool for 5 minutes under a cloth, then peel off the skin and scrape out the core and seeds, taking care to retain as many of the juices as possible (so don't do this under the tap). Finely chop the flesh and stew in the remaining butter over a gentle flame for a few minutes. Pour over the port, allow to bubble, and then add the $^1/_2$ pint (300 ml) of hot duck stock. Simmer uncovered for 10 minutes.

When the duck has been cooking for 1 hour, drain the fat again, place it breast side up and sprinkle the skin with salt. Turn the oven up to 160°C/325°F/Gas 3.

Chop the duck liver finely and add to the sauce. Cook for a further 5 minutes then push the sauce through a sieve or give a quick whizz in the processor. If it is too liquid, reduce to the required consistency by fast boiling. Season well.

When the duck skin has crisped (which should take about 15 minutes), carve and serve with the sauce. A few potatoes and parsnips roasted in the fat as the duck cooks are an excellent addition.

GUINEAFOWL WITH CABBAGE

Guineafowl are now being reared in this country, and free-range French birds are available from some supermarkets. Often described as tasting like a cross between a pheasant and a chicken, the guineafowl is traditionally cooked in France with cabbage – pintade aux choux. This produces a tender bird surrounded by cabbage flavoured with the cooking juices – a world away from the overcooked cabbage of school memories. For an especially authentic flavour, use goose or duck fat left over from roasting a bird, or bought in jars from some delicatessens.

1 large guineafowl (*or 2 small ones if you and your guests are very hungry*)	2 tablespoons marc, brandy or Calvados (*optional*)
	6 juniper berries
	1 bayleaf
1 large Savoy cabbage	several sprigs of fresh thyme
1 onion	4 rashers of smoked streaky bacon
2 cloves of garlic	
2 tablespoons goose or duck fat, or dripping	1/2 bottle white wine (*I use an Alsatian wine, such as a Riesling or a Sylvaner*)
1/2 oz (15 g) butter	

Choose a heavy-based lidded pan into which the guineafowl and cabbage will fit comfortably. Chop the onion roughly and the garlic finely. Melt the fat and sweat the onion and garlic gently for 10 minutes, until the onion takes on a little colour.

Meanwhile, shred the cabbage, discarding the tough outer leaves and the hard core. Add the cabbage to the pan, stirring well to make sure it is thoroughly coated with the fat. Cook over a very low heat for 5 minutes, making sure the cabbage doesn't take colour.

In a separate frying-pan, melt the nugget of butter over a high heat and fry the bird(s) briefly so that they take colour on all sides. Warm the spirit (if you are using it) in a ladle over a flame, light with a match, stand well back and pour over the bird(s). Shake the pan until the flames die down.

Season the cabbage and add the juniper berries and bayleaf. Make a well in the centre of the dish, put the sprigs of thyme in the cavity of the bird and place it breast side down on the cabbage. Cover the top of the bird with the rashers of bacon, pour the white wine into the cabbage around the bird, cover and cook in a low oven (120°C/250°F/ Gas $^1/_2$) for about 2 hours. Check occasionally that there is sufficient liquid for the cabbage to cook; if it looks low, add a little water. When both the cabbage and the bird are tender, carve the meat and lay over the bed of cabbage and juices. I like to serve this dish with a purée of potatoes made with stock.

LAMBS' KIDNEYS IN SHERRY

If calves' liver has introduced you to the delights of offal (or if you need no introduction), the next choice should be lambs' kidneys. Small and sweet, they are a neglected source of cheap, nourishing and delicious dishes. Lambs' kidneys are easy to prepare and take well to quick cooking, unlike their larger cousins such as veal kidneys, which need long, slow braising. The Spaniards have many ways with lambs' kidneys – here is one of my favourites.

16 lambs' kidneys
4 rashers of smoked streaky
  bacon
8 shallots
4 oz (115 g) brown cap
  mushrooms
1 tablespoon olive oil
$^1/_2$ tablespoon flour

salt and freshly ground
  black pepper
$^1/_2$ teaspoon cayenne pepper
1 wine-glass dry sherry
  (*fino or manzanilla*)
1 tablespoon chopped fresh
  parsley

Prepare the lambs' kidneys by first breaking them out of their casing of fat, if that is the way they have been sold. Peel off the transparent skin. With a pair of scissors, cut out the central white core, making sure you do not leave any behind. Cut the kidneys across into 2 or 3 slices.

Cut the bacon into dice and finely chop the shallots. Wipe the mushrooms clean and slice finely. Gently heat the oil and bacon together in a heavy-based frying-pan. When the fat from the bacon begins to run, add the mushrooms and shallots and fry until they are soft (about 5 minutes). Meanwhile, season the flour with salt, black pepper and the cayenne pepper and roll the kidney slices in it.

Turn the heat up and throw the kidney slices into the pan. Fry for a minute or two, stirring, until the slices are browned on all sides. Pour over the sherry, stir it in well and bubble fiercely for a minute or two. Turn down the heat to low, cover and cook for 10 minutes. Season well with plenty of freshly ground black pepper, sprinkle over the parsley and serve.

Diced potatoes fried from scratch in olive oil with whole cloves of garlic and a green vegetable such as beans go well with the dish.

MEDITERRANEAN RABBIT CASSEROLE

Rabbit is a lean and cheap meat which deserves greater popularity in Britain. I find the meat of the smaller wild rabbit more flavoursome than that of the domesticated rabbit, but it does need long slow cooking unless you are sure you have a young animal in which case you can marinate the legs before smearing them with mustard and grilling them (see spring recipe, page 95). This casserole, for an older rabbit, uses olives and herbs to give a Mediterranean flavour to the dish.

2 wild rabbits

³/₄ pint (450 ml) rabbit stock (*made from saddles and giblets*)

2 cloves of garlic

freshly ground black pepper

1 teaspoon turmeric

2 tablespoons fruity extra virgin olive oil

1 lb (450 g) plum tomatoes or a 14 oz (400 g) tin

1 Spanish onion

1 orange

2 glasses dry white wine

2 sprigs of thyme or ¹/₄ teaspoon dried thyme

4 sprigs of oregano or marjoram or ¹/₂ teaspoon dried

1 sprig of rosemary

1 bayleaf

4 oz (115 g) black olives (*look for the variety preserved in oil rather than brine, preferably unpitted, which tend to have more flavour*)

Ask the butcher to joint the rabbits for you. When you get home, use the bony rib cages and the giblets, excluding the liver, to make a stock, with a little onion and a carrot or two.

Rub the rabbit legs and saddles with the cut side of a piece of garlic, black pepper and the turmeric. Leave to marinate in the olive oil for at least 30 minutes, turning once.

Peel and de-seed the tomatoes if you are using fresh ones. Chop the onion and garlic finely. Fry the onion gently for 10 minutes in the drained oil from the marinade, until soft. Now add the chopped garlic and fry for a further 3 or 4 minutes, making sure that the garlic doesn't brown. Turn the heat up slightly and add the rabbit pieces; fry on all sides until lightly browned. Add the tomatoes, orange juice and white wine and the herbs if you are using dried ones; bubble for 5 minutes.

Pour over sufficient rabbit stock to cover and tuck in the herbs if you have fresh ones, together with a small slice of orange peel. Place in a medium low oven (130°C/275°F/Gas 1) for 1 hour.

Meanwhile, blanch the olives. After an hour, add the olives to the casserole. Cook for another 15 minutes. Remove the rabbit pieces and put to keep warm; sieve the sauce and sprinkle the olives, tomatoes, onions, etc. over the rabbit, fishing out the herbs and orange peel. Boil the liquid down to the required consistency. Check for seasoning and add salt as necessary.

Serve the rabbit with tagliatelle and perhaps a roasted red pepper salad.

PORK BRAISED IN MILK

Pork is one of my favourite autumn meats. The very best pork comes from the household pig, fed on scraps, and slaughtered at home, but since you are unlikely to find such meat in the shops, look out for meat from animals which have been traditionally reared, allowed to roam and feed on natural ingredients. The difference in taste is extraordinary.

An excellent Italian way with a joint of pork is to braise it in milk. The longer you can marinate the meat in advance, the more tender it will be.

For 6
1 boned leg of pork, approx. 3 lb (1.5 kg)

FOR THE MARINADE

$^1/_2$ a bottle cheap, fruity, dry white wine (*a Pinot Grigio or similar wine from the Trentino area of northern Italy from which* *this dish originates would be perfect*)
4 bayleaves (*fresh if possible*)
8 black peppercorns

FOR THE COOKING

1 oz (25 g) butter
1 sprig of rosemary
4 fresh sage leaves
freshly ground black pepper
$1^1/_2$ pints (850 ml) full-cream milk
salt

Trim the pork of its skin and all excess fat and plunge the point of a sharp knife deep into the meat at regular intervals. Marinate at least overnight with the wine, bayleaves and peppercorns, turning occasionally.

To cook, remove the meat from the marinade and dry thoroughly. Keep the wine to use in making stock or soup, and reserve the bayleaves.

Melt the butter in a large, heavy-based casserole into which the meat just fits. Fry the meat on all sides until browned, then add the herbs, including the bayleaves from the marinade, and some black pepper, but no salt at this stage, as this would toughen the meat.

Pour over sufficient milk to just cover the meat, put on the casserole lid and simmer very slowly. After 1 hour, add salt to taste. Cook very slowly for 3–3½ hours, until the meat is meltingly tender. Do not be tempted to speed up the cooking time or you will end up with tough pork.

When the meat is ready, remove it from the casserole and keep it warm. Boil down the remaining milk until it thickens slightly. Carve the meat into thick slices, strain the sauce and pour over the meat.

This dish is good served with plain vegetables such as carrots steamed with a little butter and sugar, or French beans cooked in water and then fried with a little garlic. Potatoes boiled in their skins are also good.

LAMB CASSEROLE WITH DRIED APRICOTS AND PERSIAN RICE

North African cooking bears a strong resemblance to medieval British dishes, in which meat was cooked with fruit and spices were in regular use. In Morocco such combinations are common in tagines, long, slowly cooked stews named after a special kind of cooking pot, a shallow earthenware dish with an extraordinary conical lid tapering into a small chimney. This tagine recipe, where lamb is combined with dried apricots, is one of my favourites. Instead of apricots, you can substitute other autumn fruit – quinces are particularly good. I like to serve tagines with rice cooked in the Persian style; this produces tender rice with a delicious crispy butter crust topping.

4 oz (115 g) dried apricots
(*I like to use the wild
variety from Pakistan that
require pre-soaking, but for
convenience you can use
those which don't require
soaking*)
1¹/₂ lb (675 g) cubed lamb,
preferably shoulder
1 teaspoon cumin seeds or
ground cumin
1 teaspoon ground ginger

¹/₂ teaspoon turmeric
1 teaspoon ground
cinnamon
salt and freshly ground
black pepper
1 large Spanish onion
1 tablespoon vegetable oil
a few sprigs each of
coriander and parsley,
tied in a bunch
2 or 3 strands of saffron

Soak the apricots if necessary, according to the instructions on the packet. Trim any excess fat off the lamb.

If you are using cumin seeds (which always give a better flavour than the ground spice), toast them briefly in a dry pan then grind. Mix together all the spices except the saffron and add salt and pepper to taste. Peel and coarsely grate the onion.

Roll the cubes of lamb in the spices. Heat the oil over a low heat and fry the meat very gently in the oil to release the spicy fragrance for 3 or 4 minutes; you are stewing rather than searing, and the meat should not brown. Add the grated onion and the bunch of herbs and sufficient water to cover. Cook in a medium low oven (130°C/275°F/Gas 1) for 30 minutes.

Allow the saffron to stand for a minute or two in a little warm water. Add the saffron liquid and the drained apricots to the stew after it has cooked for 30 minutes, then cook for another 30–45 minutes, until the meat is tender. Remove the bunch of herbs, reduce the sauce to taste and serve with Persian rice.

PERSIAN RICE

12 oz (350 g) basmati rice
(*the variety is important*)

3 oz (85 g) unsalted butter

Wash the rice and soak in warm water for an hour or two to release the starch. Drain and rinse well.

Bring a large pan of salted water to the boil. Boil the rice hard for 4 or 5 minutes, until it is about two-thirds cooked – it should still have quite a bit more bite to it than you would normally like. Exact cooking times will vary according to the freshness of the rice, so make sure you taste to test.

Melt three-quarters of the butter in a heavy-based pan with a lid. Place the drained rice on top, without stirring it in, and dot the surface with the remaining butter. Place a clean tea-towel over the pot then add the lid, folding the corners of the tea-towel over it. Leave over a very low flame for 20–30 minutes.

When you are ready to eat, remove the lid and tea-towel and turn the rice out of the pot. Make sure you scrape out any of the crispy butter crust adhering to the base of the pan, which is a particular delicacy.

ROAST PARTRIDGE WITH ELDERBERRY AND RED WINE SAUCE

Partridge is one of my favourite game birds, taking second place only to woodcock. Epicureans claim that the smaller British grey-legged variety is superior to the French red-legged partridge, but I am not fussy. Older birds can be casseroled, but if you can get hold of young birds you should roast them to enjoy their full succulence. I like to serve roast partridge with this unusual sweet-and-sour rich red sauce made from elderberries, which are not available unless you pick them yourself. On autumn walks, look out for the heavy clusters of purple black berries, which also make excellent wine and jellies.

1 partridge per person
fresh pork fat (for
    preference) or unsmoked
    streaky bacon, for larding
1 oz (25 g) butter per bird

salt and freshly ground
    black pepper
1 slice of crustless bread per
    bird

FOR THE SAUCE (SUFFICIENT FOR 2 BIRDS)

8 oz (225 g) elderberries,
  stripped from their stalks
2 oz (55 g) sugar (*or to taste
  depending on the tartness of
  the berries*)
2 glasses red wine

1 dessertspoon red wine
  vinegar
freshly ground black pepper
1 oz (25 g) butter
a few drops of soy sauce

To make the sauce, wash the elderberries very thoroughly and put in a pan with the sugar and a very little water. Cook until the berries are mushy, then strain the juice through a sieve into a separate pan. Add the vinegar, the red wine and some black pepper and boil together for 5–10 minutes, until reduced to the required consistency, which should be syrupy. Just before serving, finish the sauce by stirring in the butter and a few drops of soy sauce.

I prefer to roast my game birds wrapped in fresh pork fat rather than bacon, as the latter's flavour can overpower a delicate bird. In either case, tie the fat around the bird so that it cannot curl away from the breast. Pre-heat the oven to very hot (220°C/425°F/Gas 7). Place the lump of butter, seasoned, inside each bird. Lay the bird on its side on a piece of bread and roast for 8–10 minutes; then turn it over to the other side, baste with the buttery juices and roast for a further 8–10 minutes with the oven heat slightly reduced (200°C/400°F/Gas 6). Turn the bird upright, cut away the fat and baste the breast well with the buttery juices. Roast for a final 5–10 minutes, depending on the size of the bird and how pink you like it.

Serve on the bread, with a pool of sauce to one side.

SAUSAGE AND BEAN CASSEROLE

As a nation, we eat a lot of sausages. But have you looked at the ingredients list for an ordinary British sausage? Meat takes a back seat to bread, artificial flavourings and preservatives and even those with a high meat content don't state what is meant by that ubiquitous term, meat. It could, literally, be anything. Of course there are old-fashioned local butchers who make their own sausages, but they are far too few. If you have one locally, make sure you patronize his shop.

In France and Italy, Spain and Greece and many of our other European neighbours, the sausage is not a dumping ground for unwanted by-products of butchering, but a delicacy in its own right. As a result, one of the most reliable ways at the moment to find a good sausage in Britain is to go to a delicatessen which imports them from continental Europe. Here you will find 100 per cent meat sausages, made with lamb, beef and pork, flavoured perhaps with fennel seeds or chilli, sold raw or smoked. Cook them with beans for a highly flavoured supper dish.

6 oz (170 g) dry weight of cannellini or haricot beans	2 cloves of garlic
	14 oz (400 g) tin plum tomatoes
2 onions	2 sprigs of fresh or $1/2$
2 cloves	teaspoon dried marjoram
1 bayleaf	or oregano
1 tablespoon olive oil	1 teaspoon fennel seeds
2 carrots	8 sausages
1 or 2 dried red chillies, to taste	$1/2$ pint (300 ml) beef or lamb stock

Soak the beans overnight. The next day, drain them and put them in a large pan of water (do not add salt or you will toughen the beans) together with 1 whole onion studded with a couple of cloves and a bayleaf. Boil hard for 10 minutes then simmer for 1 hour, until the beans are tender but still al dente (the exact cooking time will depend on the freshness of the beans – make sure you taste them regularly towards the end of cooking and check occasionally to ensure that there is sufficient water to cover the beans).

To cook the casserole, chop the second onion and fry in a heavy-based pan in the oil for 10 minutes until translucent. Meanwhile chop the carrots into fine rings and finely chop the chillies and garlic. When the onion is ready, add the carrot, chilli, garlic and fennel seeds to the pan and cook for a further 5 minutes or so. Now add the chopped tomatoes and the herbs. Cook for 5 minutes over a lowish heat.

In a separate pan, heat a little oil and sear the sausages on all sides.

When the tomato mixture is ready, add the sausages and turn well to make sure they are well coated.

Ideally this dish is cooked in the oven in a large flat earthenware dish. If you have such an item, transfer the ingredients at this stage; if not make do with the pot you have used to date. Pre-heat the oven to medium low (130°C/275°F/Gas 1). Add the well-seasoned cooked beans to the casserole, so that they completely cover the sausages and pour over the stock. Bake in the oven uncovered for about 1 hour. Serve with good bread and a green salad.

SPICED PORK KEBABS

This is a Spanish recipe for small cubes of pork marinated in spices and quickly grilled. Traditionally, the little kebabs are cooked over charcoal braziers on street corners or in tapas bars; the effect of the grill is not so authentic, but the kebabs are still very good. They are served with bread, a slice of lemon and a pile of rock salt for dipping the meat in; they can be either a starter or a main dish, in which case a bowl of white beans stewed with tomatoes would accompany them well. Another good idea is a glass of cold beer, to wash down the fiery spices.

To make 16 kebabs

1¹/₂ lb (675 g) pork escalope, cut into slices about 1 inch (2.5 cm) thick

16 metal or wooden skewers
2 lemons
rock salt

FOR THE MARINADE

1 teaspoon whole cumin seeds
1 teaspoon coriander seeds
¹/₂ teaspoon cayenne pepper
1 teaspoon paprika

1 teaspoon black peppercorns
¹/₂ teaspoon ground mace
1 dried red chilli pepper
4 tablespoons olive oil

If you have time, let the pork marinate overnight; if not, leave it in the marinade for a minimum of 3 hours. Trim the pork escalopes of any excess fat and cut into cubes approximately $3/4$–1 inch (2–2.5 cm) square. Grind all the spices together with the dried chilli (I use a coffee grinder kept especially for this purpose, but the more traditional method would be a pestle and mortar) and then mix in the oil. Leave the cubes of pork to marinate in this mixture until you are ready to cook them, turning the meat occasionally.

To cook, pre-heat the grill to absolute maximum. Thread the cubes of pork on to the skewers. (If you are using wooden skewers, sprinkle them with water to make sure they don't catch fire.) Grill as close as possible to the element or flame, with a dish underneath to catch the juices; turn the kebabs after a few minutes and baste with the juices. Total cooking time will be around 7 minutes. Serve immediately, with lemon quarters and a bowl of coarse sea salt.

VENISON CASSEROLE

The lean meat of venison has gained enormously in popularity in the last decade, so much so that it is now available in supermarkets as well as from game butchers. Much of the meat now sold is from farm-reared deer; it is this farming of deer which has done so much to bring down the price of venison and make it an available choice. If you can get hold of a whole haunch of venison, it makes a splendid roast, an excellent dish for a large family occasion (see winter recipe, pages 373–7). Much cheaper, however, than joints or fillets are the packs of stewing venison. This meat does need marinating before cooking; it is worth the trouble, for the eventual casserole will be tender and flavoursome.

For 6

2 lb (900 g) stewing venison

FOR THE MARINADE

¹/₂ a bottle red wine (*a heavy, fruity wine from the South of France, Spain or Portugal is ideal – as always, it must be fit to drink or you will ruin the dish*)

2 tablespoons olive oil
1 teaspoon juniper berries
1 teaspoon black peppercorns
1 teaspoon coriander seeds
¹/₂ an onion
1 clove of garlic, crushed

FOR THE CASSEROLE

4 oz (115 g) belly pork
4 rashers of smoked streaky bacon
¹/₂ tablespoon goose or duck fat or good quality beef dripping
1 onion
1 large carrot

1 clove of garlic
1 level tablespoon plain flour
salt and pepper
1 sprig of thyme
³/₄ pint (450 ml) game or beef stock

FOR THE GARNISH

1 oz (25 g) butter
6 oz (170 g) shallots (*or small pickling onions if shallots are unavailable*)
6 oz (170 g) brown cap or button mushrooms *or*

6 oz (170 g) shelled, cooked chestnuts (*for convenience, buy ready-prepared chestnuts from a delicatessen*)

Trim any fat from the meat and cut into large cubes or strips, if the butcher has not already done so. Mix together all the marinade ingredients, pour over the meat and leave overnight if possible.

To cook the casserole, remove the skin from the belly pork and strip the rind from the bacon. Chop the pork and bacon coarsely. Melt the fat in a large pan and add the pork and bacon; when the fat runs, add the chopped onion, carrot and garlic. Cook over a gentle heat for 15 minutes until soft. Turn up the heat and add the venison, together with the flour and some seasoning. Cook for 5 minutes, until the venison is browned. Strain the marinade and pour into the pan. Tuck in the thyme and add enough stock to cover, bring to a simmer and transfer to a low oven (120°/250°F/Gas $^1/_2$). Cook for 2–2$^1/_2$ hours.

When you are nearly ready to serve, melt the butter for the garnish in a pan. Add the peeled whole shallots and fry gently for 10 minutes until they are browned. Add the washed mushrooms (whole, if they are small) or the cooked chestnuts and continue to fry over a very low heat until they are soft. When the onions and mushrooms or chestnuts are ready, add them to the casserole for the last 5 minutes of cooking. Serve very hot, with boiled or baked potatoes.

PUDDINGS

The most characteristic scent of autumn, at least in my memory, is the sweet sharp smell of the apple shed, filled with the best of the crop stored to last through the winter. Apples were the vital ingredient of so many of the comforting puddings I remember from my childhood – apple pie, blackberry and apple crumble, baked apples stuffed with sultanas, simple apple purées. Autumn meant walks along the hedgerows to pick black-berries and elderberries, and sloes after the first frost. It meant gathering the windfall apples and plums, then teetering on a ladder to get at the perfect ripe fruit, and stacking slatted trays marked with labels bearing the glorious names of the fruit. The reward came later in the kitchen, in the form of jams and jellies, puddings and cakes.

Childhood memories are often rose-tinted but one look at a fruiterer's today might convince me that mine are a mirage. Where are the apples I remember – the Ellison's Orange and Michaelmas Red, the Beauty of Bath and the Saint Edmund's Russet, the Sturmont Pippin and the Worcester Pearmain? These perfectly formed, overgrown and un-blemished fruits which take their place all taste the same, of little but water. For that matter, what happened to quinces and damsons, early Ribers and Czar plums?

The British apple species which have evolved over the centuries each has its own season and culinary value. The difference in flavour between varieties can be astonishing to the uninitiated. Yet despite the fact that there are over 6,000 varieties listed in the National Apple Register, fewer than half a dozen regularly find their way to the retailer.

At New Covent Garden market, the central source of supply for so many of our market stalls, there are as many apples imported from America and France as there are native-grown fruit. These imports are often more expensive, but according to Covent Garden traders they are what we, the public, want. Imported apples are larger, brighter, more perfectly formed than our native varieties – never mind what they taste like, they look better on the shelves. As one trader commented: 'We eat with our eyes, not our mouths.'

The received wisdom continues: if the public does buy English apples, they buy what they know, Cox's and Bramleys. Certain super-markets are now making an effort to introduce additional strains to the shelves, such as varieties of russet. Yet apparently even these are taking time to become recognized by the shopper.

Apples are not of course the only thing to use in autumn puddings, but they are one of the best choices, along with plums, pears, and the new season's nuts. If it is true that we, the consumers, have lost interest in the more unusual varieties of native-grown fruit, then we are missing a great deal. If we are no longer offered the choice of varieties, due to constraints of shelf and stall space, a new generation of shoppers will grow up in ignorance of the treasures of autumn.

Salisbury – Saved by the Women's Institute

I came to Salisbury as part of my quest for old-fashioned British apple varieties. It may not seem an obvious choice, for it is on the very edge of the West Country apple-growing region – but then I had already learned that local orchards do not necessarily mean good markets. The markets of Canterbury and Faversham, a city and a town at the heart of the orchards of the Weald of Kent, are both bitterly disappointing for autumn fruit – nothing but imported Golden Delicious from France and the optimi-stically named American Red Delicious, Conference pears and Victoria plums. A visit to Taunton, of cider fame, had also failed to produce anything more promising on the apple front than a few Cox's and Bramleys, and I was beyond surprise when I learned that much of our English cider production comes from French apple juice, shipped ready pressed. But good cathedrals and good markets often go hand in hand, the medieval ecclesiastical establishment encouraging the development of the town as a trading centre. Salisbury is worth a visit for the beauty of its thirteenth-century cathedral and the eclectic architecture of the Close alone – and it still retains its old market square at the heart of the city.

The square is small, and on Tuesdays and Saturdays the traders are clustered together with little room to move. One of the largest of the stalls on the outskirts of the square is an encouraging sight for the market shopper, a butcher and game dealer from a local farm displaying haunches of wild venison, free-range quail, locally reared lambs and 100 per cent venison sausages. There are three good fish stalls too, as well as a cockle stall selling shellfish as mid-morning snacks, to be eaten with a toothpick from a little saucer. The fruit stalls, however, are less promising – the odd Spartan and russet apples creep in among the familiar display of Cox's, bananas and Conference pears, but there is little to get excited about. If, however, you bore in towards the centre of the market, an unexpected treat is in store.

On the Saturday of my visit, a large queue had formed in front of an old-fashioned mobile van sporting branches of holly red with early berries. Shoppers were bearing away trophies in clear plastic bags, leaving others to hunt through piles of fruit in wicker baskets on the front of the stand, peering each time at small freezer labels on the packages. Labels which bore the time-honoured names, Beauty of Bath and Lord Derby, Ellison's Orange and Laxton's Fortune, James Grieve and Charles Ross. On this particular day there were about twenty different varieties of apple on offer, over the course of the season 100 or more find their way to the market. I had found my source of apples – the Women's Institute stall.

Britain and Ireland are unique in the world with their network of Women's Institute markets. There are currently over 550 in Britain and more than seventy in Ireland. They can range from a single stall in an open market, as in Salisbury, to whole village halls taken over with WI stalls; others take place in garages or even pub yards. WI markets are co-operatives, selling the produce of local inhabitants. The food on sale is the result of long hours at work in the garden or the kitchen and comes freshly picked or baked to the market.

The apples on sale in Salisbury market were therefore the produce of local orchards and gardens, which accounted for their variety. The women serving were only too eager to describe the provenance of the fruit, and to tell me how each type was best used. The Lord Derbys, I learned, were just right for stuffing with dried fruits and baking, perhaps coated with a little of the local honey also on sale. The Laxton's Fortunes were late sweet eaters, best just on their own, like the Ellison's Orange. The Cox's Orange Pippins were very good for cooking with – did I know there are twenty-five different varieties of Cox alone? Perhaps I should try the Bramley's Seedlings for an apple pudding, for they had the right blend of tart and sweet flavours, or use the Worcester Pearmains in an open apple tart. And if I didn't feel like cooking, there were some ready-made apple turnovers to be bought.

The apples were just one of the many treasures of the WI stall. A small pile of furry quinces were being held for a special customer, I should have liked them for slicing into savoury stews, or simply baking with cream and honey, but had to make do with a jar of spiced quince jelly. It was too late in the season for greengages, and unfortunately the woman who used to supply mirabelle plums had recently died, but I could choose between damsons and Marjorie Seedling plums, as well, of course, as Victorias for my favourite nursery food, plum crumble. Rows of different-shaped glass jars held jams and chutneys; all, I was assured, made from local garden produce. It was only two months to Christmas, so what about some home-made mincemeat – much spicier than the commercialized versions. Oh, and if I came back next week there would be some home-made ginger wine, and perhaps even a few bottles of last year's sloe gin.

The WI stall is not the only pleasure of Salisbury market. Several stalls in the autumn season sell nothing but nuts and dried fruits – the new 'wet' walnuts, which make an excellent pudding when ground and then boiled with milk and sugar for a Spanish walnut cream; sweet chestnuts from Italy, which can be toasted, roasted or boiled and used as the base for that rich pudding, Mont Blanc; almonds, both in the shell and ready-flaked for sweet and savoury dishes; several different grades of dried apricot, the best to be used in a winter fruit salad sprinkled with orange-flower water; piles of dried figs, dates, even dried apples. One of the fruit and vegetable stalls on the day I visited had fresh figs from Turkey, not in perfect condition after their long journey, but good when baked. If you want cheese, before or after the pudding, Salisbury has several good cheese stalls, with excellent selections of Cheddars of varying degrees of maturity, local goats' cheeses, blue Cheshires and Stiltons as well as imported French and Italian cheeses. Combine cheese with a bowl of well-chosen, perfectly ripe autumn fruit, especially pears, figs and fresh dates, and you have the simplest and most delicious of ends to a meal, especially if you add home-made fruit and nut breads, which you can buy from that WI stall.

APPLE CHARLOTTE

This method of cooking apples in a sort of bread-and-butter pudding case is one of my favourite ways of dealing with the most popular, and prolific, of autumn fruits. The crisp bread, which for further flavour can be flamed in rum or calvados, encases a juicy centre of spicy, soft apples. A pudding for a cool evening or a Sunday lunch after a long walk, this is nursery food of the best sort.

Apple Charlotte is best made in quantities for 6 or more, to give the right ratio of fruit to bread, although this pudding for 6 could well find itself devoured by 4 hungry people.

3 lb (1.5 kg) good English eating apples (*e.g. Cox's Orange Pippin, Worcester Pearmain, Egremont Russet, Laxton Superb, Ellison's Orange, Orleans Reinette and many more*)	4 cloves
	2 sticks of cinnamon
	4 oz (115 g) sultanas
	1 small loaf stale white bread (*use good country bread rather than the watery, tasteless sliced variety*)
3 oz (85 g) unsalted butter	
4 oz (115 g) brown sugar	2 tablespoons dark rum or calvados (*optional*)

Peel and core the apples and slice into half-moons. Melt $^1/_2$ oz (15 g) of the butter in a pan and gently fry the apples together with half the sugar. When the apples have taken a little colour, barely cover with water, add the spices and sultanas, and simmer until the apples are soft but not falling apart – a matter of 5–10 minutes depending on the ripeness of the fruit. Allow to cool in the liquid.

Pre-heat the oven to medium hot (180°C/350°F/Gas 4). Cut the bread into thin slices and remove the crusts. Mix the remaining butter and sugar and spread on one side of the slices of bread. In a heatproof dome-shaped bowl, 8 inches (20 cm) across by 4 inches (10 cm) deep, well buttered, arrange the slices of bread around the base and sides, buttered sides against the bowl. Make sure there are no gaps. Pick the spices out of the apple and sultana mixture and spoon the mixture into the bread case. Cover the top with more slices of bread, buttered side up. Put a light weight on top and bake for $1^1/_4$ hours; remove the weight after 30 minutes.

When the pudding is cooked, turn it out of the bowl, heat the spirit if you are using it, set light to it, pour it over the pudding and bring it flaming to the table.

APPLE PUDDING

This French recipe is somewhere between a pudding and a cake; the apples are encased in a light batter, the whole topped with a crispy coating of butter and sugar. Although I usually prefer to use eating apples for baking, in this dish I find the tartness of a cooker works well. A substantial but delicious pudding, it is much appreciated on cold days. For indulgence, you can serve it with whipped cream.

$^1/_2$ pint (300 ml) full-cream milk
1 vanilla pod
8 oz (225 g) plain white flour
4 oz (115 g) white sugar (*vanilla sugar if you have it – keep a special jar of sugar with a vanilla pod in it*)
2 teaspoons baking powder
2 tablespoons vegetable oil
pinch of salt
4 large cooking apples (*e.g. Bramley, James Grieve, Lord Derby, Victoria*)
2 oz (55 g) butter
1 egg
1 teaspoon ground cinnamon

Bring the milk to the boil with the split vanilla pod and leave to cool. When cool, strain to remove the skin.

Pre-heat the oven to medium ($150°C/300°F$/Gas 2). Mix together the sifted flour, half the sugar, the baking powder, the oil, and the pinch of salt, make a well in the centre and slowly pour in the cooled, strained milk, stirring all the time. Peel and core the apples, slice them very finely, and then add them to the mixture. Butter an oblong baking dish and carefully spoon in the mixture. Bake for 30 minutes in a medium oven.

Melt the butter and stir in the remainder of the sugar, the beaten egg and the cinnamon. Spread this mixture over the tart and bake for another 30–40 minutes, until the topping is crisp. Serve immediately.

AUTUMN FRUIT CRUMBLE

A crumble is one of those old-fashioned British puddings that almost everybody likes. The rich, buttery topping over a layer of juicy fruit makes a serious dish. My favourite crumbles are made with a mixture of plums, perhaps with greengages and damsons thrown in. The slight tartness of the fruit sets off the crisp top perfectly.

2 lb (900 g) mixed plums	2 tablespoons whisky
3^1/$_2$ oz (100 g) unsalted	(*optional*)
butter	pinch of salt
3 oz (85 g) white sugar	1 teaspoon ground
6 oz (170 g) plain flour	cinnamon

Wash, halve and stone the plums. Melt ^{1}/$_2$ oz (15 g) of the butter in a pan, add the plums and fry gently for 5 minutes. Add 1 oz (25 g) of the sugar. If you are using it, heat the whisky in a ladle, set light to it and pour it over the fruit. Shake the pan to make sure the flames touch all the plums.

Sieve the flour with a good pinch of salt. Stir in the rest of the sugar and the cinnamon. Crumble in the rest of the butter, softened, with your fingertips, until you have a pile of crumbs.

Pre-heat the oven to medium hot (180°C/350°C/Gas 4). Put the fruit in the base of a baking dish and spoon over the topping. Bake for 30–40 minutes, until the crumble is lightly browned. Serve piping hot.

AVOCADO AND COCONUT CREAM

Large, thin-skinned avocados, often from Israel, are common in the shops in autumn, before the small, purply ones with rough skins reappear in winter. The avocado pear is a fruit rather than a vegetable and can be used as the base for drinks, ice-creams and delicate creams. This Indonesian pudding combines the avocado flesh with coconut milk in a simple-to-make dish. On no account leave out the lime juice, or your elegant pale green cream will turn a dirty shade of brown. For the same reason, do not make it more than 2 hours or so in advance.

4 very ripe, unbruised
    avocados
2 limes
1 oz (25 g) caster sugar or
    to taste

4 tablespoons coconut milk
    (*available in tins from
    Indian and West Indian
    stores*)
2 oz (55 g) toasted hazelnuts

Peel the avocados and remove the stones. Cut out any pieces of darkened flesh, which would spoil the colour of the cream. Mash the avocado flesh and the lime juice together with a fork (a liquidizer bruises the fruit) and then stir in the sugar and coconut milk. Taste to check sweetness (the amount of sugar needed will depend partly on the sweetness of your brand of coconut milk). Spoon into individual serving dishes and chill. Before serving, top with the toasted hazelnuts.

BAKED BANANAS IN RUM

Bananas and rum are two of the mainstays of the Caribbean, so it is not surprising that West Indian cooks regularly combine the two. As autumn moves on and locally grown fruit becomes scarcer, bananas correspondingly increase in number and quality. Look out for fat, well-ripened but not mushy fruit for this dish; if you can get hold of the coarse, dark brown, unrefined sugar called jaggery, the taste will be more authentic.

4 large bananas	$^1/_2$ teaspoon ground allspice
$1^1/_2$ oz (45 g) butter	2 limes
2 oz (55 g) jaggery or brown sugar	3 tablespoons dark rum

Pre-heat the oven to hot (200°C/400°F/Gas 6). Prick the unpeeled bananas deeply several times on each side with a skewer. Place on a baking tray and cook for 10–15 minutes depending on size, until the skins have darkened and the fruit feels soft.

Melt the butter and stir in the sugar and allspice; cook over a low heat for a minute or two. When the bananas are cool enough to handle, peel off the skins and sprinkle the fruit with the juice of the limes. Warm the rum in a ladle, set light to it and pour it over the fruit. When the flames die down, pour over the spicy sugar and butter mix and serve immediately.

BAKED FIGS WITH SAFFRON CREAM

Imported fresh figs are a particular treat of early autumn, their purply black skins concealing sweet red glutinous fruit and tiny yellow seeds. Of course, the best figs are those picked in the early morning from the tree by your terrace and served for breakfast, but for most of us that is the stuff of dreams. If you can buy perfectly ripe figs, squidgy to the touch but their skin unmarked, their flesh juicy, then cut them into quarters and eat them straight away, with parma ham, or on their own for the perfect end to a meal. But if you find your figs are a little old, a little tough, or a little under-ripe, then try baking them before serving with a saffron-scented cream.

8 fresh figs	a few strands of saffron
1 orange	$^1/_4$ pint (150 ml) double cream
1 oz (25 g) caster sugar	

Place the washed figs in a baking tray into which they will just fit, squeeze over the orange juice and sprinkle with caster sugar. Add a very little water to moisten the bottom of the pan, and bake in a medium oven (150°C/300°F/Gas 2) for 15 minutes.

Meanwhile soak the saffron in a tablespoon of warm water, so that the flavour infuses. Whip the cream until very stiff. When the figs are ready to serve, strain the saffron water and whip into the cream. Cut a cross in the centre of each fig, put in a dollop of the yellow, fragrant cream and serve immediately.

BAKED QUINCES WITH CREAM AND HONEY

The quince, an import from central Asia, was extremely popular in medieval British cooking, where it was used in both savoury and sweet dishes. As time went on, however, it became an ever rarer sight, so that in recent years it seemed almost to have disappeared from our dishes. Not so abroad: in Morocco, for example, tagines of chicken with quince are regularly served, as well as delicious quince jams. I hope that Britain is in the throes of rediscovering the quince, for I have seen it in several autumn markets recently, the odd-shaped greeny-yellow fruits with their fluffy white down proudly displayed in wicker baskets at the front of the stall. Before moving on to the more exotic savoury dishes, try this excellent recipe from Provence for baked quinces.

2 oz (55 g) raisins	4 tablespoons clear honey
2 glasses sweet white	(*flower-scented is best*)
pudding wine (*a Muscat*	$^1/_4$ pint (150 ml) single
is particularly good)	cream
4 large quinces	1 wine-glass water
16 cloves	1 teaspoon ground
	cinnamon

Pre-heat the oven to medium (150°C/300°F/Gas 2). Soak the raisins in the wine for 30 minutes to plump them up. Meanwhile, peel and core the quinces using a slim knife or a corer.

Stud the quinces with the cloves and stuff with the raisins. Mix the remaining ingredients and pour in and over the quinces. Bake for about $1^1/_2$ hours until the quinces are very soft and golden brown. Early on in the cooking, the sauce may separate – don't worry, it will reconstitute itself if you leave well alone.

BLACKBERRY SORBET

Although I love the flavour of fresh blackberries, I find the pips a nuisance, adding a tartness which detracts from the fruit. This problem is avoided if the berries are first cooked and then sieved, as in blackberry fool, the sieved purée whipped into sweetened fresh cream. Another alternative is blackberry sorbet. Ices are not normally an autumn choice, but the fresh taste of this one makes it a good end to a rich meal.

2 lb (900 g) blackberries
6 oz (170 g) sugar (*or more if you have a sweet tooth – I like the sorbet a little tart*)
$^1/_2$ a lemon

2 tablespoons kirsch (*if you don't have any kirsch, a good-quality Russian or Polish vodka also goes well*)

Wash the berries very thoroughly and put them in a small pan. Cook, stirring, over a low heat until the juices run, then cover and cook for a further 10 minutes, until the fruit is very tender. Meanwhile, mix together the sugar and $^3/_4$ pint (450 ml) of water and bring to the boil. Boil for 5 minutes, then leave the syrup to cool.

Push the cooked fruit through a very fine sieve. Strain the juice from the lemon and add it to the sugar syrup with the kirsch and the fruit purée. Mix together very well.

Pour the mixture into a freezer-proof container with a lid. Freeze with the lid on, stirring a couple of times during the freezing process to break up the ice granules. Remove from the freezer at least 30 minutes before serving – it should have a slightly slushy consistency.

DAMSON AND MASCARPONE FOOL

Tiny purple damsons seem to be regaining popularity. Look out for them in your local market and choose firm-fleshed fruit with no brown patches. Damsons are tart and need quite a lot of sugar, which is why they are popularly used for jams and damson cheese. They can also be good in savoury dishes, as in the damson and okra curry suggested for serving with grilled mackerel (pages 241–3). I find that the damson's powerful flavour and bright colour combines well with the rich Italian cream cheese mascarpone in this fool.

1 lb (450 g) damsons	8 fl oz (250 ml) mascarpone
4 oz (115 g) sugar	(*if you can't get this, use an*
1 vanilla pod	*unsweetened cream cheese*)
juice of 1 orange	2 oz (55 g) toasted hazelnuts

Wash the damsons and remove their stalks (no need to stone them). Put them in a pan with the sugar, the vanilla pod and the orange juice. Add half a wine-glass of water and bring to the boil. Simmer covered for 15 minutes, until the fruit is dissolved and you have a thick syrup. If the syrup seems too thin, boil uncovered for a few minutes; if too thick, dilute with a little more water.

Sieve the syrup and allow to cool. When it is cool, whip it into the mascarpone. Spoon into individual serving dishes and chill thoroughly. Scatter with the toasted hazelnuts before serving.

GINGERED APPLES AND PEARS

Apples and pears stewed in lemon juice and fresh ginger make a wonderful compote, the spice bringing out the flavour of the fruit. I like to serve this pudding with a real custard, made with vanilla-scented milk and fresh eggs, but if you have less time try it with Greek yoghurt into which you have whipped some brown sugar.

FOR THE CUSTARD

1 pint (575 ml) full cream milk	4 egg-yolks
	2 oz (55 g) white sugar
1/2 a vanilla pod	

FOR THE FRUIT

1 lb (450 g) good-quality
English eating apples,
slightly underripe

1 lb (450 g) slightly
underripe pears (*French
Poire Williams are
especially good here*)

1 inch (2.5 cm) piece of
fresh ginger

1 large lemon

1 oz (25 g) brown sugar

To make the custard, boil the milk with the vanilla pod for 5 minutes. Leave to cool for 10 minutes. Meanwhile, beat the egg-yolks and sugar together until the cream lightens in colour. Remove the vanilla pod and any skin from the boiled milk and stir it very slowly with a wooden spoon into the egg and sugar mix, until it is all incorporated. Heat over a very low flame, stirring all the time, until the mixture thickens sufficiently to coat the back of the spoon (about 20 minutes). On no account let the custard come anywhere near boiling or it will curdle.

Peel the fruit and chop into bite-sized cubes. Peel the ginger and grate into a cooking pan, making sure you catch all the juices. Add the juice of the lemon and the fruit and cook over a low flame for 20 minutes. Then stir in the brown sugar and cook for another 10 minutes.

Serve the compote warm with the custard.

LEMON TART

The bright sharpness of a lemon tart is a welcome reminder of summer sunlight on a cooler day. The lemon tarts of Provence seem to have a delicate fragrance which it is difficult to re-create in Britain, where our lemons are hardly fresh from the tree. I have found a stunning improvement in results, however, when using the unwaxed lemons which are now available from shops and supermarkets. In a lemon which has not been sealed with chemically treated wax, the zest retains its natural oils, which are essential to the success of this dish.

6 oz (170 g) plain flour   3 oz (85 g) unsalted butter
pinch of salt   1 egg-yolk
1 oz (25 g) sugar

FOR THE FILLING

2 unwaxed lemons   *my tart sharp)*
4 oz (115 g) sugar (*or more*   4 eggs, separated
   according to taste – I like   1 teaspoon cornflour

To make the pastry, sieve together the flour, salt and sugar then blend in the butter with your fingers. Add the egg-yolk and a tablespoon of chilled water; form the dough into a ball. Allow to rest, wrapped in foil or paper, for an hour or so in a cool place.

Roll the pastry out very thinly and line an 8–10 inch (20–25 cm) buttered flan case. Prick the pastry with a fork all over and bake blind in a medium oven (150°C/300°F/Gas 2) for 15 minutes.

To make the filling, first grate the rinds of the lemons then squeeze out their juice. Combine three-quarters of the sugar with the egg-yolks and then add the lemon zest and juice. Carefully stir in the cornflour and cook over a low heat until the cream thickens, stirring all the time – this should take about 15 minutes in all. Beat the egg-whites with the remaining sugar until stiff and fold very gently into the cream. Turn the oven up to medium hot (about 180°C/350°F/Gas 4). Lay the filling over the pastry base and cook for 20–25 minutes, until brown on top. Serve warm.

MONT BLANC

This pudding from the foothills of the Alps takes its name from the finished appearance of the dish. The base of brown chestnut mixed with chocolate is the mountain itself; the topping of liquored whipped cream is meant to resemble the winter snows. This very rich dish makes a spectacular end to a dinner party.

1¹/₂ lb (675 g) fresh
chestnuts (*chestnut purée
really isn't an adequate
substitute here,
unfortunately, having too
fine a consistency*)
¹/₂ pint (300 ml) double
cream

1 tablespoon caster sugar
2 tablespoons brandy
1 vanilla pod
pinch of salt
1 pint (575 ml) full cream
milk
4 oz (115 g) best-quality
dark chocolate

Wash the chestnuts and score each across the round side. Put in a large pan, cover with water, bring to the boil and boil hard for 20 minutes. Remove from the pan and peel as soon as they are cool enough to handle, ensuring that you remove all the bitter skin. Do not wait until the nuts are completely cold or they will be impossible to peel. Whip the cream with the sugar and brandy, and chill.

Put the peeled chestnuts in a pan with the vanilla pod and a pinch of salt and cover with the milk. Bring to the boil and simmer uncovered for 20 minutes or so. By this time the chestnuts should be thoroughly tender and the milk almost absorbed.

Remove the vanilla pod and either push the chestnuts through a sieve or give them a quick whizz in the food processor (the former will give a more authentic result, for the chestnuts shouldn't be too smooth, but of course the latter is easier – take care not to process for more than a moment or two, though). Keep back a little chocolate for grating over the pudding and melt the rest in a double boiler. Stir the melted chocolate into the chestnuts.

Roughly pile the just warm chestnut and chocolate mixture in the centre of a serving dish and spoon the chilled cream over so that it comes about two-thirds of the way down the sides. Sprinkle over a little grated chocolate. Serve immediately, unless you want a mountain so authentic that the snow melts.

OPEN PLUM TART

French open tarts are a decorative and tasty way to use autumn fruit. They can be made with apples, pears, or, my favourite, plums. In Alsace, the tiny purple plums called quetsch are used, but any small dark plum will do well. Other excellent fruits for this pudding are the golden plums known as mirabelles, or the early autumn greengages.

The tart tastes best a day or two after it is made, when the flavours have blended – the coating of boudoir biscuits stops the juice of the fruit making the pastry soggy. The quantities given here are for a large flan or tart dish (about 12 inches (30 cm) diameter).

FOR THE PASTRY

8 oz (225 g) plain flour	3 oz (85 g) unsalted butter
pinch of salt	2 eggs
2 oz (55 g) sugar	

FOR THE FILLING

2^1/$_2$ lb (1.25 kg) plums	1 egg-white
6 oz (170 g) boudoir	caster sugar
biscuits	ground cinnamon

To make the pastry, sift the flour with a pinch of salt and the sugar. Crumble in the softened butter with your hands and then add the beaten eggs. Add a tablespoon or two of chilled water and form a dough. Wrap in greaseproof paper and allow to rest for an hour or so in a cool place.

Roll the pastry out thinly and line the buttered flan or tart dish. Bake blind in a pre-heated medium hot oven (180°C/350°F/Gas 4) for 10 minutes.

Wash the plums well, halve and remove the stones. Crumble the boudoir biscuits very finely.

Sprinkle the biscuit crumbs in a layer across the pastry base and lightly brush with egg-white. Arrange the plums in concentric circles on top, starting from the middle. *Note*: the plums should be cut side upwards. Sprinkle with caster sugar and cinnamon and bake in a medium hot oven (180°C/350°F/Gas 4) for 30–40 minutes

Leave to cool thoroughly before serving.

PEAR AND DATE STRUDEL

The traditional Austrian filling for strudel is apples and sultanas or raisins, but I also like a combination of pears and dried dates. The natural sweetness of the dates eliminates the need to add sugar and combines well with the delicate fragrance of the pears.

4 slightly underripe pears	8 sheets filo pastry
2 oz (55 g) dried dates	1 teaspoon ground allspice
3 oz (85 g) unsalted butter	

Peel the pears and chop the fruit into pieces. Finely chop the dried dates. Cook the pears and dates with a tablespoon of water for a few minutes, to allow the fruit to soften and the dates to absorb the juices. Set aside.

Pre-heat the oven to medium low (130°C/275°F/Gas 1). Melt the butter, without allowing it to brown, and skim off any scum. Grease a flat baking tray and have ready a clean damp tea-cloth. To assemble the strudel, lay a sheet of filo pastry flat on the baking tray and brush the upper side with a little melted butter. Meanwhile, keep the rest of the pastry covered with the damp cloth. Lay another sheet of filo on top, brush again with butter, and so on until you have used 4 sheets.

Now spread the fruit and date mixture in a thin layer across all of the pastry surface. Sprinkle the fruit with the allspice and lay another sheet of filo on top. Brush with butter and continue until you have used all the pastry. Now take one of the two short ends of the pastry rectangle and fold it inwards so that the edge is at the centre of the rectangle. Fold the other short end over, so that you have a small oblong which contains 3 layers of fruit. This may not be the traditional strudel shape, but it works just as well and is much easier to put together. Brush the surface of the pastry with the remaining butter.

Bake the pastry for 45–60 minutes in the oven, until it is crisp and lightly browned. Serve warm, perhaps with some cream.

SPICED PEARS IN RED WINE

Pears are another fruit where only recently has the range available to the British shopper begun to open out. There are too many delicious and different varieties for us to be content with Conference pears, good though they can be. Look out for my favourite, the French Doyenne de Comice, usually distinguishable by the red blob of sealing wax put on top to stop the stalk bleeding when the fruit is picked. Another good imported variety is the Poire William, which gave its name to the famous Alsatian eau-de-vie. If you get hold of a perfectly ripe pear, do nothing more than slice it and eat it, perhaps with a little blue cheese such as the Italian dolcelatte. But if you have pears which refuse to ripen, try cooking them in spicy red wine to produce a burnished red, juicily tender fruit.

4 slightly underripe pears
$^1/_2$ oz (15 g) butter
3 tablespoons brown sugar
$^1/_3$ bottle red wine (*a heavy wine high in alcohol such as the Portuguese Dão is*

good here)
1 stick of cinnamon
4 cloves
4 cardamom pods
pinch of grated nutmeg

Peel the pears, leaving their stalks on. Melt the butter in a pan big enough to take all 4 pears. Gently fry the pears for a few minutes until coloured on all sides. Add the sugar, the wine and the spices. Bring to the boil, bubble for a minute or two, and then cover and turn down to a slow simmer. Cook for about 45 minutes, turning the pears occasionally, until they are soft but not soggy. When the pears are done, remove from the sauce. Pick out the whole spices and boil the sauce down to a syrupy consistency. Pour over the pears.

Serve the pears hot or cold – I like them just warm and on their own, but you can accompany them with some whipped cream, preferably vanilla-scented (leave a piece of vanilla pod in a small carton of cream for 30 minutes before whipping).

WINTER

THE CHRISTMAS FEAST HAS A TENDENCY TO DOMINATE THE COOK'S WINTER. DECEMBER IS A MONTH OF

preparation leading up to the big day, interspersed by the round of parties, placing constant demands on the kitchen. By January the cook is exhausted and often only in February does enthusiasm for food return, with the imminent advent of spring.

The national obsession with Christmas is fuelled by the retailers, and the major food sellers are no exception. In December your local supermarket suddenly turns into an Aladdin's cave, stacked with extraordinary goods. Too often these are totally unseasonal: new potatoes are now grown for the Christmas market, as are peaches, strawberries and asparagus.

The market shopper will escape the majority of these unseasonal aberrations and rely on local producers for the many delights of the winter season. Game is excellent. This is one of the best times of the year for the white fish which predominates in our fishing catches. Shellfish too are still abundant, especially oysters. Root vegetables need not be boring: they make wonderful salads to help you recover from the excesses of December. Winter-grown salad leaves are crunchy, with a hint of bitterness. There is plenty of fruit left over from the autumn, and when that runs out, you can turn to dried fruits and nuts. The long dark winter evenings make the warm kitchen positively attractive; now is the time for slow-cooking dishes, which you can prepare in advance. There is more to the winter season than the feast of Christmas itself.

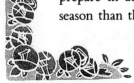

STARTERS

In this book, the theme of starters concentrates on vegetables. I am no lover of the overcrowded plate of meat and three veg and prefer where possible to serve meat, fish and vegetables as distinct courses. So a recipe which many might consider as a side dish for a main course may well be found here in the starter section. This rule wavers a little in the winter, when meaty pâtés, plates of charcuterie and solid terrines acquire a particular attraction. But then there are winter soups, or assortments of winter salads to consider.

At first sight, the range of traditional British winter vegetables seems limited. But there are plenty of root vegetables which are under-appreciated: celeriac and Jerusalem artichokes, for example. There are local vegetables which we scandalously neglect, like the delicious seakale, which is virtually impossible to find, or salsify, the 'vegetable oyster'. And in recent years we have also come to consider as our own a number of vegetables which, although not native to Britain, have their season in winter and grow well here, or at least survive the rigours of import without too many ill-effects, like fennel and chicory, or the many varieties of winter salad leaves.

Sadly, many traditional markets feature few of these delights, relying instead on the cheaper but boring winter trio of cabbages, potatoes and onions. Nowhere is this more true than in Dublin's Moore Street. Even with this limited choice, however, there are plenty of options for the cook to kick off a winter's meal.

A Step Back in Time to Moore Street

Dublin's main retail fruit and vegetable market takes place six days a week in a small and scruffy street on the north side of the Liffey. Turning off the main O'Connell Street into pedestrianized Henry Street, the entrance of the market is heralded by travellers selling lighters and packs of tobacco. On the corner of Moore Street there are usually a few mobile stalls set up on old-fashioned prams, which can be wheeled away at the first sign of the Garda. Molly Malone, in statue form, may be allowed to stand in front of Trinity College selling her wares, but everyone else has to have a licence.

The stalls of Moore Street are ranged back to back with a wide thoroughfare through the middle, forcing you to walk up one side and then down the other in order to be able to examine what is on offer. As you wander along, soft lilting voices mutter: 'Would you be wanting some of the oynions?' 'How about a pound of musharooms?' 'Try me caulies at 40 pence.' 'What will you be wantin', me darlin'?' A far cry from the strident noise of the London street markets, these gentle persuasions come, you suddenly realize, from female voices. The traders of Moore Street are almost all women, strong tough ladies with the weather etched in their faces and the look of farmers' wives, aunts or sisters. Which they almost all are, for they are selling the produce of the farm.

And this, you realize, is another thing which is peculiar about Moore Street market: all the stalls seem to be offering the same goods. Of course, there are minor differences of price and quality. This lady's sprouts seem to have had a touch of frost, the cauliflowers on the next stall are particularly cheap, the cabbage over there looks especially hearty. But there the variety ends. There is no stall selling exotic imported vegetables, unless you count the odd red pepper or aubergine. No one offering a selection of winter salad leaves, such as mâche or frisée – it's unseasonal butterhead lettuce or nothing, for the Irish are not big salad eaters. There is little fennel or chicory, the type of winter vegetable we no longer think of as exotic. Where are the chillies, limes, or herbs for ethnic cooking? The vegetable stalls of Moore Street in winter offer the type of produce which, with the odd exception (those aubergines and peppers again), might have been found in an English country market in the early 1950s. Root vegetables, cabbages, onions and potatoes take up most of the space.

Of course, not everything can come from the farm. A good proportion of the produce is bought in from the early-morning wholesale market at Smithfield, itself a popular stop for budget-conscious Dublin shoppers. From there much of it is delivered up the road in traditional style – horse and cart. On the day I visited a shaggy skewbald stood at one end of the central thoroughfare, stretching out his neck to nose through boxes for discarded cabbage leaves and earning a 'Git on, be Jaysus' from his owner, who was busy distributing cases of vegetables amongst the stallholders. The other end of the street was blocked by a big Irish dray horse, clothed in bright orange plastic sheeting against the soft rain, his cart loaded with empty crates. A scene for the calendar photographers, perhaps, but also a reflection of everyday life in Dublin.

Nostalgia apart, what does Moore Street represent of the food of Ireland? The limited range of produce on offer in winter is a good reflection of the traditional diet at this time of year. Potatoes remain vital – although when I visited only one variety was on offer, albeit in enormous quantities. The potato introduced by Sir Walter Ralegh in the sixteenth century was the sweet variety, but the Virginian potato followed hard on its heels and by the late eighteenth century had become the staple diet of the poor. That overdependence was of course to have tragic consequences when blight struck in the 1840s. No one today lives on potatoes alone, but they are still an important element of Irish cooking. Potatoes form the base for many of the thick soups which are the traditional Irish starter: onion and potato, leek and potato, fish chowder, watercress and lovage soups, even garlic soup. Potato soup itself is popular. Potato pancakes take many forms, including the boxty, which according to Gallagher's Boxty House in Dublin was developed during the famine as a way of using potatoes once the starch in which the blight was contained had been removed. Gallagher's serve these potato pancakes as a main course with various fillings but I like coarser, crispier, smaller versions as a base for a starter, heaped with tomatoes or covered with smoked salmon. It has to be said, though, that Irish cooks do not seem to be too adventurous with their potato. They might do well to copy the

Spanish, who like them for tapas – try potatoes spiced with paprika and cumin. Gnocchi, the potato dumplings from Italy, are distinctly non-Irish, but served in a creamy blue cheese sauce I am pretty sure they would find favour.

Moore Street in winter displays even more cabbage than it does potatoes – Savoy, white or 'Dutch' and spring cabbage being the most popular varieties. Red cabbage, although popular before the war, now has something of a novelty value. Cabbage too is used in soups. Again, the Irish use of cabbage cannot be said to be especially creative; most popular is to combine it with that other staple, the potato, in colcannon, or to serve it buttered as a plain vegetable. Yet the cabbage has excellent potential for winter starters. Try the marvellous bean and cabbage soups of Tuscany, enriched with olive oil; the delicately patterned cabbage terrine of France, stuffed with pork and carrots; or the winter salads of the Turks, finely sliced red cabbage combined with raisins and olive oil.

Onions and members of the family such as the leek and wild garlic have long been important in Irish cuisine. Try the Dublin technique of baking onions in their skins, thus preserving many of the vitamins: this is the perfect vegetable for a Sunday roast. Moore Street had plenty of the tiny pickling onions on offer, not just for preserving but for braising and combining with sugar and vinegar to make a sweet-and-sour sauce. Root vegetables were popular too, but the turnips straight from the farm had grown too large for my liking – I prefer them smaller so that I can braise them with butter and sugar and combine them with strips of duck for an earthy starter. Parsnips by now were also overgrown and woody: make sure you squeeze them before buying to check they are firm to the touch. Good ones can be used for one of my favourite winter starters, creamy parsnip soup spiced with a little turmeric and cumin.

Of course, it is unfair to Irish food to talk only of their use of winter vegetables. Ireland is the source of some of the best-quality seafood in western Europe. Her oysters are magnificent, her smoked salmon gives the Scots serious competition, her fishing fleet catches some of the best fish to be had. Her dairy produce reaps the benefit of good grass and a damp climate. Irish meat, beef, pork and lamb, can be of exceptional quality. Such good quality that much of it is exported, with the substantial backing of the Irish government. For that which stays behind, there are some wonderful traditional recipes – a good Irish stew or a

Dublin coddle is no poor thing. The country certainly has the raw material for the gourmet.

And there are exciting things a cook can do with winter vegetables as offered in Moore Street. Taking lessons not just from Ireland but from Italy and Spain, France and Belgium, Germany and Scandinavia, there is endless potential for the potato, the cabbage and the root vegetable. There is also, however, a lesson that in preaching seasonality one can become precious. In this global market, seasonal food is not just what is available locally, but what is best at that time of year from the various countries in which the produce is grown. Farming means growing not just traditional crops, but those which although not native are suited to local conditions, provided of course there is a market for them. This should not be a new idea for Ireland – after all, the potato itself is no native here.

CABBAGE TERRINE

Few gastronomic pulses race at the thought of one of the best of the winter vegetables, cabbage. For many of us our potential enjoyment of the cabbage in its many forms was spoilt at school by the sight, smell and appalling taste of cabbage boiled to death. But if you ignore those memories and revisit the world of the cabbage, you could be pleasantly surprised. Try red cabbage slowly braised with vinegar, cider and spices or served raw, very thinly sliced and dressed with lemon juice and olive oil; white cabbage tossed in mustard oil Gujerati style with cumin and mustard seeds, sugar and lemon juice, or blanched and served in a salad with plump sultanas and toasted nuts; Savoy cabbage braised in white wine with bacon, and perhaps a plump game bird sitting on top.

This terrine displays the unexpected beauty of the cabbage leaf. The finely veined light green leaves encase a juicy filling of pork studded with carrots, producing a visually impressive first course which tastes even better. I like to serve slices of the terrine cold on a pool of hot, slightly sweet-and-sour tomato sauce.

Serves 6–8

FOR THE TERRINE

4 shallots

1 clove of garlic

1 lb (450 g) minced pork

2 large eggs

2 tablespoons finely
   chopped fresh parsley

1/4 teaspoon ground mace

pinch of grated nutmeg

salt and freshly ground
   black pepper

1 glass dry white wine

(*a fruity wine such as an
Alsatian Riesling or
Sylvaner or an Italian
Pinot Grigio is good*)

1 large Savoy cabbage

2 large carrots

goose or duck fat, or lard,
   for greasing

6 rashers of smoked streaky
   bacon

FOR THE TOMATO SAUCE

2 onions

1 tablespoon olive oil

14 oz (400 g) tin plum
   tomatoes

1 tablespoon finely chopped
   fresh parsley

1 teaspoon sugar

1 tablespoon red wine
   vinegar

salt and freshly ground
   black pepper

1/2 pint (300 ml) vegetable
   or chicken stock

To make the terrine, finely chop the shallots and garlic. Mix together with a wooden spoon the pork, eggs, shallots, garlic, parsley, mace, nutmeg, plenty of freshly ground black pepper, a little salt and half the wine. Allow to stand for an hour or so, for the meat to absorb the flavours.

Peel the tough dark green outer leaves off the cabbage and discard. Carefully remove the inner leaves, trying as far as possible to keep them whole. Cut out any tough stalk ends in a V shape.

Fill a large pan with cold water and add the cabbage leaves. Heat slowly and when the water comes to the boil drain, being careful not to break the leaves. Allow the cabbage leaves to cool slightly.

Peel the carrots, cut them in half across and slice very thinly lengthways. Bring a pan of water to the boil and blanch the carrots for 1 minute.

Pre-heat the oven to medium (150°C/300°F/Gas 2). Choose an oblong earthenware terrine dish about 10 inches (25 cm) long and grease it with lard, goose or duck fat. Line the base of the dish with 3 slices of the bacon. Lay the largest of the cabbage leaves across the base of the dish, so that they run up the sides and overlap the edge. Lay half the pork stuffing mix on top of the leaf base. Cover the stuffing with half the thinly sliced carrots and top with a layer of the smaller cabbage leaves.

Lay the other half of the stuffing on top of the cabbage; top with the remaining carrots in a single layer. Fold over any cabbage overlapping the sides and top with a final layer of cabbage leaves. Lay 3 slices of bacon on top and pour over the remainder of the wine.

Cover the terrine with foil or greaseproof paper and tie it round with string. Place the terrine in a baking tray and half fill the tray with water, so that it comes about a third of the way up the terrine dish. Place in the pre-heated oven and cook for 2 hours.

Remove the cooked terrine from the oven, untie the string and place a heavy weight on top of the foil. Leave to cool at room temperature and then transfer to the fridge to set. When the terrine is firm, turn out on to a large plate. Discard the bacon but make sure you scrape out any jelly in the dish.

To make the sauce, roughly chop the onions. Heat the oil and gently fry the onion until tender and lightly browned (about 15 minutes). Add the tinned tomatoes and fry gently for another 5 minutes, until the tomatoes start to break up. Add the chopped parsley, the sugar, the vinegar, plenty of freshly ground black pepper and a pinch of salt. Allow the vinegar to just come to the boil then pour over the stock. Bring back to the boil then allow to simmer uncovered for 20 minutes, by which time the liquid should almost have evaporated.

Push the sauce through a fine sieve, return to the heat and boil until you have the right consistency.

Slice the cold terrine thickly and serve 1 slice per person in a pool of the hot tomato sauce, with plenty of bread.

CHICORY AND HAM GRATIN

Chicory is at its best from November through to March. Look for firm heads with light green outer leaves and white stems, and avoid any with a tinge of brown. Chicory makes an excellent winter salad – top the bitter leaves with toasted nuts and dress them with walnut oil and balsamic vinegar. For a more substantial starter or lunch dish, I cook this favourite from Belgium, where much of the chicory we buy is grown. It is important to use good-quality ham, preferably home-cooked – the processed version will give off too much liquid and ruin the sauce.

The quantities given here are for a starter for 4.

4 heads of chicory
juice of $^1/_2$ a lemon
2 oz (55 g) butter
1 oz (25 g) plain flour
1 tablespoon mild grainy French mustard (*halve the quantity if using Dijon and use far less if you only have the fiery English mustard*)

$^1/_2$ pint (300 ml) full-cream milk
3 oz (85 g) strong hard cheese, coarsely grated (*I prefer Gruyère but you can also use mature farmhouse Cheddar*)
salt, pepper and cayenne
4 slices of cooked ham

Wash the chicory heads well and sprinkle them with the lemon juice to prevent them from discolouring. Melt half the butter in a pan with a lid and gently fry the whole chicory until it takes on a little colour. Add a tablespoon or two of water and cover the pan. Cook until the chicory is tender (check with a skewer) – this should take 20–30 minutes, depending on the size of the heads. Shake the pan occasionally to make sure the chicory isn't burning and add a little more water if necessary. When cooked, remove the chicory and leave to drain upside down for 5 minutes. (Many recipes for chicory gratin call for the chicory to be boiled – this makes it waterlogged and is not a good idea.)

Meanwhile make the sauce. Melt the remaining butter and stir in the flour. When the roux is lightly coloured, stir in the mustard and then add the milk, very slowly at first and stirring all the time. When you have added all the milk, bring slowly to the boil. Simmer for 5 minutes, still stirring, until the sauce has thickened and you have cooked off the taste of the flour. Take off the heat and stir in the grated cheese. Add salt, pepper and cayenne to taste (a pinch of the latter should do the trick).

Pre-heat the oven to medium hot (180°C/350°F/Gas 4). Wrap a slice of ham around each cooked chicory head. Arrange the chicory in a gratin dish into which it will just fit, with the join of the ham slice underneath. Pour over the sauce. Cook in the oven for 15 minutes, until the surface is bubbling and lightly browned. Serve immediately, with warm crusty bread.

FILO PASTRY PARCELS

The Ottoman Empire produced one of the great cuisines of the world, which stretched out its fingers to influence all Middle Eastern cooking as we know it today. One of my favourite features of this style of food is the mezze served at the beginning of the meal, rows of little coloured bowls of vegetables cooked in olive oil or pickled in vinegar, olives marinated with lemons and herbs, crumbly white cheeses, tiny delicately spiced meatballs and the famous pastries or boreks. Boreks are made with many different kinds of pastry – I like the crispy effect of filo.

Traditional fillings for boreks include spinach and cheese – I give two examples here, but you can experiment. Try raisins in the spinach, different herbs instead of olives with the cheese, and so on. The parcels make good winter starters, the buttery flaky pastry hiding a juicy, hot interior. If you want to serve them as part of a winter mezze, follow the Turkish example with pickled vegetables, salads of red cabbage with raisins and nuts or blanched grated turnips with a yoghurt and cumin dressing, and a few spicy lamb meatballs.

For 24 parcels
8 sheets filo pastry (*a packet usually contains about 15 sheets*)
3 oz (85 g) unsalted butter

FILLING 1

1 lb (450 g) fresh spinach
1 onion
1 tablespoon olive oil

salt and freshly ground
black pepper
pinch of grated nutmeg
2 oz (55 g) pinenuts

FILLING 2

fresh dill (*or parsley if dill is
unavailable*)
2 oz (55 g) stoned black
olives

4 oz (115 g) feta cheese
freshly ground black pepper

To make the first filling, wash the spinach very well and cook it in a very little water (just enough to cover the base of the pan) for 5 minutes, until it has completely broken down. Chop the onion very finely and fry in the oil for 10 minutes or so, until tender. Squeeze any excess water from the spinach and season with salt, pepper and nutmeg. Add the spinach and the pinenuts to the onion and fry for a few minutes, stirring. Leave to cool.

To make the second filling, finely chop the herbs and the olives. Crumble the cheese and stir in the olives and herbs thoroughly. Season with plenty of black pepper but no salt, as feta is very salty.

To assemble the pastries, cut each piece of filo pastry into 3 long strips lengthways. Keeping the rest of the pastry covered with a damp cloth, brush a little melted butter along the length of one strip. With the strip pointing away from you, put a heaped teaspoon of the filling in the bottom right-hand corner, about $^1/_2$ inch (1 cm) from the edge. Taking the left-hand corner, fold it over the filling so that you have a triangle. Now pick up the right-hand corner and move it through 180 degrees so that the triangle moves up the sheet of pastry. Pick up the new right-hand corner and fold it across to the left side. Now pick up the left-hand corner and fold it over through 180 degrees. Continue until you reach the end of the strip of pastry.

Brush each triangle with a little melted butter. When all are assembled, bake in a medium hot oven (180°C/350°F/Gas 4) for 15–20 minutes, until browned. Serve warm.

Note: you can make the pastries in advance and re-heat them before serving.

FLAT ONION BREAD

This Roman version of the flat Italian olive oil bread, focaccia, is the perfect accessory to a little plate of bought antipasti such as salami, olives, pickled anchovies or buffalo mozzarella. The hot, oniony bread makes such a starter more attractive on a winter's day; or you can eat it as the Romans do, on its own as a snack at any time of the day. Of course, cooked in a conventional oven it will not have quite the same quality as the bread baked in the wood-fired pizza ovens of Italy, but it is a pretty good imitation. For those in awe of baking bread, this is a very easy version.

¹/₂ oz (15 g) dried yeast	1 teaspoon salt
1 teaspoon sugar	8 oz (225 g) white onions
1 lb (450 g) strong white bread flour	1 large sprig of fresh rosemary (or 1 teaspoon dried)
8 tablespoons olive oil	

Soak the dried yeast in ¹/₄ pint (150 ml) of warm water with the teaspoon of sugar – check the packet instruction – stirring to make sure it dissolves (unless you are using easy blend yeast). Put the flour in a very large bowl or on a clean work surface and make a well in the centre. Pour in half the olive oil, the yeast liquid and the salt. Working quickly, blend the flour into the liquid with your hands. The dough will initially be very sticky, but as you continue to knead will become more malleable. Add more water only if strictly necessary – better to keep kneading. After 10 minutes or so you should end up with a nice, pliable ball of dough. Put it to rest in a bowl, cover it with a clean cloth and leave it to rise in a warm place. After 45 minutes, knock the dough back with your fist (I always enjoy this bit). Cover and leave to rest for a further 30 minutes.

Slice the onions into thin half-circles and soak for 10 minutes in warm water. Pre-heat the oven to absolute maximum. When the dough is ready, oil a large metal baking tray, of the sort which just fits into the oven. Spread the dough out with your fingers across the tray, pushing it right into the corners. A little of the remaining olive oil poured over the surface helps this process. Make sure the dough is spread right across the tray, then drain the onions, dry them thoroughly and arrange them across the surface of the bread, right up to the edges. Sprinkle over the rest of the olive oil and the needle-like leaves from the sprig of rosemary. Season well.

Bake the bread in the hottest possible oven (240°C/475°F/Gas 9) for 15–20 minutes, until the onions are just brown and the bread lightly coloured. Serve hot, cut into thick wedges, with the antipasti of your choice (these can be as simple as a few olives or pickled vegetables).

GNOCCHI WITH GORGONZOLA SAUCE

When I lived in Rome, one of my favourite dishes was potato gnocchi. Our local trattoria only served them once a week, on Thursdays, since it took a long time to make the quantity of gnocchi their customers would consume. Nowadays, of course, you can buy vacuum-packed pre-prepared gnocchi, and many restaurants serve them every day. But they do not have the same lightness as those prepared by hand. If you are making them in smaller quantities, it is a relatively quick and simple task.

Home-made gnocchi are good enough to serve just with freshly grated parmesan and a knob of butter. But for an especially comforting winter starter, make a creamy blue cheese sauce to bathe them in.

FOR THE GNOCCHI

1 $^1/_2$ lb (675 g) red-skinned potatoes (*Desirée are a good variety for gnocchi*)

$^1/_2$ teaspoon salt
6 oz (170 g) plain white flour

FOR THE SAUCE

6 oz (170 g) Gorgonzola (*for a milder sauce use Dolcelatte; you can also make the sauce with Stilton*)

1 teaspoon plain flour
1 oz (25 g) unsalted butter
$^1/_4$ pint (150 ml) full-cream milk

Wash the potatoes and boil them in their skins until soft. This can take between 20 and 45 minutes, depending on the size and freshness of the potatoes. The skin splitting is usually a sign that they are ready – but avoid the temptation to prick them with a fork to check, as this will waterlog the potatoes. Instead, after 20 minutes hold a potato in a tea-towel and squeeze to see if it is soft.

As soon as you can handle them, peel the potatoes and mash the flesh very thoroughly. Season with the salt. With your fingers, blend in the flour, adding a little at a time, until you have a pliable, slightly sticky dough. You may not need to use all the flour, depending on the potatoes. Knead the dough as little as possible, to keep it light (for the same reason, do this by hand, rather than in a processor).

Sprinkle flour over a large work surface. Again using your hands, roll the dough out into long sausages about as thick as your thumb. With a sharp knife, cut the 'sausage' at 3/4 inch (2 cm) intervals. Now shape the gnocchi by pressing each one with your thumb against the flat side of the prongs of a fork, held towards you. The result should be a thumb-shaped indentation on one side, grooves on the other and a slightly concave overall shape. The hollow helps the gnocchi to cook through quickly; the grooves are to hold the sauce. Put the formed gnocchi on a floured tray; do not pile them on top of each other or they will stick together.

Now make the sauce. Remove any rind from the cheese and discard it; with a fork break the cheese into pieces. Work the flour into the butter. Bring the milk to the boil and stir in the cheese. When the cheese has melted, add the knob of flour and butter, still stirring continuously. Allow the sauce to bubble for a few minutes, until it has thickened slightly. Put the sauce in the bottom of the serving dish and place in a low oven to keep warm.

To cook the gnocchi, bring a large pan of slightly salted water to the boil. Cook the gnocchi in 3 or 4 batches. They are done when they rise to the surface of the water – a matter of 2 or 3 minutes, so keep your eye on them. Lift them out of the pan with a slotted spoon and transfer to the serving dish. Serve as soon as the last batch is ready, with nothing more than black pepper.

HOT CHICKEN LIVER SALAD

Sometimes in winter you long for the greenery of summer. But if you look hard there are still plenty of salad ingredients which can to some extent satisfy the craving. Florentine fennel is at its best in the winter months – it is good simply sliced and sprinkled with lemon juice and oil, and can be crisped up with onion to make a crunchy, sweet salad topping. The small lamb's lettuce or mâche and the bitter frisée are also at their best in winter and make excellent bases for a salad. In the cold months I like to top my salads with something warm and meaty. Chicken livers are a cheap and underrated food: rolled in mustard and spicy flour, they quickly become crisp on the outside while retaining a moist, creamy interior, providing a contrast of flavours and textures in this substantial salad.

FOR THE SALAD

12 oz (350 g) chicken livers	1 teaspoon ground cumin
1 large onion	1/4 teaspoon cayenne pepper
1 large fennel bulb	1/4 teaspoon ground mace
4 oz (115 g) lamb's lettuce (mâche)	salt and pepper
1 small frisée lettuce	1 tablespoon Dijon mustard (*if using English mustard use far less, as it is very strong*)
3 tablespoons vegetable oil	
1 tablespoon plain flour	

FOR THE DRESSING

red wine vinegar	salt and freshly ground
extra virgin olive oil	black pepper

Trim the chicken livers of any fat or gristle and chop in half. Slice the onion and the fennel into fine half-rings. Wash the salad leaves.

Heat 2 tablespoons of the vegetable oil and fry the sliced onion and fennel slowly, until crisp and caramelized – this will take about 30–40 minutes, and you only need to stir occasionally. Meanwhile make the dressing, using 1 part vinegar to 4 parts olive oil and adding seasoning (I do not use sugar for this dressing, as the caramelized onions and fennel give the sweetness). Season the flour with the spices, salt and pepper. Put the washed salad leaves in a bowl.

When the onion and fennel are ready, remove them from the pan and drain off the oil. Roll the chicken livers in the mustard and then in the seasoned flour. Heat the remaining oil until very hot in the same pan and stir-fry the livers until they are crisp but still pink on the inside – a matter of no more than 3 or 4 minutes. Sprinkle the livers over the salad leaves and top with the crisp onion and fennel. Serve immediately.

LENTIL SALAD

Well-cooked lentils are one of the most delicious of dishes in the sparse times of winter. A few basic rules apply: make sure you choose green lentils, preferably those from Le Puy in France, ensure that they are fresh by buying either from a stockist with a high turnover or in sealed packets, and add a little fat before serving. Lentils go well with game, with roast joints, even with fish, and they also make an excellent base for simple warm salads.

8 oz (225 g) green lentils	1 tablespoon brown sugar
1 red onion	2 tablespoons balsamic
1 carrot	vinegar
1 oz (25 g) butter	8 oz (225 g) smoked streaky
freshly ground black pepper	bacon, cut in thick slices
1¹/₂ pints (850 ml) game or	8 oz (225 g) brown cap
chicken stock	mushrooms
8 oz (225 g) shallots	1 tablespoon chopped flat-
6 tablespoons extra virgin	leaved parsley
olive oil	

Rinse the lentils well. Finely chop the onion and carrot and soften in the butter for 5 minutes. Add the lentils and stir well to coat with the fat; season with black pepper. Add sufficient stock to cover by an inch or so and bring to the boil, then turn down to simmer and cook for 30 minutes, checking occasionally to ensure that the lentils are not sticking and adding more liquid if necessary. At the end of this time the lentils should be soft but not falling apart, the liquid absorbed. You may need to vary the cooking time according to the freshness of the lentils: add more stock if they are not cooked, boil off any excess liquid if they cook more quickly.

While the lentils are cooking, prepare the other salad ingredients. Peel the shallots, leaving them whole, and heat the olive oil in a wide frying-pan. Add the shallots and the sugar and leave to fry gently for 20 minutes, turning occasionally. Then add the balsamic vinegar and boil off quickly. Keep the caramelized shallots warm in the oven, together with their juices.

Chop the bacon into small chunks and fry briefly to release the fat. Meanwhile finely slice the mushrooms. Add to the pan and fry quickly until the mushrooms soften.

Stir the shallots, bacon and mushrooms into the cooked lentils, together with the parsley. Season with plenty of freshly ground black pepper. Serve with virgin olive oil and balsamic vinegar, to allow your guests to dress the salad to their taste. Plenty of good bread to mop up the juices is essential.

PAPRIKA POTATOES

The Spaniards readily adopted the potato when it was brought back from South America by the conquistadores, and today they often serve potato dishes on their own as the starter for a meal. This spicy red version comes from the Castilian region, where it is popular in the tapas bars. It is fine on its own, but even better with a plate of sliced salami or chorizo.

2 lb (900 g) firm potatoes (*I use the red-skinned Desirée for this dish*)	1 teaspoon ground cumin
	$1/2$ teaspoon freshly ground black pepper
1 large Spanish onion	$1/4$ teaspoon cayenne pepper
1 large clove of garlic	2 bayleaves
3 tablespoons olive oil	$1/2$ teaspoon salt
3 teaspoons paprika	1 tablespoon plain flour

Peel the potatoes and slice them thickly (about $^1/_2$ inch (1 cm) across). Slice the onion into fine rings and chop the garlic. Heat the oil in a heavy-based pan and fry the onions and garlic until they are golden. Add the potatoes, spices, bay leaves, salt and flour, and cook, stirring, for a few minutes. Cover the potatoes with boiling water and cook, uncovered, until the potatoes are tender and have absorbed almost all the liquid. Serve very hot.

Salsify Salad

The salsify is a root vegetable shaped like a very long thin panatella cigar and is at its best in the winter months. It has a delicate, unusual flavour, which may explain its occasional nickname of vegetable oyster although in shape or taste it bears no resemblance to that shellfish. I think winter asparagus would be more appropriate.

Salsify is too rarely seen in the shops; it is not grown on a large scale in Britain and most of the produce seems to come from the Low Countries. If you can get hold of it, however, snap it up, for it is delicious and good enough to be served all on its own as a first course. You can also serve it with a white sauce, although in my view this masks the flavour. If you are hesitant to serve a plain vegetable as a starter, think of asparagus.

1 tablespoon white wine vinegar
1 lb (450 g) salsify roots
2 oz (55 g) unsalted butter
salt and freshly ground black pepper
juice of 1 lemon
1 tablespoon finely chopped fresh parsley or $^1/_2$ tablespoon dill (*I prefer to use the latter but it can be difficult to get hold of in winter*)

Half-fill a bowl with cold water and add the vinegar. Under cold running water, peel the salsify of its dark brown skin; as you finish each root, chop it in half and place it in the acidulated water. Cut any particularly thick roots in half lengthways as well.

Bring a large pan of salted water to the boil and add the salsify. Boil for 15 minutes, by which time it should be just tender. Melt the butter in a large pan and add the drained salsify. Fry on both sides until the roots take a little colour – about 5 minutes. Spoon on to a plate with the melted butter, season and sprinkle with the lemon juice and the chopped herb of your taste.

Serve with plenty of bread.

STILTON SOUP

Stilton is an essential element of the British Christmas feast and at its best beats many of the French cheeses hands down. Unfortunately, there are now too many 'imitation' Stiltons – make sure you seek out a traditionally made, fully matured cheese. A hunk from a full-size cheese is generally better than the mini or baby versions which are now popular, or, better still, acquire a quarter or half cheese, which will allow you to admire the wonderful gradation from the knobbly brown rind through the creamy white outer cheese to the blue-veined centre. A round of Stilton will keep for a long time, as long as you avoid the peculiar and not especially tasty practice of pouring in port, and keep the cheese covered in a cool place (but not the fridge, which kills the cheese). Any leftovers can be made into this delicious creamy soup.

12 oz (350 g) Stilton, the more mature the better	2 pints (1.1 litres) full cream milk
1¹/₂ oz (45 g) unsalted butter	¹/₂ pint (300 ml) chicken stock
2 tablespoons plain white flour	salt and white pepper
	2 sticks of celery

Remove any rind from the Stilton and chop the cheese roughly. In a large heavy-based pan, melt the butter and stir in the flour; cook over a low heat until the roux takes on a little colour. Stir in the pieces of cheese and continue to cook until the cheese just starts to melt.

Stir in the combined milk and stock, very slowly at first to make sure that the mixture amalgamates and there are no lumps. Bring to the boil, still stirring, and turn down to a gentle simmer for 15 minutes. Stir occasionally to prevent the cheese sticking to the base of the pan.

Season with a little white pepper (black would spoil the beautiful creamy colour of the soup) and salt to taste. Wash the celery sticks thoroughly and chop the white part into very fine pieces. Serve the celery with the soup, to be sprinkled over it. Granary bread warmed in the oven goes best.

SWEET-AND-SOUR ONION AND DUCK SALAD

Small pickling onions are a common sight in the shops in winter. You can use them as a vegetable, roasted in their skins beside a joint of lamb or gently stewed in butter and stock as a side dish for a roast chicken. I simmer them with sugar, vinegar and raisins to make a sweet-and-sour onion salad which can be served as a starter. Cooked this way, the little onions are even better combined with shreds of roast duck and bitter chicory leaves. Many supermarkets now sell duck legs separately, or you can buy a whole duck, grilling the breasts for a main course and using the carcass for soup.

1 lb (450 g) pickling onions	4 cloves
4 tablespoons red wine vinegar	salt and freshly ground black pepper
2 tablespoons olive oil	3 heads of chicory or other bitter leaf (*frisée also goes well*)
1 tablespoon brown sugar	
4 oz (115 g) raisins	
2 duck legs	1 orange

Peel the onions carefully, making sure you do not split the flesh. Put them in a pan in which they just fit in one layer, and add the vinegar, olive oil, sugar and raisins. Add sufficient cold water to cover and simmer gently for about 45 minutes, uncovered. The onions are ready when they are soft but not falling apart. By this time the liquid should just about have evaporated.

Pre-heat the oven to very hot (220°C/425°F/Gas 7). Stud each leg of duck with 2 cloves and put to roast until just cooked through – this will take 25–30 minutes depending on size. Drain off any fat half-way through cooking. When the duck legs are ready, remove the cloves and peel off the skins. Sprinkle the skins with salt, shred them and put the shreds to crisp in a dry frying-pan over a high heat – be careful they do not burn. Shred the cooked meat and keep warm.

Slice the chicory into rings or shred the salad leaves, and stir in the warm onions and raisins. Sprinkle the shreds of cooked duck meat on top and squeeze over the juice of the orange. Season well. Finally, sprinkle each plate with the crispy shreds of duck skin.

TUSCAN BEAN AND CABBAGE SOUP

Italian cooking is by no means all pasta dishes, char-grilled vegetables and lightly grilled meats. There are just as many hearty peasant dishes, using cheap ingredients designed to warm and fill, usually enriched with olive oil. In the Tuscan region such dishes are often based around beans, as befits a people called the bean-eaters by their neighbours. One of my favourites is the classic bean and cabbage soup of Florence, a thick, strongly flavoured soup which does equally well as a lunch or supper dish or a starter. In Tuscany 'black cabbage' or 'cavolo nero' would be used, but this, like another favourite Italian vegetable, the cardoon, is virtually impossible to find in Britain; Savoy cabbage is an adequate substitute. It is important to use dried beans to achieve the right texture.

8 oz (225 g) dried cannellini beans
3 small or 2 large onions
6 tablespoons fruity extra virgin olive oil
4 cloves of garlic
2 carrots
2 sticks of celery
14 oz (400 g) tin plum tomatoes
1 ham bone or 1 pig's trotter (*the latter are available from most butchers*)
2 oz (55 g) pancetta or unsmoked streaky bacon, in one thick slice
7 or 8 leaves of Savoy cabbage
salt and freshly ground black pepper
1 sprig of fresh rosemary or a pinch of dried
2 sprigs of fresh thyme or $1/4$ teaspoon dried
4 slices of dry white country bread
2 tablespoons freshly grated parmesan

Soak the beans overnight in plenty of water. The next day, boil them hard in plenty of water for 10 minutes, drain and rinse. Slice the onions and fry in 1 tablespoon of the oil until soft. Add 2 cloves of garlic, chopped, and fry for another few minutes. Roughly chop the carrots, celery and tinned tomatoes. Add the vegetables to the pan together with the beans, ham bone or pig's trotter and piece of pancetta or bacon. Cover with 3 pints (1.75 litres) of cold water.

Bring the water to the boil and simmer, covered, for an hour or until the beans are tender. Fish a ladle or two of whole beans and other vegetables out of the pan and reserve; remove the ham bone or pig's trotter and the pancetta or bacon. Liquidize the rest.

Tear the cabbage leaves into fairly large pieces and blanch for 1 minute in a pan of boiling water. Return the soup to the heat and add the cabbage leaves and the reserved whole beans. Season to taste and simmer, covered, until the cabbage is tender. In a separate pan, heat the remaining 5 tablespoons of olive oil with a peeled clove of garlic, whole but crushed, and the sprigs of herbs or the dried herbs. When the oil is very hot, take the pan off the heat and allow to stand for 10 minutes for the flavours to infuse.

Rub the slices of bread with the cut side of the remaining clove of garlic and toast them. Just before serving, strain the olive oil and carefully stir it into the soup. Put a piece of toast in the bottom of each serving bowl, spoon over the very hot soup, sprinkle with the parmesan and serve.

VENISON PÂTÉ

Home-made pâtés are easy to make and worth the small amount of trouble involved – the difference in flavour and texture between a home-made and a commercial pâté is astonishing. Pâtés can also be an excellent way to use up leftovers from roasts of game, provided you add sufficient fat to ensure the meat stays moist. One of the best meats to use in this way is venison. The pâté will keep well for up to a week in the fridge.

To make 1 large or 2 medium pâtés

1 lb (450 g) venison (*either raw or leftovers from a rare roast*)	8 black peppercorns
	¹/₂ teaspoon salt
	¹/₄ teaspoon ground mace
1 lb (450 g) belly pork	1 clove of garlic (*optional*)
4 oz (115 g) pork fat (*if you are using cooked meat; otherwise use half the amount, as the meat will not be so dry*)	2 glasses dry white wine
	2 tablespoons brandy (*optional*)
	8 oz (225 g) smoked streaky bacon
6 juniper berries	

Mince the venison, belly pork and pork fat very finely together – this is best done with a knife if you like a chunky texture; if you use a processor for speed make sure you don't whizz the meats to a paste. Crush the juniper berries and black peppercorns together with the salt, the mace and the garlic if you are using it, and add to the minced meats with the wine and brandy. Mix well together and allow to stand for an hour or so to allow the flavours time to blend.

Put the mixture into one large or two small earthenware pâté dishes to a depth of about 2 inches (5 cm) and cover the surface with the bacon. Pre-heat the oven to medium low (around 130°C/275°F/Gas 1) and place the pâté dish(es) in a baking tray half filled with water. Cook for 1¹/₄ hours. The pâté is done when it starts to come away from the sides of the dish.

Remove the bacon and put a weight on top of the pâté while it is cooling; this will make it easier to carve. When the pâté is completely cool, turn out and decorate the surface with a few juniper berries and a bayleaf. Serve with toast and perhaps a few pickled gherkins.

WINTER CRUDITÉS

There comes a time after the excesses of Christmas feasting when your stomach yearns for simple salads, for raw vegetables, crunchy textures and straightforward flavours. Just because it is winter, crudités should not be off the menu. Root vegetables in particular make some of the nicest salads. Try putting together a selection served in prettily coloured bowls, with different dressings. Given the effort, this is best done for larger groups, or you can just pick one or two of the salads. Serve with the best bread available.

BEETROOT SALAD

For 1 lb (450 g) beetroot in their skins

$^1/_2$ teaspoon salt
$^1/_4$ teaspoon freshly ground
   black pepper
juice of $^1/_2$ a lemon
1 teaspoon whole dill seeds,
   toasted
$^1/_2$ teaspoon ground cumin

2 tablespoons extra virgin
   olive oil
6 fl oz (175 ml) thick
   natural yoghurt (*I like to
   use Greek sheep's milk
   yoghurt*)

Bake or boil the beetroots in their skins until tender (I prefer the former method but it takes longer – about $1^1/_2$–2 hours as opposed to 45 minutes). Peel as soon as they are cool enough to handle and chop into coarse chunks. Season with the salt, pepper and lemon juice and leave to stand for 10 minutes. Stir the toasted dill seeds, the cumin and the olive oil into the yoghurt and pour over the beetroot.

CARROT SALAD

For 1 lb (450 g) carrots

4 shallots
2 tablespoons white wine
    vinegar
6 tablespoons extra virgin
    olive oil

1 teaspoon sugar
$^1/_4$ teaspoon coarsely
    ground black pepper

Scrub the carrots and then grate them on the finest hole of the grater, so that they almost become a purée. Discard the hard yellow central core. Finely chop the shallots and mix into the carrots. Make a dressing with the remaining ingredients and dress just before serving.

Note: If you grate the carrots some time before serving, squeeze over a little lemon juice to preserve their colour, and correspondingly reduce the vinegar in the dressing.

CELERIAC SALAD

For 1 lb (450 g) celeriac

juice of $^1/_2$ a lemon
2 teaspoons Dijon mustard
1 teaspoon black mustard
    seeds

6 tablespoons mayonnaise
    *(home-made is best of
    course)*

Peel the celeriac and grate coarsely. Bring a large pan of salted water to the boil and blanch the celeriac for 30 seconds. When cool enough to handle, squeeze very dry and dress with the lemon juice to prevent discoloration. Mix the mustard into the mayonnaise and stir into the celeriac at least an hour before serving. Heat a dry frying-pan and put in the mustard seeds until they pop. Sprinkle into the celeriac just before serving.

FENNEL SALAD

2 bulbs of Italian fennel   walnut oil
juice of 1 lemon

Slice the fennel very thinly, leaving out the hard outer leaves and the core. Bring a large pan of water to the boil and blanch the fennel for 30 seconds. Dress with the lemon juice and walnut oil.

MARINATED OLIVES

1 tablespoon fresh coriander   olives preserved in oil
1 clove of garlic   4 tablespoons extra virgin
1 small green chilli   olive oil
4 oz (115 g) unstoned black

Chop the coriander, garlic and chilli very finely. Mix into the olives and pour over the oil. Leave to stand for at least a day.

Or, for the faint-hearted:

zest of $^1/_2$ a lemon and $^1/_2$ an orange
4 tablespoons extra olive oil

Mix the fruit zests and the oil into the olives and leave to stand for a day at least.

RED CABBAGE SALAD

For 1 lb (450 g) red cabbage (unpeeled weight)

2 oz (55 g) salted pistachio
  or cashew nuts
juice of 1 lemon

juice of 1 orange
4 tablespoons extra virgin
  olive oil

Peel the outer leaves from the cabbage and slice the inner leaves into the thinnest possible ribbons, discarding the white central core. Mix in the nuts. Mix the fruit juices with the oil and dress the salad just before serving.

WHITE RADISH SALAD

Ethnic shops and supermarkets now often stock white radishes or moolis in winter.

For 1 lb (450 g) white radish or mooli

juice of 1 lemon
2 teaspoons French mustard
  (less if using the stronger
  English mustard)

1 teaspoon sugar
$^1/_2$ teaspoon salt
4 tablespoons sunflower oil

Coarsely grate the peeled radish. Mix together the remaining ingredients and dress. Leave to stand for up to $1^1/_2$ hours before serving.

FISH

The fishing trade takes a break over the Christmas season, so the first week of January is perhaps the worst time of the year to buy fish. The weeks leading up to Christmas, however, see a flurry of activity. Some households choose to make a whole fish rather than a bird or a roast the centrepiece of the table, at least on Boxing Day if not 25 December. Salmon is the most popular choice, but the delicate and delicious sea bass makes an excellent alternative, and is very impressive when roasted in a sea-salt crust. Smoked salmon is as much of a feast-day necessity in many British households as are oysters over the Channel on the Veille, or Christmas Eve. Another French Christmas special, the sea urchin, has yet to make a hit in Britain, but maybe its time will come.

It is not just at Christmas time, though, that we should turn to fish for winter food. Traditionally the long lean months of winter are a time for preserved fish, smoked or salted. Don't ignore undyed cold-smoked Finnan haddock, salt cod from Grimsby, oak-smoked kippers from Craster. These are some of the very best of British food. Fresh white fish from British waters are at their best at this time of year and cod in particular is of excellent quality; try it roasted in olive oil or marinated and grilled to rediscover its fine flavour and texture. Winter is an excellent time of year too for the fish from tropical waters which our fish trade describes as the 'exotics'. Some of course are more exotic than others: most of us are familiar with, say, tuna or red snapper, but a visit to some of the more adventurous fish shops, as in London's Chinatown, or the Caribbean-influenced Ridley Road market in Hackney, reveals an amazing, and largely unrecognizable, variety. For interesting results, ask the fishmongers or the local shoppers how each fish is best cooked.

Winter, then, offers plenty of opportunities for fish enthusiasts. But, as always, the best quality seafood can be difficult to find in this country. To find out what is happening to the British fish trade I visited the market which was its largest for many centuries, Billingsgate, now in London's Docklands.

Billingsgate – Under Threat?

London has had a central fish market known as Billingsgate since the fourteenth century. Until 1982 Billingsgate occupied a site on the River Thames, in the centre of the City of London, most recently in a beautiful arcaded building. The site was a splendid one but impractical for modern times, since fish was no longer brought to the market by boat but by lorries, which had to negotiate the congested streets of the City. So the old market was partly converted to a dealing room, though it is rumoured that some floors had to be left empty due to the ineradicable smell of fish. And Billingsgate moved East to Docklands.

The market today is housed in a long low building overshadowed by the ivory tower of Canary Wharf. Perhaps by moving to Docklands, Billingsgate hoped to share in the planned rejuvenation of the area. But just as regeneration has been slow in coming to Docklands, the fortunes of Billingsgate remain on the wane. The issues facing the market are a microcosm of those in the UK fishing industry as a whole. The prime concern is for the declining fish stocks in the North Sea. As supply has become more uncertain, so prices have destabilized, leading some customers to turn to the more reliable frozen fish suppliers. Billingsgate has been able to mitigate this effect by increasing other lines, such as shellfish, which now represent nearly a third of total sales, and exotic fish. But the fact remains that the top three species sold are still cod, plaice and haddock in that order, and their supply is under threat.

Just as important an issue for the market has been the changing pattern of retail trade in the UK. Supermarkets may have been late in coming to fresh fish, but they are now working hard to increase their sales in this area. Hardly any of the fish sold in supermarkets comes via Billingsgate – central purchasing and distribution systems mean the supermarkets prefer to buy direct, although this policy hardly seems to have had a positive impact on the freshness of the fish they offer, which is too often frozen or subjected to preserving processes. And the problem is not just that the supermarkets cut out Billingsgate, but that their stranglehold on the retail trade is threatening the existence of many independent high-street fishmongers, Billingsgate's traditional customers.

Not that the consumers have helped matters. The decline in the consumption of fish, which reached an all time low in the 1970s, may have been turned around, but we continue to display a worrying tendency to prefer our fish delivered ready to cook or even frozen. The argument is convenience, but I suspect it is more often ignorance. A good fishmonger will advise his customers on how to cook a particular fish; but such traders are a rarity today, although there are exceptions, for example the famously excellent Steve Hatt in Islington. Supermarket staff are no replacement, lacking as they do experience if not training.

These problems have had a serious impact on the volume of Billingsgate's trade. In 1958 there were 165 merchants dealing with an estimated 123,000 tonnes of fish in a year; thirty years later the number of merchants had dwindled to sixty-seven, and tonnage to 35,750, according to a Seafish report. And there are new threats on the horizon: the prospective opening of the Channel Tunnel has brought fears of imports from the French markets, while at the same time Continental buyers are picking up much of the UK's best fish at the ports. New distribution systems make direct delivery ever more likely, cutting out the inland markets.

But how does all this affect you, the individual consumer? Well, if you live in London it actually has a positive side. As its traditional wholesale customer base declines, Billingsgate has actively sought to encourage retail trade. Despite open days for the public, it remains a little-known fact that anyone can go to Billingsgate and buy fish. Of course, you have to get up early in the morning. The market opens five days a week at 5 a.m., excluding Sundays and Mondays, and the day's trading is all but over by 9. You may also have to buy in larger quantities than normal, although this is offset by the low prices. But these inconveniences are more than outweighed by the freshness and variety of the fish on offer.

Where else in Britain can you find for sale in one place whole crates of live lobsters; sacks of scallops in their pink-tinged, fluted shells; cases of oysters from Ireland, large grey shells packed tight in dark green seaweed; tiger prawns, Dublin bay prawns, grey shrimps and bags of mussels; crayfish and crabs angrily waving their claws in the air? Parrot fish, red snapper, kingfish, swordfish and tuna from tropical seas; boxes of slithering eels, the odd valiant escapee making it to the floor; sides of smoked salmon; whole farmed salmon of every size as well as wild ones in season; enormous cod, eyes bright in the ugly face, monkfish tails, flat fish of all varieties? You name it, they've got it. And at a price that will make you wonder who's making the money out of fish.

So where does all this fish go, and why is it so difficult to obtain good-quality fresh fish at the retail end? Unlike the trade at the ports, little of Billingsgate's sales are for export. Fishmongers and market stalls remain the largest sector of customers, still accounting for nearly half the turnover. The main sales to these customers, however, are in the traditional white fish, with some mackerel and herring thrown in, or perhaps some farmed salmon. White fish are the preserve, too, of the institutional caterers and the fish-fryers who together account for over a fifth of Billingsgate's trade. It is depressing to think of those excellent cod being encased in soggy batter and fried in stale oil, or drowned in a flour-thickened white sauce before serious overcooking.

The shellfish and more expensive wet fish are largely the preserve of the hotels and restaurants who buy direct from the market, or the wholesalers who supply them. You will be lucky to see those oysters or lobsters, sea bass or turbot on the shelves of any but the best fishmongers. Instead, they will be served to you (at a price) in smart restaurants.

And here, I believe, lies the nub of the problem for the retail customer of fish. Stocks may be declining, but good fish and shellfish are still being caught or reared in quantity off the British Isles. Yet very little of this catch reaches the cook. It may be exported direct from the port; it may be shipped direct to a processing factory; it may go to the supermarkets for freezing or turning into ready-to-cook dishes; it may be bought by the catering trade. There is precious little of any quality that makes it through the net to your fishmonger, who in any case seems to believe that you don't want to buy the more expensive varieties. Go to Billingsgate in any season to see what you are missing.

MALABAR MUSSELS

On India's beautiful Malabar coast, the former Dutch trading colony of Cochin remains the spice capital. Here black pepper futures are still traded and the old warehouses in Jewtown are piled high with fragrant heaps of ginger, cardamom, cumin and chillies. Cochin is also a major fishing centre, the ramshackle fleet bringing in daily huge hauls of prawns, crabs and mussels from the Arabian Sea, while poorer fishermen work the spiderweb Chinese fishing-nets which ring the harbour mouth. The tortuous backwaters south of the city are lined with dense groves of coconut palms, the source of the third major product of the Malabar region, coconut oil.

This local recipe combines the Malabar trio of spice, seafood and coconut and is perhaps my favourite way of cooking mussels. Despite the large quantities of spice used, the end result is surprisingly mild, the creamy yellow sauce flecked with green coriander complementing the mussels perfectly. In India this dish would be served as a main course with rice but I prefer it as a starter, served with spoons for the sauce and plenty of bread.

4 lb (2 kg) mussels
1 large Spanish onion
2 tablespoons groundnut or peanut oil (*or coconut oil if you can get it – it is available in many Indian and West Indian shops*)
4 large cloves of garlic
1 oz (25 g) piece of fresh ginger
2 small fresh green chillies

2 teaspoons ground cumin
$^1/_2$ teaspoon turmeric
$^1/_2$ teaspoon salt
$^1/_2$ teaspoon ground black pepper
15 oz (425 g) tin unsweetened coconut milk
1 tablespoon chopped fresh coriander

Prepare the mussels as on page 246. Finely chop the onion and heat the oil in a pan large enough to take all the mussels. Fry the onion until it is soft but not browned – about 10 minutes. Meanwhile, peel the garlic cloves and chop the ginger into several chunks. De-seed the chillies. Process all

334

three together with a little water to make a paste. When the onions are soft, add the garlic-ginger-chilli paste to the pan, along with the cumin, turmeric, salt and pepper. Fry for 5 minutes, stirring, then pour in the coconut milk and bring to the boil. You can do all of this an hour or two in advance, so that all you have to do when you want to eat is add the mussels.

When the coconut milk mixture comes to the boil, add the mussels and the chopped coriander leaves and cover. Cook over a medium heat for 5–6 minutes, until the mussels have opened. Discard any which haven't and serve immediately, in soup bowls, with plenty of juice.

COD ROASTED IN OLIVE OIL AND GARLIC ON A BED OF MASHED POTATO

Despite concern about declining stocks in the North Sea, cod remains the largest and most valuable catch for British fishermen. Unfortunately, too much cod is consigned to the processor or the fish-and-chip shop, so that many of us have forgotten how good a fresh piece of cod can be. Try chunky cod steaks roasted in olive oil for a reappraisal of the merits of the most popular of British white fish.

6 oz (170 g) belly pork
1 teaspoon coriander seeds
4 juniper berries
salt and freshly ground
   black pepper
1 lb (450 g) potatoes (*King Edward are good for mashing*)
1 large sweet potato, approx. 8 oz (225 g)

4 tablespoons extra virgin olive oil
2 dried red chillies
1 head of garlic (*that's right, a head*)
8 shallots
4 thick cod steaks, total weight 1¹/₂–2 lb (675–900 g)

It is easiest to prepare the mashed potato before the cod, which is quick to cook.

Chop the belly pork into large chunks, leaving on all the fat. Put in a heavy-based casserole over the lowest possible heat. Add the whole coriander seeds and the juniper berries, together with plenty of black pepper. Cover and cook for 30–45 minutes, until the fat melts. Stir occasionally to prevent the meat from sticking.

Bring a large pan of salted water to the boil and cook the ordinary and sweet potatoes whole in their skins until tender (25–40 minutes according to size). Do not prick the potatoes during the cooking time or they will become waterlogged. Instead test them by squeezing with a heatproof cloth – they should feel very soft when done. Drain and leave for 10 minutes to cool.

Chop the cooked pork into small pieces and salt well. Strain the fat from the pan in which the pork cooked. Peel the potatoes and mash together with the fat from the pork and more seasoning to taste. Put the pork pieces back into the pan over a low heat to crisp.

Pre-heat the oven to very hot (220°C/425°F/Gas 7). Put the olive oil in an earthenware dish into which the cod steaks will just fit. Add to the oil the chillies, the whole head of garlic and the shallots still in their skins split into individual cloves, left unpeeled. Roast for 10 minutes. Remove the chillies from the oil and discard. Put the cod steaks in the dish with the garlic and the shallots and return to the oven. Roast for 10 minutes, turning once. Put the potato in the oven at the same time, to heat through.

When the fish is cooked, remove the papery skin from the cloves of garlic and put 2 or 3 cloves on the side of each plate together with a couple of roasted shallots still in their skins. Pile some mashed potato in the centre of each plate and place a cod steak on top. Pour over the oil from the roasting pan. Sprinkle with the crispy pork and serve immediately.

FISH COUSCOUS

There are so many ways of preparing the North African dish couscous that whole books have been written on the subject. Couscous refers to a type of semolina made with durum wheat grain; the key to the dish is the stewed vegetables and meat or fish served with it. The recipe here is for winter vegetables cooked with raisins or sultanas and delicate spices to form a light broth, served with rather unauthentic but very good marinated cod kebabs (you could use monkfish). You can also serve couscous with lamb or chicken, which should be cooked in the vegetable broth and then finished with a honey glaze. The couscous is prepared right at the end, as almost all couscous sold in this country is pre-cooked. This is the ideal meal for a large group and is perfect cold weather food, being warming, filling and comforting.

For 6–8

6 oz (170 g) dried chickpeas
  soaked for 24 hours
  (*canned chickpeas, although
  time-saving, will not
  achieve the same effect*)
4 large carrots
6 small turnips
5 onions
2 sticks of cinnamon
4 or 5 strands of saffron
6 tablespoons olive oil
1 teaspoon ground ginger
1/2 teaspoon turmeric
salt and freshly ground
  black pepper
4 or 5 sprigs each of fresh
  coriander and flat-leaved
  parsley

4 lb (2 kg) cod tail
2 lemons
2 limes
4 fresh green chillies
1 1/2 lb (675 g) tomatoes,
  skinned
6 oz (170 g) raisins or
  sultanas
1 small tin harissa paste (*or
  if you can't get it, some
  tomato paste and red
  chillies*)
1 teaspoon ground cumin
1 lb (450 g) couscous (*or
  more depending on how
  many guests you have and
  how hungry they are*)
butter

First prepare the vegetable broth. Bring a large pan of unsalted water to the boil and boil the chickpeas hard for 10 minutes, then drain. In the largest casserole you possess, pile the drained chickpeas, the peeled carrots chopped into thick rings, the peeled and quartered turnips, 4 of the onions sliced finely in half-moons, the cinnamon sticks, saffron, 2 tablespoons of the olive oil, the ginger and turmeric and plenty of freshly ground black pepper. Tie half the coriander and parsley together and dangle into the pot. Do not add salt at this stage, as it will toughen the chickpeas. Three-quarters fill the pot with water and simmer for 1 hour. (*Note:* Although some recipes call for pre-frying of the vegetables, I find simply boiling them gives a more delicate flavour.)

Skin the cod and cut into chunks about 1 inch (2.5 cm) square. Marinate for 1–2 hours in the remaining olive oil, with the lemon and lime juice and the de-seeded chopped green chillies.

After an hour's cooking, add the skinned tomatoes, cut in half, and the raisins to the broth. Simmer for another 30 minutes then add salt and black pepper to taste. The broth should be ready by now, all the vegetables still separate but very tender. It improves if it is taken off the heat to stand for 30 minutes or so to allow the flavours to mingle. Chop the remaining coriander and parsley leaves and float on the surface just before serving the broth.

To cook the fish, thread the marinated chunks of cod on to metal or wooden skewers, 3 or 4 to each stick. Pre-heat the grill to maximum, and when you are nearly ready to serve, grill the kebabs for a few minutes on each side (the fish needs little time under the grill, as it will already have started to 'cook' in the citrus juices).

To make a fiery sauce for the fish, mix a couple of teaspoons of the harissa paste with a ladle of liquid from the broth, the strained marinade (do not include the green chillies or the sauce will be too hot) and a teaspoon of cumin. Boil briefly and pour over the fish kebabs. If you cannot get harissa, substitute a mixture of dried red chillies and tomato paste and fry it for 5 minutes before adding the liquid.

Finally, to steam the couscous use a double boiler with a sieve or put the couscous in a colander which will fit over the pan in which the vegetables are cooking. Soak the couscous briefly and then steam according to the instructions on the packet (5–7 minutes is usual for pre-cooked couscous). Before serving, fluff up the couscous with a fork and add plenty of butter. I like to fry the remaining onion until it is caramelized and sprinkle it on top of the couscous.

I serve the couscous and kebabs on large platters in the centre of the table, with a ladle in the vegetable broth, so that everyone can help themselves. Put a little harissa in a side dish for those who like it hot.

HERRINGS MARINATED IN CIDER

Herrings are one of the cheapest fish in the market and are at their best in the winter months. They are oily fish, and one of the best ways of cooking them is grilling, as in the autumn recipe (pages 244–5). There are also endless recipes for marinated or preserved herring – in vinegar, in white wine, with dill, with onions. My favourite, for herring fillets in cider with winter vegetables, comes from Normandy. The fish is 'cooked' in the cooling liquid, producing tender flavourful fillets. The dish can be eaten as soon as it is thoroughly cooled, but is best left for a day or two for the flavours to mingle.

For 4 herrings, filleted, total weight approx. 1 1/2 lb (675 g)

2 carrots
2 small onions
1 bulb of fennel
1 pint (575 ml) cider
  (*the non-carbonated version is best – try to get cider from Normandy or use West Country scrumpy*)

1 teaspoon black peppercorns
2 cloves
2 juniper berries
a few sprigs of thyme and sage and a bayleaf, tied together
pinch of salt
1/4 pint (150 ml) cider vinegar

Peel the carrots and onions and remove any brown outer leaves from the fennel. Slice the vegetables coarsely. Put the vegetables, cider, spices, herbs and salt into a pan with a lid and bring to the boil. Simmer for 20 minutes or so, covered, until the vegetables are soft but not collapsing. Add the vinegar and bring to the boil; simmer for another few minutes.

Wipe the herring fillets dry and remove any stray bones. Place them in an earthenware dish in which they will just fit. Pour over the boiling liquid and the vegetables and leave until completely cold – the herrings will cook as the cider cools.

Serve the fillets with the vegetables, accompanied by brown bread and butter or hot potatoes boiled in their skins.

KIPPER PÂTÉ

The verb 'to kipper' was originally used in application to a variety of fish such as salmon, mackerel and herring which were cured in salt and pepper and then dried either in the open air or over smoke. Today if you ask for a kipper you will usually get a smoked herring. The best kippers are smoked over oak chips and are juicy and not too salty. I never understood how anyone could eat them for breakfast until I was given not one but two at a B & B right next to the smoking factory in the tiny port of Craster, Northumberland. The cries of the gulls over the harbour filled the sitting-room, the mist rolled back to reveal the ruined Dunstanburgh Castle along the cliff, every breath was filled with the pungent smell of kippers cooking next door. When they came, they were delicious.

But apart from these rare occasions, the kipper is a difficult fish to appreciate. Too strong, too salty are common criticisms. Tempered with soft cheese, however, and perked up with lemon juice and spice, it makes a powerful pâté which is a long way from the delicate but sometimes tasteless fish terrines beloved of restaurateurs.

2 whole kippers
1 oz (25 g) unsalted butter
$^1/_2$ teaspoon freshly ground
   black pepper
$^1/_4$ teaspoon cayenne pepper
$^1/_4$ teaspoon fish masala
   spice mix (*optional – this*

is an Indian spice mix,
generally containing cumin,
cinnamon, ginger and
cloves)
juice of 1 lemon
8 oz (225 g) low-fat cream
   cheese

Dot the kippers with the butter and cook in a medium oven (150°C/300°F/Gas 2) for 15 minutes. As soon as they are cool enough to handle, remove the skin and bones. Mash the flesh with a fork and pick over to remove any small lingering bones.

Beat the spices and lemon juice into the cheese. Mash in the cooled kipper flakes with a fork. Put into individual serving dishes or a pâté dish. Chill well until needed.

Serve with hot brown toast, chunks of lemon and chopped cucumber.

MONKFISH ROASTED WITH ROSEMARY-FLAVOURED OLIVE OIL

Monkfish has come a long way from the days when it was regarded as a substitute for lobster, and now commands high prices. Deservedly so, for the firm-textured white flesh can be delicious, particularly in this recipe from Provence for a whole monkfish tail, studded with garlic and roasted in a fragrant olive oil, just as if it were a piece of lamb. Small onions, shallots and heads of garlic, roasted whole in their skins alongside the fish, are a good addition.

1 lemon (*preferably unwaxed*)
1 large sprig of rosemary
1 large clove of garlic
$1/_4$ pint (150 ml) extra

virgin olive oil (*preferably from Provence*)
a whole piece of monkfish tail, approx 2 lb (900 g)
salt and pepper

Peel a strip from the lemon and blanch. Leave the rosemary, peeled garlic and strip of lemon to infuse in the oil for at least an hour.

Pre-heat the oven to very hot (240°C/475°F/Gas 9). Strain the oil, reserving the rosemary and garlic. Remove any skin from the monkfish and put it in a roasting dish on top of the sprig of rosemary. Cut slivers from the clove of garlic and with the point of a sharp knife make slits in the fish; push in the garlic. Season the fish well and pour over the oil.

Roast for 25 minutes, basting frequently. Check that the fish is ready by inserting a skewer – the juices should run clear. Sprinkle with lemon juice and serve very hot, with the juices from the roasting pan.

POTTED SALMON

Although the flavour of farmed salmon is inferior to that of the wild fish, the larger-scale farming of salmon in the British Isles has brought with it a major price advantage. At least, it would do if wholesale prices were being passed on to the retail customer – on one day recently I saw whole fish at just over £1 a pound in Billingsgate, and a few hours later at over four times that price from a market stall, whose holder admitted he had bought at Billingsgate that morning.

Despite such outrageous mark-ups, salmon is slowly losing its luxury image and becoming more affordable, allowing cooks to move beyond simple poached or grilled salmon cutlets. Salmon was traditionally potted to preserve it, but even if you want to serve it the same day this dish is worth making. The fatty tail end of the fish is best for potting and should be reasonable in price.

I like to serve home-pickled cucumbers with the potted salmon – they are easy to make and need to be left for only a week or so before serving. They will keep for several months.

For 1 lb (450 g) salmon you need

4 oz (115 g) unsalted butter $^1/_4$ teaspoon white pepper
$^1/_4$ teaspoon ground mace   (*black spoils the*
pinch of ground allspice   *appearance*)
$^1/_4$ teaspoon salt

Skin the salmon and remove any bones. Flake the flesh with a fork. Clarify the butter by melting it and skimming off any froth (if you have any muslin handy you can drain it through that). Pre-heat the oven to very low (about 75°C/175°F/Gas $^1/_4$).

Stir the spices and salt into the flaked salmon. Put the salmon and melted clarified butter in a heavy lidded pot. Cook covered at the bottom of the oven for an hour – the aim is for the salmon to slowly melt in the butter.

Pack the salmon into a terrine from which you will serve it. Leave to cool for an hour or so, then put a weight on top and transfer to the fridge. Serve when it is thoroughly chilled, with hot toast.

If you want to keep the potted salmon for a few days, cover it with a thin layer of clarified butter.

PICKLED CUCUMBERS

For 1 lb (450 g) small pickling cucumbers you need

6 fl oz (175 ml) white wine
  or cider vinegar
1 oz (25 g) sugar
1 oz (25 g) salt

4 sprigs of dill or 1 teaspoon
  dill seeds
1 clove of garlic (*optional*)

Bring ¾ pint (450 ml) of water to the boil. Add the vinegar, sugar and salt and bring back to the boil. Wash the cucumbers and prick each one several times with a fork. Put them in a sterilized preserving jar into which they just fit, with the dill and the garlic if you are using it. Pour over the hot brine and seal. Leave for at least a week before serving.

SCALLOPS IN VERMOUTH WITH A HERBED POTATO CRUST

Scallops are at their best from autumn to early spring. Unfortunately, too many of our scallops go straight to the processing unit for freezing. If you do see live scallops on the shell, make sure you buy some, for their flavour and texture are far superior to the frozen variety – you will acquire a useful serving receptacle as well.

Scallops can be fried, grilled, baked or poached. In all cases the essence is quick cooking or the scallop flesh will toughen. I often fry scallops in olive oil with a little garlic and parsley before stirring them into fresh tagliatelle. In winter, I poach them in a herby vermouth before topping them with a potato crust, to make a more substantial starter or light lunch dish.

1 lb (450 g) potatoes (*King Edward are good for mashing*)

2 oz (55 g) butter

2 tablespoons full cream milk

2 tablespoons chopped fresh dill, or parsley if dill is unavailable

salt and pepper

8 scallops, preferably in their shells

3 fl oz (75 ml) dry white vermouth (*I use Noilly Prat, as I find it has the most herby flavour*)

2 tablespoons double cream

1 teaspoon paprika

Boil the potatoes whole in their skins until they are soft. Take care not to prick them or they will become waterlogged – squeeze one of the largest potatoes in a cloth to see if it is done (it should be soft to the touch). Drain the potatoes and leave until cool enough to handle, then peel them and mash them with $1^1/_2$ oz (45 g) of the butter and the milk. When the purée is very smooth, season well and stir in the chopped dill.

If the scallops are still in their shells, prise them open with a knife. Cut the muscle attaching the scallop to the shell and remove the fringe which surrounds the meat. Being careful not to damage the coral, cut off the dark intestinal sac and remove the black thread which runs down the scallop. Rinse well under gentle cold running water. Scrub the deeper side of the shells very thoroughly; discard the flat side. Cut the white part of the scallop into 2 or 3 flat discs, depending on thickness.

Bring the vermouth to the boil in a small pan in which the scallops will just fit; slip in the slices of scallop and the corals. Turn down to a simmer and allow to cook for a minute or two, no more or they will toughen. Lift out carefully with a slotted spoon. Stir the double cream into the vermouth; do not allow it to come back to the boil.

Pre-heat the grill to three-quarters of its maximum. Divide the scallops between the 4 deep shells (if you don't have scallop shells, use heatproof saucers). Pour a little of the vermouth and cream mixture into each shell, and mould the mashed potato over the top. Make a hole in the centre of the potato crust and pour in any remaining vermouth and cream. Dot the surface with the rest of the butter and sprinkle with the paprika.

Cook under the grill until the potato crust is browned – about 10 minutes, but be careful it doesn't burn. Serve immediately.

SEA BASS IN A SEA SALT CRUST

The sea bass is in my view the king of fish. This superiority is reflected in its price, making it a dish for a special occasion. Fishmongers report increasing interest in sea bass as part of the Christmas feast. Cooking the fish in a crust of sea salt is very impressive – you can crack the crust open at the table to cries of wonder. More to the point, the crust keeps in all the juices, so that the fish stays very moist. The accompanying sauce is rich, creamy and spiked with tarragon, a herb which dries well. You can serve this dish as a fish course, in which case no vegetables are necessary, or as the centrepiece of the meal, in which case a purée of potatoes, some braised celery and fennel and glazed carrots would go well.

1 sea bass, approx. 3 lb (1.5 kg) (*ask the fishmonger* not *to scale it*)

4 lb (2 kg) coarse sea salt (*yes, 4 lb*)

10 oz (285 g) plain white flour

1/2 pint (300 ml) water

1/2 pint (300 ml) vegetable stock (*made with a stick of celery, an onion, a carrot and some parsley*)

1 glass dry white wine

8 oz (225 g) crème fraîche (*if you can't get crème fraîche, try a mixture of two-thirds double and one-third sour cream*)

1 teaspoon freeze-dried tarragon (*the unseasonal fresh tarragon available at this time of year often has an overpowering taste of liquorice and is best avoided*)

Gut the fish and wash thoroughly. With a sharp knife remove the dorsal spine – be careful, as it is very sharp. Do not scale the fish as the skin will be removed before serving and the scales help keep in the moisture while the bass is cooking.

In a large bowl, mix together the salt and the flour (it seems a phenomenal amount of salt but don't worry, the fish won't be over-poweringly salty – the crust serves to keep the moisture in). Add the water slowly, until the flour and salt stick together. Lay some aluminium foil on a tray large enough for the fish and put half the salt mixture on it, to cover the base of the fish. Lay the bass on top and smear the remaining salt and flour all over it, working down the sides to meet the base.

Pre-heat the oven to hot (220°C/425°F/Gas 7). Cook the fish in the middle of the oven for 25–30 minutes.

To make the sauce, reduce the stock with the wine by fast boiling to half the quantity. Stir in the crème fraîche and tarragon and reduce again until the sauce is thick enough to coat the back of the spoon. Keep warm.

When the fish is cooked, break open the salt crust with a sharp knife – be careful, as it will be very hard. Remove the fish from the crust and peel off all the skin. Strain the sauce into a separate jug.

SINHALESE KINGFISH CURRY

Fish curry is a splendid dish for a cold winter's day. I was first served this recipe in a rather different climate by a splendid Sri Lankan cook who runs a restaurant on the Indian coast below Madras, aptly named the Ideal Beach Resort. The fish had been caught that day and was served under the palm trees within earshot of the surf, which made for idyllic memories. But it is a dish which translates well back to the UK, especially given the availability in winter of what the trade calls 'exotics', such as kingfish. The recipe also works well with other firm-fleshed fish which can be served in steaks, such as tuna or swordfish. Provided you live in or near a city with ethnic food shops, you should be able to find all the ingredients – the hardest may be the curry leaves, which are not vital. You cannot, however, do without the tamarind, which adds a vital sour element. As with many curries, the list of ingredients is long, but the actual execution is not complicated.

1 teaspoon chopped
preserved tamarind or
tamarind paste
1 teaspoon salt
4 kingfish steaks
2 onions
2 or 3 small green chillies
(*the authentic recipe uses
more*)
14 oz (400 g) tin plum
tomatoes
2 tablespoons vegetable oil
1 teaspoon whole black
mustard seeds

3 or 4 curry leaves
1 teaspoon ground cumin
1 teaspoon cayenne pepper
(*again, tempered – you can
increase the quantity
according to taste*)
$^1/_2$ teaspoon turmeric
1 teaspoon ground
coriander
3 tablespoons coconut milk
(*tins can be found in most
ethnic shops – make sure it
is unsweetened*)
freshly ground black pepper

Finely chop the tamarind and soak it in a little water if using the preserved variety. Blend with the salt to make a paste and smear this over the fish steaks. Leave to stand for 10 minutes. Grate the onions; de-seed and chop the chillies, drain the tomatoes and chop.

Heat the oil in a pan large enough to take all the fish in one layer. When the oil is hot, add the mustard seeds, chillies, curry leaves and cumin. Fry for a minute or two then add the grated onion and the tomato. Cook over a medium heat, stirring, until the tomatoes and onions are browned. Add the cayenne pepper, turmeric and coriander together with the fish. Fry briefly on each side to seal, then pour in enough water to cover the bottom of the pan. Cover and cook over a low heat for 15–20 minutes, depending on the thickness of the steaks.

Take out the fish and put it to keep warm. Boil off any remaining water and stir in the coconut milk. Add a little freshly ground black pepper, spoon the sauce over the fish and serve with plain rice.

SMOKED SALMON AND EGGS ON A PANCAKE

Due to the large scale on which salmon are now farmed, smoked salmon has become an affordable luxury, and, if the pre-Christmas trade is anything to go by, almost a necessity in many households. If you have perfect thin-cut slices of traditional oak smoked salmon, a delicate browny-pink glistening with oil, then of course serve them with nothing more than a twist of lemon and a grind of pepper. But if you have offcuts, or simply smoked salmon which seems to have lost a little of its glory in the processing, then try serving it on a small crispy pancake of potato and turnip, topped with a creamy baked egg. This is a good brunch dish.

3 large potatoes	1 tablespoon vegetable oil
3 small turnips (*avoid very large ones, as they have an overpowering flavour and a woolly texture*)	1 oz (25 g) butter
	4 eggs
	4 tablespoons single cream
	4 oz (115 g) smoked salmon
salt and pepper	1/4 teaspoon cayenne pepper

Peel the potatoes and turnips and grate coarsely. Sprinkle with salt and leave to drain for 30 minutes, then squeeze out any excess liquid. Heat the oil in a wide non-stick heavy-based frying-pan and add the grated vegetables. Stir-fry for a few minutes, then pack down with a wooden spoon into 4 roughly round pancakes (or you can make 1 large pancake and cut it into 4). Fry for 5–7 minutes on each side, pressing down with the spoon occasionally to release any liquid. The pancakes should be lightly browned.

Pre-heat the oven to medium hot (180°C/350°C/Gas 4). Butter 4 small ramekins very well, to make sure the eggs slip out when cooked. Break an egg into each, season well, and pour in the cream. Bake for 5–8 minutes in a bain-marie, until the egg is set.

To serve, spread a slice of smoked salmon on top of each pancake. Slip a knife round the edge of the ramekins, turn upside down and carefully unmould an egg on top of each slice of salmon. Sprinkle with cayenne pepper and serve immediately.

SMOKED HADDOCK SOUP

Look out for undyed Finnan haddock. The fish should be firm to the touch, a pale cream in colour, the skin a light grey and undamaged. Choose a middle rather than a tail piece for preference. Smoked haddock is most often found in kedgeree, but there are lots of other uses for it – in summer try slicing it very thinly, marinating it in lemon juice and olive oil and serving it raw topped with olives or spring onions. In winter I make this smoked haddock soup, which is surprisingly delicate.

1 lb (450 g) undyed smoked haddock
1 oz (25 g) unsalted butter
1 tablespoon flour
$^1/_2$ teaspoon turmeric
$^1/_4$ teaspoon ground ginger

$^1/_4$ teaspoon white pepper (*black pepper spoils the creamy appearance*)
2 pints (1.1 litres) full-cream milk
4 fl oz (100 ml) single cream

Skin the haddock and chop coarsely. Melt the butter in a pan and add the flour. Cook over a low heat for 3–4 minutes, until the roux just takes colour, then add the skinned chopped haddock and the spices. Cook for a further couple of minutes, then slowly add the milk, stirring all the time to avoid lumps. Simmer for 20 minutes then liquidize. Reheat with the cream and check the seasoning before serving.

Tuna Steaks with Seville Orange Sauce

Seville oranges have a very short season, generally appearing in the shops only in the month of February, and are promptly snapped up by the marmalade makers. The bitter oranges can also be used to sauce game, meat and fish, as in the sauce bigarade for duck. They go particularly well with tuna steaks, enhancing rather than overpowering the fish's strong, meaty flavour. Try to buy steaks which have been thick-cut (up to 1 inch/2.5 cm) as they will remain juicier under the grill.

3 Seville oranges
3 tablespoons olive oil
4 tuna steaks
freshly ground black pepper
2 onions
14 oz (400 g) tin plum tomatoes

4 or 5 sprigs of parsley, preferably flat-leaved
a few celery tops
sugar
balsamic vinegar

Squeeze the juice from the Seville oranges. Keep one half skin for later use. Mix the juice with 2 tablespoons of the olive oil and pour over the fish. Season well with freshly ground black pepper and leave to marinate for 2 hours, turning half-way through.

To prepare the sauce, chop the onions and fry gently in the remaining olive oil. When the onion is soft and lightly browned, add the drained chopped tomatoes, the parsley and the celery tops. Fry for 5 minutes then add the juice from the tomatoes and a tablespoon of water. Season and simmer, covered, for 15 minutes.

Strain the sauce through a sieve, pushing the tomatoes and onions with the back of a wooden spoon to make sure you extract their juice. Peel the pith from a strip of the Seville orange skin and cut the skin into 12 very thin slivers. Add these to the sauce together with the marinade from the fish and a teaspoon or two of sugar.

Pre-heat the grill to maximum. When it is very hot, grill the tuna for 5–10 minutes on each side, depending on the thickness of the steaks. The fish is done when it is opaque all the way through and just beginning to break into flakes.

Heat the sauce through very gently. When it is nearly boiling check for acidity – you may need to add more sugar, depending on the oranges. Finish with a few drops of balsamic vinegar.

When the fish is cooked, pour over the sauce, making sure each plate gets a few slivers of orange peel. Serve immediately. Good side dishes are fried polenta, mashed potato or simply bread; and a winter salad, such as grated red turnips or slivers of blanched white cabbage dressed with lime juice and olive oil.

SWEET-AND-SOUR FISH

The classic sweet-and-sour sauce is an excellent way of serving the exotic varieties of fish which are widely available in the winter: the sauce is light years away from that which we have become used to from Chinese takeaways. In most Chinese recipes for this dish the fish is deep-fried; in a Chinese restaurant in Bombay, however, I was served that city's favourite fish, a pomfret, grilled and topped with a sweet-and-sour sauce. This is their recipe.

1 or 2 whole fish, approx. 3–3¹/₂ lb (1.5 kg) total weight – if you can't get pomfret, try red snapper or sea bream	1 oz (25 g) fresh ginger
	1 or 2 green chillies
	2 teaspoons cornflour
	1 small glass dry sherry (*or rice wine if you have it*)
¹/₂ teaspoon salt	2 tablespoons dark soy sauce
¹/₂ teaspoon freshly ground black pepper	6 tablespoons vinegar (*rice wine vinegar is most authentic, otherwise use white wine vinegar*)
¹/₄ teaspoon cayenne pepper	
3 tablespoons vegetable oil	
2 large onions	3 tablespoons caster sugar
4 cloves of garlic	¹/₂ a lemon

Clean and gut the fish thoroughly and make 3 deep slashes on either side. Mix together the salt, black pepper and cayenne pepper together with 1 tablespoon of the oil and rub this mixture all over the fish. Leave to stand for 30 minutes.

Meanwhile, make the sauce. Chop the onions, garlic, ginger and chillies very finely. In a shallow frying-pan heat the remaining oil and add the onion and garlic (usually you should avoid browning garlic but this recipe requires the slightly bitter taste of toasted garlic). When the onion and garlic are light brown, add the ginger and chilli. Fry for another few minutes, stirring all the time.

Dilute the cornflour in 6 tablespoons of warm water and add to the pan, followed by the sherry, soy sauce, vinegar, sugar and juice of the lemon. Stir all together, turn down the heat and simmer for 5–10 minutes until the sauce has a thick, creamy consistency.

Pre-heat the grill to maximum. Cut a couple of slices from the squeezed lemon and pop them in the cavity of the fish. Grill the fish close to the grill, until the skin bubbles up and blackens. Depending on the size and thickness of the fish, allow between 5 and 10 minutes a side – the flesh should come easily away from the bone.

When the fish is cooked, peel off the blackened skin. Spoon over the sauce and serve immediately. Plain boiled rice and Chinese greens in oyster sauce or lightly fried butterhead lettuce go well.

MEAT

For many families the most important meat purchase of the year is the bird for the Christmas table – and of course the ham, the stuffing meat, the sausages and the bacon which are all part of the feast. A big fat turkey is still the most popular and economic choice, but an increasing number of Christmas tables now sport a goose, which was the traditional bird in medieval times, or a brace of pheasant for smaller parties. Some families won't serve a bird at all, sitting down instead to a haunch of venison or a sirloin of beef on the bone. Few families will see a meatless table on 25 December although a whole sea bass or salmon can make an excellent alternative.

The Christmas ritual has a tendency to reach such gargantuan proportions that the January cook is left feeling jaded and penniless. Now is the time for slow-cooking casseroles which need little attention, for spicy dishes to revive tired palates, for meals which use leftovers or cheap cuts of meat. By February, energy and pockets should have been replenished, so that you can enjoy the very last of the game, the fuller-flavourered hogget or mature lamb, or dishes which combine the excellent winter shellfish with meat in the Spanish style. By the end of the month, as the crocuses push through the ground and the first lambs appear in the fields, the worst of the winter should be over and the need for warming, filling meaty casseroles diminishes.

But back to the feast. It is a good idea to start thinking about the Christmas centrepiece at the beginning of December or you may well be disappointed, for good producers and butchers sell out early, as I found when I visited one of my favourite markets, in Oxford. This is a British market about which I have few grumbles – there is little you can't find here. In particular, the meat section is well served, with no fewer than seven butchers. Why has Oxford market survived and even flourished when so many others have fallen by the wayside?

Oxford Covered Market

I have a soft spot for Oxford market. It was here that the *Independent* sent the finalists in their cookery competition to buy the ingredients for the lunch that they were to cook at the Manoir aux Quat' Saisons, for none other than Raymond Blanc. Not that this particular visit is an especially happy memory, as I for one was a little weak from the excesses of the night before, a hazy vision of champagne and glorious food. The ebullient Mr Blanc dispatched us at seven-thirty the following morning, and I was too fragile to protest that the market didn't open before nine, so that I had plenty of time for panic to set in while we sipped thick tea in a market café. As the stallholders unpacked, I wandered round in a daze debating what I could possibly buy to cook in those frightening kitchens which had turned out such a revelation of a meal just a few hours before. Through the mental fog I realized that here was produce, meat and fish fresh enough to need little treatment beyond good cooking and that if I bought well, I would cook well. So it turned out, and fortunately my simple spring dishes of asparagus, squid with samphire, lamb cooked with apricots and, to finish, a citrus cream found favour with the judges.

Revisiting Oxford market as I have done many times since, I always get the feeling of being spoilt for choice. Admittedly, that choice has declined over the years, for from the time when the market was first established in the late eighteenth century on its current covered site right up until the middle of this century, it sold predominantly meat and was almost entirely dedicated to food products. Today only about half the shops sell food, as rent increases and simple changes in demand have forced out some of the old suppliers, replacing them with higher-margin clothes and shoe shops or fast-food outlets. As you enter the market through a narrow alleyway off the High, just down from Carfax, traditional food retailers seem few and far between.

But on a cold winter's day approach instead from the northern end off the Turl and the prospects are altogether more promising. Instead of the greasy tang of fast-food shops and the sour smell of leather at the other entrance, here at the trade end you are greeted by the overpowering smell of roasted coffee, the fragrant scents of teas and the ammoniac tang of farmhouse produce from the nearby cheese stall. Or perhaps you get a whiff of seaweed and salt from one of the two fish stalls, bright with glossy salmon and sea bass, boldly striped parrot fish and meaty red tuna steaks, scallops on the shell and garlic buttered snails. Penetrate into the heart of the market and things really look up. Above your head on the butchers' forecourts hang ranks of vibrantly coloured game birds alongside creamy white turkeys, juicy fat geese and boiling fowl, whole roe and fallow deer, still in their brown and grey fur, white bobtails on show. Inside the shops dangle joints of Angus beef from Scotland, the deep red of the meat denoting proper hanging, alongside huge blackened hams the colour of molasses and strings of plump sausages.

Looking at these meaty displays, it is but a short step in the mind to the candlelit fineries of the college dining-rooms and then on to medieval images of roast haunches of venison on silver platters, geese stuffed with capons stuffed with guineafowl stuffed with pheasant, barons of beef served bloody rare, all washed down with jugs of college ale, claret, port. Of course, it's not like that today, cry the impoverished Oxford dons; well, not unless it's a feast day at All Souls or Christchurch. But a quick survey of market shoppers on a cold winter's Saturday suggests that the Oxford intelligentsia, be it from academia or business, still plays a vital part in sustaining the life of this market, in sharp contrast to so many British cities where the market has been downgraded to the province of the bargain-hunter. The shoppers of Oxford are demanding but enthusiastic eaters, who play a great part in maintaining the range and quality of goods on offer. There can't be many markets in Britain where a single butcher can boast of an annual turnover of something close to 30,000 brace of pheasant, can sell 350 geese in the week leading up to Christmas and have requests for at least another 100 more, can use up over 100 turkeys (each weighing up to 40 lb) every week of the winter months, let alone the 1,200 turkeys sold in the pre-Christmas week, and can stock between six and eight whole deer a week in season. And this is only one butcher among seven in the market – though perhaps the best.

For this is M. Feller & Sons, the butcher to which most first-time visitors to the market are drawn by its always impressive display over the long shopfront. Billed as High Class University and Family Butchers, its traditional appearance suggests a longer history than is actually the case, for the current management took over only at the beginning of the 1980s. New management or not, the values are old-fashioned. This is meat that has been carefully selected, properly treated, and only offered for sale when it is ready. All the buying is done direct from the producers, many of whom are small local concerns, or from shoots. Not just the game but the joints of beef, pork and lamb are well hung, so essential for sweetness. Those serving know their meat, for they are all involved in the purchasing. They seem to know their ovens as well, if their willingness to give rather good cooking instructions is anything to go by. The atmosphere of the family butcher is cleverly preserved in what is after all a mini-empire: for opposite the main shop is a separate outlet for cooked meats, and next door the same management owns another butcher operating under a separate name, as well as providing other retailers in the market with game – oh, and supplying half of the Oxford colleges. All credit to them – a better fate has befallen Feller's than its neighbour, once a vast old-fashioned pork butcher whose emblem of a stuffed fox sporting an ancient pair of glasses has been shunted to one end of the shop to make way for a sweet department at the other end. Such is progress. But Feller's is reaping the reward of commitment — this was one of the few butchers which I have encountered where the staff believe that there is a trend *away* from purchasing of meat in the supermarket.

Maybe it is true in Oxford, however, for this is a carnivore's paradise. And when you have acquired the vital ingredients for your winter pâtés, civets, roasts and casseroles, don't just rush home to cook. Spend some time instead wandering round the eclectic Palm's delicatessen, managed by a Czechoslovakian lady brought up in Germany, whose aunt started the shop in 1954. There aren't many places outside London where you can find over a dozen vinegars, from aneth to Xérès, even if winter isn't the time for her delicious home-made salads which can make a summer picnic beside your punt on the Cherwell so memorable. Pick up a little smoked eel as a starter from one of the fishmongers, or perhaps a live lobster, or even a whole sea bass as an alternative to the Christmas bird. Buy some raclette from the Oxford Cheese Shop for the perfect winter supper, the grilled cheese served by the fireside spread on potatoes boiled in their jackets, accompanied by pickled onions and gherkins and maybe the leftovers of a roast. And don't forget the coffee or tea of your taste – you're bound to find it here. Then go home via the quadrangle of at least one of the colleges, or perhaps take a look at the Bodleian or the Sheldonian. Admire the architecture and the taste. For I have a sneaking suspicion that the dietary habits of Oxford fellows mean that there will always be a demand from at least one quarter of the city for the finer foods of life.

BAECKEOFFE

This Alsatian dish derives its name from the housewives' practice of taking their casserole dishes to the baker's oven for long slow cooking after the bread had been baked. Until recently this was common practice in much of France and Italy, for few people had large ovens at home. Baeckeoffe is a country dish, just the sort you would want to come home to after a long, cold day working in the field. It bears a certain resemblance to Lancashire hotpot, but the local Alsatian wine provides the cooking medium and traditionally three different meats, lamb, pork and beef, are combined. On special days a piece of goose or veal might be added to the pot, which must be earthenware to achieve the right flavour. Not a sophisticated dish, it is perfect winter fodder for hungry crowds and can be put in the oven and forgotten about.

To serve 6–8

1 lb (450 g) shoulder of lamb, off the bone
1 lb (450 g) beef bladebone, off the bone
1 lb (450 g) pork sparerib, off the bone
1 pig's trotter (*this is optional, but it gives a good flavour and makes the juice gelatinous: most butchers will supply them*)
8 oz (225 g) white onions
2 leeks
1 bouquet garni, composed of a few sprigs of parsley, 1 sprig of thyme and 2 bayleaves
1 pint (575 ml) Alsatian white wine (*Sylvaner, Riesling, Pinot Blanc*)
salt and freshly ground black pepper
2 lb (900 g) potatoes
good pinch of ground cloves

356

You will need a large earthenware pot with a close-fitting lid, and flour and water paste to seal the pot (see below).

Trim all the meat of its fat. Cut the meat into pieces, except for the pig's trotter. Leave to marinate overnight with the onions sliced into rings, the whole whites of the leeks, the bouquet garni, the wine and plenty of freshly ground black pepper.

The next day, peel the potatoes and cut them into very thin rounds – it is best to use a processor or mandoline for this, so that you get equal thickness. Cover the base of the cooking pot with a layer of potatoes. Put the beef on top, cover with a layer of potatoes, then add the pork, the pig's trotter and the bouquet garni. Cover the pork with another layer of potatoes and place the lamb on top. Finally, top the lamb with a layer of potatoes, mixed with the sliced onions which you have picked out of the marinade. Strain the wine from the marinade and add the pinch of cloves and salt to taste. Pour the wine into the pot, adding sufficient water to bring the liquid half-way up the pot. Make a paste by mixing flour with sufficient water for it to stick together. Cover the pot and seal the gap between lid and pot with strips of the paste.

Bake in a medium low oven (130°C/275°F/Gas 1) for 3 1/2–4 hours then break open the flour and water paste with a knife and serve the baeckeoffe piping hot with just a green salad.

BEEF MEATBALLS WITH EGGS

This Moroccan dish of spicy beef meatballs stewed in a thick tomato sauce and finished with eggs has its origin, like so much Middle Eastern cooking, in medieval tradition. The result is a substantial dish which makes an excellent winter one-course meal. It needs nothing more with it than bread or rice and a winter salad.

FOR THE MEATBALLS

1 lb (450 g) minced beef
1 teaspoon ground cumin
1 teaspoon ground
  coriander
1/2 teaspoon ground
  cinnamon

1/4 teaspoon cayenne pepper
1/2 teaspoon freshly ground
  black pepper
1/2 teaspoon dried mint
salt
1 tablespoon olive oil

FOR THE SAUCE

1 lb (450 g) plum tomatoes
  or a 14 oz (400 g) tin
  peeled plum tomatoes
1 large onion
1 small green chilli
1 clove of garlic
2 tablespoons olive oil
1/2 teaspoon ground allspice
1 teaspoon ground cumin

1/2 teaspoon freshly ground
  black pepper
2 teaspoons tomato purée (*if
  you are using fresh
  tomatoes*)
2 tablespoons chopped fresh
  coriander, or parsley if
  that is unavailable

4 eggs (1 per diner)

Mix together the minced beef, spices and mint, and add salt to taste. Form the mixture into small meatballs about the size of a walnut. Choose a heavy-based pan with a lid and deep sides which you can take to the table, and fry the meatballs briefly in the oil until they are coloured all over. Put to one side.

Peel and de-seed the tomatoes if you are using fresh ones. Chop the onion, chilli and garlic. Heat the oil in the pan and fry the onion until soft; add the garlic and chilli. As soon as the garlic starts to take on a little colour, add the spices, together with the tomato purée if you are using it. Fry for a minute, then add the fresh tomatoes together with a few tablespoonfuls of water or the tin of tomatoes. Cook uncovered for 30 minutes, until the sauce is thick.

Add the meatballs to the sauce and cook over a low heat, covered, for 10 minutes. When the meatballs are done, stir in the chopped coriander or parsley. Make 4 small holes in the sauce. Carefully break an egg into each of these holes, cover the pan, and cook over a low heat until the eggs are set. Serve immediately, straight from the pan.

CHICKEN WITH OLIVES AND LEMON

The Moroccans produce high-quality lemons and olives, and for centuries have combined them in their cooking with lamb, chicken and fish. To make sure they could enjoy their lemons all year round, they preserved them in salt and spices. To me the taste and smell of those preserved lemons is one of the most distinctive features of Moroccan food. They are very easy to make and look pretty bottled in glass jars but you do need to leave them for a month before you can use them. If you haven't made any, don't be put off: this delicately spiced chicken simmered in lemon juice, onions and herbs and served with olives is still a winter treat, bringing a taste of warmer climes to the kitchen.

$1/2$ teaspoon ground ginger
$1/2$ teaspoon paprika
$1/4$ teaspoon ground cumin
$1/4$ teaspoon turmeric
$1/4$ teaspoon freshly ground black pepper
a few strands of saffron
2 tablespoons olive oil
1 free-range, corn-fed roasting chicken
1 clove of garlic
3 large onions (*the mild Spanish variety are best*)
a few sprigs of fresh parsley
and coriander, tied in a bunch
1 lemon (*or 2 if you are not using the preserved lemons*)
$1/2$ teaspoon salt
4 quarters of preserved lemon (*optional – recipe given below*)
4 oz (115 g) olives (*the best variety for this dish are small unpitted green ones, available from Italian delicatessens*)

Mix together all the spices except the saffron and add the oil. Clean the chicken, removing any excess fat from the cavity, and rub inside and out with the cut side of the clove of garlic. Smear the oil and spice mixture all over the chicken and leave to stand for 4–6 hours (or overnight).

When you are ready to cook, grate the onions coarsely. In a casserole just large enough to take the chicken, put the onions, bunch of herbs, fresh lemon juice, saffron, any remaining marinade and $^1/_2$ pint (300 ml) of water. Bring to the boil, add the salt and put in the chicken on its side. Simmer, covered, for 20 minutes then turn the chicken over on to its other side.

When the chicken is nearly ready (about another 20 minutes, but check with a skewer), add the olives to the sauce, and the rinsed quarters of preserved lemon if you are using them. Cook for another 10 minutes to allow the perfumes to mingle. Take the chicken out of the pot, keep it warm, and reduce the sauce a little if necessary (though there should be plenty of liquid). Remove the bunch of herbs. Serve with rice and a green vegetable or salad.

Preserved Lemons

For 6 lemons you need

4 oz (115 g) coarse sea salt	$^1/_2$ teaspoon whole black
$^1/_2$ teaspoon whole	peppercorns
coriander seeds	4 cloves
	1 bayleaf

If you can get unwaxed lemons, they are by far the best to use. Soak the whole lemons in cold water for 2 days, changing the water after 24 hours. This softens the skins.

Cut the lemons into quarters. Choose a preserving jar into which the lemons will just fit and sprinkle some of the salt in the base. Pack in the lemons, alternating with salt and the spices and pressing down on each layer to extract juice. There should be enough juice to cover the lemons completely – if there is not, top up with a little extra fresh lemon juice. Tuck in the bayleaf. Seal the jar and leave for a month, shaking it occasionally.

Before using the lemons, rinse thoroughly under cold running water to remove excess salt. The lemons will keep for up to 6 months.

CHICKEN IN RED WINE

The origin of this recipe is the traditional French dish of coq au vin, as bastardized in many a so-called bistro. But what is the classic recipe for coq au vin? Which wine should be used, and should the bird be marinated? Should the onions be added at the start or later, and at what point are the mushrooms to be included in the casserole? Is stock needed and should the blood of the bird be used to thicken the sauce? There is of course no definitive recipe, for this is one of those peasant dishes devised to fit as needs must. So if you are in Burgundy you use Burgundy wine, in the Loire perhaps Chinon, in Gascony Madiran and so on. As for the marinade, the onions, the mushrooms, the stock, well, that depends on who taught you to make the dish in the first place. On two points, however, all recipes agree: a mature cockerel and a bottle of good red wine are vital.

The fact is that unless you run a farm or a smallholding a mature cockerel is hard to get hold of in Britain, so you are going to find it difficult to cook a traditional coq au vin in any case. The red wine is not difficult to acquire but it is a wrench to use a good bottle, given the cost in the UK. Be assured that it is worth it. The following is my own best effort at a coq au vin substitute; it is also one of my favourite recipes for a friendly supper in winter.

1 large boiling fowl
6 oz (170 g) pancetta or unsmoked streaky bacon, cut in 1 or 2 thick slices
1 bottle red wine (*I prefer to use a full-bodied red – it doesn't have to be French, I have successfully used Chianti and Dão; however, the dish will be a failure if you use a bottle of wine which is unfit to drink*)
2 sprigs of thyme
1 bayleaf

3 sprigs of parsley
2 tablespoons of brandy or Armagnac
1 tablespoon flour
1 clove of garlic
salt and freshly ground black pepper
8 oz (225 g) shallots
2 oz (55 g) unsalted butter
8 oz (225 g) button mushrooms, preferably brown cap
juice of 1/2 a lemon

Have the fowl jointed into 8 pieces by your butcher. When you get home, pick over the joints to remove any excess fat (poke under the skin to check). Heat a heavy-based frying-pan and fry the chicken pieces gently, with no added oil, for 5 minutes, to release any excess fat. Pick out the chicken and wipe dry. Discard the fat.

Chop the pancetta or bacon into small but relatively thick oblongs (lardons). Bring a large pan of water to the boil and blanch the pancetta or bacon for 1 minute. Drain and pat dry.

Put the wine, the leaves pulled off the sprigs of thyme, the crumbled or chopped bayleaf and the finely chopped parsley leaves in a separate pan to heat gently. Choose another large, heavy-based pan with a lid, put it over a gentle heat and add the lardons and the pieces of chicken. Fry the chicken for a couple of minutes on either side. Meanwhile heat the brandy in a ladle; stand well back, set light to it in the ladle and pour it into the pot. As the flames subside, shake well to make sure all the chicken is touched. Add the flour, the clove of garlic, crushed and chopped, and seasoning to taste (remember the bacon when adding salt), and cook for another few minutes. Pour over the hot wine and bring to the boil; boil for 2 minutes, then turn down to a slow simmer and cover. If, as with many modern gas hobs, you find it difficult to maintain a slow steady simmer, transfer the covered pot to a low oven at this stage.

You now leave well alone for an hour. At the end of this time, peel the shallots and fry them whole in half the butter for about 15 minutes, stirring occasionally, until they are softened and lightly browned. With a ladle skim off any fat on the surface of the casserole, check for seasoning and add the shallots. Return to the hob or oven.

Wipe the mushrooms clean and fry gently in the remaining butter for 5 minutes. When they are soft and lightly browned, squeeze over the lemon juice and allow to rest for a minute or two. Add the mushrooms to the casserole.

Cook for another 5 minutes and serve. Traditionally, fried bread would be served with the dish; I prefer plain boiled long-grain Italian rice, with a knob of butter and some fresh chopped parsley.

LAMB CASSEROLE WITH YOGHURT AND PAPRIKA

A lamb can be up to a year old before slaughtering, and the English meat available in the shops through the winter months usually comes from older animals, when it should be called hogget. It needs slower cooking for a tender result; keep quick roasts of lamb or chops flashed under the grill for spring and summer. The reward, however, is a fuller flavour. The use of yoghurt with lamb is traditional in many cuisines, for the yoghurt helps to break down the fibres of the meat to produce a melting dish. Yoghurt is often used as a marinade for kebabs, but it can also be excellent as the cooking medium itself. Despite the use of the chilli, this dish of Turkish origin tastes delicately spiced and makes an excellent supper. Serve it with a nutty pilau, buttered rice finished with fried onions, raisins and some almonds or pinenuts.

2 mild onions (*red ones are best*)
2 tablespoons olive oil
1 clove of garlic
1 dried red chilli
6 green cardamom pods
4 cloves
1 stick of cinnamon
1 1/2 lb (675 g) boned shoulder of mature

British lamb, chopped into chunks about 1 1/2 inches (3.5 cm) thick
1 teaspoon paprika
8 fl oz (250 ml) Greek yoghurt (*the sheep's milk variety is most authentic*)
2 tablespoons warm water
salt and freshly ground black pepper

Pre-heat the oven to medium low (130°C/275°F/Gas 1). Finely chop the onions and cook gently in half the oil until very soft (about 20 minutes). Add the chopped garlic, the red chilli, the cardamom, cloves and cinnamon. Fry for another couple of minutes then transfer to the casserole (use a covered earthenware dish, or even a tagine, if you have one).

Trim the lamb pieces of any fat and roll in the paprika. Heat the remaining oil and fry the meat over a high heat, until browned on all sides. Transfer to the casserole and stir in the yoghurt and warm water. Season with salt and plenty of freshly ground black pepper.

Cook covered for 1¹/₂ hours. Don't worry if the yoghurt looks like separating or the meat seems tough – it will right itself. To avoid unnecessary worries, simply don't look at it during the cooking. Serve piping hot.

PAPRIKA STEAK WITH SOUR CREAM, CAPERS AND POTATO CAKE

The addition of capers to the classic Hungarian combination of paprika, sour cream and steak may not be authentic, but it works rather well, giving the dish extra bite. The potato cakes, flavoured with caraway, go particularly well with the dish; you might also like to add a dish of blanched cabbage tossed in oil and finished with lemon juice and sugar.

FOR THE STEAKS

1¹/₂ lb (675 g) silverside, cut into thick slices about 1¹/₂ inches (3.5 cm) long and ¹/₂ inch (1 cm) wide (*even better, use rump or even fillet*)

3 tablespoons paprika (*it must be very fresh*)
2 tablespoons capers
a nugget of goose fat or lard
6 fl oz (175 ml) sour cream

FOR THE POTATO CAKES

1 lb (450 g) floury potatoes
salt and freshly ground black pepper

3 teaspoons caraway seeds
1 tablespoon goose fat (*or lard if unavailable*)

Trim the steaks of any fat and beat them hard with a wooden object to tenderize the meat. Cut them into bite-sized chunks and roll them in the paprika. Leave to stand for 30 minutes.

Boil the potatoes whole in their skins until soft (about 25–40 minutes, depending on the potatoes). Peel them as soon as they are cool enough to handle. Mash the potatoes thoroughly, season very well and stir in the caraway seeds, making sure they are evenly distributed through the mixture. With your hands, form small cakes about 2 inches (5 cm) across and 1 inch (2.5 cm) thick.

Rinse the capers very thoroughly, to remove any traces of brine (or soak them in advance if they have been preserved in salt). In a heavy-based pan, melt 1 tablespoon of goose fat or lard and when it is sizzling add the potato cakes. Fry for 5–6 minutes on each side, until they are very crisp. Transfer to the oven to keep warm.

Melt some more goose fat or lard in the pan and when it is very hot throw in the pieces of meat. Fry very quickly until browned on all sides (no more than a couple of minutes) and transfer to a warmed dish in the oven. Add the capers to the pan and pour in the sour cream; heat through for a minute or two. Season to taste, pour the sauce over the steak and serve immediately, with the potato cakes on the side.

PHEASANT STEWED WITH CALVADOS AND APPLES

Pheasant is at its best in November and December, being both plentiful and cheap as well as of good quality. If there are two of you it can make an excellent dish for Christmas Day. In my opinion, it is best served braised or casseroled, especially later in the season, for unless you can be sure you have a young bird, roast pheasant has a tendency to dryness. This luxurious recipe from Normandy is good for a feast day, but in recent years the price of pheasant has also made it affordable as an everyday dish, as in the recipe for salmis (pages 377–8).

Serves 2

1 large pheasant (*look out for dark patches on the flesh, which indicate bruising and will impair the flavour*)
1 oz (25 g) butter
2 tablespoons Calvados
1 wine-glass medium dry cider (*farmhouse is best, especially if you can get a French variety*)
3 small eating apples (*try Cox's Orange Pippin or a Russet*)
6 fl oz (175 ml) very thick double cream
salt and pepper

Wipe the pheasant clean, making sure you pick out any remaining feathers. Melt the butter in a heavy casserole into which the bird will just fit and brown the bird on both sides. Heat the Calvados in a ladle over a candle or gas flame, set light to it and pour over the bird, standing well back. Shake the casserole to ensure that the flames touch all parts of the bird. When the flames die down, arrange the bird on its side in the casserole and pour over the cider. Bring to the boil, turn down to a simmer, cover and cook for 20–25 minutes, depending on the size of the bird. Then turn the pheasant over on to its other side, cover and cook for a further 20 minutes.

Pre-heat the oven to medium low (130°C/275°F/Gas 1). Peel and core the apples and cut them into half-moon slices. Take the pheasant out of the casserole and carve it; put it in a serving dish in the oven. Bring the juices in the pan to a slow boil and add the apple slices. When these are just tender (a few minutes), take the pan off the heat and stir in the cream together with a little salt and pepper. Carve the pheasant and serve with the apples and sauce spooned over. To go with the dish, I like a purée of potato and Jerusalem artichoke (in a ratio of four parts of potato to one of artichoke) and some sprouts lightly cooked with chestnuts or some caramelized carrots.

PORK WITH CLAMS

In Portugal, fried pork is often served with the small local clams, still in their shell. In this version of the Portuguese dish, I use cider rather than the white wine which would be traditional. Not only is this cheaper, I like the slight appley taste which the cider lends to the sauce. If you can't get clams, cockles are a good substitute.

1¹/₂ lb (675 g) boned loin
  of pork
1 large carrot
¹/₂ a large Spanish onion
1 clove of garlic
2 tablespoons cider vinegar
¹/₂ pint (300 ml) flat cider
  (*I use medium dry scrumpy
  from Devon – French ciders
  are also good*)

1 tablespoon chopped flat-
  leaved parsley
¹/₂ teaspoon freshly ground
  black pepper
a few strands of saffron
1 lb (450 g) clams (or
  cockles) in the shell
2 tablespoons olive oil

Trim the pork of any fat and chop into cubes about 1 inch (2.5 cm) across. Grate the peeled carrot and finely chop the onion and the garlic. Combine the cider vinegar, cider, carrot, onion, garlic, parsley, pepper and saffron. Leave the meat to marinate in this mixture for at least 4 hours, turning once or twice (if you can leave it overnight, it will be even better). Put the clams or cockles in a large bowl of salted water to allow them to clean themselves. When you are ready to cook, rinse them very thoroughly under cold running water, scrubbing the shells.

In a large frying-pan with a lid, heat the olive oil. Drain the marinade liquid away from the pork and reserve. When the oil is hot, add the pork and the vegetables from the marinade. Fry quickly over a high heat, stirring constantly – 6 or 7 minutes should be sufficient. Do not overcook the pork or it will toughen.

When the pork is almost cooked through (if you are unsure, cut a cube in half), add the reserved cider from the marinade. When it bubbles, add the clams or cockles and cover the pan. As soon as the shellfish open, the dish is ready. Season with salt to taste and serve. A plain risotto and some fennel baked in olive oil go well.

PORK WITH PRUNES

The marriage of pork with prunes is an old-fashioned one from the Touraine region of France, using as it does what were once two of the département's most popular products. Sadly, the prunes of Tours which were once famous in Paris are now a rare sight, although pigs are still reared in the region and rillettes de Tours, potted pork, is made on a large scale. The combination of meat and dried fruit is an excellent one, the prunes in the dish adding a smoothness and richness to the pork. This is an easy dish to prepare and should be served with plain boiled potatoes and a green vegetable such as French beans.

12 best-quality dried prunes (*canned prunes will not do, as their consistency is too soggy*)

2 glasses white wine (*a Loire wine such as a Vouvray would be ideal*)

4 thick slices of loin of pork
white flour
salt and freshly ground black pepper
1 oz (25 g) butter
4 fl oz (100 ml) double cream

Soak the prunes overnight in sufficient water to cover. Next day, drain the prunes and simmer gently, covered, in the wine for 30 minutes until tender. Pick the prunes out and remove the stones; put them in the oven to keep warm and reserve their cooking liquid.

Dust the pork slices with flour and season well with salt and black pepper. Melt the butter in a heavy-based frying-pan large enough to take all 4 pork slices and when the butter is bubbling add the meat. Fry quickly for a minute or two on each side to seal, then turn down the heat and cook for 5–6 minutes on each side, until the pork is cooked through (the exact cooking time will depend on the thickness of the slices, but take care not to overcook the meat or it will become dry and tough).

Put the pork steaks in a warmed serving dish in the oven, arranging the stoned prunes on top of the meat. Pour the cooking liquid from the prunes into the pan and stir in the cream; allow to bubble for a minute or two, season to taste and pour over the meat. Serve immediately.

ROAST STUFFED GOOSE

The goose is regaining its earlier popularity as the centrepiece of the Christmas table, although it still has a long way to go before it threatens the popularity of that sixteenth-century intruder from the Americas, the turkey. Goose is more expensive, and may be impractical if you have a big family party to feed, as even the largest bird will not stretch beyond 6 people. But for taste I find it far preferable to the turkey, which however carefully roasted always seems to end up with a dry breast. And there are delicious by-products from the roast goose; plenty of fat for roasting potatoes in the winter months to come, the giblets to make an unbeatable gravy, the bird's liver and neck to make a separate pâté.

Do make sure you buy your goose from a reliable supplier. The most tender birds will be those hatched in the late spring or summer, brought up on a free-range or semi-free-range regime with a diet of grass and corn and specially fattened for the feast day, be that Michaelmas when 'green' geese were traditionally eaten, America's Thanksgiving or Christmas Day itself. Make sure you order your goose well in advance: one of the largest free-range suppliers, Goodman's of Warwickshire, sold 1,800 geese last season but were overwhelmed with demand in the last few weeks of the year. When you order, make sure you will get the whole bird, giblets and neck included, or you will be missing out.

I prefer to cook my stuffings separately from the bird, to ensure that they neither become drenched with fat nor interfere with the roasting process. I offer two so-called stuffings, one made with dried fruits and vegetables and the other a richer meatier version. Although the gooseberry is of course out of season in mid-winter, the fruit did not acquire its name for nothing and even the frozen berries make an excellent sauce. Take advantage of the fat dripping from the bird to roast wonderful potatoes. As a vegetable, red cabbage or choucroute is ideal.

TO ROAST THE GOOSE

The most important thing when roasting the goose is to stand it on a mesh tray in a deep roasting dish, otherwise the bird will stew in its own fat.

Remove any loose fat from the cavity of the bird and wipe it clean. Pre-heat the oven to medium (150°C/300°F/Gas 2). Butter a piece of foil or greaseproof paper and spread it over the breast of the bird, making sure you cover the wings and legs. After 1 hour, remove the foil or paper, drain off excess fat (and keep it), add parboiled potatoes for roasting to the pan, and turn the bird breast-side downwards on the grid. After a further hour, turn the bird breast-side uppermost again, baste it with the fat, sprinkle with salt and pepper, turn the potatoes and season them as well, and replace in the oven. Cook for another 30–60 minutes, depending on the size of the bird, allow 15 minutes to the pound (30 minutes to the kilo) – the juices should run clear when you prick the flesh between the breast and leg. Allow to stand for 10 minutes before carving.

TO MAKE THE GRAVY

The gravy can be made the day before the feast, which has the added advantage of letting you skim off any fat when it cools.

2 carrots	goose giblets, excluding
2 small onions or 1 large	the liver
2 leeks	1 bouquet garni containing
$^1/_2$ oz (15 g) clarified butter	a bay-leaf, a sprig of
or goose fat	parsley and a sprig of sage
1 glass dry white wine	salt and pepper

Pre-heat the oven to very hot (220°C/425°F/Gas 7). Roughly chop the vegetables. Melt the butter or goose fat in a large deep pan and add the roughly chopped vegetables; cook in the oven until the vegetables are lightly browned, shaking the pan occasionally. Add the giblets and cook for a further 10 minutes, turning over once. Transfer the pan to the hob and pour over the wine; allow to bubble for 5 minutes. Pour over $2^1/_2$ pints (1.5 litres) of water, add the bouquet garni and seasoning, and bring to the boil; skim off the scum, turn down to a simmer and cook for $1^1/_2$ hours, skimming regularly, until well reduced. Allow to cool and skim off the fat.

Before serving, strain and return to the heat. Boil fiercely to reduce to the required consistency (try to avoid thickening with flour, which impairs the flavour, unless you must have a thick gravy).

FRUIT AND VEGETABLE STUFFING

The choice is endless when choosing the ingredients for a stuffing for goose, as the meat has an affinity with a great many fruits and vegetables.

My favourite is a mix of celery, apple and dried apricots with citrus fruits, but other good recipes use prunes, chestnuts, walnuts and quinces (although not all mixed together). I have strong feelings about the use of herbs in stuffings for goose: the flavour of sage is too overpowering and brings nothing to the dish. Stick instead to parsley and thyme. I use breadcrumbs as the base, but you can also use potato. Finally, if you do not want to cook the stuffed goose's neck, then add 8 oz (450 g) of pork or pork and veal mince and the bird's liver to the stuffing to make it more substantial.

(*Note:* If you do want to cook the stuffing inside the goose, do not pack it tightly or it will affect the cooking time.)

2 small white onions	2 sprigs of thyme (or
1 oz (25 g) butter	$^1/_4$ teaspoon dried)
4 large sticks of celery	pinch of grated nutmeg
2 Bramley apples	$^1/_4$ teaspoon ground
6 oz (170 g) dried apricots,	cinnamon
soaked	salt and black pepper
$^1/_2$ a lemon	8 oz (225 g) fresh
1 orange	breadcrumbs (*preferably*
1 tablespoon chopped	*from good white country*
fresh parsley	*bread*)

Finely chop the onions and stew in the butter until translucent. Meanwhile clean the celery and chop the white part finely. Add to the onion and continue to stew gently until both are tender. Peel the apples and chop coarsely; add to the pan and fry for a further minute or two.

Chop the soaked apricots into small pieces. Grate the zest from the lemon and orange. In a large bowl, combine with a wooden spoon the onion, celery, apple, apricot, orange and lemon zest, the juice of the orange, the parsley and the leaves from the thyme, the spices, salt and black pepper. Gently stir in the breadcrumbs and combine thoroughly.

Grease a baking tray with a little of the fat from the goose, which should already be roasting. Pack in the stuffing and dot with more melted goose fat. Bake, covered with foil, alongside the roasting goose for 45 minutes. Take off the foil, add a little more fat and cook for another 20 minutes before serving.

Stuffed Goose Neck

The stuffed goose neck together with the bird's liver makes a delicious dish hot or cold. This can be served separately from the roast goose (perhaps on Christmas Eve or Boxing Day) or hot with the bird itself. Preparation needs to start a day before, and a day longer if you intend eating the pâté cold.

the neck of the goose	1 egg
coarse salt	1 tablespoon Cognac or
the goose's liver	Armagnac
8 oz (225 g) lean coarsely	good pinch of ground mace
minced pork, or half	and ground cloves
pork and half veal	freshly ground black pepper

With a very sharp knife or a pair of scissors, cut the skin away in a circle as close to the bird's breast as possible. Do the same at the head end, as close to the beak as possible. With a chopper, detach the bird's neck from the body and head. Peel the skin down the neck like a glove, starting from the thicker breast end and taking care not to split the skin. Alternatively, if you think this is too difficult (and it is tricky), cut the skin straight up the neck with a pair of scissors and then peel off, so that you have a long oblong which you will then have to roll up into a sausage shape. Remove the fat adhering to the inside of the skin and reserve. Remove any flesh from the neck bone and mince. Sprinkle the skin with a tablespoon of coarse salt and leave in a cool place for 24 hours.

Trim any greenish-tinged pieces from the goose liver and chop it into small pieces. Combine any goose meat from the neck and the pieces of liver with the pork or pork and veal mixture in a large bowl. Add the egg, the brandy, the spices and salt and pepper to taste. Allow the mixture to rest for at least 4 hours to let the flavours mingle.

When you are ready to make the pâté, wipe any remaining salt from the goose skin and pat dry. If you have succeeded in removing the goose neck without cutting it, tie up the broader end with string and very gently fill the tube with the stuffing. Do not try to stuff in too much at once or pack too tightly, or the skin will burst during cooking. If you have cut the skin, lay it on a flat surface and arrange the stuffing along one side of the oblong, leaving a gap at each end; then carefully roll it up into a sausage shape.

Find a dish or terrine into which the sausage will just fit, or make an open foil parcel. Put plenty of goose fat in the base and lay the sausage on top, cut side down and end flaps tucked over if you have used the second method of stuffing. Dot the top with goose fat and bake in a medium low oven (130°C/275°F/Gas 1) for 45–60 minutes until the top is lightly browned. If you are serving the pâté with the goose, roast it alongside. Either serve immediately or leave to cool for a day, before slicing.

GOOSEBERRY SAUCE

1 lb (450 g) gooseberries	1–2 oz (25–55 g) sugar
2 cloves	1 teaspoon orange-flower
1/2 a lemon	water (*optional*)
2 oz (55 g) butter	

Cook the gooseberries with the cloves and a couple of slivers of lemon peel in just enough water to cover the pan until they are very tender. Pick out the cloves and lemon peel, and push the fruit through a fine sieve to eliminate pips. Whip in the butter in little knobs and season to taste with the juice of the lemon, the sugar and the orange-flower water if you are using it. Serve warm.

ROAST HAUNCH OF VENISON WITH PORT WINE SAUCE AND ORANGE FRUITS

One of the finest dishes to celebrate Christmas is a haunch of venison. Birds may be traditional in Britain today, but in many parts of the Continent a roast of venison is considered a far superior feast, and we don't have to look too far back in British culinary history to find a similar enthusiasm. The best-flavoured venison comes from wild deer. If you have a game dealer who is in touch with local shoots, order a haunch and have it hung a good 10 days before eating. Best of all, ask for a young fallow doe, which to my taste provides the sweetest and most tender flesh. Deer farmers will also provide haunches of venison, but in this case make sure you hang the meat a little longer to acquire a sweetly gamy taste.

If you can acquire the right quality of venison, marinating the meat should not be necessary and indeed in my view can overwhelm the delicate taste of the meat. If you are unsure of the deer's age, however, marinate the haunch for 24 hours in a mix of 3 parts red wine to 1 part olive oil, with spices and herbs such as juniper berries, bay, black peppercorns and thyme, and a few sliced onions.

Having acquired your haunch of venison and made sure it is being properly treated to bring out the full succulence of the meat, turn your attention to the accompanying dishes. Venison was traditionally served with fruits; I like to use pickled apricots and spiced kumquats. The Germans serve red cabbage with venison, the French lentils; both, I find, can take their place on the Christmas table. Finally, make sure you have a little port on hand for the sauce, preferably *not* the vintage variety.

Venison is a lean meat, which makes it healthy eating but also means it is difficult to keep juicy. It needs relatively short cooking, with plenty of fat, best achieved by larding it with pork fat. If you don't have a larding needle, ask someone to buy one for your stocking.

To serve 8–10

1 haunch of venison, approx. 8–10 lb (4–5 kg)	2 or 3 large strips of pork fat
2 teaspoons juniper berries	1 larding needle

To ensure that the meat stays moist during cooking, it must be well larded. Cut the pork fat into thin strips about 2 inches (5 cm) long and, using the larding needle, sew a strip of fat through the meat at regular intervals, leaving each end of the strip of fat just poking out. Continue until the meat is regularly dotted with strips of fat.

Despite the size of the joint, venison cooks surprisingly rapidly; 12–15 minutes per pound (450 g) in a hot oven is sufficient. Pre-heat the oven to very hot (220°C/425°F/Gas 7), and cook the meat for 1 hour, covered with a sheet of buttered greaseproof paper. At the end of the hour, remove the paper, drain off any fat and reserve, and cover the surface of the meat with the crushed juniper berries. Turn the oven down to 200°C/400°F/Gas 6 and cook for a further $1-1^1/_2$ hours, depending on the size of the joint – test with a skewer, the juices should run pink not red. Rest the joint in a warm place for 20 minutes before carving.

PORT WINE SAUCE

1 tablespoon plain white flour	1 pint (575 ml) game stock
	4 fl oz (100 ml) ruby port

Pour a little of the fat you have drawn off the joint into a pan and stir in the flour. Cook over a low heat for a minute or two then slowly add the game stock, stirring well. Bring to the boil then add the juices from the venison (some juices will flow while the joint is resting, and more after carving). Season to taste and add the port; reduce by fast boiling to the required consistency.

SPICED APRICOTS
(prepare a week in advance)

2 lb (900 g) apricots	2 teaspoons allspice berries
12 fl oz (350 ml) white wine vinegar	1 teaspoon black peppercorns
4 oz (115 g) brown sugar	1 teaspoon coriander seeds
1 teaspoon cloves	

Wash the fruit and dry well. Put the vinegar in an enamelled pan together with the sugar and spices and bring to the boil, stirring to dissolve the sugar. Add the fruit to the pan and simmer for 5 minutes, then take off the heat and allow the fruit to cool in the vinegar. Bottle in a sterilized preserving jar, leaving all the whole spices in the jar and set aside for at least a week. Serve cold, brushing off the spices.

SPICED KUMQUATS

2 lb (900 g) kumquats	1 teaspoon allspice berries
2 oz (55 g) butter	4 cracked green cardamom
2 tablespoons brown sugar	pods
8 cloves	1 tablespoon white wine
	vinegar

Wash and dry the fruit. Melt the butter in a large flat pan and add the sugar and spices. Briefly fry the fruit over a gentle heat then add the vinegar and sufficient water to cover the base of the pan. Cover and cook over a low heat for 10–15 minutes until the fruit is soft. Brush off the spices and serve the fruit warm.

SPICED RED CABBAGE COOKED IN CIDER
(prepare at least a day in advance)

3 lb (1.5 kg) red cabbage	(e.g. Bramley)
2 tablespoons goose or duck	8 cloves
fat or lard	2 sticks of cinnamon
4 tablespoons red wine	1 pint (575 ml) sweet or
vinegar	medium dry cider
1 tablespoon brown sugar	8 oz (225 g) prepared
salt and pepper	chestnuts, cooked and
1 cooking apple	peeled

Red cabbage improves greatly in flavour if it can be made a day or two in advance and left to stand in a cool place – in fact, cooked red cabbage will keep for up to a week, which can be a boon to a busy Christmas cook.

Peel the tough outer leaves from the cabbage and chop into shreds, discarding the white central core. In a large heavy-based pan which will take all the cabbage, melt the goose or duck fat or lard (if you can get bird fat, it will give greater flavour). Add the cabbage to the pan and stir to make sure that it is all well coated in the fat. Add the vinegar, sugar, salt and pepper, the whole unpeeled apple studded with the cloves and the sticks of cinnamon. Pour over the cider and bring to the boil, then cover and leave barely to simmer or transfer to a low oven. Stir occasionally and add water if necessary to make sure the cabbage does not stick. After 2 hours, add the peeled, cooked chestnuts. Total cooking time will be 3–3¹/₂ hours, by which time the cabbage will be very tender. Remove the cinnamon stick and keep the cabbage until you are ready to use it; it can be reheated on the stove or in the oven.

LENTILS AND PARSLEY BUTTER

12 oz (350 g) green lentils, preferably the Le Puy variety

1 carrot

1 onion

4 cloves

4 rashers of smoked streaky bacon

1 tablespoon fresh flat-leaved parsley

2 oz (55 g) butter

Rinse the lentils very thoroughly and put them in a large pan with the carrot, the peeled whole onion studded with the cloves and the rashers of bacon. Just cover with boiling water and simmer uncovered until the lentils are tender, adding more water if necessary. Remove the carrot, onion and bacon from the pan and boil off any remaining liquid.

Chop the parsley finely. Just before serving, stir the parsley and the butter into the lentils and season well.

SALMIS OF PHEASANT

Pheasant is at its best in November and December, and recently has been both plentiful and cheap. Some butchers now sell pheasant legs separately, and these are ideal for this dish. If you have a whole bird, however, strip it of its breasts and grill, fry or roast them separately, thereby avoiding the dryness which is too often a feature of a whole roast pheasant. Then use the legs another day to make a salmis, a traditional English treatment which produces a gravy of succulent intensity.

1 carrot
8 oz (225 g) shallots
1 tablespoon vegetable oil
4 rashers of smoked streaky
    bacon
4 legs of pheasant
1 tablespoon plain white
    flour
1 glass red wine
$^1/_4$ pint (150 ml) chicken
    stock

1 teaspoon black
    peppercorns
4 juniper berries
2 sprigs of parsley
1 sprig of thyme
2 oz (55 g) butter
4 oz (115 g) brown cap
    mushrooms
salt and pepper

Pre-heat the oven to medium hot (180°C/350°F/Gas 4). Chop the carrot and a few of the shallots and brown them in the vegetable oil in a shallow earthenware dish in the oven. When the vegetables are browned, add the bacon chopped into pieces and the pheasant legs. When the meat takes on a little colour, dredge with the flour; cook for a further 5 minutes before pouring over the red wine and stock. Crush the peppercorns and juniper berries and add them to the dish with the parsley and thyme. Turn down the oven to medium (150°C/300°F/Gas 2) and cook uncovered for an hour or so until the meat comes off the bone.

Skin the pheasant and strip the meat from the bones. Put the bones back in the pan together with the juices and vegetables to cook for another 30 minutes. Meanwhile, peel the remaining shallots and cook them in the butter for about 20 minutes until soft and lightly brown. Then add the mushrooms, chopped in half. Stew until soft.

Strain the juices from the pheasant, pushing the bones to make sure you extract the maximum juice. Add the pheasant meat, shallots and mushrooms to the juice and gently reheat. If you were Victorian, at this stage you would pour in a glass of Madeira, but personally I find this a little excessive. Adjust the seasoning and serve with triangles of bread lightly fried in butter.

SPICED BRAISED OXTAIL

Braised oxtail is the archetypal winter dish. This is not a dish for those in a rush and the end result is not elegant, but it is packed with flavour and is the perfect antidote to those put off oxtail by the soups which masquerade under that name. It is best made in advance and reheated, so that you can skim off the fat when the stew has cooled.

3 lb (1.5 kg) oxtail, cut into pieces
2 tablespoons plain white flour
1 tablespoon vegetable oil
1 lb (450 g) onions
1 oz (25 g) butter
1 teaspoon chopped fresh ginger
3 large carrots
1 lb (450 g) small turnips
4 cloves
8 allspice berries
1 teaspoon coriander seeds
1/4 pint (150 ml) red wine
1 1/2 pints (850 ml) beef stock
1 teaspoon tomato purée
herbs (*ideally 2 or 3 sprigs of parsley, a bayleaf, a sprig of thyme and a sprig of rosemary, tied together with string*)
salt and freshly ground black pepper

Trim the oxtail of excess fat and roll in the seasoned flour. Fry the meat in the oil in a large, heavy-based casserole until browned on all sides, then remove. Discard the oil.

Pre-heat the oven to medium low (130°C/275°F/Gas 1). Chop the onions into half-rings and gently fry in the butter until soft. Add the ginger, the carrots chopped into fine rings and the peeled, quartered turnips. Fry for 3–4 minutes, stirring, then add the cloves, allspice berries and coriander seeds. When the seeds pop, pour over the red wine and bring to the boil. Boil for 1 minute then add the beef stock, into which you have stirred the tomato purée. Bring back to the boil and add the fried oxtail and the herbs, leaving the string hanging out of the pot for easy removal. Season with plenty of black pepper and salt, taking account of the saltiness of the stock. Cover the pot and leave in the oven for 3 hours.

Leave to cool so that you can skim off the fat from the surface of the casserole. If you like, you can remove the pieces of oxtail and pull the meat off the bone (you should be able to do this using just a fork). Return the meat to the casserole, keeping the bones for stock. Serve very hot, with mashed or plain boiled potatoes.

TURKEY MEXICAN STYLE

The turkey was first introduced to Europe from Mexico soon after the Spanish Conquest. The conquistadores were so overcome by the beauty of the wild turkey that they thought it a species of peacock, and hastened to take one home to their king. At the time of the Conquest, the domesticated turkey was also widespread throughout Central and South America and it is this bird with which we are familiar today. Turkey is still a very popular dish in Mexico, and is traditionally cooked with another local product, chocolate, in a dish known as a mole. The Aztec origins of the recipe show in the combination of nuts, fruit and chocolate (and in its rather time-consuming preparation). The end result is a wonderfully dark-coloured, rich dish truly fit for a feast.

4 skinned, thick-cut fillets of turkey breast, $1^1/_2$–2 lb (675–900 g) in total

4 tablespoons red wine vinegar

1 tablespoon sugar

1 teaspoon salt

1 teaspoon coarsely ground black pepper

3 large dried red chillies

1 teaspoon tomato purée

2 pints (1.1 litres) light turkey stock (*ask your butcher for some turkey bones or substitute chicken stock*)

2 large cloves of garlic

4 oz (115 g) raisins

1 lb (450 g) tomatoes (*the plum type give the best flavour, but don't use a tin as you need to roast the tomatoes in their skins*)

1 oz (25 g) sesame seeds

3 tablespoons groundnut or peanut oil

2 oz (55 g) whole almonds in their skins

8 oz (225 g) onions

2 teaspoons ground cinnamon

$^1/_2$ teaspoon ground allspice

4 ground cloves

2 oz (55 g) good-quality bitter chocolate

Marinate the turkey breasts for an hour or two in the vinegar, sugar, half the salt and half the pepper. Meanwhile, de-seed and split the dried chillies and briefly toast them in a dry pan until they just start to brown. Stir the tomato purée into the turkey or chicken stock, bring to the boil and add the toasted chillies. Simmer, covered, for 30 minutes until the chillies are very tender.

Roast the garlic cloves in their skins in a medium oven until just soft (15–20 minutes). Soak the raisins in warm water for 20 minutes. Pre-heat the grill to maximum and cook the whole tomatoes in their skins for 10 minutes, turning once, so that the skins darken. Toast the sesame seeds in a dry pan for 5 minutes or so, stirring constantly, until they pop and brown but are not burnt. Remove the sesame seeds and heat 1 tablespoon of the oil in the pan. Quickly toast the whole almonds until they brown, taking care that they do not burn, then grind them. Finally, roughly chop the onions.

You are now ready to assemble the sauce. The preparation of its ingredients may be time-consuming, but it is vital to the flavour of the dish. Squeeze the roasted garlic out of its skins and mix with the spices in a pestle and mortar. Process the tomatoes, chillies, ground almonds and toasted sesame seeds to a paste, and stir this paste, the spice and garlic mixture, the onions and the drained raisins into the liquid in which the chillies have simmered. Process again.

In a deep-sided, heavy-based pan large enough to take the meat and sauce, heat the remaining oil. Lift the turkey breasts out of the marinade and when the oil is hot, fry quickly on each side to seal. Remove from the oil and reserve. Pour the sauce through a sieve into the pan and fry over a medium high heat for 5 minutes, stirring constantly. Then stir in the chocolate, broken into small pieces, and when it has melted place the turkey breasts in the sauce. Simmer uncovered for an hour or so, until the turkey is tender and the sauce has thickened.

I like to serve this very rich dish with sweet potatoes baked in the oven until soft, and an avocado and red onion salad, dressed with lime juice and fresh coriander and perhaps spiked with a little green chilli.

PUDDINGS

For most of the year my puddings are based around the fruit bowl: tropical fruits in the spring, Mediterranean soft fruits and British strawberries in the early summer, Scottish raspberries in August, blackberries, apples and pears in the autumn. When fresh fruit is in season, puddings are easy. But in the depths of the winter months the choice is reduced.

In the days before air freight, winter puddings relied to a great extent on dried fruits, spices and nuts. Not that some of the fruits weren't exotic – apricots, figs, dates, raisins all dry well, besides our own apples, pears and plums. Fruits dried in the autumn are at their best a month or two later, when they still retain their juiciness. Nuts too do not keep for ever, as anyone who has kept a Christmas bowl of nuts until Easter will know, but autumn-gathered nuts eaten in January still have their essential oils. Dried fruits and nuts are traditionally combined in British winter baking in Christmas cake, plum pudding and mince pies. They are also used in puddings from further afield, in the Turkish baklava, raisin ice-cream from Spain or prune mousse from the south-west of France.

Dried fruits require just as careful shopping as the fresh variety, their provenance and age being equally important. Sadly, this is rarely recognized by the British shopper. A visit to the markets of Paris showed me the difference in the French approach.

Parisian Markets

It is hard in Paris to draw a dividing line between market and shop. All along the boulevards, down the narrow side streets, the produce of the stores spills out on to the pavements, displayed in the open air on ramshackle stalls. This practice is not confined to the smaller, more traditional shops – even supermarkets do it. Go to the famous Rue de

Buci market off the Boulevard St-Germain, where well-heeled Parisians do their shopping on their way home from work, and you will see a stall selling sausages and choucroute, fruit and vegetables as part of the large supermarket on the corner of the Rue de Seine.

Paris has covered markets and street markets, occasional markets and those that are open all day, every day. It has specialist markets, like the one for birds which on Sundays takes over the site of the plant market on the banks of the Seine, and it has flea markets, selling almost anything you can think of. Above all, it has food markets, over sixty at the last count. The 'ventre' or belly of Paris, as the now defunct Les Halles were called, may have been dispersed but it has not disappeared.

All the markets offer treats for the British cook. In winter one of the greatest delights are the displays of shellfish, cheap oysters, live crabs, scallops on the shell, spiky purple sea urchins. In case you are wondering, the French crack the urchins open with special scissors and eat the powerfully iodine-flavoured insides raw, or stir them into scrambled eggs. The urchins usually come from Brittany, but how much of the shellfish, I wonder, has found its way to Paris from British waters? There are charcuterie stalls, hung with sausages for the choucroute, and fat or thin salamis for serving as a starter with a hunk of farm butter and a few gherkins. Beneath the ranks of sausages sit chunky glass jars of pâtés, rillettes and terrines, made from pork, goose and duck.

With all this to choose from, why on earth should I come to the markets of Paris to look for ideas for puddings? Shouldn't I be talking about French cuts of meat, the massive consumption of oysters on Christmas Eve, or the different sorts of pâtés? Well, perhaps, but the Parisians do manage to maintain their standards to the end of the meal. I dined one night at La Procope, famed for its revolutionary connections, with a young English banker who had recently moved to the city. After his meal of 'petites perles de Bretagne' (oysters), coq au vin made with Hermitage wine, and a perfect slice of Brie de Meaux, he tucked into his crème marronnière, a confection of chestnut purée and meringue floating on crème anglaise, or custard. Eyes closed in bliss, he murmured, 'The puddings are always the best bit in France.' Maybe this reflects simply the British obsession with the pudding, but surely this at least is an area where we, the Brits, ought to be able to take on the French, especially in winter, the season of baking.

The Paris markets show why we often lose the culinary battle even on our home turf. Almost every market I visited had a stall dedicated to dried fruits and nuts, those essential ingredients for baking. Take the market in the pretty Place Monge, in the 5th arrondissement, just up the road from the more famous street market of the Rue Mouffetard. The Place Monge market takes place three mornings a week, on Wednesdays, Fridays and Sundays, and so attracts small producers, like the market gardener who sells courgette flowers in summer. The dried fruit stall is there only in winter; in summer its owner switches to fruit from the Mediterranean.

Of course, we have such stalls in British markets – there is a good one in Salisbury, for example. But how often do you see six different qualities of dried apricot on offer, priced according to their provenance, plumpness and time of drying? These wild ones (the most expensive, from Afghanistan) are so good that they can be eaten just as they are, the stallholder informs me; these, from Italy, need a little soaking and would be best for a cake. Or how about some of the figs, sold threaded together on strings, or perhaps these dates, the best from Morocco, or these highest-quality prunes from Agen? Plump sultanas and raisins are sold not packed into mean little plastic bags but by the scoop from the huge trays he has set out in the weak winter sunshine. Smaller trays display candied fruits – whole clementines, fat slices of mango, kumquats, perfumed lemons from the South of France and, in a striking contrast of colour, strips of green angelica. Buy a selection and chop them up for your own candied peel for the Christmas cake. There are bags of peeled, cooked chestnuts, packed 'sous vide' to retain their freshness. And every nut you can think of, in the shell, in the skin or blanched. Not ground, though, as we often buy them: the stallholder explains that they lose their oils too quickly that way, and it would be far better for Madame to grind them at home.

One reason for the preponderance of such produce is the large population of Arab descent in Paris. Arab cuisine makes good use of dried fruits and nuts, not just in puddings, but in couscous, in salads, with meats in tagines. Barbès, the Arab quarter in the 18th in the shadow of the Sacré Coeur, is a fascinating if rundown part of the city where tourists rarely venture. The main market, on Wednesday and Saturday mornings, huddles under the overhead railway and is best for cheap fruits and vegetables – if you are a marmalade maker in Paris, this is where you buy your Seville oranges in February. Just off the boulevard is the famous Rue de la Goutte d'Or, the drop of gold, where every day except Friday and in Ramadan there is a market feel, as small shops open out on to the street and little stalls sell breads and bunches of mint. This is the best place in Paris to buy spices: cardamom, nutmeg, ginger, cinnamon, allspice berries, all are sold cheaply, loose from sacks on the street or from large spice boxes inside the shops. These spices feature just as strongly in old English pudding recipes as they do in current Middle Eastern and North African cooking. Pick up as well a bottle of rosewater or orange-flower water for flavouring yoghurt, for adding to the syrup for your baklava, for giving a Middle Eastern flavour to your baking. Then, if you dare, take your purchases into one of the predominantly male cafés for a glass of sweet mint tea, poured from a silver teapot, and a slice of sticky pastry.

So Paris is a good place for the winter baker. But what if you are short of the time needed to make such puddings? Here again, the Parisians score. They have a quite different approach to fast food: there is no shame in buying in the pudding, for quite often it will be of higher quality than you would produce at home; unless of course you also happen to be a master pâtissier. It sometimes seems as if every street in Paris has a pâtisserie, its window displaying artistic fruit-filled tarts in summer, darker nut and chocolate cakes or light Austrian streusels in winter. The prices, however, reveal the work that has gone into these creations: they are special treats rather than everyday purchases. A cheaper alternative is found in the markets, where little bakers' stalls are often set up. Back to the Place Monge to find home-made rhubarb tarts, pink and green strips of rhubarb poking out of eggy custard, in a flaky pastry which does not quite have the perfect cut of that from the pâtisseries, but is just as good. One stallholder sells nothing but honey (from bees feeding on acacia flowers or chestnut trees, so the labels say) and home-made pain d'épices, spice bread which is perfect at teatime or with a dried fruit salad. The baker has the Alsatian kugelhopf, made in a special mould and studded with dried peel, galettes from Brittany which ooze butter, almost black linzertortes filled with almonds and raspberry jelly. The only possible rivals in Britain's markets are the home-made cakes of the WI stalls, a good but rare commodity. Unfortunately there can be no comparison between French pâtisseries and the vast majority of our bakers.

There is one other aspect of the Parisian markets which incites great jealousy in me. In winter, with a good bottle of red wine, there is great pleasure in simply ending a meal with a selection of cheeses. And we in Britain make great cheeses: serve a Frenchman a slice of perfectly ripe Stilton or mature farmhouse Cheddar and he will be pleasantly surprised. We do not, however, except with rare exceptions, have great cheese stalls in our markets. They do in Paris. The one in the Place Monge boasted wicker trays of fresh goat's cheeses, rolled in cinders, wrapped in vine-leaves, or just plain. It had goat's cheeses in differing stages of maturity, ranging in colour from pure white to a dark yellow. The exact degree of hardness of the cheese Madame should buy was a matter for 10 minutes' discussion. There were whole Reblochons and Tommes from Savoie, massive sides of Gruyère, farmhouse Bries so ripe that they would have to be dribbled on to the plate, heart-shaped sweetened fromages blancs for a Valentine's day pudding with fruits bottled in Armagnac. No little bits of plastic were wrapped round the cheeses making them sweat; most were open to the air, and passed on in thick paper. The stallholder knew every cheese, where it came from, who made it, when it should be eaten and with or after what. Little mouthfuls for tasting and subsequent discussion were happily dispensed.

This was a good cheese stall, but not an exceptional one in Paris. There are others in every market, in the Raspail open market, famous for its organic and farmhouse produce, in the covered market of St-Quentin, between the transport hubs of the Gares du Nord and de l'Est, in the Rue Mouffetard just to the south of the Place Monge, in the Lecourbe market of the 15th – the list is endless. Until we breed stallholders who have such pride in and knowledge of their produce, until we become customers who demand, and can recognize, the very best, until we live in a society where to be a master pâtissier is an honour, then we in Britain shall remain jealous of the markets of France – whatever the season, whatever the course.

ALMOND CAKE

This cake of Italian origin has a light buttery case filled with a rich almond centre, the whole topped by crisp whole almonds. It is an impressive dish which can be served with cream as a pudding, as an excellent mouthful with an early glass of sherry or as a cake at teatime.

FOR THE PASTRY CASE

4 egg-yolks
3 oz (85 g) white sugar
3 oz (85 g) butter
a few seeds from a vanilla pod or a few drops of vanilla essence

8 oz (225 g) self-raising flour
1/4 teaspoon salt (*if you are using unsalted butter*)

FOR THE FILLING

8 oz (225 g) whole skinned blanched almonds
3 oz (85 g) unsalted butter
pinch of salt

4 oz (115 g) white sugar
3 whole eggs
1/2 teaspoon baking powder
1 oz (25 g) potato starch

First, make the pastry case. Cream together the egg-yolks, sugar and butter and stir in the seeds from the vanilla pod or the essence. Carefully sieve in the flour and salt and form into a ball. Allow to rest in the fridge for an hour or so. Butter a cake tin with a detachable base, and when the pastry is firm, carefully roll it out and line the tin to half-way up the sides. Prick the pastry with a fork and put back in the fridge for another 10 minutes or so.

Pre-heat the oven to medium hot (180°C/350°F/Gas 4). Grind half the almonds; toast the other half whole in 1/2 oz (15 g) of the butter until they are lightly browned. Mix the ground almonds, salt and sugar together and beat in the eggs one by one, so that the mixture is light and fluffy. Meanwhile, slowly melt the remaining butter. Sieve the baking powder and the potato starch into the egg, sugar and nut cream and fold in carefully; then fold in the melted butter.

Fill the lined pastry case with the mixture and bake in the pre-heated oven for 10–15 minutes, until the filling rises and begins to set. Quickly scatter the toasted almonds over the surface of the cake and return to the oven for another 20 minutes, by which the time the filling should be set and the pastry lightly browned.

Remove the cake tin and leave the cake to cool on a rack.

BAKED ORANGE CUSTARD

Towards the end of the winter months, the new season's sweet oranges start to appear, some of the best coming from North Africa. February also sees the short season of the bitter Seville orange, friend of the marmalade maker. This Spanish recipe for baked orange custard is a very popular pudding at this time of year.

4 oz (115 g) caster sugar	1 Seville orange
5 small or 4 large eggs	2 teaspoons orange-flower
4 small or 3 large sweet	water (*optional*)
oranges	

Heat two-thirds of the sugar in a small pan with 1 teaspoon of water. Stir until the sugar caramelizes. Spread the caramelized sugar over the base of 4 ramekins or an 8 inch (20 cm) oval flan case and leave to cool.

Heat the oven to medium (150°C/300°F/Gas 2). Whisk together the eggs, the remaining sugar, the juice of all the oranges, the grated zest of one of the sweet oranges and the orange flower water if you are using it. Pour into the ramekins or flan case and place in a tray of water (bain-marie).

Cook for an hour until set (test with a skewer, which should come out clean). Leave to cool before turning out just before serving. The caramelized sugar will form its own sauce.

BAKLAVA

Despite its Middle Eastern associations, baklava was first created by the Christian Armenians, who served this luxurious pudding on Easter Sunday. The early recipes used forty sheets of filo pastry, one for each day of Lent – the name is derived from baki-halva, or Lent sweet. The dish was soon being prepared in the kitchens of the Sultans of the Ottoman Empire, and today is symbolic of Turkish cuisine in particular.

Never mind tradition, baklava has always seemed to me to be a winter pudding, with its lavish use of nuts. Walnuts are usual, but you can substitute almonds or pistachios, or a mixture. As served in Turkey, baklava is too sweet and sticky for my taste. Instead of using nearly 1 lb of sugar, I make honey the main ingredient of my syrup. And there is less pastry – if you use forty sheets of filo, you also need to use nearly 1 lb (450 g) of butter (which may be why fat pashas liked it so much). The result is a flakier, thinner pastry which still goes very well with a cup of cardamom coffee.

4 oz (115 g) sugar	4 oz (115 g) unsalted butter
6 tablespoons clear honey	18 sheets filo pastry
1 lemon	8 oz (225 g) shelled walnuts
2 tablespoons rosewater	1 teaspoon ground
1 orange	cinnamon

The first step is to make the syrup. Stir together the sugar, honey and juice of the lemon and then add 3/4 pint (450 ml) of water. Bring to the boil, stirring all the time, and then simmer for 10 minutes or so, until the syrup sticks to the back of the spoon. Stir in the rosewater and leave to cool.

Pre-heat the oven to medium hot (180°C/350°F/Gas 4). Skin the orange and peel off any pith. Cut the peel into very thin strips and blanch for 1 minute. Butter a baking tray large enough to take an entire sheet of filo pastry (if you haven't got one large enough, you will have to cut off any pastry which falls over the side). Melt the remaining butter and skim off any foam which rises to the surface.

Place 2 layers of filo on top of each other on the tray. Dribble a tablespoon of the melted butter over the surface. It is best not to paint the butter on with a brush, as this presses down on the layers of pastry, and your aim is to leave air between them; for the same reason, do not smooth creases out of the pastry. Apply another sheet of filo; dribble over a little more butter. Continue until you have used up 6 sheets, then scatter half the chopped walnuts and the orange peel over the surface. Sprinkle over half the cinnamon. Lay another 6 layers on top, dribbling over a little butter each time, then sprinkle over the remainder of the walnuts, orange peel and cinnamon. Finish with the remaining 6 sheets, again applying butter, including on the top of the final layer.

It is easier if you cut the baklava up at this stage, rather than waiting until the pastry has crisped. It is traditionally cut into lozenges.

Cook the baklava in the pre-heated oven for 30 minutes, then turn the temperature down to medium (150°C/300°F/Gas 2). Cook for another 40 minutes or so, until the surface is a golden colour.

Allow the pastry to cool for 10 minutes then pour over the cooled syrup, making sure it flows into the gaps between lozenges. Leave the baklava for at least 24 hours, longer if you can, so that the syrup is absorbed. It will keep for up to a week.

CHESTNUT CREAM

This is an easy-to-put-together pudding which relies on store-cupboard ingredients as a base. The French manufacture a range of chestnut purées as well as selling whole chestnuts bottled in glass jars or vacuum-packed. Although British manufacturers have yet to follow suit, the purées are available from good delicatessens and some supermarkets, and are good standbys. I also keep a tin of coconut milk in the store cupboard for puddings and curries. Combine the two with yoghurt and cream for a rich, unctuous sweet.

4 tablespoons sweetened chestnut purée (*a confectioner's purée is best*)
4 tablespoons coconut milk (*I use unsweetened, as the sweetened version can be a little sickly and the remainder of the unsweetened tin can be kept for curries*)

6 fl oz (175 ml) Greek
yoghurt

4 fl oz (100 ml) thick
double cream
2 oz (55 g) toasted hazelnuts

Whip together the chestnut purée and the coconut milk. Stir in the yoghurt and cream. Check for sweetness and add a little caster sugar if necessary. Spoon into glasses or glass bowls and chill. Just before serving, toast the hazelnuts and sprinkle over.

CHRISTMAS BREAD

Christmas breads rather than cakes are popular in many parts of Europe. These breads share features in common with our own Christmas cake: they use dried fruits, nuts and peel, are enriched with butter and are often made on a grand scale. However, they are neither as sweet nor as rich and consequently I prefer them (although I realize I may be in the minority). This particular recipe produces a huge flat bread and therefore plenty of crust, in the Italian style.

1 lb 10 oz (750 g) plain
flour
1 oz (25 g) dried yeast (or
2 oz (55 g) fresh yeast)
6 fl oz (175 ml) full cream
milk
4 oz (115 g) dried apricots
4 oz (115 g) sultanas
3 tablespoons brandy (or
whisky)
1 orange
1 lemon (preferably
unwaxed)

4 oz (115 g) skinned,
chopped almonds (*flaked
almonds are not appropriate
as they do not give the right
texture in the bread*)
4 oz (115 g) caster sugar
pinch of salt
3 egg-yolks
8 oz (225 g) unsalted butter,
softened
icing sugar
ground cinnamon

Sieve the flour and put it in a warm place in a large bowl. If using the dried variety, reconstitute the yeast according to the instructions on the packet (this usually involves mixing it with a little sugar and warm water). Warm the milk to tepid. Make a well in the centre of the flour, pour in the yeast and milk and mix to a dough (it will be sticky at first). If using easy blend yeast, you may need to add a little water. Sprinkle the surface with flour, cover with a cloth and leave in a warm place for an hour or so to rise.

Finely chop the apricots and combine with the sultanas. Pour over the spirit. Peel the zest from the orange and lemon (this is best done with a potato peeler, to make sure you do not get any pith), and chop coarsely. Bring a pan of water to the boil and plunge in the zest; drain as soon as the water returns to the boil. Sprinkle the zest over a large baking tray and put in the bottom of a low oven for 10 minutes to dry out. If you are using whole almonds, chop them coarsely.

Add the zest, almonds, sugar, salt and egg-yolks to the apricot and sultana mixture. Chop the very soft butter into little pieces. When the dough has risen, work in the pieces of butter with your fingers, a little at a time (this is a messy job, as the dough is very sticky to work with – however, try to resist using a processor as it will knock the air out of the dough). When all the butter has been incorporated, add the apricot and almond mixture. Keep working the dough until all is amalgamated, sprinkling your hands with flour as necessary.

Pre-heat the oven to medium hot (180°C/350°F/Gas 4). Put the dough on a large metal baking tray and fashion into a crescent shape. Cover with a cloth and leave in a warm place to rise again. When the dough has doubled in volume, spreading itself across the tray so that it is almost heart-shaped, place in the middle of the oven. After 30 minutes, turn down to medium (150°C/300°F/Gas 2).

The bread will take about an hour to cook, its large flat shape ensuring that it cooks evenly and that there is a good ratio of crust to bread. Keep an eye on it and turn down the oven if it browns too fast. Test with a skewer after an hour – it should come out clean. Leave it to cool on the baking tray, then dust it with icing sugar and cinnamon. Cut it into long thin slices and serve it after the meal with cheese or pudding, for breakfast, at tea-time, as an appetizer with a glass of sherry, as you like. The bread keeps well for some days.

DRIED FRUIT SALAD

Dried fruits come into their own in the middle of winter, when the fresh variety are at their scarcest. They are useful store-cupboard foods, which as well as being used for puddings can be popped into meaty casseroles. Dried apricots have a great affinity with lamb, prunes and dried apple rings are good with pork, sultanas go surprisingly well with beef. For a pretty Christmas gift, simmer a mixture of dried fruits in red wine, spiced as if for mulling, and bottle in an attractive preserving jar. For a more everyday pudding, try this recipe, which gives the fruit a slightly Turkish flavour through the use of rosewater.

mixed dried fruits such as apples, apricots, figs, prunes, raisins, sultanas (*but not bananas*), to a total dried weight of 12 oz (350 g) (*dried fruit is very rich and you do not need a great quantity*)

the juice of 2 oranges
2 tablespoons rosewater
1 stick of cinnamon
4 cardamom pods
4 tablespoons clear honey
12 fl oz (350 ml) Greek yoghurt

Soak the fruits overnight in the orange juice, rosewater, spices and sufficient water to cover. The next day bring the liquid and the fruits to the boil and simmer gently for 20 minutes or so, until the fruits are very tender. Remove the fruits to cool and boil the liquid down to a syrupy consistency. Strain and pour the liquid over the fruits.

Whip the honey into the yoghurt and spoon into glass serving dishes. Spoon over the cooled fruits (they are nice just tepid) and serve. You can sprinkle some toasted nuts over the dish, if you like.

FLAMED DRIED FRUITS AND NUTS

In Spain dried fruits and nuts are doused in brandy, set alight and brought still flaming to the table, to be eaten as soon as they are cool enough to handle. In Turkey the same treatment is given to pistachios, using the local spirit, raki. It is an excellent way to end a meal if you haven't time to prepare a proper pudding, and looks very impressive.

a mixture of walnuts, almonds, hazelnuts, dried figs, raisins, sultanas
1 tablespoon brandy to 2 oz (55 g) fruit and nuts
(*cheap cooking brandy, preferably Spanish, should be used*)

Arrange the fruit and nuts on a heatproof platter. Heat the brandy in a ladle, pour it over the fruit and nuts and set light to it. Carry flaming to the table.

LYCHEES IN GINGER SYRUP

Until recently, most of us were familiar with lychees only in their tinned form, served in a rather sickly syrup as a pudding in Chinese restaurants. Fresh lychees, however, are now widely available in winter, the knobbly pink skins encasing a juicy, rose-scented fruit of surprising delicacy. Lychees are beautiful additions to a fruit bowl, but are messy to eat at a dinner party. Peel the fruit and bathe it in a syrup of greater delicacy than that in the tins and you have a simple but elegant pudding.

1 lime
1/2 pint (300 ml) water
4 oz (115 g) white sugar
1 oz (25 g) fresh ginger, peeled and chopped into several pieces
1 1/2 lb (675 g) fresh lychees

Squeeze the juice from the lime and mix with the water. Add the sugar and heat slowly until the sugar dissolves, then add the pieces of ginger and the skins of the lime; boil together for 10 minutes, strain and allow to cool.

Peel the lychees and remove the stones. When the syrup is cool, add the fruit and leave for at least 6 hours before serving.

Mulled Wine Jelly

This very adult jelly is a long way from the fluorescent moulds I remember from childhood birthday parties. It is also extremely simple to put together and is therefore a good standby dinner party pudding.

For 4 individual servings

$^1/_2$ pint (300 ml) red wine	stick of cinnamon
$^1/_3$ pint (200 ml) water	3 allspice berries
juice of 1 orange	1 sachet gelatine (to set
juice of $^1/_2$ a lemon	1 pint (575 ml) liquid)
2 cloves	2 tablespoons sugar

Heat the wine with the water, fruit juices, spices and sugar, stirring until all the sugar has dissolved. Simmer for a few minutes, then take off the heat and strain (through muslin if you have some – if not, don't worry, but the jelly will be a little cloudier). Stir in the gelatine, pour into individual serving dishes and chill until set.

Raisin and Sherry Ice-cream

Ice-cream may not seem very suitable for winter, but this version from the sherry-producing regions of Spain is rich enough to cope with cold weather. Sherry is in my opinion vastly underrated in this country, especially the rich dark sherries which can be served equally well before or after the meal. Dark does not necessarily mean sweet: olorosos and palo cortados, for example, have a dry finish but a rounded, full taste in the mouth.

4 oz (115 g) good-quality
    raisins
4 tablespoons good-quality,
    rich dark sherry (*I use the
    dry but full and fruity
    oloroso; you could also use
    amontillado or at a pinch a
    cream sherry, but definitely*

*not the bone-dry finos or
    manzanillas)*
$^1/_2$ pint (300 ml) full cream
    milk
3 egg-yolks
4 oz (115 g) caster sugar
$^1/_2$ pint (300 ml) double or
    whipping cream

Put the raisins to soak in the sherry for a few hours at least, preferably overnight. When the raisins have soaked, bring the milk to the boil. Allow to cool for 10 minutes and remove any skin. Whisk together the egg-yolks and caster sugar until pale and creamy, then whisk into the milk. Over a low heat, stir continuously with a wooden spoon until a thick custard forms, taking care not to let the mixture boil. (This is best accomplished using a thin saucepan, which does not retain heat, so that you can lift it off the fire if it gets too hot.) When the custard coats the back of the spoon, take it off the heat and allow to cool.

Whip the cream until stiff. Fold it into the cooled custard, along with the sherry and raisins. Pour the mixture into a shallow freezer container with a lid and put it, covered, in the freezer for 2–3 hours. Take the mixture out and whisk it up again to break up any ice crystals. Cover again, and place back in the freezer for another couple of hours.

Make sure you take the ice-cream out of the freezer at least 30 minutes before you serve it, or the raisins will be too hard. If you like, you can pour a little more sherry over the ice-cream when you serve it.

SPICED RICE PUDDING

Winter is a good time for solid and comforting nursery food. The texture of rice pudding fulfils all the nursery characteristics, and I add a few spices to increase its appeal to the adult palate. The end result is deeply satisfying on a very cold day.

1 oz (25 g) unsalted butter

3 oz (85 g) pudding rice

1 teaspoon ground
cinnamon

1 teaspoon ground allspice

1 oz (25 g) brown sugar

4 cardamom pods

1 tablespoon orange-flower
water

1¹/₂ pints (850 ml) full-
cream milk

Pre-heat the oven to low (110°C/225°F/Gas ¹/₄). Butter an 8 inch (20 cm) dish with half the butter and put in the rinsed rice. Mix in the cinnamon, allspice and sugar and add the cardamom pods. Pour over the orange-flower water and the milk and dot the surface with the remaining butter.

Cook the pudding in the bottom of the oven for 2¹/₂ hours, until a brown crust has formed and all the milk has been absorbed. The cardamom pods will rise to the surface; pick them out of the skin before serving.

PRUNE AND BRANDY MOUSSE WITH ALMOND PETITS FOURS

The difference between a soggy prune canned in sweet syrup and a good-quality dried prune is quite astonishing to the uninitiated. Some of the best prunes come from the south-west of France, where they are combined with the local liquor, Armagnac, to make an unctuous mousse. If you have a bottle of Armagnac to hand, splendid, otherwise you can use its more common cousin, Cognac. The result will be a rich and delicious pudding for a dinner party, especially if you make some almond petits fours for scooping up the mousse.

1 lb (450 g) good-quality
dried prunes (*available
from delicatessens*)

2 strips of lemon rind

4 tablespoons Armagnac or
Cognac

sugar

1 pint (575 ml) double
cream

2 egg-whites

Soak the prunes in plenty of water overnight (for other dishes I often soak prunes in weak tea, but here water is best). To cook, simmer the prunes in the water in which they soaked, using just sufficient to cover the fruit, and adding the lemon peel. When the fruit is tender, which should take 30–45 minutes, remove the stones and process the prunes to a purée (you may need to add a little of the cooking liquid) or push them through a sieve. Stir the brandy into the purée, together with sugar to taste. Allow the purée to cool.

Whip the cream until stiff. Whip the egg-whites with a little sugar until they stand in peaks. Fold the cooled purée into the cream, then fold in the egg-whites. Spoon into individual serving dishes and chill well before serving.

Almond petits fours go well with the mousse. They are easy to make, and the dough can be kept in the fridge or freezer until you are ready to use it.

ALMOND PETITS FOURS

4 oz (115 g) butter	pinch of baking powder
4 oz (115 g) white sugar	pinch of salt
4 oz (115 g) ground almonds	1 teaspoon ground cinnamon
juice of 1 orange	8 oz (225 g) self-raising flour
zest of $^1/_4$ of a lemon	
1 egg	1 egg-yolk

Mix together the butter, sugar, almonds, orange juice, lemon zest, egg, baking powder, salt and cinnamon. When they are thoroughly blended, stir in the sieved flour. Allow the dough to rest for at least 2 hours in a cool place.

Roll the dough out to a thickness of $^1/_2$ inch (1 cm) and cut into rounds. Arrange on a buttered baking tray and brush the surface with egg-yolk. Bake in a medium oven (150°C/300°F/Gas 2) for 15 minutes.

Rhubarb with Orange and Stem Ginger

Although I find it a little odd to describe rhubarb as a winter fruit, the early forced stems, grown largely in Yorkshire, reach the shops in January. Unlike much other early fruit they are rather good, the pale pink stems having a greater delicacy than the later outdoor version. Make sure the rhubarb is crisp when you buy it, rather than soft and flabby, which can indicate age or exposure to cold. I prefer to steam rather than stew rhubarb and often serve it plain, with a few drops of orange-flower water. Rhubarb is also an excellent fruit to use in a tart (see spring recipe, page 119) or a clafoutis. A favourite dish is gently steamed rhubarb with stem ginger, served with plenty of cream or Greek yoghurt mixed with honey.

$1^1/_2$ lb (675 g) rhubarb	1 orange
1 oz (25 g) butter	4 or 5 pieces of stem ginger
2 oz (55 g) sugar or to taste	in syrup
(*I like the fruit tart*)	

Clean the rhubarb and cut off the leaves. Peel thinly if the outer skin is fibrous. Chop into 1 inch-long (2.5 cm) pieces, cutting any particularly broad stems in half lengthways. Find a heatproof glass bowl which will fit over a saucepan of boiling water, or a double boiler. Bring the water to a soft boil and place the rhubarb pieces in the bowl together with the butter, sugar and juice of the orange. Leave to cook for 30 minutes, stirring from time to time. Although this takes longer than stewing the fruit immediately over the heat, the slow cooking preserves a greater delicacy of flavour.

When the fruit is tender (the exact cooking time will depend on the freshness and thickness of the rhubarb and the thickness of the bowl), slice the stem ginger very finely and add it to the dish to warm through. Check the sweetness, addding more sugar if you like, and serve.

INDEX

Index